PACEMAKER®

World Geography and Cultures

GLOBE FEARON

Pearson Learning Group

Pacemaker® World Geography and Cultures Second Edition

Pacemaker Curriculum Advisor: **Stephen Larsen**, formerly of the University of Texas at Austin

PROJECT STAFF
Executive Editor: Jane Petlinski
Lead Editor: Wendy Svec
Editors: Alisa Brightman, Brian Hawkes, Tara Lynch
Production Editor: Marcela Maslanczuk
Lead Designer: Tricia Battipede
Cover Design: April Okano
Photo Researcher: Jenifer Hixson
Electronic Specialists: Leslie Greenberg, Susan Levine
Manufacturing Supervisor: Mark Cirillo

About the Cover: *World Geography and Cultures* is the study of the world and the world's people. The images on the cover are cultural objects that represent the different regions of the world. A Mexican mask shows a common theme in Latin America, the sun. South African money displays a drawing of a native animal, the elephant. An Asian ship, a junk, is an important mode of travel. A South Pacific lei is woven from fresh flowers. Wooden clogs originate in the Netherlands. The decorated pot was made by the Anasazi, North American Indians. What images would represent objects made where you live?

ISBN 0-130-23674-8

Printed in the United States of America

8 9 10 11 12   09 08 07

Globe
Fearon
Pearson Learning Group

1-800-321-3106
www.pearsonlearning.com

Contents

UNIT 2   THE UNITED STATES AND CANADA   43

Chapter 4 An Overview of the Region   44

Chapter 5 Native Americans   56

Chapter 6 Settlers From Other Lands   70

| UNIT 4 | AFRICA SOUTH OF THE SAHARA | 145 |

Chapter 11 West Africa   146

Chapter 12 The Sahel and Central Africa   160

Chapter 13 East Africa   174

Maps and Diagrams

Reference Center

Using Globes and Maps

A globe is a model of the Earth. Looking at the globe, you can see that the Earth is round. You can see the Earth's features and surfaces. A globe is the best way to show the Earth. However, how do you show the round features of a globe on a flat page? You use a map.

You also can see that geographers divide the Earth into halves or **hemispheres**. The **equator** divides the Earth into the Northern Hemisphere and the Southern Hemisphere. The equator is an imaginary line that circles the middle of the Earth.

The **prime meridian** divides the Earth into the Eastern Hemisphere and the Western Hemisphere. The prime meridian is an imaginary line that circles the Earth from the North Pole to the South Pole.

Geographers measure distances from the equator and the prime meridian. These distances are imaginary lines called **latitude** and **longitude**.

The Hemispheres

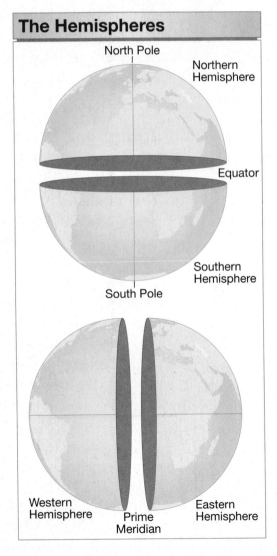

North Pole

Northern Hemisphere

Equator

Southern Hemisphere

South Pole

Western Hemisphere

Prime Meridian

Eastern Hemisphere

Cartographers, or **mapmakers**, have created different map projections. Some of these map projections show the true size of a place, but distort, or change, the shape. Others show the true shape, but distort the size. All maps show some kind of distortion. Therefore, geographers must choose the best maps for their purposes.

A **Mercator projection** stretches the lines of latitude apart. It does not show the true size of landmasses. A Mercator projection does show true shape, however.

Landmasses in a **Robinson projection** are not as distorted as in a Mercator projection. However, there is some distortion in the size of the landmasses.

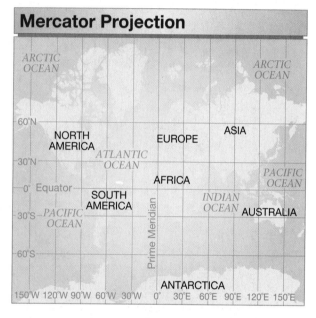

Mercator Projection

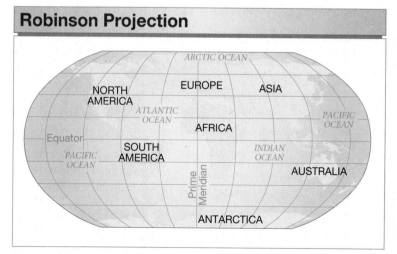

Robinson Projection

CRITICAL THINKING

Why would a mapmaker choose to use a Robinson projection instead of a Mercator projection?

Reading a Map

To understand geography, you need to know how to read maps. To read a map, you need to understand its parts. The main parts of a map are a title, a key, a compass rose, and a scale. Many of the maps you see are **general purpose maps**. These are political map and physical maps. A **political map** shows features determined by people, such as country boundaries, cities, and capitals.

The **title** of a map tells the subject.

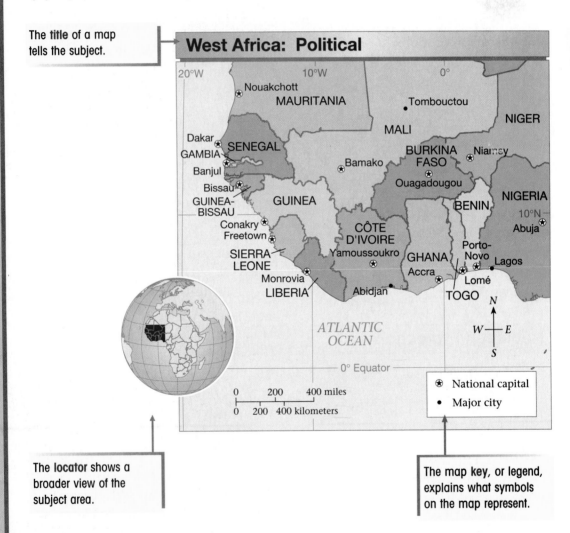

The **locator** shows a broader view of the subject area.

The **map key**, or legend, explains what symbols on the map represent.

A **physical map** shows how high a landmass is. It also shows natural features such as rivers and oceans. Some of the maps you see show specific kinds of information. These maps are called **special purpose maps**. There are many types of special purpose maps. For example, a climate map is a special purpose map. It shows the temperature of a place.

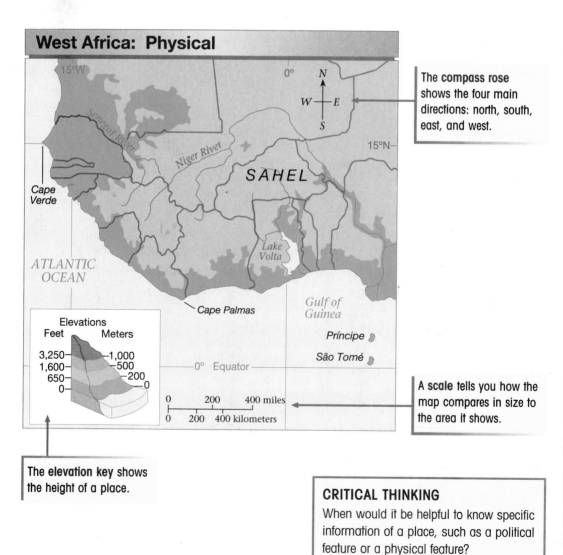

West Africa: Physical

The **compass rose** shows the four main directions: north, south, east, and west.

A **scale** tells you how the map compares in size to the area it shows.

The **elevation key** shows the height of a place.

CRITICAL THINKING

When would it be helpful to know specific information of a place, such as a political feature or a physical feature?

Reading Graphs and Charts

Graphs and charts organize and present information in a visual way. There are different types of graphs and charts.

A **circle graph** is sometimes called a pie graph. It is a good way to show the sizes of parts as compared to a single whole. This single whole is represented as a circle. Each piece of the circle represents a part of the whole.

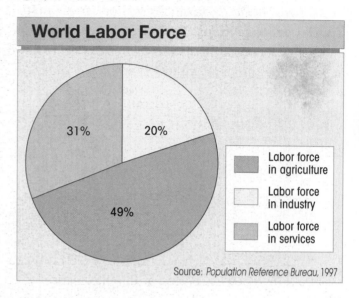

World Labor Force

- Labor force in agriculture
- Labor force in industry
- Labor force in services

Source: *Population Reference Bureau*, 1997

A **bar graph** is a good way to show information visually. Each bar represents a set of facts. You can compare sets of facts by looking at the different sizes of the bars.

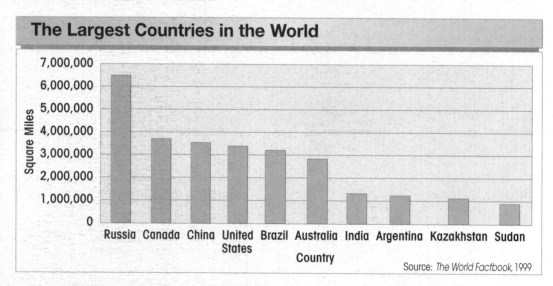

The Largest Countries in the World

Source: *The World Factbook*, 1999

World Facts

Fact	Place	Location	Size
Highest Mountain	Mount Everest	Nepal/China	29,034 feet
Highest Volcano	Guallatiri	Chile	19,876 feet
Longest River	Nile	North/East Africa	4,160 miles long
Largest Island	Greenland		822,700 square miles
Largest Body of Water	Pacific Ocean		64,186,300 square miles

Source: *Global Statistics, 2000*

A **chart** can also be called a table. Charts are organized into rows and columns. Charts can help you to compare information.

A **line graph** shows the relationship between two sets of information. A point is placed at the intersection of every fact. When all points are made, a line is drawn connecting the points. You can get a quick idea as to the trend, or direction, of information by looking at the ups and downs of the line.

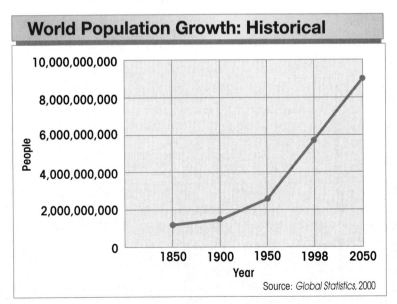

World Population Growth: Historical

Source: *Global Statistics, 2000*

CRITICAL THINKING
If you were to organize information about your classmates into categories such as age and gender, would you use a chart or a graph? Explain.

The World: Political

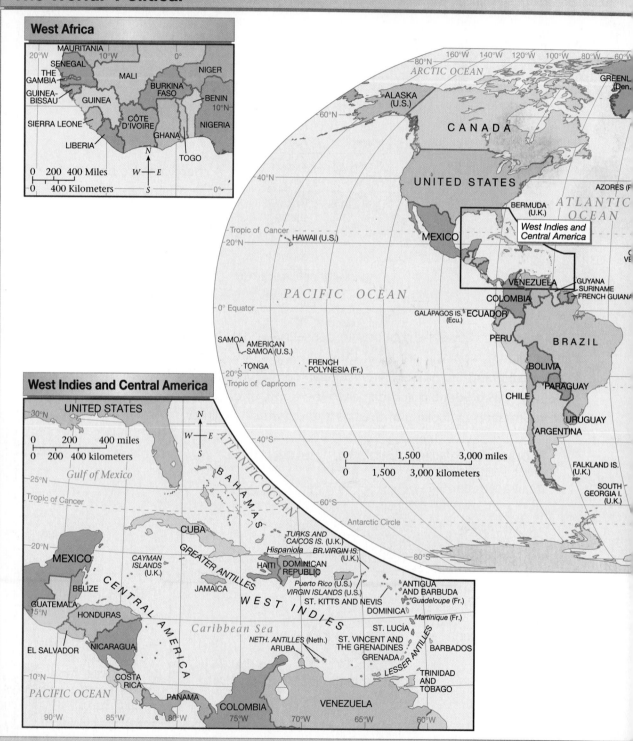

West Africa

MAURITANIA
20°W   10°W   0°
SENEGAL
THE
GAMBIA   MALI   NIGER
GUINEA-   BURKINA
BISSAU   GUINEA   FASO
                                    BENIN   10°N
SIERRA LEONE   CÔTE   NIGERIA
            D'IVOIRE
            LIBERIA   GHANA   TOGO

0   200   400 Miles
0   400 Kilometers

N
W   E
S

West Indies and Central America

UNITED STATES
30°N
0   200   400 miles
0   200   400 kilometers
Gulf of Mexico
25°N
Tropic of Cancer

N
W   E
S

ATLANTIC OCEAN
BAHAMAS
CUBA
CAYMAN
ISLANDS
(U.K.)
GREATER ANTILLES
TURKS AND
CAICOS IS. (U.K.)
Hispaniola   BR. VIRGIN IS.
(U.K.)
HAITI   DOMINICAN
REPUBLIC
Puerto Rico (U.S.)
VIRGIN ISLANDS (U.S.)
ANTIGUA
AND BARBUDA
Guadeloupe (Fr.)
MEXICO
BELIZE
JAMAICA
20°N
ST. KITTS AND NEVIS
DOMINICA
CENTRAL
WEST INDIES
Martinique (Fr.)
GUATEMALA
HONDURAS
15°N
ST. LUCIA
EL SALVADOR
Caribbean Sea
NICARAGUA
AMERICA
NETH. ANTILLES (Neth.)
ARUBA
ST. VINCENT AND
THE GRENADINES
GRENADA
LESSER ANTILLES
BARBADOS
COSTA
RICA
10°N
PACIFIC OCEAN
PANAMA
TRINIDAD
AND
TOBAGO
COLOMBIA
VENEZUELA
90°W   85°W   80°W   75°W   70°W   65°W   60°W

ARCTIC OCEAN
160°W   140°W   120°W   100°W   80°W   60°
80°N
ALASKA
(U.S.)
GREENL
(Den.
60°N
CANADA
40°N
UNITED STATES
AZORES (P
BERMUDA
(U.K.)
ATLANTIC
OCEAN
West Indies and
Central America
Tropic of Cancer
20°N   HAWAII (U.S.)
MEXICO
GUYANA
SURINAME
FRENCH GUIANA
VENEZUELA
C
VE
COLOMBIA
0° Equator
PACIFIC OCEAN
GALÁPAGOS IS.   ECUADOR
(Ecu.)
SAMOA
AMERICAN
SAMOA (U.S.)
PERU
BRAZIL
TONGA
FRENCH
POLYNESIA (Fr.)
20°S
BOLIVIA
Tropic of Capricorn
PARAGUAY
CHILE
URUGUAY
ARGENTINA
0   1,500   3,000 miles
0   1,500   3,000 kilometers
FALKLAND IS.
(U.K.)
40°S
SOUTH
GEORGIA I.
(U.K.)
60°S
Antarctic Circle
80°S

ARCTIC OCEAN

Arctic Circle

ICELAND

Europe

R U S S I A

KAZAKHSTAN

MONGOLIA

GEORGIA
ARMENIA
CYPRUS
TURKEY
UZBEKISTAN
KYRGYZSTAN
TURKMENISTAN
TAJIKISTAN
SYRIA
AZERBAIJAN
LEB.
AFGHANISTAN

CHINA

N. KOREA
S. KOREA
JAPAN

PACIFIC OCEAN

MOROCCO
ISRAEL
IRAQ
IRAN
JORDAN
KUWAIT
BAHRAIN
QATAR

ALGERIA
LIBYA
EGYPT
ESTERN SAHARA (lor.)
MALTA

NEPAL
BHUTAN

MALI
MAURITANIA
NIGER
CHAD
SUDAN
SAUDI ARABIA
OMAN
YEMEN
ERITREA
DJIBOUTI
UNITED ARAB EMIRATES

West Africa

NIGERIA
CENTRAL AFRICAN REP.
CAMEROON
ETHIOPIA
SOMALIA
INDIA
BANGLADESH
MYANMAR (BURMA)
LAOS
VIETNAM
THAILAND
CAMBODIA
MALDIVES
SRI LANKA
PHILIPPINES

PAKISTAN

TAIWAN
Hong Kong

NORTHERN MARIANA IS. (U.S.)
GUAM (U.S.)
MARSHALL IS.

EQUATORIAL GUINEA
SÃO TOMÉ & PRÍNCIPE
GABON
CONGO
DEM. REP. OF THE CONGO
RWANDA
UGANDA
KENYA
BURUNDI
TANZANIA
COMOROS
MAYOTTE (Fr.)
SEYCHELLES

BRUNEI
MALAYSIA
PALAU

FEDERATED STATES OF MICRONESIA
KIRIBATI
NAURU
TUVALU

CABINDA (Ang.)
ANGOLA
ZAMBIA
MALAWI
ZIMBABWE
MADAGASCAR
MAURITIUS
RÉUNION (Fr.)

SINGAPORE

I N D O N E S I A

PAPUA NEW GUINEA
SOLOMON ISLANDS

INDIAN OCEAN

VANUATU
FIJI

NAMIBIA
BOTSWANA
MOZAMBIQUE
SWAZILAND
SOUTH AFRICA
LESOTHO

AUSTRALIA

NEW CALEDONIA (Fr.)

NEW ZEALAND

ATLANTIC OCEAN

N
W   E
S

A N T A R C T I C A

ALB.= ALBANIA
BELG.= BELGIUM
B. H.= BOSNIA AND HERZEGOVINA
CRO.= CROATIA
EST.= ESTONIA
LAT.= LATVIA
LIECH.= LIECHTENSTEIN
LITH.= LITHUANIA
LUX.= LUXEMBOURG
MAC.= MACEDONIA
MON.= MONACO
NETH.= NETHERLANDS
RUS.= RUSSIA
SLOV.= SLOVENIA
S. M.= SAN MARINO
SWITZ.= SWITZERLAND
YUGO.= YUGOSLAVIA

0   200 400 miles
0   400 kilometers

Europe

FINLAND
NORWAY
SWEDEN
RUSSIA

North Sea

IRELAND
UNITED KINGDOM
DENMARK
NETH.
EST.
LAT.
LITH.
RUS.
BELARUS

N
W   E
S

60°N

Baltic Sea

50°N

GERMANY
POLAND
BELG.
LUX.
CZECH REP.
SLOVAKIA
UKRAINE
MOLDOVA

ATLANTIC OCEAN

FRANCE
LIECH.
SWITZ.
AUSTRIA
HUNGARY
SLOV.
CRO.
S. M.
B. H.
YUGO.
ROMANIA

Black Sea

40°N

PORTUGAL
SPAIN
ANDORRA
MON.
ITALY
MAC.
ALB.
BULGARIA
TURKEY
GREECE

Mediterranean Sea

The World: Physical

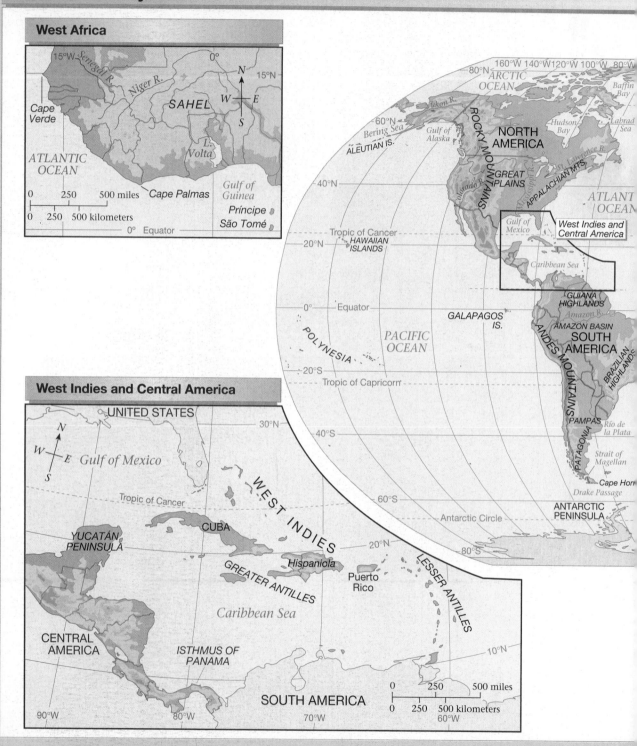

West Africa

15°W
Senegal R.
Niger R.
0°
15°N
N
W — E
S
Cape Verde
SAHEL
L. Volta
ATLANTIC OCEAN
Cape Palmas
Gulf of Guinea
Príncipe
São Tomé

0 250 500 miles
0 250 500 kilometers
0° Equator

West Indies and Central America

UNITED STATES
30°N
N
W — E
S
Gulf of Mexico
Tropic of Cancer
YUCATÁN PENINSULA
CUBA
WEST INDIES
20°N
Hispaniola
GREATER ANTILLES
Puerto Rico
LESSER ANTILLES
Caribbean Sea
CENTRAL AMERICA
ISTHMUS OF PANAMA
SOUTH AMERICA
10°N

0 250 500 miles
0 250 500 kilometers

90°W 80°W 70°W 60°W

160°W 140°W 120°W 100°W 80°W
80°N
ARCTIC OCEAN
Baffin Bay
60°N
Yukon R.
Bering Sea
Gulf of Alaska
ALEUTIAN IS.
ROCKY MOUNTAINS
NORTH AMERICA
Hudson Bay
Labrador Sea
St. Lawrence R.
40°N
GREAT PLAINS
Colorado R.
Mississippi R.
APPALACHIAN MTS.
ATLANTIC OCEAN
Gulf of Mexico
West Indies and Central America
Tropic of Cancer
20°N
HAWAIIAN ISLANDS
Caribbean Sea
GUIANA HIGHLANDS
0° Equator
GALAPAGOS IS.
Amazon R.
AMAZON BASIN
SOUTH AMERICA
POLYNESIA
PACIFIC OCEAN
ANDES MOUNTAINS
BRAZILIAN HIGHLANDS
20°S
Tropic of Capricorn
40°S
PAMPAS
Río de la Plata
PATAGONIA
Strait of Magellan
60°S
Cape Horn
Drake Passage
Antarctic Circle
ANTARCTIC PENINSULA
80°S

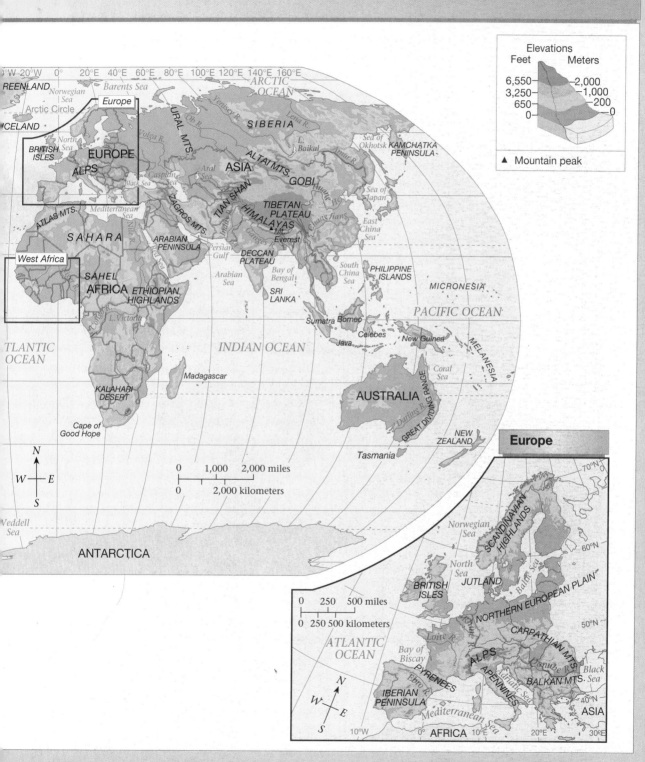

Elevations
Feet   Meters

6,550 ——— 2,000
3,250 ——— 1,000
650 ——— 200
0 ——— 0

▲ Mountain peak

GREENLAND

Norwegian Sea

Barents Sea

ARCTIC OCEAN

Arctic Circle

ICELAND

North Sea

BRITISH ISLES

EUROPE

ALPS

Europe

ATLAS MTS.

Mediterranean Sea

SAHARA

West Africa

SAHEL

AFRICA

ETHIOPIAN HIGHLANDS

ATLANTIC OCEAN

Congo R.

L. Victoria

KALAHARI DESERT

Cape of Good Hope

Weddell Sea

ANTARCTICA

URAL MTS.

Ob R.

Yenisey R.

Volga R.

Caspian Sea

Aral Sea

Black Sea

ZAGROS MTS.

ARABIAN PENINSULA

Persian Gulf

Red Sea

Nile R.

Arabian Sea

SIBERIA

Lena R.

Amur R.

L. Baikal

ALTAI MTS.

ASIA

TIAN SHAN

GOBI

Huang He

TIBETAN PLATEAU

HIMALAYAS

▲ Mt. Everest

Indus R.

Ganges R.

DECCAN PLATEAU

Bay of Bengal

SRI LANKA

Chang Jiang

Sea of Okhotsk

KAMCHATKA PENINSULA

Sea of Japan

East China Sea

South China Sea

PHILIPPINE ISLANDS

Sumatra

Borneo

Celebes

Java

New Guinea

MICRONESIA

PACIFIC OCEAN

MELANESIA

Coral Sea

AUSTRALIA

GREAT DIVIDING RANGE

Darling R.

NEW ZEALAND

Tasmania

INDIAN OCEAN

Madagascar

N
W — E
S

0   1,000   2,000 miles

0   2,000 kilometers

Europe

70°N

Norwegian Sea

SCANDINAVIAN HIGHLANDS

60°N

North Sea

JUTLAND

Baltic Sea

BRITISH ISLES

NORTHERN EUROPEAN PLAIN

CARPATHIAN MTS.

50°N

Rhine R.

Loire R.

ATLANTIC OCEAN

Bay of Biscay

PYRENEES

ALPS

Danube R.

APENNINES

Adriatic Sea

BALKAN MTS.

Black Sea

Ebro R.

IBERIAN PENINSULA

Mediterranean Sea

40°N

ASIA

AFRICA

10°W   0°   10°E   20°E   30°E

0   250   500 miles

0   250 500 kilometers

N
W — E
S

North America

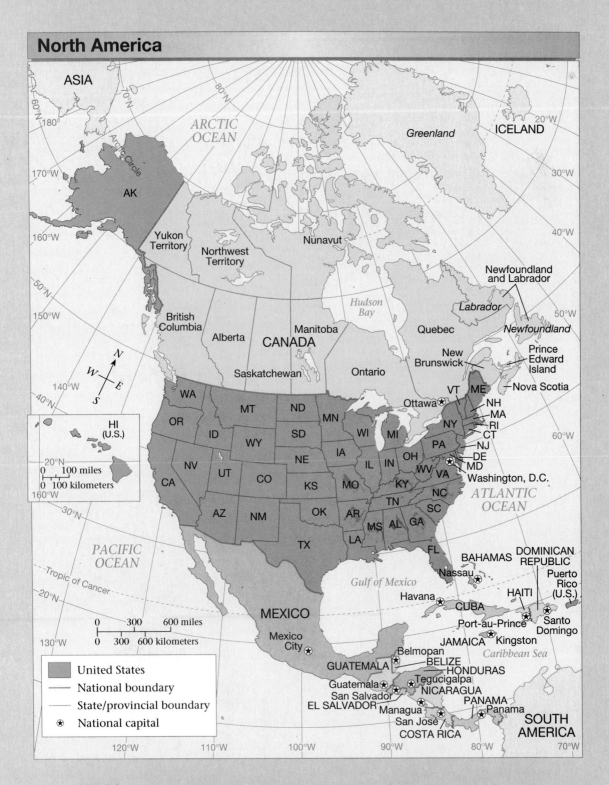

ASIA

ARCTIC OCEAN

Greenland

ICELAND

AK

Yukon Territory

Northwest Territory

Nunavut

Newfoundland and Labrador

Hudson Bay

Labrador

Newfoundland

British Columbia

Alberta

Saskatchewan

Manitoba

CANADA

Ontario

Quebec

New Brunswick

Prince Edward Island

Nova Scotia

N
W E
S

WA

MT

ND

MN

WI

MI

Ottawa ⊛

VT ME
NH
MA
RI
CT

HI (U.S.)

20°N

0   100 miles
0   100 kilometers

OR

ID

WY

SD

NE

IA

IL

IN

OH

PA

NY

NJ
DE
MD

Washington, D.C.

NV

UT

CO

KS

MO

KY

WV

VA

CA

AZ

NM

OK

AR

TN

NC

SC

GA

ATLANTIC OCEAN

MS

AL

PACIFIC OCEAN

TX

LA

FL

Tropic of Cancer

0   300   600 miles
0   300   600 kilometers

MEXICO

Mexico City ⊛

Gulf of Mexico

Nassau

Havana ⊛

BAHAMAS

DOMINICAN REPUBLIC

Puerto Rico (U.S.)

HAITI

CUBA

Port-au-Prince ⊛

Santo Domingo ⊛

JAMAICA

Kingston ⊛

Caribbean Sea

Belmopan ⊛

GUATEMALA

BELIZE

HONDURAS

Guatemala ⊛

San Salvador ⊛

EL SALVADOR

Tegucigalpa ⊛

NICARAGUA

Managua ⊛

PANAMA

Panama ⊛

San José ⊛

COSTA RICA

SOUTH AMERICA

	United States
	National boundary
	State/provincial boundary
⊛	National capital

120°W   110°W   100°W   90°W   80°W   70°W

South America

Caribbean Sea

10°N

GUYANA

Caracas

VENEZUELA

Georgetown SURINAME
French Guiana
(Fr.)

Bogotá

Cayenne

COLOMBIA

Paramaribo

Equator 0°

GALÁPAGOS
ISLANDS
(Ecuador)

Quito
ECUADOR

PERU

BRAZIL

10°S

Lima

La Paz

Brasília

BOLIVIA

Sucre

PARAGUAY

20°S

Tropic of Capricorn

Asunción

N

CHILE

W   E

S

URUGUAY

30°S

Buenos Aires

ATLANTIC OCEAN

Santiago

Montevideo

ARGENTINA

PACIFIC OCEAN

0   400   800 miles

0   400   800 kilometers

National boundary

⊛ Capital city

FALKLAND (MALVINAS)
ISLANDS (U.K.)

40°S

50°S

100°W   90°W   80°W   70°W   60°W   50°W   40°W   30°W   20°W

Europe

30°W 20°W 10°W 70°N 0° 10°E 20°E 30°E 40°E 50°E

Reykjavík
ICELAND

Arctic Circle

60°N

Norwegian Sea

0   300   600 miles
0   300   600 kilometers

N
W   E
S

North Sea

SWEDEN

FINLAND

NORWAY
Oslo
Helsinki
Stockholm
Tallinn
ESTONIA
Baltic
Sea
Riga LATVIA
RUSSIA
Moscow

DENMARK
Copenhagen
LITHUANIA
Vilnius
Minsk
BELARUS

Dublin UNITED
KINGDOM
IRELAND
NETHERLANDS
RUSSIA
Warsaw
Kiev
London
Amsterdam
Berlin
POLAND
UKRAINE
BELGIUM
Brussels
GERMANY
ATLANTIC
OCEAN
Paris
Luxembourg
Prague
7
SLOVAKIA
MOLDOVA
Chisinau
1
Vienna
Bratislava
2
FRANCE
Bern
6
AUSTRIA
Budapest
HUNGARY
ROMANIA
Ljubljana
Zagreb
Bucharest
Black Sea
MONACO
SLOVENIA
CROATIA
4
Belgrade
PORTUGAL
ANDORRA
3
8
BULGARIA
40°N
Madrid
Sarajevo
Sofia
Lisbon
SPAIN
ITALY
Rome
Skopje
TURKEY
5
Tirana
ASIA
GREECE
ALBANIA
Athens

MALTA

30°N
AFRICA
Mediterranean Sea

50°N

1. LUXEMBOURG
2. LIECHTENSTEIN
3. SAN MARINO
4. BOSNIA and
   HERZEGOVINA
5. MACEDONIA
6. SWITZERLAND
7. CZECH REPUBLIC
8. YUGOSLAVIA

—— National boundary
⊛ Capital city

Africa

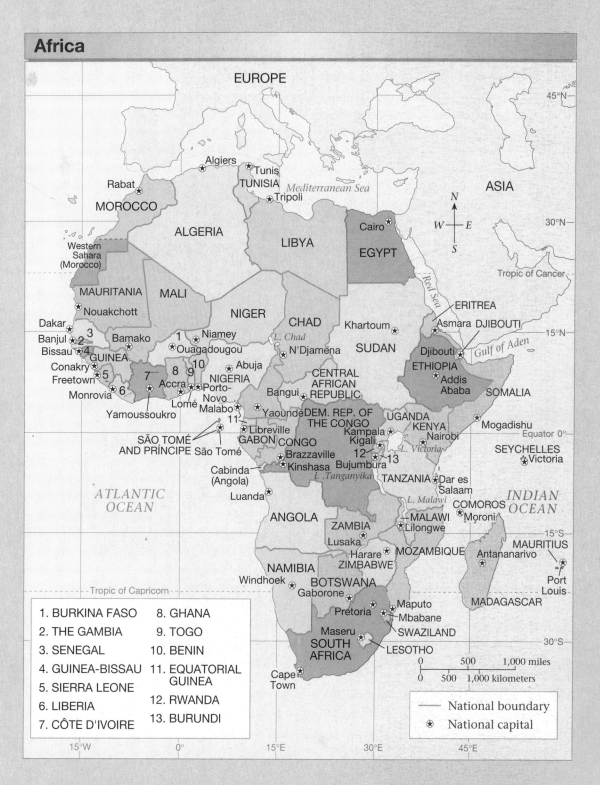

EUROPE

Algiers ✴

✴ Tunis
TUNISIA
Rabat ✴
MOROCCO   ✴ Tripoli   Mediterranean Sea   ASIA

Western   ALGERIA   LIBYA   Cairo ✴   30°N
Sahara   EGYPT
(Morocco)   Tropic of Cancer

MAURITANIA   MALI   ERITREA
Nouakchott ✴   NIGER   Khartoum   Asmara ✴ DJIBOUTI
Dakar ✴   L. Chad   ✴   ✴ 15°N
Banjul ✴   3   1 ✴ Niamey   CHAD   SUDAN   Djibouti ✴ Gulf of Aden
   ✴ 2   Bamako   ✴ Ouagadougou   N'Djamena ✴   ETHIOPIA
Bissau ✴ 4   10   ✴
       GUINEA   8 9 ✴ Abuja   CENTRAL   Addis
Conakry ✴   NIGERIA   AFRICAN   Ababa   SOMALIA
Freetown ✴ 5   7 ✴ Accra   Porto-   REPUBLIC
       ✴ 6   Yamoussoukro Novo Lomé Bangui ✴   UGANDA   Mogadishu ✴
Monrovia   Malabo ✴   Kampala ✴ KENYA Equator 0°
       Yamoussoukro   11 ✴ Libreville Yaoundé DEM. REP. OF   Nairobi ✴ SEYCHELLES
       SÃO TOMÉ   GABON   CONGO   THE CONGO Kigali ✴ L. Victoria ✴ Victoria
       AND PRÍNCIPE São Tomé ✴   Brazzaville ✴ 12   13
                                   Cabinda ✴ Kinshasa Bujumbura ✴   INDIAN
       ATLANTIC   (Angola)   L. Tanganyika TANZANIA ✴ Dar es OCEAN
       OCEAN   Luanda ✴   L. Malawi Salaam
                                                                        COMOROS
                                   ANGOLA   MALAWI ✴ Moroni
                                                        ZAMBIA   ✴ Lilongwe   15°S
                                                        Lusaka ✴   MAURITIUS
                                                               Harare   Antananarivo ✴
       Tropic of Capricorn   NAMIBIA ✴ ZIMBABWE MOZAMBIQUE   Port
                                   Windhoek ✴ BOTSWANA   MADAGASCAR Louis
                                              Gaborone ✴   Maputo ✴
                                                        Pretoria ✴ Mbabane
                                                        Maseru   SWAZILAND   30°S
                                                        SOUTH   LESOTHO
                                                        AFRICA
                                                        Cape Town ✴

N
W E
S

1. BURKINA FASO	8. GHANA
2. THE GAMBIA	9. TOGO
3. SENEGAL	10. BENIN
4. GUINEA-BISSAU	11. EQUATORIAL GUINEA
5. SIERRA LEONE	
6. LIBERIA	12. RWANDA
7. CÔTE D'IVOIRE	13. BURUNDI

0   500   1,000 miles
0   500   1,000 kilometers

—— National boundary
✴   National capital

15°W   0°   15°E   30°E   45°E

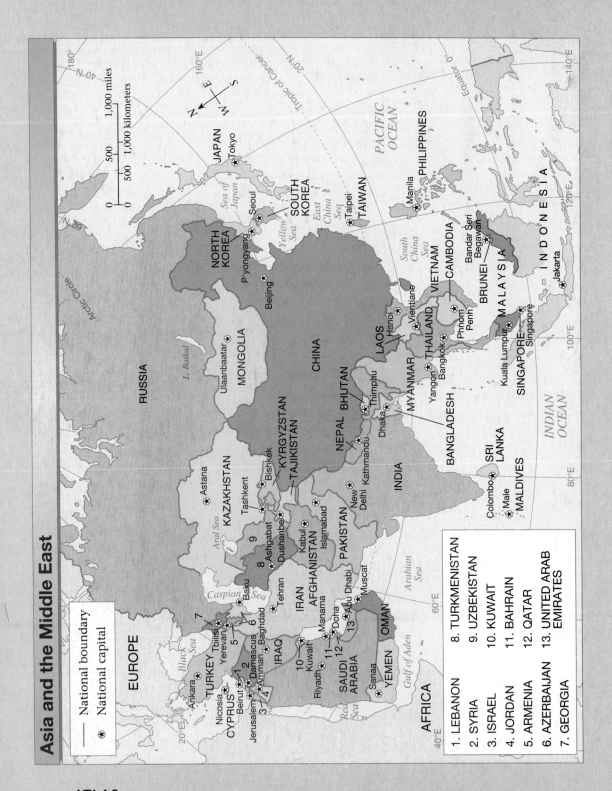

Asia and the Middle East

Legend:
— National boundary
⊛ National capital

1. LEBANON
2. SYRIA
3. ISRAEL
4. JORDAN
5. ARMENIA
6. AZERBAIJAN
7. GEORGIA
8. TURKMENISTAN
9. UZBEKISTAN
10. KUWAIT
11. BAHRAIN
12. QATAR
13. UNITED ARAB EMIRATES

EUROPE

AFRICA

RUSSIA

MONGOLIA   Ulaanbaatar

KAZAKHSTAN   Astana

KYRGYZSTAN   Bishkek
TAJIKISTAN

Tashkent

Aral Sea

Ashgabat   Dushanbe
8   9

Kabul
AFGHANISTAN   Islamabad

IRAN   Tehran

PAKISTAN

Caspian Sea
Baku

TURKEY   Tbilisi
Yerevan
7
5
6
Ankara
Nicosia   Beirut   Damascus
CYPRUS   1   Baghdad
Jerusalem   2   Amman   IRAQ
3   4
10   Kuwait
11   12
Riyadh   Manama   Doha
SAUDI   13   Abu Dhabi
ARABIA   Muscat
Sanaa   OMAN
YEMEN
Red Sea   Gulf of Aden

Black Sea

New Delhi
INDIA

NEPAL   BHUTAN
Kathmandu   Thimphu

CHINA

NORTH KOREA   P'yongyang
Beijing

SOUTH KOREA   Seoul

Yellow Sea

Sea of Japan

JAPAN   Tokyo

Dhaka
BANGLADESH   MYANMAR
Yangon

SRI LANKA   Colombo

MALDIVES   Male

Arabian Sea

INDIAN OCEAN

LAOS
Hanoi
VIETNAM
Vientiane
THAILAND
Bangkok
CAMBODIA   Phnom Penh

South China Sea

East China Sea

TAIWAN   Taipei

PHILIPPINES   Manila

BRUNEI   Bandar Seri Begawan

MALAYSIA
Kuala Lumpur
SINGAPORE   Singapore

INDONESIA   Jakarta

PACIFIC OCEAN

Tropic of Cancer

Arctic Circle

L. Baikal

180°   40°N
40°N
60°N   160°E
20°N
Equator   0°
140°E
120°E
100°E
80°E
60°E
40°E
20°E

1,000 miles
1,000 kilometers
500   1,000
0   500

N E
S W

Australia and Oceania

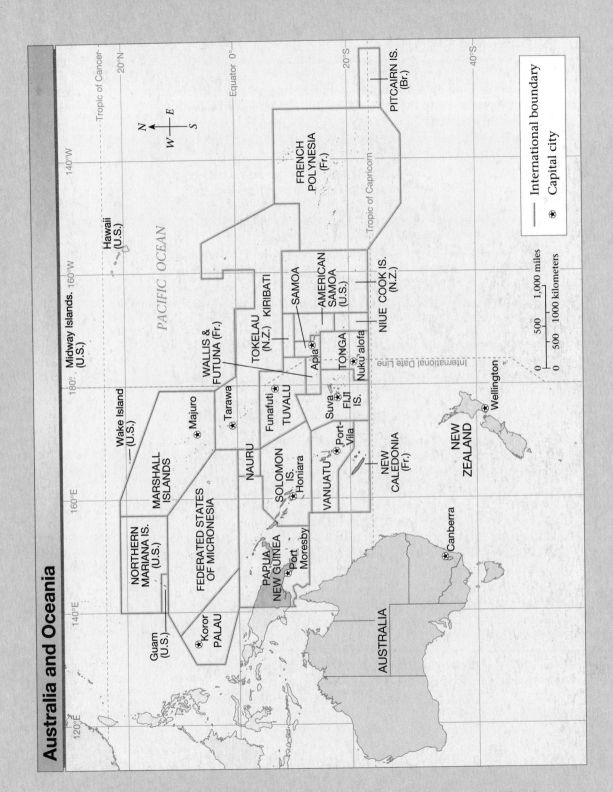

PACIFIC OCEAN

PITCAIRN IS. (Br.)

FRENCH POLYNESIA (Fr.)

Hawaii (U.S.)

Midway Islands. (U.S.)

SAMOA

AMERICAN SAMOA (U.S.)

COOK IS. (N.Z.)

NIUE (N.Z.)

KIRIBATI

TOKELAU (N.Z.)

WALLIS & FUTUNA (Fr.)

Apia

TONGA

Nuku'alofa

Wake Island (U.S.)

Majuro

Tarawa

Funafuti

TUVALU

Suva

FIJI IS.

Wellington

NEW ZEALAND

MARSHALL ISLANDS

NAURU

SOLOMON IS.

Honiara

Port-Vila

VANUATU

NEW CALEDONIA (Fr.)

NORTHERN MARIANA IS. (U.S.)

FEDERATED STATES OF MICRONESIA

PAPUA NEW GUINEA

Port Moresby

Canberra

AUSTRALIA

Guam (U.S.)

Koror

PALAU

International Date Line

Tropic of Cancer

Equator 0°

Tropic of Capricorn

20°N

20°S

40°S

120°E   140°E   160°E   180°   160°W   140°W

N
W E
S

Legend:
— International boundary
⊛ Capital city

Scale:
0   500   1,000 miles
0   500   1000 kilometers

A Note to the Student

It is useful and important to understand the many different regions of the world—and the people who live in them. As you read, you will learn about the geography of the various regions of the world. You will study the physical features of the earth, such as mountains, deserts, and oceans. You will study climate and the land's resources. You will also learn about the people on the Earth and the ways in which they live and interact with the environment.

In every chapter of this book, there are special features that show you how geography and culture relates to your life. For example, the **Celebrations** feature describes festivals and other ceremonies. The **Spotlight On** feature focuses on geographic and cultural topics of special interest. The **Global Issues** feature discusses current concerns around the world, such as ways to help the environment, world famine, and world literacy.

World Geography and Cultures has many activities that allow you to practice key geography skills. Whether you are reading a map or understanding time zones, you will need these skills to guide you. These skill activities can be found in the **Geographer's Tool Kit** and **Geography in Your Life** pages of your book.

Throughout the book you will find notes in the margins of the pages. The **margin notes** are there to make you stop and think. Some notes comment on the material you are learning. Sometimes the notes remind you of something you already know.

You will also find several study aids in this book. At the beginning of every chapter, you will find **Learning Objectives**. These objectives will help you focus on the important points covered in the chapter. The **Words to Know** section will give you a preview of vocabulary you may find challenging. The **Places to Know** section will highlight important places covered in the chapter. At the end of every chapter, the **Summary** will give you a quick review of what you have just read.

We hope you enjoy reading about the geography and cultures of the world. We wish you well in your studies.

Unit 1 ▶ What Is Geography?

NORTH AMERICA

EUROPE

ASIA

ATLANTIC OCEAN

PACIFIC OCEAN

AFRICA

PACIFIC OCEAN

SOUTH AMERICA

INDIAN OCEAN

ATLANTIC OCEAN

AUSTRALIA

ANTARCTICA

There are seven continents, or areas of land. What are the names of the seven continents?

TRAVEL LOG

You are about to travel the world. Your suitcase is packed for your trip. Where will you go? Write a paragraph about a place in the world that you would like to visit and why.

Ready for world travel

This satellite image of the Earth was taken from space. How would you describe the photograph?

The Five Themes of Geography

Words to Know

geography	a study of the Earth's surface, focusing on descriptions of places and the people who live in them
location	where a place is
latitude	distance, measured in degrees, north and south of the equator
longitude	distance, measured in degrees, east and west of the prime meridian
equator	an imaginary line around the middle of the Earth
prime meridian	the line of 0 degree longitude from which east and west locations are measured
climate	the pattern of weather in a place over many years
migration	the movement of a group of people from one place to another

Places to Know

equator

prime meridian

Learning Objectives

- Name the five themes of geography.
- Compare longitude and latitude.
- Describe the ways in which people affect the Earth.
- Describe the ways in which the Earth affects people.
- Locate places on a globe or map.

What Is Geography?

Geography has two branches. One branch studies physical features of the Earth, such as mountains, valleys, oceans, lakes, and rivers. This branch is called physical geography.

The other branch of geography describes the people on the Earth and the ways that people live in different places. This branch is called human geography.

You Decide

How does geography affect the way you live?

Most geographers travel a lot. They measure distances and draw maps. They collect information about different places and about the people who live in these places. Geographers want to know how people relate to the world around them. They also want to know how the Earth affects people and their ways of life.

To explore these questions, geographers look at five themes. Each theme is a broad idea—a different way of looking at the Earth and its people. The five themes are location, place, interaction, movement, and region.

Location

Every place on the Earth has a **location**, or where a place is. People often describe the location of a place by referring to another place. This is called the relative location of a place. Suppose you wanted to explain where Peoria, Illinois, is. You might say, "It's about 110 miles southwest of Chicago." Anyone who knows where Chicago is would then know where Peoria is. Yet to a person who has never heard of Chicago, this description means nothing.

Geographers have another way to describe location. They use imaginary lines on a map or globe called **latitude** and **longitude.** This way, the location of a place can be given without mentioning any other place. This is called the absolute location of a place.

Lines of Latitude and Longitude

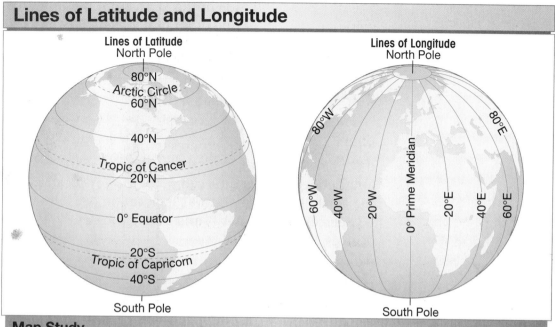

Lines of Latitude
North Pole
80°N
Arctic Circle
60°N
40°N
Tropic of Cancer
20°N
0° Equator
20°S
Tropic of Capricorn
40°S
South Pole

Lines of Longitude
North Pole
80°W
60°W
40°W
20°W
0° Prime Meridian
20°E
40°E
60°E
80°E
South Pole

Map Study

1. **LOCATION** What is the latitude measurement of the equator?
2. **LOCATION** What is the longitude measurement of the prime meridian?

Lines of latitude run from side to side. The **equator** runs around the middle—the widest part—of the Earth. All lines of latitude run parallel to the equator. They are measured in degrees from 0 to 90. Latitude marks how far north or south of the equator a place is. The equator is at 0 degrees. The South Pole is at 90 degrees S, and the North Pole is at 90 degrees N.

Above and below the equator, the Earth can be divided into imaginary halves called hemispheres. The upper half is called the Northern Hemisphere, and the lower half is called the Southern Hemisphere.

Lines of longitude stretch from the North Pole to the South Pole. The **prime meridian** marks 0 degrees. Longitude lines are not parallel. They run like the sections of an orange and come together at both poles.

Geography Fact

Hemisphere means "half a ball." The Earth can be divided into two halves along the equator.

On the opposite side of the Earth from the prime meridian is another line of longitude, which marks 180 degrees. The lines in between are numbered from 0 to 179 degrees. Each one is east or west of the prime meridian. So longitude tells us how far to the east or west of the prime meridian a place is.

Degrees of longitude and latitude are divided into minutes. There are 60 minutes in one degree. Minutes describe a location very exactly. Therefore, latitude and longitude, used together, can pinpoint any location on the Earth. Remember Peoria? Its location is a latitude of 40 degrees, 42 minutes N and a longitude of 89 degrees, 36 minutes W.

Place

The second theme of geography is place. Location answers the question, "Where is it?" Place answers the question, "What do you find there?"

Every place has features that make it special. Is the land flat? Is it hilly? Does it have cliffs? What is the weather like? What kinds of plants and animals can be found there? These are all questions about physical features.

Natural events can help explain physical features. For example, the Colorado River formed the Grand Canyon after millions of years of its water wearing away at the rock. Understanding this event helps describe what the Grand Canyon looks like.

A place usually has human features, too. Knowing about people leads to an understanding about a place. Questions such as: "How many people live there? Who are they? What language do they speak? What customs do they follow?" are about human features.

> **HISTORY FACT**
>
> The first sighting of the Grand Canyon by a European was made by Francisco Coronado's expedition in 1540. Its cliff-dwellings, though, proved humans had lived there long before.

Interaction

Human activities can change what a place is like. People may have cut down trees. They may have built factories. The human features of a place may include changes that humans have brought about.

These changes are caused by the interaction of people and their environment. People affect their natural surroundings and are, in turn, affected by it. Geographers explore this relationship. They look for connections between how people live and where they live.

People adjust their way of life to fit their surroundings. In northern Alaska, where the weather is very cold, many people protect themselves from the **climate** by wearing clothing made from sealskins. Climate is the pattern of weather over many years. Yet if a family from northern Alaska moved to a warmer climate, they would start wearing clothes made of cotton, or other light fabrics. In short, they would adapt, or change, to blend in with their environment.

Movement

Most people move several times in their lives. In the United States, for instance, everybody has family members or ancestors who moved from somewhere else. People have always moved from place to place.

Geographers are interested in two kinds of movement. One type is trade. People may go to another place to do business. Trade is necessary, because people rarely have everything they need in their own area. They must trade what they have in order to get what they need.

Trade helps to spread goods around the world. It also helps to spread ideas. While people are trading, they learn about other lands and other ways of life.

Villagers fish on wooden poles in Sri Lanka. Their livelihood was threatened when an oil and fertilizer spill on Sri Lanka's southern coast in 1999 devastated the local environment.

Another type of movement is **migration**. Migration is the movement of a group of people from one place to another. When people migrate, they move to new areas to settle. Like trade, migrations also help to spread ideas. Usually, people take their customs, beliefs, and way of life with them.

People have many different reasons for migrating. They may migrate to escape wars or other dangers. They may move to find political or religious freedom. Sometimes people move because they are hungry. An area may be going through a drought, or time of no rain. Without rain, people cannot grow enough food. Therefore, a drought can drive people into migration.

These people from Kosovo in Eastern Europe fled their homes to escape war.

Region

It is hard to study the whole world at once. So geographers divide the world into regions, or areas that have shared features. There are many ways to define a region.

One way to define a region is by its physical features. Physical features include mountains, lakes, and valleys. We call these physical features landforms. An area with many volcanoes, for instance, could be considered a region.

Climate is another way to define regions. Climate influences many aspects of a place. Climate controls what kinds of plants and animals can live in a region. Climate can even control the activities of people.

Regions can also be defined by human features. For example, we can group together areas where people speak the same language. We can group together areas that have the same religion. Politics can define regions, too.

Economics is another way of defining regions. Economics is everything that has to do with work and money. For example, countries where most people make their living by herding or farming could be grouped together as a region.

✓ Check Your Understanding

Write your answers in complete sentences.

1. What are the five themes of geography now?

2. What physical features describe where you live?

3. How does environment affect the way you live?

4. Why do geographers divide the world into regions?

Remember
Climate is the pattern of weather over many years.

$ Economics Fact

Changes in climate can change the economics of a place. In the 1930s, some of the Great Plains states suffered through severe droughts. The soil blew away. Thousands of farm families who could not make a living moved west.

GEOGRAPHER'S TOOL KIT
Understanding Political and Physical Maps

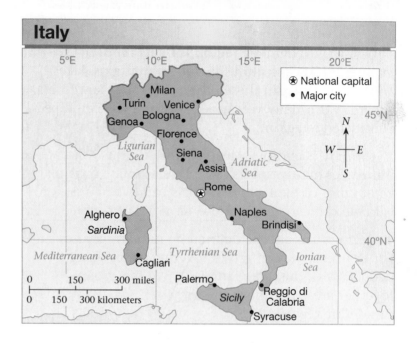

Italy

Two important kinds of maps are *political* and *physical* maps.

A *political* map shows the features that people have created on land. These include the boundaries of states and countries. A political map also shows cities and towns.

A *physical* map shows the natural features of a place. On a physical map, you can find oceans, lakes, and rivers. The map key often shows the elevation, or height, of different areas of land. Look at the map key to see what the symbols and colors mean.

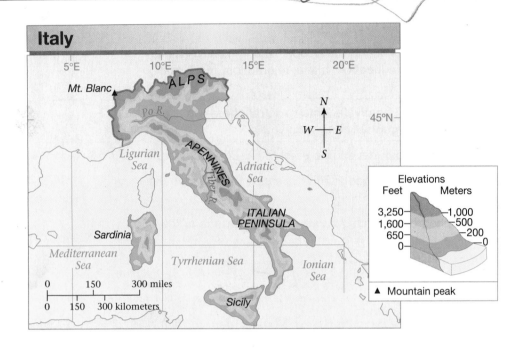

Italy

Elevations

Feet	Meters
3,250	1,000
1,600	500
650	200
0	0

▲ Mountain peak

Answer the questions below.

1. What mountain ranges are shown on the physical map?

2. What is the national capital of Italy?

3. What are two major cities in Italy?

CHALLENGE What are the names of the islands off the mainland of Italy?

Apply the Skill

From memory, draw a map of your state showing political and physical features. Check an atlas to see how close you came.

Chapter

1 Review

Summary

Geography describes the Earth and the people who live on it. The five themes of geography are location, place, interaction, movement, and region.

The study of geography can be divided into two branches—physical geography and human geography.

Both human and physical features can be used to describe a place.

Migration and trade interest the geographer because they involve the movement of people.

Regions can be defined by physical features and by features of the people living there.

Vocabulary Review

Write *true* or *false*. If the statement is false, change the underlined term to make it true.

1. The pattern of weather in a place over many years is called <u>climate</u>.

2. Distance north and south of the equator is measured by lines of <u>longitude</u>.

3. An imaginary line around the middle of the Earth is the <u>prime meridian</u>.

4. The movement of a group of people from one place to another is <u>migration</u>.

5. The study of the Earth's surface, focusing on descriptions of places and the people who live in them, is <u>geography</u>.

Chapter Quiz

Write your answers in complete sentences.

1. What is physical geography?

2. What marks 0 degrees latitude?

3. What are three ways to define regions?

4. Critical Thinking How are lines of longitude and latitude different?

5. Critical Thinking How would you define the region in which you live?

Write About Geography

Complete the following activities.

1. Using each of the five geographic themes, write a description of your hometown.

2. Create a poster encouraging tourists to visit your hometown.

Group Activity

With your classmates, form two groups—human geographers and physical geographers. Have a meeting to discuss the geography of your school and school grounds. Make a list at the meeting that includes information about location, place, interaction, movement, and region.

Many forces make changes to the Earth's surface. What might have shaped this Costa Rican landscape?

Chapter 2 — Physical Geography

Words to Know

glacier	a huge, moving mass of ice
erosion	the wearing away of the Earth's surface by wind or water
delta	a flat, sandy area where a river enters an ocean
plain	a flat landform
plateau	a high, flat landform
map projection	a way to draw the curved areas of the Earth on a flat surface
tropical	related to regions near the equator; a tropical climate is very warm and moist
fossil fuel	coal, oil, or natural gas that formed over millions of years from the remains of plants and tiny animals
renewable resource	a resource that can be replaced as it is used
nonrenewable resource	a resource that cannot be replaced by natural resources or is replaced extremely slowly

Places to Know

North Pole
South Pole

Learning Objectives

- Identify some landforms on the Earth's surface.
- Explain why the seasons change.
- Explain what causes different climates.
- Explain the difference between renewable and nonrenewable resources.

Inside the Earth

The Earth is not just a solid ball. It has three separate layers: the crust, the mantle, and the core. The crust is a thin layer of rock, sand, and soil. It covers the Earth like a skin and even lines the floor of the oceans. Below the crust is a thick layer of rock called the mantle. The outer part of the mantle is melted, but deeper inside it is solid. At the center of the Earth is the core, which is made of two metals: nickel and iron. In the outer core the metals are more fluid, but the very heart of the Earth is solid.

The inside of the Earth is a very busy place. Melted rock and other materials are always moving—flowing and rubbing together. This activity builds up heat and pressure that cause movements in the crust. Sometimes, these movements can be felt as earthquakes. Mountains and volcanoes also are made by forces deep in the Earth. Most of these changes happen too slowly for people to notice. A volcanic eruption, however, causes sudden change. Forces deep within the Earth, then, do affect life on the surface. There is no way to stop these forces.

On the Earth's Surface

Land covers about 30 percent of the Earth's surface. Water covers about 70 percent. The water is in oceans, lakes, rivers, and **glaciers.** A glacier is a huge moving mass of ice. Water is also found underground.

The oceans and seas hold most of the water on our planet. This water is salty, and we cannot drink it or use it for farming. Ocean water evaporates, however, and turns into water vapor. Most of the salt stays behind, and the water vapor becomes part of the air. Wind carries the water vapor over the land, where it may drop back to the Earth as rain or snow. In time, the water flows back to the sea. This process is known as the water cycle.

Inside the Earth

Crust
3–30 miles thick

Mantle
1,800 miles thick

Inner core
860 miles thick

Outer core
1,300 miles thick

The Earth has three separate layers.

The atmosphere is the layer of air around the Earth. It is about 1,000 miles thick. It is made up mainly of two gases—nitrogen and oxygen—along with small amounts of other gases.

Water and air are always changing the surface of the Earth. Wind, ice, and flowing water break down rocks. We call this process weathering. Wind and water also carry away bits of rock and soil in a process called **erosion.** For example, through erosion, a river may wash soil downstream. The soil ends up in a **delta**—a flat, sandy area where a river enters an ocean.

Weathering and erosion shape the Earth's surface. They wear mountains down to hills and create valleys and canyons. They create the flatlands called **plains** and the high, flat landforms known as **plateaus**.

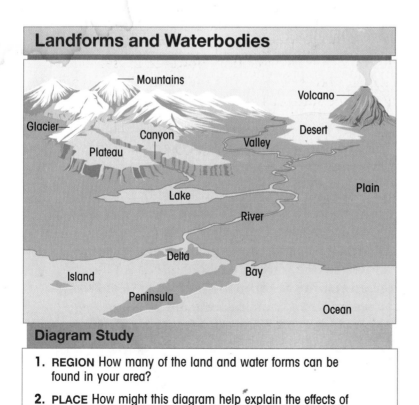

Landforms and Waterbodies

Mountains

Volcano

Glacier

Desert

Canyon

Valley

Plateau

Plain

Lake

River

Delta

Island

Bay

Peninsula

Ocean

Diagram Study

1. **REGION** How many of the land and water forms can be found in your area?

2. **PLACE** How might this diagram help explain the effects of weathering and erosion?

Map Projections

The Earth—shaped like a ball—has a curved surface. A globe can represent this curved surface. Suppose you could remove the outer layer of a globe. Could you smooth it out flat to make a map? Not quite. It would stretch and split in many places.

Try this experiment. Take a flat piece of paper and see if you can cover a round ball with it. Notice how the paper wrinkles and overlaps. Now you know what problem mapmakers face when they draw maps of the Earth. A flat map cannot really show the curved surface of the Earth. That is why geographers have invented **map projections**.

There are many kinds of map projections. Each one shows a different way to draw the curved areas of the Earth on a flat surface. However, all map projections have some distortion. Some of these maps change the shapes of continents or make their sizes look incorrect. In some map projections, the distances between places look wrong. Some of these maps do not accurately show directions (north, south, east, and west). The distortions are more noticeable on maps that show larger areas. A map of the world has much distortion. A map of your town would have almost none.

A Mercator projection shows the true shapes of continents and islands. To make the shapes correct, a Mercator projection stretches the lines of latitude apart. As a result, the map does not show the true sizes of landmasses. The farther a landmass is from the equator, the greater the distortion. However, a Mercator projection is a good kind of map to use for travel on the ocean because it shows directions accurately.

Most maps in a geography book are based on the Robinson projection. This type of projection map shows only small distortions. Only the landmasses near the South Pole and the North Pole look distorted.

GEOGRAPHY IN YOUR LIFE
Making Maps

Every day, you create maps in your mind. These maps help you get from place to place. For example, you know how to get from school to the library. You can use this skill when you study geography. As you read, make a map in your mind of the place you are studying.

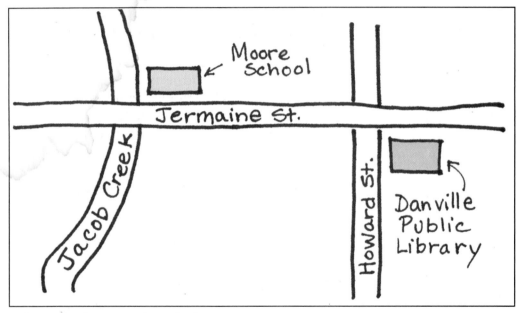

Answer the questions below.

1. How do you get from Moore School to the Danville Public Library?

2. Draw an example of a map you have in your mind that helps you get somewhere day to day.

   CHALLENGE How can making a map of a place you are studying help you understand it better?

Apply the Skill
Picture a building on the same street as your school. Draw a map of your route from the school to that building.

Rotation and Revolution

Remember
The force of gravity keeps the planets in orbit around the sun.

You Decide

Why are the days longer during part of the year?

There are nine planets in the solar system. All of the planets travel around the sun. The Earth is the third planet in orbit away from the sun. It takes a year for the Earth to make a full trip, or revolution, around the sun.

Revolution is one way in which the Earth moves through space. The Earth also spins on its axis in a motion called rotation. The Earth makes one complete rotation in 24 hours. However, the Earth's axis does not point straight up and down. It is slightly tilted.

During some months, this tilt aims the North Pole a little toward the sun. In these months, the sun shines more directly on the Northern Hemisphere for more hours of each day. These are the summer months in the Northern Hemisphere. In the Southern Hemisphere they are the winter months, because the South Pole is tilted away from the sun.

During the summer months in the Southern Hemisphere, the South Pole is tilted toward the sun. When neither pole is tilted toward the sun, it is spring or fall. The Earth's tilt and its revolution together cause the changing seasons.

✓ Check Your Understanding

Write your answers in complete sentences.

1. What causes earthquakes and volcanoes?

2. Explain the water cycle.

3. Why did geographers invent map projections?

4. What is the difference between the rotation and the revolution of the Earth?

GEOGRAPHER'S TOOL KIT
Understanding Latitude and Longitude

The following information will help you to understand latitude and longitude.

- *Latitude* lines run east and west of the equator around the Earth. The equator is always 0° latitude.

- Lines of *longitude* travel north and south from the prime meridian around the Earth. The prime meridian is always 0° longitude.

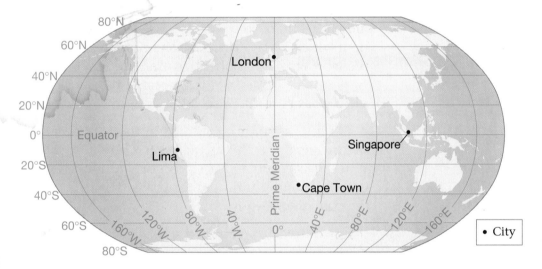

Answer the questions below.

1. In which direction do lines of latitude run?

2. In which direction do lines of longitude run?

CHALLENGE Which city on the map is closest to the equator?

Climate Around the World

The weather changes every day. One day it might be warm and sunny, and the next day it might rain. The weather in any one place follows a general pattern, however. For example, Denver, Colorado, can expect some snowfall each winter. Los Angeles, California, can expect warm, dry winds every fall.

Why is climate different from place to place? Three main factors shape climate. Latitude is one factor. The closer a place is to the equator, the warmer it tends to be. Another factor is elevation. In general, the higher a place is above sea level, the cooler it is.

Remember
The lines that run east and west around the Earth measure the latitude of a place. The equator is always 0° latitude.

The World: Climate Regions

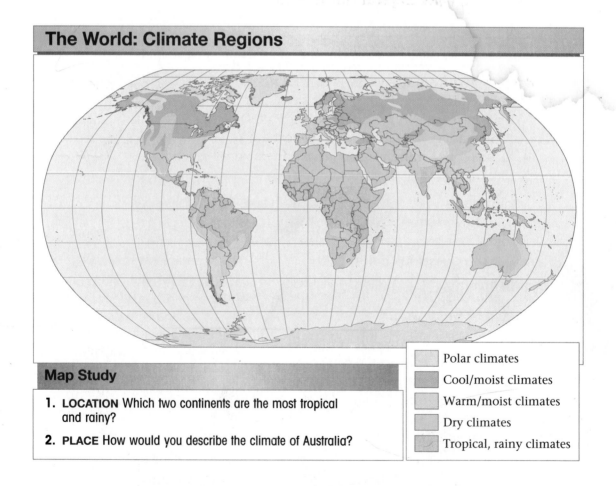

Polar climates
Cool/moist climates
Warm/moist climates
Dry climates
Tropical, rainy climates

Map Study

1. **LOCATION** Which two continents are the most tropical and rainy?

2. **PLACE** How would you describe the climate of Australia?

Finally, the ocean plays a part. The temperature of the ocean does not change easily. When cold air blows over the ocean, the air warms up. When hot air blows over the ocean, the air cools down. Therefore, it is the ocean that prevents the extremes of great heat and cold. That is why places near the ocean tend to have milder climates than inland areas.

Some geographers divide the Earth into five climate regions. In the far north and far south are the polar regions. Near the poles and in the middle of continents are the cool/moist regions. Closer to the equator and near oceans and seas are the warm/moist regions. Here and there are deserts that have a dry climate. Along the equator is the hot, rainy **tropical** climate region.

Using the Earth's Resources

Anything we use from the Earth is considered a natural resource. Air is one natural resource. Water is another. Without these two natural resources, nothing could live. The plants and animals that we eat are resources. So are rocks, minerals, soil, **fossil fuels**, and many other things.

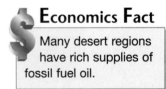

Economics Fact

Many desert regions have rich supplies of fossil fuel oil.

Some resources can be replaced as they are used. For example, when we cut down trees for lumber, we can plant new ones to replace them. Trees, then, are a **renewable resource.** Some resources were formed millions of years ago, such as fossil fuels like oil, natural gas, and coal. They cannot be replaced. These are considered **nonrenewable resources.**

The Earth's resources are spread out unevenly. In desert regions, for example, fresh water is scarce. Without water, food is hard to grow. People in these areas may have to trade the resources they have to get food. Most people depend on trade to get at least some of the resources they need.

In the United States, most people work in factories and businesses. A lot of natural resources are needed to support this way of life. Factories, power plants, and cars use a lot of energy. Much of that energy comes from burning fossil fuels.

However, the world may soon run out of fossil fuels. Furthermore, burning fossil fuels does damage to the environment. Cars, factories, and power plants put harmful smoke and gases into the air. Over the years, the air around the world has become dirty and is killing some of our forests.

The smoke and gases have affected the atmosphere high above the Earth, too. The damaged atmosphere may be letting in more of the sun's harmful rays, which could change the climate of the Earth. Problems such as these are of interest to geographers.

These trees have been damaged over the years by harmful smoke and gases in the air.

✓ Check Your Understanding

Write your answers in complete sentences.

1. What are the main factors that influence climate?

2. Why do places near the ocean tend to have mild climates?

3. What is the difference between a renewable and a nonrenewable resource?

4. How is trade related to the Earth's resources?

GLOBAL ISSUES
The Ozone Layer

Ozone is a form of oxygen. On the ground, it is a dangerous gas. Yet, high up in the atmosphere, ozone is useful. A layer of ozone in the upper atmosphere protects the Earth from the sun's harmful rays.

Scientists have discovered a hole in the ozone layer. In the early 1900s, industry began using chemicals called chlorofluorocarbons (CFCs). Over time, CFCs break down. When they do, they release a chemical that destroys the ozone.

What will happen if the hole in the ozone layer gets bigger? Ultraviolet rays from the sun will pour down onto the Earth. Millions of people each year may then be blinded by diseases related to harmful rays or may get cancer.

Answer the questions below.

1. What is the ozone layer?

2. What happens if the hole in the ozone layer gets bigger?

MAKE A DIFFERENCE
Organize a group cleanup. Search your neighborhood for discarded products that may contain CFCs, such as air conditioners, refrigerators, carpets, spray cans, and plastic foam packages. Explain to your friends why these products are harmful to the environment.

Summary

The Earth is changing all the time. Forces within the Earth cause movements that build mountains and cause earthquakes, while wind, ice, and moving water change the Earth's surface from the outside.

The Earth's revolution around the sun and the tilt of the Earth's axis cause the changes in seasons.

A projection map shows the curved surface of the Earth on a flat plane.

The Earth can be divided into five main climate regions—polar, cool/moist, warm/moist, dry, and tropical.

Natural resources are from the Earth, and we need them to stay alive.

tropical

delta

plain

glacier

fossil fuel

Vocabulary Review

Write a term from the list that matches each definition below.

1. A flat landform

2. A warm and moist climate

3. Coal, oil, or natural gas that formed over millions of years

4. A flat, sandy area where a river enters an ocean

5. A huge, moving mass of ice

Chapter Quiz

Write your answers in complete sentences.

1. What are the three layers that make up the Earth?

2. Are natural gas, oil, and coal products examples of nonrenewable or renewable resources?

3. Where do weathering and erosion occur?

4. **Critical Thinking** How are people affected by events and forces inside the Earth?

5. **Critical Thinking** What is the climate where you live?

Write About Geography

Complete the following activities.

1. What landforms do you see where you live? Write what you think might have caused them.

2. Make a chart that lists the nonrenewable and renewable resources you use daily.

Group Activity

Should people be able to use as much of the world's nonrenewable resources as they want? Within your group, form two teams. One team should research and write an argument for one side of the question. The other team should research and write an argument for the other side of the question.

These people are running in a race across California's Golden Gate Bridge. What are some other reasons people gather in large groups?

Chapter 3 / Human Geography

Words to Know

culture	everything people make, think, and do
nuclear family	a social unit consisting of parents and their children
extended family	a social unit consisting of parents, their children, and other relatives
subsistence	providing only the basic needs of life
commercial	done for the purpose of making money
industry	businesses that make finished products
rural	in the country
technology	the use of science for practical purposes
urban	in or around a town or city
population	the whole group of people in an area
custom	a pattern of behavior followed by a whole group of people
nomad	a person who travels all the time in search of food

Places to Know

rural areas

urban areas

Learning Objectives

- Identify the main aspects of culture.
- Identify differences in ways of farming.
- Describe trends in world population and industrialization.

What Is Culture?

Remember
There are two branches of geography: physical geography and human geography.

Culture is everything that people make, build, think, believe, and do. Human geography focuses on culture. It looks at how cultures differ from place to place.

Geographers sometimes divide the world into cultural regions. They group together people who share the same broad way of life. In some cases, the line between one cultural region and another may be hard to define. Even so, dividing the world into cultural regions is useful. It is a good way to explore how different people live on the Earth.

Families and Social Structure

The family is the most basic unit of social structure. It is one of the ways people organize themselves. Every culture has this type of unit. Yet cultures define the family in different ways. For example, a family consisting of a mother, a father, and their children is a **nuclear family**. A family that also includes aunts, uncles, and cousins is an **extended family.**

Geography Fact

There are clans in many cultures. Among the best known are the many clans of the Highland region of Scotland.

In some cultures, the family can be a whole clan—a large group of relatives. A clan, in fact, can include hundreds of people. Some cultures are organized into tribes as well. A tribe is a group of related families or clans.

People may belong to other groups as well as to a family. For example, they may belong to clubs, unions, or political parties—all of which are part of the social structure of a culture.

Government is another part of the social structure. Every culture has a government, which makes laws and tries to bring order to human life.

Agriculture and Industry

Almost every person on the Earth depends on agriculture. However, not everyone on the Earth is a farmer. Nor is farming done the same way in all places. In some regions, **subsistence** farming is common. Subsistence farmers grow food just for themselves and their families. They often work with simple tools and grow several different crops. They eat what they grow and have nothing left over to sell to others.

Another type of farming is **commercial** farming. Commercial farmers grow crops to sell. They often use machines, as well as chemicals, to fertilize the soil and to kill insects. They grow one crop over a large area.

Some commercial farming, such as this vegetable harvest in Africa, cannot be done by machines.

Commercial farmers in developed countries often have full use of science and modern inventions. In developed countries, only a few people work as farmers. That is because there are many other types of jobs.

Developed countries usually have a lot of **industry**, including businesses that make things out of raw materials. Most of these products are made in factories, where machines do much of the work.

Life is generally more comfortable in an industrialized country. There is more food and safer drinking water than in nonindustrialized countries. There are more health workers and hospitals, and most people own things like cars and televisions. Most developing countries are working to become industrialized countries.

Rural and Urban Life

Hundreds of years ago, most people lived in **rural** areas. They lived in the country or in small villages. Farming was the main type of work.

Then **technology** improved. Industries began to grow, and people started working in factories. Trade became more important, too. More and more people began to sell things for a living. People left the farms and moved to towns, which grew into big cities, or **urban** areas.

✓ **Check Your Understanding**

Write your answers in complete sentences.

1. Why do geographers divide the world into cultural regions?

2. Explain nuclear families.

3. What is a subsistence farmer?

4. Why did urban areas develop?

Population

In 1990, there were over 5 billion people in the world. By the year 2000, the **population**, or the whole group of people in an area, exceeded 6 billion. By the year 2025, it is expected to be about 8 billion. Every year, the world's population increases.

Today, all over the world, urban areas are growing quickly. In 1960, only about 25 people out of every 100 lived in urban areas. In the 1990s, about 45 people out of every 100 lived in urban areas. Cities are more crowded than rural areas. A geographer would say that cities have greater population density. That is, more people live in each square mile than ever before.

You Decide

Why is the world's population growing so quickly?

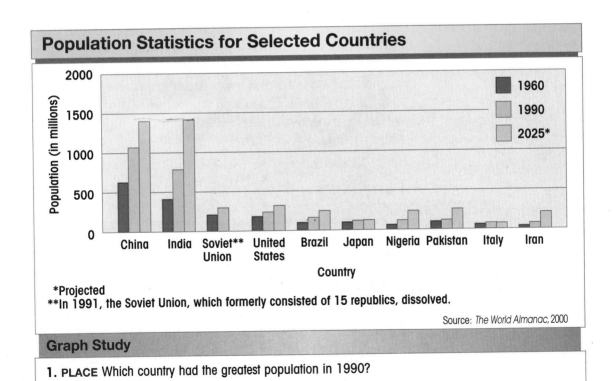

Population Statistics for Selected Countries

Population (in millions)

Legend: 1960, 1990, 2025*

Countries: China, India, Soviet** Union, United States, Brazil, Japan, Nigeria, Pakistan, Italy, Iran

*Projected
**In 1991, the Soviet Union, which formerly consisted of 15 republics, dissolved.

Source: *The World Almanac*, 2000

Graph Study

1. **PLACE** Which country had the greatest population in 1990?

2. **PLACE** Which country shows the most rapid growth of population between 1960 and 2025?

Population growth is not a new problem. However, the world is no longer producing enough food for everyone. People are using up the natural resources of the Earth very quickly. We are running out of space to dump our waste.

Population growth and density are not the same everywhere, though. The quickest growth is taking place in some of the poorest regions. Right now, some of the most heavily populated parts of the world are in Asia and Africa. As a result, in these places hunger is replacing disease as the major killer of humans.

The Arts

Music, dance, literature, and folk tales are forms of art. They express what is important to people. Every culture has some form of art. Even in cultures that have no written language, people tell folk stories. One purpose of art is to make life more enjoyable. The arts also give people a chance to share their culture with others. Through the arts, people can develop their ideas, beliefs, and values.

Language

Language is one of the most important features of a culture. People who share a language can share information. They can share ideas and beliefs. Language helps tie people together.

Thousands of different languages are spoken around the world. In fact, more than 1,000 languages are spoken in Africa alone. The many languages of the world can be grouped into 13 major language families. The largest is the Indo-European language family. English, German, Polish, and Russian belong to this family, and so do about 75 other languages.

All the languages in the same family are related. They may have the same alphabet and grammar. They may share some words. This is because they started out as the same language.

Suppose that long ago, a group of people spoke the same language. Then this group split into two groups. Perhaps the two groups migrated to different areas. In those days, people could not communicate across long distances. They had no phones and could not send letters. Once people were separated, they lost touch with each other.

Meanwhile, within both groups, the language that they shared kept changing. New words crept in. Old words came to have new meanings. At last, after hundreds of years, the two groups spoke entirely different languages. In this way, a few languages branched into many.

Spotlight On

WORLD LANGUAGES

There are six major languages spoken by more than 200 million people around the world.

Look at the chart. The most popular language spoken is Mandarin Chinese. The second most popular language spoken is English.

It is not uncommon for people to speak more than one language.

Critical Thinking Why do you think English is spoken by so many people around the world?

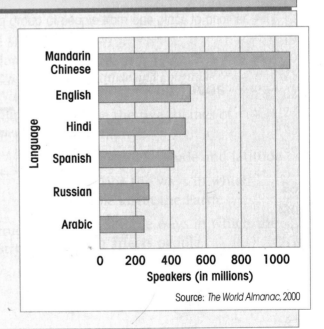

Source: *The World Almanac*, 2000

Customs and Traditions

In parts of Asia, some people use chopsticks. In other parts of the world, they use silverware. Patterns and habits like these are called **customs**. Every culture has its own set of customs. Every culture also has its own traditions, or customs handed down from the past.

Customs include what clothes are worn and how hair is styled. These customs may be affected by physical geography. In warm climates, people tend to wear less clothing.

Celebrations and ceremonies are also customs. Two cultures may celebrate the same event but they may do so in different ways. A wedding in Nigeria is quite unlike a wedding in Greece.

Celebrations

EARTH DAY

The first Earth Day was held on April 22, 1970. Senator Gaylord Nelson was the organizer. His idea was that everyone would take a day to learn about taking care of the Earth. An estimated 20 million people celebrated the first Earth Day.

Earth Day is now celebrated every year around the world on April 22. In 1990, more than 200 million people from 141 countries participated in Earth Day celebrations.

Celebrations vary from place to place. Some people plant trees on Earth Day. Others recycle trash or clean up the oceans. Musicians and other artists often come together on Earth Day to raise awareness and celebrate the Earth.

Critical Thinking How does your school or community participate in Earth Day?

33 USA Earth Day Celebrated

The Earth Day Stamp is part of the "Celebrate the Century—1970s" U.S. Stamp Collection.

Housing

Because everyone needs shelter, all people build housing. Some people live in grass huts, some in stone buildings. Some houses are round, and some are square. Such differences are not random. They reflect differences in culture.

Physical geography affects the kinds of houses that people build. For one thing, people use whatever materials are available to build their houses. In the Arctic, for example, houses are not built of wood but of such things as animal skins and whale bones. Why? It is because no trees grow there.

These houses are made of grass and reeds because those are easy-to-find building materials in Cambodia.

Houses may also reflect how people live. In Mongolia, for example, some people are **nomads**. They move from place to place, so they build houses that can easily be taken apart and put back together.

Religion

Religion is an organized set of beliefs about a god or gods. Most religions have rules about how people should behave. Muslim people, followers of the religion of Islam, and Jewish people must not eat pork because their religions consider pork unclean. Hindu people must not eat beef because their religion teaches that cows are sacred.

Religion can affect much more than what people eat, however. It can shape family life, influence art, and mold a culture's form of government. In fact, religion can affect an entire culture.

Christianity and Islam are the most widespread religions. Christians and Muslims live all around the world.

✓ **Check Your Understanding**

Write your answers in complete sentences.

1. What is population density?

2. Explain how people who live in different places and speak different languages might know some of the same words.

3. What is an example of a custom?

4. Why would people in a community build stone houses rather than wooden houses?

5. What do different religions have in common?

GEOGRAPHER'S TOOL KIT
Using Bar Graphs

A bar graph shows information in a visual way. A bar graph helps you to compare information. Here is how to read a bar graph. First, read the title to learn the subject of the graph. Then, read the labels at the side and across the bottom of the graph. They will tell you what the bars show. Finally, draw conclusions from the graph.

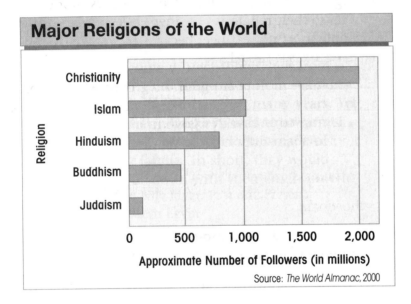

Major Religions of the World

Approximate Number of Followers (in millions)

Source: *The World Almanac*, 2000

Write your answers in complete sentences.

1. Which religion in the world has the most followers?

2. Which religion has approximately 750 million followers?

   CHALLENGE The world's population is approximately 6 billion. Use the bar graph to determine what percentage of the world's people practice a major religion.

Apply the Skill

Create a bar graph that shows the amount of homework you did each day last week. On which day did you do the most?

Summary

| Human geography looks at cultures around the world. |
| Culture includes such things as social structure, farming, industry, population patterns, language, religion, housing, and the arts. |
| More than six billion people live on the Earth, and this number is increasing rapidly. |
| People express their culture through the arts. |
| Thousands of languages are spoken around the world. |
| Clothing, food, and celebrations are examples of customs. |

nuclear family
rural
industry
subsistence
nomad

Vocabulary Review

Write a term from the list that matches each definition below.

1. The type of farmers who grow crops only for their own use and not to sell to others

2. A person who travels all the time in search of food

3. A social unit consisting of parents and their children

4. A business that produces goods or services

5. An area found in the country

Chapter Quiz

Write your answers in complete sentences.

1. Why is life generally more comfortable in industrialized countries?

2. Does population grow more quickly in rural or urban areas?

3. How can religion affect someone's daily life?

4. **Critical Thinking** In what ways is population growth a problem?

5. **Critical Thinking** Do you think commercial farming is more common in developed or developing countries?

Write About Geography

Complete the following activities.

1. Find a photograph of a family in a newspaper or magazine. Decide whether or not the family is most likely an extended family or a nuclear family. Explain your reasoning in a short essay.

2. You are a radio reporter from another country. Write a short report about a custom of that country.

Group Activity

With your group, choose a country. Write an oral report about the human geography of that country. Each person can choose a different subject, such as religion, industry, or the arts. Present your report to the class.

Unit 1 Review

Comprehension Check

Answer each question in a complete sentence.

1. What are the two branches of geography?

2. What are the five themes of geography?

3. In your own words, what is the definition of culture?

4. What are customs?

Building Your Skills

Answer each question in a complete sentence.

1. What is a physical map?

2. What do lines of longitude and latitude measure?

3. Why would you make a map in your mind?

4. When is a bar graph useful?

Where Is It?

Write the name of the place based on the information below.

1. It is 0° latitude.

2. The place farthest north on the Earth

3. Places where there are cities

Writing an Essay

Answer one of the following essay topics.

1. Discuss the difference between physical geography and human geography.

2. Explain why geographers invented map projections.

3. Discuss the difference between subsistence farming and commercial farming.

Geography and You

Discuss the problems that come from the use of fossil fuels. What can be done to lessen these problems?

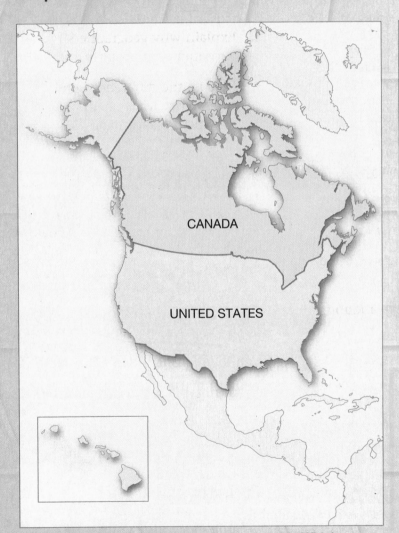

CANADA

UNITED STATES

The United States and Canada share a border. Which country do you think has warmer weather?

TRAVEL LOG
You are a traveler visiting North America. Write notes to a friend who will soon visit. Tell your friend what a tourist should make sure to see. Write what type of people live here, and where they came from.

Native American moccasins

The tourist attraction Niagara Falls is on the border between the United States and Canada. How should two countries that share a natural border get along?

Words to Know

hurricane	a violent tropical storm
immigrant	a person who moves to another country to settle
democracy	a form of government in which people choose their own leader
export	to sell goods or resources to other countries; the goods sold are called exports
mineral	a natural resource found inside the Earth
ore	a natural mixture of rocks or soils that contains metal
manufacturing	the making of products
import	to buy goods or resources from other countries; the goods bought are called imports
service	a useful task that people perform to earn a living without making a product

Places to Know

Gulf of Mexico

Appalachian Mountains

Canadian Shield

Rocky Mountains

Mississippi River

Learning Objectives

- Identify the major landforms of the region.
- Describe the climate of the region.
- Describe the human features of the region.
- Describe the economy of the United States and Canada.

The Land

The United States and Canada are the two largest countries in North America. They cover about 90 percent of the continent. The Rio Grande marks the southwestern border of the United States. The St. Lawrence River marks a part of the border between the United States and Canada.

If you could see this region from outer space, you might notice a number of major landforms. Refer to the map below as you read about these landforms.

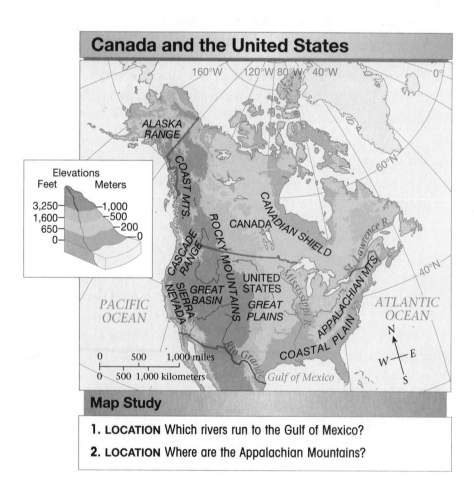

Canada and the United States

Elevations
Feet   Meters
3,250 — —1,000
1,600 — —500
650 — —200
0 — —0

Map Study

1. **LOCATION** Which rivers run to the Gulf of Mexico?
2. **LOCATION** Where are the Appalachian Mountains?

In the east is a flat, rolling landscape called the Coastal Plain. It stretches down the Atlantic Coast and west along the Gulf of Mexico. A little to the west of the Coastal Plain is a long strip of hills. These are called the Appalachian Mountains.

Then there is a vast flat area—the biggest landform in the region. In Canada, much of this flat area is a high, rocky plateau called the Canadian Shield. Farther south, where the elevation drops, the flatlands are known as the Interior Plains.

West of the plains, there is a broad band of mountains. The first and biggest are the Rocky Mountains. It is part of a mountain range that starts in Alaska and runs almost to Mexico. This mountain range contains many peaks more than 10,000 feet high. Other smaller mountain chains stretch between the Rocky Mountains and the Pacific Coast. In the south where the mountains branch apart, the bowl-shaped land between them is called the Great Basin.

In the far west is the Pacific Coast Mountain Range, stretching from Alaska to California. This strip of hills and valleys is more than 2,500 miles long, yet most of it is less than 100 miles wide.

Geography Fact

The tallest mountain in North America, at 20,320 feet high, is Mount McKinley, also known as Denali. It is located in Alaska.

Climate

Many kinds of climates are found in the United States and Canada. Generally, the temperature varies from hot in the south to cold in the north. Along most of the U.S. West Coast, the weather is mild. The Rocky Mountain area is cold in winter. In the Central Plains, seasons can vary by as much as 150 degrees.

Most parts of Canada and the United States are moist. The Pacific Northwest gets fog and drizzle more than half of the year. The Atlantic and Gulf coasts get violent, tropical storms called **hurricanes.**

Five of the world's largest lakes, the Great Lakes, lie on the border between the United States and Canada. One of the world's longest rivers, the Mississippi, runs through the Great Plains. The region does, however, have dry parts. The southwestern United States is the driest.

The People

Almost everyone in this cultural region speaks English, although other languages are spoken in some areas. Most children go to a public school. Private citizens or companies run most businesses. People are free to practice many faiths.

Remember
Geographers study movement of two kinds. They study how a group of people moves from one place to another to settle. They also study the movement of people to do business.

There is a reason for all this cultural variety. Everyone in this region is descended from **immigrants.** They have roots in some other part of the world. About 80 percent have roots in Europe. About 20 percent trace their ancestry back to Africa, Asia, and other places. The Native Americans also migrated to this land. They came from Asia long ago.

Both Canada and the United States have **democracy** as their form of government. The United States is divided into 50 states. Alaska and Hawaii are not connected to the others. Alaska is farther north. Part of Canada separates it from the "lower 48" states. Hawaii is a group of islands in the Pacific Ocean.

The United States also has several territories, including Puerto Rico. Territories have their own governments, but the people who live there are citizens of the United States. Canada is divided into ten provinces and three large territories.

Both countries are very urban. About 273 million people live in the United States, while Canada has about 31 million. Three-fourths of the population lives in or near cities. Most Canadians live within 120 miles of the U.S. border. Few live much farther north because the climate is so cold.

More than 18 million people live in the New York City area. It has the largest population of any metropolitan area in the United States.

The United States has the world's most powerful economy. Its wealth comes from many sources. The people work in many kinds of jobs. Canada has fewer people, but it has much the same kind of economy. Many people have their own electric lights, a fax machine, a computer, and more than one television and telephone.

Farming, Ranching, and Fishing

Today, most of the farmland in the United States and Canada is owned and run by companies, though some farms still belong to families. Almost all farmers in this region use machines to work the land. As a result, Canada and the United States grow more food than their citizens eat.

Both countries **export** wheat, which is grown in the Central Plains. Corn and other grains are also grown there. Farmers in the southern and southeastern United States earn billions of dollars from growing cotton, rice, and tobacco. California alone grows enough vegetables to feed the whole continent. The Pacific Northwest produces fruit and potatoes.

Both Canada and the United States have dairy farms and raise hogs, chickens, and cattle. Fishing is big business along the thousands of miles of coastline.

✓ **Check Your Understanding**

Write your answers in complete sentences.

1. What is the name of the Canadian landform that is the largest landform of its kind in North America?

2. What is the driest part of North America?

3. Compare and contrast the economies of Canada and the United States.

4. What is a crop that both the United States and Canada export?

Mining, Drilling, and Logging

North America is rich in **minerals**. Gold is just one of them. Many other **ores** are found in this region. They are found in the western mountains, in the Canadian Shield, and near the Great Lakes. There is silver, copper, iron, and much more. Coal is found in the Appalachians. The work of getting these resources out of the Earth is called mining. Canada gets much of its wealth from mining.

Both Canada and the United States have reserves of oil, which has sometimes been called "black gold." It is crucial to life in developed countries. Factories and cars run on it, and farmers depend on it.

You Decide

Why would oil be called "black gold"?

This photograph shows several of the miners who went to Alaska during the Gold Rush.

The first big North American oil fields were found in Texas and Oklahoma. Today, most of the oil pumped in this region comes out of new fields in Alaska and Oklahoma. A huge tube called the Trans-Alaska Pipeline brings the oil down the coast, where it is loaded into ships and carried south.

At one time, forests covered most of the lands we now call Canada and the United States. Only the Central Plains and the southwestern United States were bare. The first settlers used timber to make houses. Later, they made paper from trees.

Today, forests still cover quite a bit of the United States and Canada. A lot of money is made from logging. Big companies log the southeastern United States and the Pacific Northwest. Timber is also a big business across much of northern Canada.

Unfortunately, trees are being cut down faster than they can grow back. Logging companies often practice clearcutting, which means they cut down every tree in a given area. Clearcutting leaves land looking bald and wipes out the animals. In a clearcut area, the soil tends to wash away and may then choke streams and kill fish.

Clearcutting strips the land of trees. Taking out some trees and leaving others is a better—but harder—way to log an area.

Manufacturing, Sales, and Service

Every part of the United States and Canada has **manufacturing** businesses. These businesses make different things, depending on the raw materials found nearby. The Pacific Northwest and the southeastern United States, for example, have many paper factories. That is because paper is made from trees that grow in these areas. The Gulf Coast has both oil wells and factories that make products from oil: chemicals, plastic, gasoline, and paint. The Midwest has factories that make food products. These factories get their raw materials from local farms.

The area from the Great Lakes to the East Coast was once called the industrial belt. Coal and metal ores were mined nearby, and factories were built to make steel. Then factories were built to use all that steel. The car industry, for example, boomed in Detroit. Even now, this area is where most U.S. cars are made. (Just across the border, Canada produces cars, too.) Today, the United States no longer makes as much steel but **imports** most of it from abroad. To import is to buy goods or resources from other countries.

High-technology businesses are on the rise in Canada and the United States. The United States is a leader in computer manufacturing. Computer companies have sprung up near an important resource—people. Many computer scientists work and teach in universities. Some of these universities are located in Massachusetts, California, Michigan, and Texas. So today, these four areas are centers of the computer industry.

In the United States and Canada, less than 4 percent of the workers have jobs in agriculture. About 15 percent have jobs in manufacturing. So what do all the other workers do? Most of them sell things, fix things, or do things for other people. They are waiters, doctors, teachers, lawyers, bankers, actors, barbers, truck drivers, mechanics, and so on. Three out of four jobs in Canada and the United States today are in sales and **service**.

✓ Check Your Understanding

Write your answers in complete sentences.

1. What is a problem caused by clearcutting?

2. Why does the Gulf Coast have chemical plants?

3. What kind of work do most North Americans do?

GLOBAL ISSUES
Old-Growth Forests

About 10 percent of the trees in the United States are found in old-growth forests, where the trees are hundreds of years old. These areas have never been logged. Today, a battle is raging over these trees. Logging companies want to start cutting them down. Old-growth trees provide the best and cheapest wood. By cutting them down, logging companies say they can provide jobs.

On the other side stand environmentalists. These are people who work to protect the natural environment. They want to stop all logging in old-growth forests. They point out that when the trees are gone, the jobs will be lost anyway.

Recently, scientists have noticed that a bird called the spotted owl is dying out. Spotted owls live in old-growth forests. Most scientists agree that the vanishing owls are a warning sign. If they are dying out, many other forest-dwelling creatures must be dying, too.

Answer the questions below.

1. What is an old-growth forest?

2. What are the arguments for logging old-growth forest?

MAKE A DIFFERENCE
How much old-growth forest is in your state? Find out from the Department of Natural Resources. Ask what the state's policy is on old-growth forests. Then write an editorial taking a stand on what you learned.

Summary

Canada and the United States are the largest countries in North America. Major landforms in the United States and Canada include the Atlantic Coastal Plain, the Appalachian Mountains, the Interior Plains, the Rocky Mountains, and the Pacific Coast.

The climate in this region varies from hot and dry to cold and snowy.

Farming, ranching, fishing, mining, logging, and manufacturing make this a productive region. Most of the people, however, work in sales and services.

Vocabulary Review

Write *true* or *false*. If the statement is false, change the underlined term to make it true.

1. A form of government in which people choose their leader is a <u>democracy</u>.

2. To <u>export</u> is to buy goods or resources from other countries.

3. <u>Manufacturing</u> is the making of products.

4. Taking <u>minerals</u> or oil from the Earth is called mining.

5. An <u>ore</u> is a task that people perform to earn a living without making a product.

Chapter Quiz

Write the correct letter for each region.

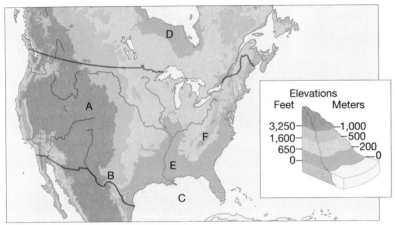

1. Rocky Mountains   **4.** Canadian Shield

2. Rio Grande   **5.** Mississippi River

3. Gulf of Mexico   **6.** Appalachian Mountains

Write About Geography

Complete the following activities.

1. Draw a postcard showing one of the major landforms in North America. Then write the caption for it.

2. Make a chart comparing the United States and Canada. Include factors such as population and climate.

Group Activity

As a group, discuss this question: How much has the human geography of North America changed in the past 200 years? Talk about how the population has changed and how the ways people make their livings have changed.

Inuit people, who live in the far north, make their homes, called igloos, from sod, rocks, or ice. Why do they use these materials?

Chapter 5 / Native Americans

Words to Know

descendant	a person born later in a family line
long house	a large wooden dwelling
constitution	the basic laws that set up the rules of government for a nation
tipi	a cone-shaped, portable dwelling made of poles and animal skins
pueblo	a dwelling with many rooms made of stone or clay
igloo	a dwelling made of sod, wood, rock, or domed ice
treaty	an agreement between nations or peoples
reservation	a piece of public land set aside by the government for use by a certain group of people; called a reserve in Canada

Places to Know

Siberia

Bering Strait

Central Plains

Arctic

Northwest Territories

Oklahoma

Learning Objectives

- Describe how Native Americans migrated to North America from Asia.

- Describe some traditional American Indian cultures.

- Explain the conflict between American Indians and European settlers.

- Describe how Europeans affected Native American populations.

- Describe Native American life today.

The First Americans

Native Americans migrated to North America from Siberia, a place in Asia. Today, Alaska is separated from Siberia by a strip of water called the Bering Strait. Long ago, during one of the Ice Ages, much of the world's water was "locked" into glaciers. The water level of the oceans sank. The floor of the Bering Strait was above sea level. People could walk from Asia to North America.

No one quite knows when the first people came to North America over the Bering Strait. It might have been as long as 48,000 years ago or as recently as 20,000 years ago. These people were the first Americans. Their **descendants** are the Native Americans of today.

The first Americans were nomadic hunters. As wild animals thinned out in one area and there was less food, they would move on in search of more. By 9,000 B.C. these first Americans had spread all across North and South America. By that time, they had branched into thousands of different bands, clans, and tribes. In time, in Mexico and farther south, great Native American cities began to be built.

In 1492, the European explorer Christopher Columbus landed on an island near Florida. He thought he had arrived at the East Indies, so he called the people he met there "Indians." Today, Native Americans are often still called American Indians. The name goes back to Columbus's mistake.

Traditional Native American Cultures

You Decide

Why did people begin to build cities?

Remember

A people's culture is everything they think, make, and do.

There are many different Native American cultures. More than 2,000 languages were spoken in America when Columbus arrived. The native cultures were as varied as the ones in Europe. Each culture was shaped by its natural surroundings. Four of the many traditional American Indian cultures are the Iroquois, the Sioux, the Pueblo, and the Kwakiutl.

The Iroquois

The Iroquois lived in the forests of what is now the northeastern part of the United States. They built large wooden dwellings called **long houses.** In each long house lived an extended family. Iroquois men were hunters, and the women were farmers. The men often shaved their heads, leaving only a comb or spike of hair. Both men and women wore deerskin clothes and soft deerskin shoes. In New York, five large Iroquois tribes joined together to form a nation called the Iroquois League, which had a democratic system of government. Some of the ideas in the United States **Constitution** may have been borrowed from the Iroquois.

The Sioux

The Sioux lived in the Central Plains. By the 1700s, they had become nomadic hunters who did no farming but followed the buffalo migrations. The Sioux lived in cone-shaped, portable dwellings called **tipis,** which were made of poles and buffalo skins. Both the men and the women grew their hair long. They wore colorful clothes decorated with feathers and quills. Most Sioux lived in small bands. Within a band, leaders could give only advice, not orders.

The Pueblo

American Indians, called the Pueblo, also lived in what is now the southwestern part of the United States. They built stone or clay dwellings also called **pueblos—** which were like apartment buildings. The pueblos had many rooms, and some were four or five stories high. However, a pueblo was not just a building. It was a community. In fact, to the people who lived in one, a pueblo was the world. Life was tightly organized, and only the group mattered. Other pueblos were like foreign countries.

A pueblo in Taos, New Mexico

The Pueblos were farmers, who grew corn and squash on irrigated lands. They were also skillful potters and weavers. The most important thing in their life was religion. Their priests were their rulers.

The Kwakiutl

The Kwakiutl lived along the Pacific Coast near what is now the border of the United States and Canada. They did no farming at all but instead built their life around fishing. The Kwakiutl were fine woodworkers. They lived in large wooden houses. They carved canoes out of single logs (one canoe could be as much as 60 feet long). They also constructed huge wooden totem poles. A totem pole is a column of carved figures, both human and animal, that stands for events in a family's history.

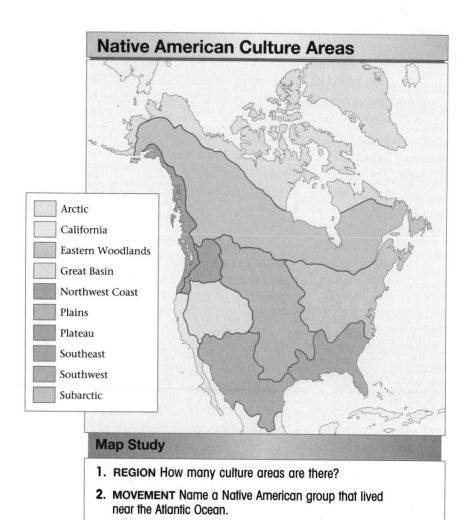

Native American Culture Areas

- Arctic
- California
- Eastern Woodlands
- Great Basin
- Northwest Coast
- Plains
- Plateau
- Southeast
- Southwest
- Subarctic

Map Study

1. **REGION** How many culture areas are there?

2. **MOVEMENT** Name a Native American group that lived near the Atlantic Ocean.

Although the Kwakiutl admired wealth, they did not care how much a person had but rather how much he or she gave away. At a great feast called a potlatch, the host would give wealth away. The more the host gave away, the more important the host became.

The Iroquois, Sioux, Pueblo, and Kwakiutl are four traditional American Indian cultures. Each can also be considered part of one of the ten North American Indian "culture areas."

Native People of the Arctic

The Inuit and Aleut are native people of the far north. They are not usually called "Indians," but like the American Indians, their ancestors came from Asia. They came much later, however, and may even have arrived as recently as 3,000 years ago. They also came by boat rather than by land. The Inuit have been called Eskimos by other people, but their own name for themselves has always been Inuit.

In the far north is an area called the Arctic. This area is covered with snow most of the year. No crops can be grown there. Human life might seem impossible in the Arctic, yet Inuit and Aleut have lived in this environment for thousands of years.

Traditional Inuit culture has been shaped by the harsh environment. In winter, for example, the Inuit live in **igloos.** These dwellings are built from sod, rocks, or domed ice. Because the entrances are below ground, igloos are warm inside—even in a blizzard.

The Inuit are nomadic hunters by tradition. Some live inland. They move around on sleds pulled by teams of dogs. They hunt animals such as caribou, a type of reindeer. Other Inuit live on the coast, as do most Aleut. Coastal Inuit travel in small, covered canoes called kayaks. They also build bigger boats called umiaks. In these boats, the Inuit hunt seals and whales.

Sculpture carved by an Inuit artist

In the 1950s, white people began moving into the Arctic. They brought with them such things as snowmobiles, television, and alcohol. White culture began to change the Inuit way of life. The Canadian government has tried to make the nomads settle down, ordering that Inuit children go to school and learn English.

The Canadian government decided that a large portion of the Northwest Territories should be given to the Inuit to govern themselves. The new territory, called Nunavut, was formed in 1999.

Native American Religions

While Native Americans have many differences, they also have some things in common. Most American Indian religions, for example, focus on nature. The American Indians believe that rocks and trees have spirits. They teach that people are connected to all other living things. Most of all, American Indian cultures hold a deep respect for the Earth.

In general, American Indians believe that people cannot own land. They believe that people belong to the Earth and not vice versa. This idea, as you might guess, brought them into fierce conflict with the Europeans.

✓ **Check Your Understanding**

Write your answers in complete sentences.

1. How did the first people migrate to North America?

2. Compare the homes the Iroquois built to those the Sioux built.

3. How has Inuit culture been shaped by environment?

4. What is a belief many Native Americans have in common?

The European Impact
on Native American Life

In 1492, at least eight million Native Americans lived in what is now Canada and the United States. Many diseases common in Europe did not exist among them. When the American Indians came into contact with Europeans, their bodies had built up no defenses against these diseases. Many American Indians died.

The survivors ended up at war with the European settlers. These settlers killed many of the American Indians in the northeastern United States and drove most of the others west and north. In the 1830s, U.S. President Andrew Jackson had the American Indians of the southeastern United States moved to what was then called Indian Territory and is now Oklahoma. The American Indians were forced to walk, and many died on the long marches. Today Oklahoma has the largest American Indian population of all the United States.

In the late 1800s, the U.S. Army fought fierce battles with the Plains Indians. The Plains Indians won some battles, but the United States won the wars. The settlers pushed west. They built railroads across the continent, killing whole herds of buffalo along the way. By 1890, they had wiped out most of the buffalo. The native people of these plains depended on the buffalo to survive. They used every part of these animals. They ate the meat, made clothing and shelter out of the skins, and made tools and weapons out of the bones. Groups such as the Blackfoot saw their whole way of life destroyed. They and other groups began to starve.

By 1900, only about 220,000 Native Americans remained in the United States. Perhaps half that many lived in Canada. Then, in 1910, the pattern began to change. The population of Native Americans began to rise again. Today, nearly two million Native Americans, including Inuit and Aleut in Alaska, live in the United States. Over 500,000 live in Canada.

HISTORY FACT

Historians now believe that most American Indians died of European diseases before they ever even saw Europeans. As many as 85 percent of American Indians may have died in this way.

Reservations and Reserves

Throughout U.S. history, American Indians fought the U.S. government and lost. Each loss led to a **treaty**, and each treaty pushed the Indians off more of their lands. In the end, they were left with just a few areas to call their own. These areas are known as **reservations.** Canada has similar areas called reserves.

There are about 300 reservations in the United States. Almost all of them are west of the Mississippi River. The largest is the Navajo reservation, located mainly in New Mexico and Arizona. About 200,000 people live on this reservation.

Reservations are run by a federal government agency called the Bureau of Indian Affairs. Yet Native Americans are supposedly free to live any way they wish on reservations. They can speak their own languages, practice their own religions, and raise their children according to their own customs.

A reservation belongs to an entire American Indian nation, not to individuals. A tribal council usually helps run schools, where children learn such subjects as math and science. They also study their own group's history and language.

Sheep are a common sight on the Navajo reservation in the American Southwest.

Most of the land set aside as reservations in the United States is barren. They are the lands the white settlers did not want. Often they have dry, rocky soil, and there is little or no way to make a living farming the land in these areas. Those who do live on reservations—about 400,000 Native Americans in the United States—have struggled to earn a living and to make a better life for themselves and their families.

Native American Life Off the Reservation

Native Americans who do not live on reservations may also find life difficult. Many cannot find jobs. In fact, the jobless rate for American Indians is seven times that of other ethnic groups. Also, the American Indians are surrounded by a culture that is not their own. This makes it difficult for them to follow their own customs and traditions.

American Indians have been struggling for years with how to keep their culture alive. The struggle has led them to reach out to one another. In the early 1900s, some groups began to unite and form political organizations.

Celebrations

POWWOWS

A powwow is a celebration of American Indian culture. At a powwow, dancers, singers, musicians, artists, and families gather to celebrate their traditions.

Usually, they are held outdoors. Food and goods are sold. Contests are held for singing and dancing. Non–Native Americans are sometimes welcome at powwows. However, they are seldom allowed to attend the religious ceremonies that are often part of such powwows.

Long ago, powwows were a special custom of the Plains Indians. Today the custom has spread to other groups. The powwow has become one feature of an ever more unified American Indian culture.

Critical Thinking How do powwows help to unify American Indian culture?

American Indian dancer Damon Polk performs at an Arizona powwow.

The largest of these is the National Congress of American Indians, founded in 1944. It continues to work to change laws that have to do with American Indian treaty rights.

The Native American Rights Fund is a legal group that tries to settle American Indian land claims in courts of law. One of many such cases was settled in Maine in 1980. It involved several nations such as the Passamaquoddy and Penobscot. These nations were paid millions of dollars for lands they had lost to white settlers.

Another organization is the American Indian Movement (AIM). AIM was founded in 1968 to promote American Indian culture. By organizing marches and demonstrations, it tries to draw attention to problems facing Native Americans.

Some nations have started successful businesses. One Chippewa community in the upper Midwest gathers and sells wild rice. A Sioux community in the Central Plains runs a successful pencil company. Such successes have inspired other Native American groups to work toward building their own businesses in their region.

$ Economics Fact

Gambling casinos have been a feature on many American Indian reservations since 1988, when a federal law allowed American Indian nations to open casinos.

✓ Check Your Understanding

Write your answers in complete sentences.

1. What happened after the American Indians and white settlers went to war?

2. Where are most of the American Indian reservations in the United States?

3. What does the Native American Rights Fund do?

GEOGRAPHY IN YOUR LIFE
Understanding Inset Maps

An inset map enlarges a section of a map. When you see an inset map, first notice what section of the main map it covers. Then look at the details in the inset map. What is the inset map showing you?

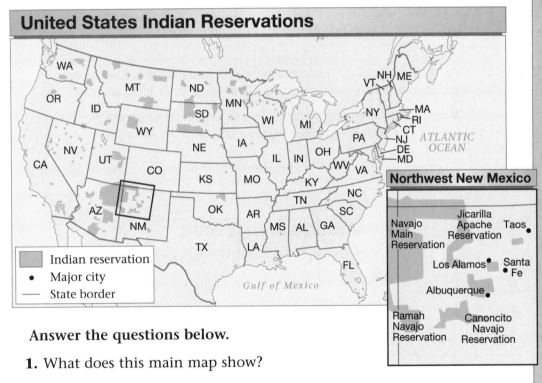

United States Indian Reservations

Indian reservation
• Major city
— State border

Northwest New Mexico

Navajo Main Reservation
Jicarilla Apache Reservation
Taos
Los Alamos
Santa Fe
Albuquerque
Ramah Navajo Reservation
Canoncito Navajo Reservation

ATLANTIC OCEAN

Gulf of Mexico

Answer the questions below.

1. What does this main map show?

2. What does this inset map show?

CHALLENGE What can you tell about New Mexico from this inset map?

Apply the Skill

Find a map in this book. Describe an inset map that would fit with the main map.

Chapter

5 / Review

Summary

The first Americans came from Asia between 48,000 and 20,000 years ago.

American Indian cultures in the United States and Canada can be grouped into culture areas.

The Inuit and Aleut of the Arctic came from Asia more recently than other native peoples.

Reservations in the United States and reserves in Canada are areas set aside for American Indians. Most have poor soil for farming or for grazing animals.

American Indian political organizations include the National Congress of American Indians, the Native American Rights Fund, and the American Indian Movement.

treaty
descendant
long house
pueblo
igloo

Vocabulary Review

Write a term from the list that matches each definition below.

1. A person born later in the family line

2. A dwelling made of sod, wood, rock, or domed ice

3. An agreement between nations or peoples

4. A dwelling with many rooms made of stone or clay

5. A large wooden dwelling

Chapter Quiz

Write your answers in complete sentences.

1. Native Americans migrated to North America from which continent?

2. The Inuit and Aleut are native to what area in North America?

3. Describe the impact of European settlers on early American Indian life in North America.

4. **Critical Thinking** How is American Indian life today different than before European settlers arrived?

5. **Critical Thinking** How are American Indians working to keep their traditional cultures alive?

Write About Geography

Complete the following activities.

1. Write an essay explaining why each of the different types of American Indian dwellings is appropriate for each culture.

2. Write the diary entry of a European settler first seeing a Native American community. Then write an entry of a Native American first seeing a European settlement.

Group Activity

Divide into groups of Native Americans and European settlers that want to trade with each other. Plan what you have to trade. Then meet and make your trades. Keep a record of the trades you make.

Millions of immigrants entered the United States in the late 1800s and early 1900s. What continent did your ancestors come from?

Chapter 6

Settlers From Other Lands

Words to Know

plantation	a large farm that grows a single crop
prejudice	judging people without knowing them
discrimination	treating some people worse than others because of prejudice
ghetto	a neighborhood where a particular ethnic group is forced to live because of prejudice
quota	a limited amount
refugee	a person who flees his or her home because of war, political danger, famine, or economic hardship
multicultural	involving many cultures mixed together

Places to Know

Acadia

Texas

Scandinavia

China

Eastern Europe

Southeast Asia

Learning Objectives

- Describe the English and French foundations of Canada and the United States.
- Explain how African Americans came to the United States.
- Describe the Hispanic heritage of the American Southwest.
- Describe the waves of immigration from Europe and Asia.
- Describe more recent patterns of immigration to this region.
- Identify contributions of various immigrant groups to the culture of this region.

The French and the English

Remember
Trade is the buying and selling or exchanging of goods.

Some of the first European immigrants to America were French fur traders. The woods of North America were full of beavers, otters, and mink. French traders would get the furs from American Indians in exchange for European-made goods. The traders could then make money selling the furs in Europe.

English settlers began arriving, too. Soon the French and English were arguing about who had the right to trade where. In 1754, war broke out between them. It was called the French and Indian War, because most of the American Indians sided with the French. The British won, and that is why English is now the main language in Canada and the United States.

Spotlight On

QUÉBEC

Québec has long had a strong separatist movement. The city includes some French-speaking people who want to separate Québec from Canada.

In 1990, Canadians voted down a plan called the Meech Lake Accord. If passed, the plan would have allowed Québec to be treated differently from other Canadian provinces.

Tension between the French- and English-speaking people of Canada continues to grow.

Critical Thinking Why does tension continue to grow in Québec?

Québec

A group of French settlers moved south. They migrated from a region in Canada called Acadia, which included what are today the provinces of Nova Scotia, New Brunswick, and Prince Edward Island. These settlers ended up in Louisiana. Today, their descendants, called Cajuns, live near New Orleans.

African Americans: Unwilling Immigrants

The ancestors of most African Americans came to America as enslaved people. The first Africans that are known to have come to North America arrived in 1619. Early settlers in the American South started growing tobacco on **plantations,** or big farms that grew one crop. The plantation owners bought Africans to do the work. Many Americans—mostly in the South, but also in the North—owned Africans as house servants.

Slavery in the United States was a terrible practice. It lasted until the Civil War of 1861 to 1865. After the war, African Americans were free. However, many African Americans were poor and had no political or economic power. They were treated with hatred and **prejudice** by former slave owners and others.

> **HISTORY FACT**
>
> The Civil Rights and Voting Rights Acts of 1964 made it against the law to discriminate against people because of their race, sex, religion, or ethnic background.

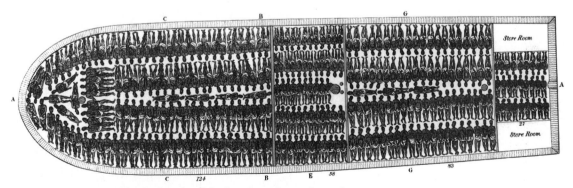

Enslaved people loaded on a ship for the trip to America.

Many African Americans moved to cities in the North to get away from the hatred and to find jobs. Yet in the North, they experienced **discrimination**. Employers would not hire African Americans because of their skin color. They had difficulty finding decent housing. They were forced to live in poor parts of town called **ghettos**.

Slavery never took hold in Canada, so Canada has fewer citizens descended from Africans than the United States does. Today, about 12 percent of the U.S. population is made up of African Americans. In recent years, African Americans have made gains, both socially and economically. African Americans can now be found in every profession. Still this group faces discrimination. In general, African Americans earn less than people of European descent, for example.

African Americans have deeply affected American culture. Their work helped to build the economy of the south. After the Civil War, many African Americans moved west and became cowboys.

Celebrations

KWANZAA

Kwanzaa is a harvest holiday. It celebrates family, community, and the values of African ancestors.

Kwanzaa was created in the 1960s. It runs from December 26 to January 1. African Americans of any religion can celebrate Kwanzaa.

Each day honors a certain principle, such as creativity, faith, working together, and purpose.

A family celebrates Kwanzaa.

Critical Thinking What are some other ways to honor the values celebrated at Kwanzaa?

African American folk tales, such as the Brer Rabbit stories, have become part of American folklore. African Americans have also influenced the kind of English spoken in the United States. In addition, almost every form of music born in the United States has roots in African American culture. This includes jazz, blues, ragtime, soul, rock 'n' roll, and rap.

The Hispanic Southwest

In the 1800s, the United States was a growing nation. However, Mexico—founded by Spanish colonists—also was growing. The Spaniards already occupied the lands from Texas to California.

Nonetheless, settlers from the United States began moving into Texas until they outnumbered the Hispanics, or people of Spanish background. Texas broke away from Mexico in 1835. It joined the United States ten years later. In 1846, the United States went to war with Mexico and won. Many Hispanics thus ended up living within the borders of the United States.

The southwestern United States still shows this Hispanic influence. Many of the people have Mexican ancestors. Many speak Spanish—some, in fact, speak Spanish as their first language. Details such as arched doorways and red tile roofs give buildings a Spanish look. Mexican styles of cooking are very popular.

✓ **Check Your Understanding**

Write your answers in complete sentences.

1. Why did French people first come to America?

2. Name one way African people helped shape American culture.

3. How did Hispanics end up living within the United States?

You Decide

Which Germans do you think were most likely to leave their homeland for America?

Germany and Scandinavia

The most common ethnic background in the United States is German. There was never a single wave of German immigration, but German immigrants came year after year. Immigrants came from other parts of northern Europe, too. Many came from Scandinavia—the countries of Norway, Sweden, Denmark, and Finland.

These immigrants came for land. In America, immigrants did not need money to own a piece of wilderness. If they could work and fight for land, it was theirs. Germans settled in Pennsylvania and across the midwestern plains. The Scandinavians settled in the plains, too, but farther north.

The German and Scandinavian heritage of the midwestern United States is everywhere. Hamburgers and hot dogs are versions of German food. So are mustard, sauerkraut, and potato salad. The Christmas tree is a custom from northern Europe. Santa Claus is based on a Scandinavian legend.

Early Immigrants From Asia

Chinese immigrants played a key role in developing the West. They helped to build the railroads, and they also worked in mining towns. Chinese communities—some called "Chinatowns"—developed in many cities. Today, Vancouver, Los Angeles, and New York all have a Chinatown.

Early Asian immigrants faced a great deal of racial prejudice. Chinese immigrants were not allowed to become U.S. citizens. From 1882 to 1943, Chinese people were not even allowed to enter the United States. Canada, too, outlawed Chinese immigration for a while.

The first wave of Japanese immigrants came to work for California's farmers in the 1890s. The newcomers quickly began leasing and buying farmland.

They did so well that, in 1913, a California law barred Japanese immigrants from buying land. A national law in 1924 went further and banned all immigrants from Japan. However, the Japanese immigrants in the United States already had built a strong community.

After Japan's attack on Pearl Harbor in 1941, the United States entered World War II. Months later, about 120,000 Americans of Japanese ancestry, most of them citizens, were imprisoned in internment camps. The same thing happened in Canada. Those sent to the camps lost their property. After the war, the Japanese community rebuilt. In 1988, the U.S. government apologized to the Japanese people sent to camps and paid each one $20,000.

Japanese people in California were sent to internment camps during World War II. They lost their land and most of their possessions.

Later European Immigrants

A great wave of European immigration started around 1860. In the next 20 years, more than seven million immigrants poured into the United States. In the 20 years after that, almost nine million immigrants came to the United States. Between 1900 and 1920, over 14 million immigrants entered the United States.

Before the Civil War, immigrants had come to this region mainly for land. After the Civil War, they came for jobs. Often, immigrants left Europe because of the growing population and lack of jobs. Industry was booming in the United States. The new immigrants had little trouble finding work.

The jobs were often in cities, where steel mills, meatpacking plants, and the clothing industry needed workers. By 1910 immigrants made up more than half the residents of the 18 largest cities in the United States. Immigrants found others from their homelands and moved near them. Within the cities, groups of immigrants spoke their native language and ate foods they knew from home.

For many, the Statue of Liberty represents freedom.

Life was not easy for these new U.S. residents. The immigrants often lived in slums. The work they did was hard, and their hours were long. The workers were not well paid. Also, many of these newcomers faced prejudice. Most had come from Eastern Europe and Italy. Many were Catholic or Jewish. At home, they had been workers and peasants. In America, the middle-class Protestant majority, mostly of Northern European ancestry, looked down on them.

The new immigrants began to improve their lives. They learned English. Parents sent their children to school so they could have a better future. Today, the descendants of these immigrants form a large part of the population of Canada and the United States.

More Recent Immigration Patterns

For a long time, Canada and the United States welcomed most immigrants. Both countries needed workers, farmers, ranchers, and miners. Immigrants tamed the wilderness and helped build cities.

However, the 1920s needed fewer workers. Prejudice was on the rise. Both the United States and Canada passed immigration laws that set **quotas** to limit immigrants of certain nationalities.

Today, both countries still limit immigration by using quotas. Immigration has not ended, however. After World War II, a flood of people poured out of Asia and Eastern Europe into North America.

Geography Fact

Many recent immigrants from Asia and Central America live in Monterey Park, California.

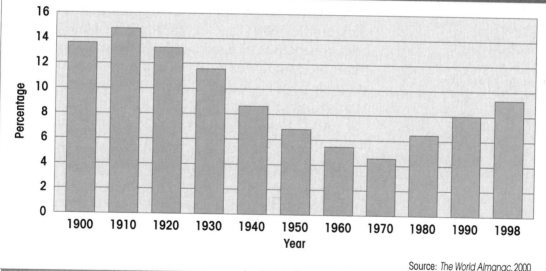

Percentage of U.S. Population That Is Foreign Born, 1900–1998

Source: *The World Almanac*, 2000

Graph Study

1. MOVEMENT In what year did the U.S. population have the largest numbers of foreign-born people?

2. MOVEMENT In what year were about 8 percent of the people in the United States foreign-born?

They came to Canada and the United States to get away from Communist rule, ethnic persecution, and economic problems. Many were **refugees**, looking for freedom and safety.

More refugees came after the Vietnam War ended in 1975. They came, by the hundreds of thousands, from such Southeast Asian countries as Laos, Cambodia, and Vietnam.

Many immigrants come to the United States from Mexico, Central America, and South America. Some are refugees, some come to work on farms, and many come into the country illegally.

What should be done about illegal immigration? That question is hotly argued in the United States. It will be a troublesome issue for years to come.

Canada and the United States have always been **multicultural.** In recent times, they have become more so. Most of the big cities have lively immigrant communities. New York and Boston have famous Italian neighborhoods. Chicago has a large Polish community. Toronto is famous for its Greek community. Vancouver has large populations of Laotian, Chinese, and other Asian people. Detroit has a large Arabic community. The music, food, arts, and customs of many cultures are all around us.

Economics Fact

Laotians come from the Asian nation of Laos. Laos is considered one of the world's poorest countries.

✓ Check Your Understanding

Write your answers in complete sentences.

1. Why did German immigrants come to America?

2. Why were Japanese Americans sent to internment camps during World War II?

3. Why did the European immigrants after the Civil War have little trouble finding jobs?

4. Why did many people from Southeast Asia begin coming to the United States in 1975?

GEOGRAPHER'S TOOL KIT
Using Pie Graphs

A pie graph shows parts of a whole. When you look at a pie graph, you can compare the amounts of the different parts. When you read a pie graph, first look at the title. Then, look at the labels and the key. They will help you to make sense of the graph.

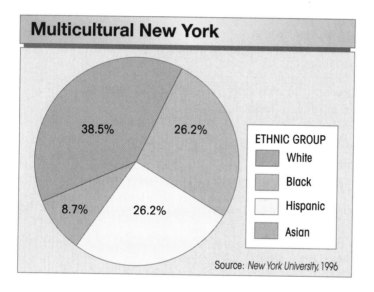

Multicultural New York

38.5%   26.2%

8.7%   26.2%

ETHNIC GROUP
- White
- Black
- Hispanic
- Asian

Source: *New York University, 1996*

Answer the questions below.

1. Which group is 38.5 percent of the population?

2. Which two groups have about the same number of people in New York?

   CHALLENGE How might this graph have looked different 200 years ago?

Apply the Skill

Think about how you spend the day. You sleep, eat, go to school, and study. Write about what percentage of the time you do each of these things. Make a pie graph that is divided to show about the amount of time you spend in each activity.

Summary

Some of the earliest Europeans in what is now the United States and Canada were French fur traders. The British won control of this region in the French and Indian War.
The ancestors of most African Americans were brought to the United States as enslaved Africans.
In the 1920s, the United States and Canada began to limit immigration, using a quota system.
Immigration to the United States and Canada from Asia and Latin America increased in the late 1900s and continues today.

quota

multicultural

plantation

prejudice

ghetto

Vocabulary Review

Complete each sentence with a term from the list.

1. A large farm that often used enslaved Africans as workers is called a ____.

2. In a ____ society, many cultures live side by side.

3. A person who judges someone without knowing him or her is practicing ____.

4. The United States uses a ____ system to limit the amount of immigrants coming into the country.

5. A neighborhood where a particular ethnic group is forced to live is called a ____.

Chapter Quiz

Write your answers in complete sentences.

1. From whom are the Cajuns of Louisiana descended?

2. Immigrants came from Cambodia and Laos after which war?

3. Which immigrant group helped to build railroads and worked in mining towns in the West?

4. **Critical Thinking** Why were enslaved Africans brought mainly to the South?

5. **Critical Thinking** What do you think attracts immigrants to the United States?

Write About Geography

Complete the following activities.

1. You are an immigrant coming to this country. Write what your first week is like.

2. Trace the history of a custom you know of or that your family follows. Write what you learn.

Group Activity

Most people have ancestors from other places. List the places from which each group member has ancestors. Put push pins in a map of the world for each place. See how widespread your group's ancestors were.

Unit 2 **Review**

Comprehension Check

Answer each question in a complete sentence.

1. What kinds of jobs do most people have in Canada and the United States?

2. How come Europeans and American Indians could not live in peace?

3. Why does the Southwest have a Hispanic heritage?

4. What drew so many immigrants to the United States in the late 1880s?

Building Your Skills

Answer each question in a complete sentence.

1. Name a major mountain range in North America.

2. What is the argument about old-growth forests?

3. What does an inset map do?

4. What is the difference between a pie graph and a bar graph?

Where Is It?

Write the name of the place based on the information below.

1. A river that runs from the Great Lakes to the Gulf of Mexico

2. The first Americans walked across this from Asia

3. Refugees from this area came to North America after the Vietnam War

Writing An Essay

Answer one of the following essay topics.

1. Describe the economy of the United States and Canada.

2. Compare how Native Americans lived in the 1700s and how they live today.

3. Explain how earlier European immigrants were different from later European immigrants.

Geography and You

How have immigrants been a positive force in North America?

Unit 3 ▷ Latin America

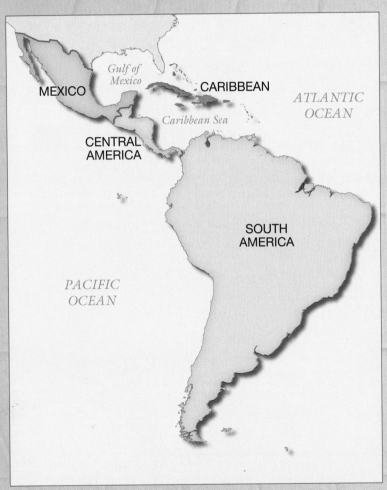

MEXICO

Gulf of Mexico

CARIBBEAN

ATLANTIC OCEAN

Caribbean Sea

CENTRAL AMERICA

SOUTH AMERICA

PACIFIC OCEAN

TRAVEL LOG
This unit has pictures of the art and culture of Latin America. Choose three and describe what you see for a friend.

Incan silver llama

The equator runs through the top of South America in this region. Where would the coldest part of Latin America be?

Skyscrapers tower over an ancient church in Mexico City. Why do you think these modern buildings were built around the church?

Chapter 7 / Mexico

Words to Know

irrigation	the watering of dry farm land by means of ditches or pipes
civilization	a high level of culture that includes writing
empire	a group of countries or cultures under a single ruler
pyramid	a structure with a square base and four triangle-shaped sides that rise to a point
staple	a main food eaten by a people
colony	a territory owned and governed by another country
mestizo	a person who has both Spanish and American Indian ancestry
hacienda	in Latin America, a large estate or ranch
ejido	a communal farm in Mexico, on which farmers either work the land together or individually

Places to Know

Mexico City
Central Plateau
Gulf of Mexico
Central America
Spain
Rio Grande

Learning Objectives

- Describe the land and economy of Mexico.
- Describe the history and culture of the Aztecs.
- Explain the role of Spain in Mexican history and culture.
- Explain the patterns of migration from and within Mexico.
- Discuss themes in Mexican art.

The Land and Its Resources

Mexico is located just south of the United States. It is part of Latin America, a region that includes North, Central, and South America. Mexico is a large country divided into 31 states. It is almost three times the size of Texas. The nation's capital is Mexico City. Like Washington, D.C., Mexico City is a separate district, and not part of a state. About one-tenth of Mexico's 100 million people live in the capital.

A mountain chain runs along Mexico's east coast. Another mountain chain runs along the west coast. Between them is the Central Plateau, where the soil is rich but water is scarce. Farmers there depend on **irrigation** to grow corn, wheat, and rice. The southern part of Mexico gets more rain. Areas in the south that are near the Gulf of Mexico are especially moist. There, Mexican farmers grow crops such as coffee, sugar cane, oranges, and pineapples. Agriculture is an important part of the Mexican economy.

The Central Plateau is dotted with volcanoes. Ash and rock from these volcanoes cover the land. The ash and rock erode and mix with the soil. This volcanic ash and rock contain the minerals that plants need to grow. As a result, the soil of Mexico is good for growing crops.

Volcanoes in Mexico also bring useful minerals such as silver, gold, copper, and lead close to the surface. In addition, Mexico has offshore oil in the Gulf of Mexico and natural gas inland. Mexico sells some of these fossil fuels to other countries and keeps some for use at home.

Other resources include warm weather and good beaches, as well as the many ruins of ancient cities. These draw tourists from around the world. The tourist trade creates jobs for builders, hotel workers, tour guides, and many others.

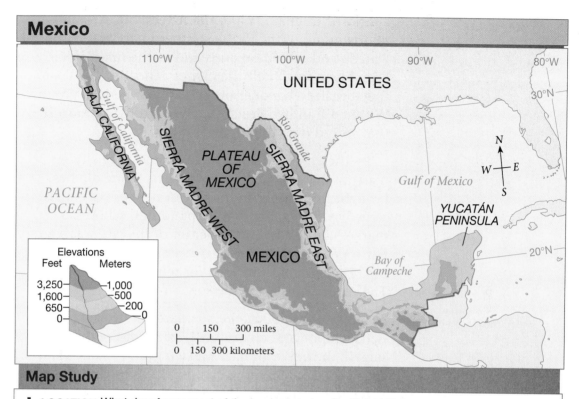

Mexico

Map Study

1. **LOCATION** What river forms most of the border between the United States and Mexico?

2. **REGION** Is the Yucatán Peninsula mountainous or flat?

The Ancient Aztecs

The earliest people in Mexico were bands of Native American hunters. They drifted south more than 10,000 years ago. Some of them settled in the Central Plateau and began to farm there. They were the first farmers in North America. By 3500 B.C., they were growing squash, corn, and beans. Over time, the great **civilizations** of the Olmecs developed.

Other great civilizations in the Central Plateau were the Zapotecs and the Toltecs. In the southeastern part of Mexico, the Maya built great temple-cities. In central Mexico, the Aztecs rose to power.

Shortly after A.D. 1300, the Aztecs, once a small roving group, came to the southern part of the Central Plateau and settled on an island in the middle of a lake. There they built the city of Tenochtitlán. Then they began to conquer other Native American groups. Within a hundred years, the Aztecs ruled an **empire** that spread over hundreds of miles.

By then, Tenochtitlán had become a big city. As many as 300,000 people lived there. Stone ditches brought fresh water to the city. A network of canals served as streets. There were buildings, schools, a market, and a zoo. At the center of the city was a large, flat-topped **pyramid** with two small temples at the top. The pyramid was used for religious ceremonies. The Aztecs worshiped the sun.

In the early 1500s, the Spaniards destroyed the Aztec empire and civilization. Traces of the Aztecs remain, however. In fact, Mexico gets its name from the Aztecs, as Mexica was another name for the Aztecs. Aztec ruins still stand in central Mexico. About one million Mexicans speak a modern dialect of Nahuatl, the language of the ancient Aztecs.

Symbols used by the Aztecs are seen throughout modern Mexico. For example, Mexico's flag shows an eagle holding a snake. This image comes from an Aztec legend that tells how the site for Tenochtitlán was chosen. According to this legend, Tenochtitlán was the place where an Aztec priest saw an eagle eating a snake. The eagle was the Aztec symbol for the sun god.

The Aztecs took much of their culture from earlier people. Perhaps the most important cultural contribution of the earlier settlers was corn. The people who came before the Aztecs were the first to plant and grow this important grain. Corn is now a **staple** throughout Central and South America.

Aztec works of art like this still inspire artists today.

A Spanish Colony

In the 1500s, a Spaniard named Hernando Cortéz heard stories that there was gold in the land of the Aztecs. He gathered about 600 soldiers and sailed to Mexico. He ordered his men to burn the ships so that they had no choice but to follow him. Cortéz then led his men in a war against the Aztecs—and won.

How did a handful of Spaniards conquer an empire? First, they had guns, while the Aztecs did not. Second, the Aztecs were afraid of the Spaniards because their legends had predicted that an angry god would attack them. The Aztecs thought Cortéz was this god. They were also frightened by Cortéz's horses, as they had never seen such large animals.

Most important, Cortéz got help from other Native Americans in this area. These Native American nations hated the Aztecs because the Aztecs had used their people as victims for human sacrifice. They were glad to help Cortéz destroy Tenochtitlán. The Spaniards then started building their own city on that same spot. Modern Mexico City sits on top of ancient Tenochtitlán.

It took only a few years for the Spaniards to conquer all of Mexico and Central America. Disease made the conquest easier. The Spaniards brought smallpox to the land. Within 80 years, the native population had dropped by up to 95 percent. Most of this damage was caused by disease.

Mexico became a **colony** of Spain. Spaniards owned all of the land. The Native Americans became enslaved and were tied to the land. They had no power, no wealth, and no rights. Mexico remained a Spanish colony for about 300 years. During that time, Spaniards and American Indians married and had children. A person who has both American Indian and Spanish ancestors is called **mestizo**. Today, about 60 percent of the population of Mexico is mestizo.

HISTORY FACT

Hernando Cortéz tasted hot chocolate while visiting the Aztec ruler Montezuma. He brought the beverage back to Europe, where it became enormously popular.

An Independent Mexico

In 1821, Mexico became independent of Spain. A priest named Father Hidalgo started the revolt that led to independence. However, the country saw little peace after independence. Governments came and went. Then, in 1876, Porfirio Díaz became president and stayed in power for 30 years. Díaz brought Mexico into the modern world by inviting companies from the United States and Europe into Mexico. The companies built railroads, power plants, and factories. They ended up controlling much of the Mexican economy.

Díaz ruled harshly. People who spoke against him were jailed. Farm and factory workers had to work like slaves and were sometimes beaten. In 1910, two men— Pancho Villa and Emiliano Zapata—called separately for a revolution. In the fighting that followed, almost a million Mexicans lost their lives.

In 1917, a new constitution was written. Still, the fighting went on. Zapata was shot in an ambush. Later, Villa was killed. Finally, in the 1920s, power settled into the hands of one party called the Institutional Revolutionary party (Partido Revolucionario Institucional, or PRI). That party remains in power today.

$ Economics Fact

In 1997, a hundred Mexican pesos were worth about $79.14 in U.S. money. At the beginning of 2000, the same amount of Mexican money was worth $10.72.

✓ Check Your Understanding

Write your answers in complete sentences.

1. Why is the Central Plateau important to the Mexican economy?

2. What was Tenochtitlán?

3. Why did the Aztecs fear Cortéz?

4. Who is Father Hidalgo?

Modern Mexico

Both the revolution and the constitution brought many changes. Until the revolution, most of the land in Mexico belonged to a few rich people and to the Catholic Church. They had large estates known as **haciendas**. Poor farmers did the work. When crops were sold, the landowners kept the money.

Mexico's constitution gave Mexicans the right to free speech. It allowed them to form political parties. It started land reform, which may have been the most important change. The new government took land away from the richest landowners and broke it up into communal farms called **ejidos**. Under this system, farmers either worked together or gained rights to farm their own land.

Trades are being made on the floor of the Mexican Stock Exchange.

Despite land reform, Mexico remains a poor country. It has valuable resources, but many people cannot earn a living—due in part to a rapidly growing population. The country cannot grow enough food to feed all of its people. That is one reason why many Mexicans are immigrating to the United States to look for jobs.

You Decide

Do you think that U.S. companies should set up factories in Mexico? Why or why not?

At the same time, many U.S. businesses are moving factories to northern Mexico, where wages, or labor costs, are lower. The U.S. companies bring in raw materials and hire Mexican workers to make clothing, toys, tools, and high-tech items such as TV sets and telephone-answering machines. The factories provide jobs and give Mexican workers a chance to stay in their own country.

All of this industry has brought some familiar problems. Towns have grown crowded. Services such as electricity, water, and sewers are poor. Waste water pollutes the Rio Grande along the Texas border.

Overpopulation is a problem in Mexico. Mexico City is the world's second most populous metropolitan area, with about 17 million people. By the year 2025, it could have 30 million people. It is currently growing by about 2,000 people a day. Much of the growth comes from migration. People keep moving to Mexico City from rural areas. They come because they do not have land or cannot find work.

Remember
A rural area is one that is in the country.

There are not enough jobs for all of them. About half of the adults in Mexico City are out of work. The city faces other problems, too. Disease travels quickly in such a crowded place. Clean water is scarce. There are not enough places for the city's garbage.

The Catholic Church in Mexico

Spanish rule brought the Roman Catholic Church to Mexico. The Church sent missionary priests to "New Spain," as the Spaniards called it. In parts of Mexico, priests were the first Spanish settlers. The priests set up schools and spread the beliefs of the Catholic Church. Some priests studied the history and religions of Native Americans. A few realized that Spanish rule in Mexico was unfair. Generally, however, the Church settled in as part of the class that ruled in Mexico.

By 1800, the Catholic Church owned about half of the land in Mexico. The Church's growing power made many Mexicans angry even though they were faithful Catholics. Reforms in the mid-1800s and the revolution of 1910 cut the power of the Church in Mexico. The Church was no longer allowed to own land. Free public schools were set up as an alternative to Catholic schools.

Celebrations

OUR LADY OF GUADALUPE

December 12 is a holiday in Mexico. More than 400 years ago, Juan Diego—a Catholic Native American—saw a vision of the Virgin Mary, whom Catholics believe is the mother of Jesus. The Virgin Mary appeared to be Native American.

For the first time, Native Americans and mestizos saw the Catholic Church as their own. They called the vision "Our Lady of Guadalupe." Musicians and dancers perform. Some people dress up as ancient Aztecs. It is a religious holiday.

Critical Thinking Why do you think Diego's vision changed the way Native Americans and mestizos thought about the Catholic Church?

Costumed man in Mexico City

Diego Rivera's mural "Our Bread" shows a family at mealtime. The painting is on a wall inside a public building in Mexico City.

The Arts in Mexico

In Mexico, the heritage of the past lives on through the arts. The Ballet Folklorico offers a striking example. This Mexican dance company travels all over the world, performing folk dances from many ethnic groups of Mexico. Musicians play both Spanish instruments such as guitars and Native American instruments such as flutes and rattles. Some of their dances are ancient, and some are modern. Some tell about Mexican history.

The Native American heritage can also be seen in Mexican architecture. For example, artists decorate buildings with scenes from Native American life done with mosaics. These are pictures made from tiny colored stones or other objects glued onto a surface.

In the 1920s, a group of Mexican artists started an important new movement. These artists were inspired by the Mexican Revolution. They did not want their art to be locked up in museums. They wanted to paint for the common people and wanted their art to be part of everyday life. So they painted murals, which are large paintings on the walls of buildings. Diego Rivera, José Clemente Orozco, and David Alfaro Siqueiros were three great muralists. They often painted scenes from Mexican history. Common people were often pictured as heroes in these murals.

✓ Check Your Understanding

Write your answers in complete sentences.

1. What are the advantages of U.S. companies building factories in Mexico?

2. How did the Catholic Church become so powerful?

3. Why did Diego Rivera paint murals instead of small paintings?

GLOBAL ISSUES
Smog

Big cities all over the world have smog. Smog is a mixture of fog and pollution. The chemicals in smog can be harmful to inhale. Mexico City is one of the smoggiest cities in the world.

The landforms around Mexico City add to the smog problem. Mountains to the east and west keep the air still, causing dust and dirt to linger in the dry air.

In addition, smoke from the factories in the city rises and mixes with the dirt and dust. Oil refineries also produce a lot of air pollution.

The city has more than three million cars that pollute the air, too. In fact, cars are the main cause of air pollution. On summer days, the skies over Mexico City are so smoggy that you cannot see farther than two blocks, and it is difficult to breathe.

Answer the questions below.

1. What is smog?

2. What is a way that Mexico might be able to reduce smog?

MAKE A DIFFERENCE

Cars are one of the main causes of pollution. There are ways to get around without driving, though. Find out what ways are available in your community. You could car pool with classmates. There may be buses or railroads. There may be bike paths. Make a booklet of the possibilities. Remember to include their advantages over driving.

Summary

About 10 percent of the population of Mexico lives in Mexico City.
Ancient Indian civilizations of Mexico included the Olmec, Maya, Toltec, Zapotec, and Aztec. The Aztecs ruled from the 1300s to the early 1500s.
Hernando Cortéz destroyed the Aztec empire in the early 1500s.
Mexico was a colony of Spain for about 300 years.
Mexico City is one of the world's fastest-growing and most populous cities.
Mexican painting, dancing, and architecture reflect the history and ancient cultures of the country.

Vocabulary Review

Write *true* or *false*. If the statement is false, change the underlined term to make it true.

1. A group of countries or cultures under a single ruler is an <u>empire</u>.

2. A <u>mestizo</u> is a person who has both Spanish and American Indian ancestry.

3. A high level of culture that includes writing is a <u>colony</u>.

4. A <u>staple</u> is a main food eaten by people.

5. An <u>ejido</u> is a large private estate in Latin America.

Chapter Quiz

Write your answers in complete sentences.

1. What city in Mexico has the fastest-growing population?

2. What grain was an important cultural contribution of the early Native American settlers?

3. What were the muralists inspired by?

4. **Critical Thinking** What role has the Catholic Church played in Mexican history?

5. **Critical Thinking** How does a growing population cause problems for Mexico?

Write About Geography

Complete the following activities.

1. Sketch a design for a mural that deals with one of the issues in this chapter.

2. You are in Mexico City. Write a note to a friend about what the city is like and what you have seen.

Group Activity

Mexico is a popular place for tourists. Choose a place in Mexico that your group would like to visit. Find out more about it. Create an ad campaign to attract tourists. Make a magazine ad, a radio ad, and a brochure.

Markets like this one in Guatemala are common throughout Central America. What can you tell about the country from what you see in this photograph?

Words to Know

adobe	a sun-dried brick made of mud and straw
sacred	deeply respected and usually having religious meaning
guerrilla	a soldier who fights outside a regular army, often against a government
rain forest	any dense forest that grows in a warm, moist area; a tropical rain forest is near the equator
cash crop	a crop grown to be sold; a cash crop usually provides a farmer's or landowner's main source of income
dictator	a leader who rules with complete power
contra	a rebel fighting the Sandinista government in Nicaragua
United Nations	an international organization whose purpose is to keep peace between nations

Places to Know

Belize

Guatemala

Honduras

El Salvador

Nicaragua

Costa Rica

Panama

Learning Objectives

- Explain how earthquakes and volcanoes affect life in Central America.
- Describe the culture of the Mayas.
- Describe the economy of Central America.
- Explain the political and social problems of this region.
- Describe some traditional handicrafts in Central America.

The Countries of Central America

Central America is a strip of land connecting Mexico to South America. Seven countries are on this strip: Belize, Guatemala, Honduras, El Salvador, Nicaragua, Costa Rica, and Panama.

The land that is Central America, like Mexico, was a colony of Spain for about 300 years. The Spanish and Native American people mixed, and today, most of the people in Central America are mestizos. Guatemala, however, is an exception. There, Spaniards and Native Americans stayed apart more. Nearly half the people of Guatemala are pure-blooded American Indians. The rest are ladinos, as mestizos are called there.

Belize is another exception. It was settled by English sailors. Even now, most people in Belize speak a form of English. Many enslaved Africans were brought to this area, too. About 40 percent of the people in Belize have African ancestry.

Nicaragua is the largest of the Central American countries, about the size of New York state. El Salvador is the smallest—but the most crowded. It has about 685 people per square mile. Compare that to the average population density of the United States, which has about 74 people per square mile.

Costa Rica stands out as a country with a stable government, which is democratic. Costa Rica's economy is in good shape, and the country is generally peaceful. Costa Rica is one of the few countries on the Earth that does not have an army. Honduras is more typical of the region. It is a poor country and has a history of military rule.

Panama occupies the thinnest part of Central America. Its best-known feature is something that people built—the Panama Canal. This waterway connects the Pacific Ocean and the Atlantic Ocean.

Remember
About 60 percent of Mexico's population is mestizo.

HISTORY FACT

Until 1981, Belize was a British colony. It was the last colony in Central America to gain its independence.

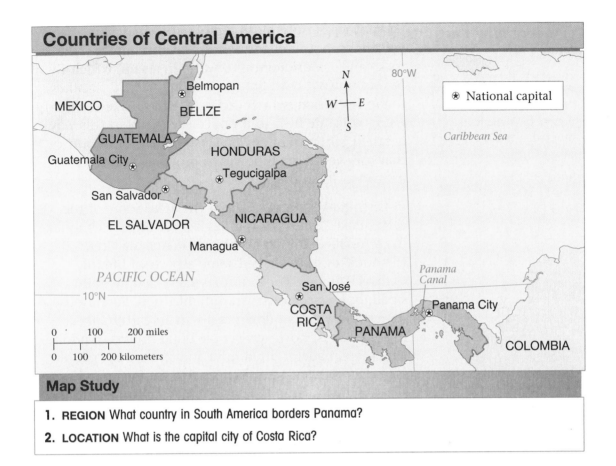

Countries of Central America

Map Study

1. **REGION** What country in South America borders Panama?
2. **LOCATION** What is the capital city of Costa Rica?

Volcanoes in Central America

Central America, like western Mexico, is dotted with volcanoes. Some are dormant—that is, they are in no danger of erupting. Many, however, are still active and could erupt at any time.

Although volcanoes can be destructive, they can also be of use to people. Soil is often very fertile near volcanoes. The rocks near volcanoes contain valuable ores and minerals such as gold, silver, copper, and sulfur. All of these minerals are mined in Central America.

Another useful volcanic product is energy. In volcanoes, hot, melted rock is near the surface. This rock can turn underground water to steam, which then pushes upward with great force. Engineers drill holes to tap the steam, which can be used to make electricity. Using volcanic heat to produce electricity in this way is called geothermal power. Costa Rica is one country that uses geothermal power to produce electricity instead of fossil fuels.

Earthquakes occur often in the area. Some of the earthquakes cause a lot of damage. A single earthquake in 1976 killed 20,000 people in Guatemala City. Earthquakes have shaped some aspects of life in Central America. For example, many people build small, one-story houses from light wood. Such houses do not break or fall down easily in an earthquake. In some areas, however, people build houses of **adobe**, which are made of dried mud and straw. Poor people use adobe because it is inexpensive. Unfortunately, in a big earthquake an adobe house may crumble and fall.

Maya: Ancient and Modern

The culture of Central America has strong roots in the great civilization of the Maya. These Native Americans lived in parts of Mexico and Central America. They built temple-cities in Belize, Honduras, and Guatemala. Descendants of the ancient Maya still live in the region. These people are called the Quiché.

Mayan civilization began about 2,200 years ago and lasted more than 1,700 years. Its peak came between A.D. 300 and 900. The Maya invented a whole system of mathematics. It was based on 20 numbers instead of 10. They developed precise calendars. For example, they figured out that a year is exactly 365.2422 days long.

The Maya had no alphabet, but they did have a writing system. The *Popul Vuh* is a **sacred** book of the Maya that was written in pictures instead of words. It tells of their history and myths and is a guide to their customs and beliefs.

Mayan artists made stone sculptures and pottery. They crafted jewelry and made gold objects. They painted scenes from their history on their temple walls and built impressive cities out of limestone. Ordinary Maya did not live in these cities, however. They lived in nearby villages, and the limestone cities were used only for religious ceremonies. They contained pyramids and temples but no houses.

A piece of ancient Mayan pottery

The modern Maya, or Quiché, still practice customs of their ancestors, the ancient Maya. They still read the *Popul Vuh*, for example, and they still honor the Mayan rain god, Chac.

Life has not been easy for the Quiché. After the 1500s, they lost most of their land to the Spaniards. In Guatemala, the ladinos controlled the army and the government. They wanted to put controls on the Quiché, too, and this led to fighting. Many Quiché were killed. Some of the Quiché formed a **guerrilla** army. A number of priests, students, political leaders, and others supported them in a war against the government that lasted 30 years. About 200,000 people died in the war. A new president took office in 1996, and a peace accord was reached. Tensions between the Quiché and the ladinos continue, however.

 **Check Your Understanding**

Write your answers in complete sentences.

1. Describe Central America.

2. What are three positive effects of volcanoes?

3. Who are the descendants of the Maya?

GEOGRAPHER'S TOOL KIT
Understanding Climate Maps

A climate map shows the weather patterns of a region. Climate is determined by the pattern of weather in a place over many years. Colors on a climate map will tell you what an area's climate is. The key tells you what different colors mean.

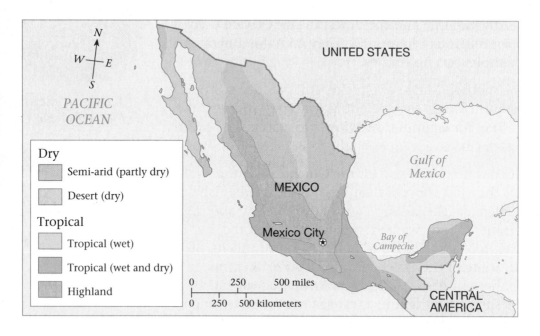

Answer the questions below.

1. What part of Mexico is the driest?

2. What is the climate near Central America?

   CHALLENGE Why might farming in the south of Mexico be easier?

Apply the Skill

What is the climate where you live? Write a description. Then, find a climate map of your state. See if you were right.

Making a Living in Central America

Rainfall is steady and plentiful in Central America, and the temperature is warm nearly all year. Plants grow quickly in these conditions, and much of the region is covered with thick forests full of trees, vines, and brush. These lush areas are called **rain forests**.

However, people are cutting down the rain forests. They do this to make money by selling the wood for building materials and paper. The warm, wet climate is also good for farming once the trees have been cut down. Unfortunately, the destruction of rain forests affects the whole world. It decreases the Earth's oxygen supply and kills wildlife.

In some coastal areas where fish and shrimp are plentiful, fishing is a growing industry. Mining is important in Honduras, where silver, gold, and many other minerals are plentiful. Unfortunately, non-Honduran companies own most of the mines. The people who work in the mines receive low wages and remain poor.

Generally, the economy of Central America is based on agriculture. Some people are subsistence farmers. Many, however, work on plantations, or commercial farms, for big landowners, growing **cash crops**. The main cash crops grown in Central America are coffee, bananas, sugar, and cotton. Many of the industries in this region make products out of these crops. The crops and other products are sold as exports. The people who own the land and the factories receive most of the money from the sale of the exports.

Because Panama has the Panama Canal, it does not depend primarily on agriculture. Shipping companies pay to use the canal to avoid a 12,000-mile trip around South America. Only about 2 percent of the people of Panama work on the canal. Many of them work in service jobs that have been created by it.

Costa Rican rain forest

The Struggle for Land Reform

A few families and companies own most of the land and wealth in Central America. Almost everyone else works for these families and companies for low wages. Such conditions lead to unrest.

Landless people in Central America have long called for land reform. However, the big landowners have refused to give up any land. Tension over land reform has led to violence. Some of the worst violence has occurred in Nicaragua and El Salvador.

The Sandinistas overthrew the ruling Somoza family in Nicaragua and held power for 11 years.

Nicaragua was ruled by one family—a **dictator** named Anastasio Somoza and then his two sons—for almost 45 years. The Somozas made themselves rich. In 1972, an earthquake hit the capital city of Managua and killed about 6,000 people. People from around the world sent money for the victims. The Somoza family ended up with most of that money.

This made many of the Nicaraguan people so angry that they united behind a rebel group called the Sandinista National Liberation Front. The Sandinistas overthrew the ruling Somozas and, in 1979, took over the country. They held power for 11 years.

The Sandinistas took land away from big landowners and gave it to groups of people to own and work together. The Sandinista government started programs for the poor. It built schools and opened health clinics. It also took over many businesses. In fact, the government took control of most aspects of life in Nicaragua. Some said that the Sandinistas limited people's freedoms.

> **You Decide**
>
> How could Central American leaders persuade big landowners in Central America to give up land?

The landowners, however, got help from the United States and formed armies of guerrilla soldiers, called **contras**, who fought the Sandinistas. By 1990, the country was devastated by this war. An election was held, and the Sandinistas lost. Many Sandinistas still hold jobs in the army and the government, however. They are opposing efforts to undo Sandinista reforms.

On the surface, El Salvador seems to be a democracy. Elections are held, and presidents come and go. However, the army holds the real power—and it is closely tied to the big landowners.

Many people became upset that the army and landowners had such power. Some of them joined a Communist-backed rebel group known as the FMLN. Throughout the 1980s the army fought a fierce war against the rebels.

The guerrillas hid in the mountains and attacked whenever they could. The rebels had secret supporters in the cities. The army, too, had supporters, called death squads, who killed people they thought were supporting the rebels. Often, the victims of death squads would just disappear.

In 1992, the Salvadoran government and the FMLN signed a peace treaty, under **United Nations** supervision. Rebels turned in their weapons. The government granted amnesty, or a governmental pardon, to political prisoners. Yet, to this day, the government is still trying to avoid carrying out land reforms.

The Arts in Central America

In Central America, many people express artistic feelings through crafts—useful items that are also beautiful. Handwoven cloth is one highly artistic craft, and some of the best handwoven cloth in the world is made in Guatemala. Designs are woven into this cloth.

Designs are also stitched onto plain fabric in a craft called embroidery. The woven or stitched designs reflect ancient Mayan art styles. For example, some have angles and patterns that lock together. Because each village or town has its own designs, you can tell where some American Indians come from by the clothes they wear.

American Indian women wear a kind of blouse called a huipil, which they also sell to tourists. A huipil is made of three flaps of cloth woven or embroidered with designs. It is worn with a skirt of many colors. Mayan women dressed this way in ancient times. Most Quiché women still dress this way today.

$ Economics Fact

The first important export to Guatemala in the nineteenth century was dye made from insects. Then coffee became the most important export. Guatemalan coffee is still shipped around the world.

Guatemalan weavers are famous for the quality and designs of their work.

✓ Check Your Understanding

Write your answers in complete sentences.

1. What is the basis of the economy of Central America?

2. Why has land led to violence in Central America?

3. What is a huipil?

Chapter

8 ⟋ Review

Summary

The seven countries of Central America are Guatemala, Belize, El Salvador, Honduras, Nicaragua, Costa Rica, and Panama.
Earthquakes and volcanic eruptions are common in Central America.
The culture of Central America shows both Spanish and Native American influences. The ancient Mayan civilization was at its peak between A.D. 300 and 900.
Much of Central America has a warm, wet climate.
Central America's economy is based on agriculture.
Unequal land ownership has created tension and unrest in Central America.

guerrilla
sacred
dictator
rain forest
cash crop

Vocabulary Review

Write a term from the list that matches each definition below.

1. Any dense forest that grows in a moist area

2. Deeply respected

3. A soldier who fights outside a regular army

4. A leader who rules with complete power

5. A crop grown to be sold

Chapter Quiz

Write your answers in complete sentences.

1. How does Belize differ from the rest of Central America?

2. What sets Guatemala apart?

3. In what ways does Costa Rica stand out?

4. **Critical Thinking** What effects do earthquakes and volcanoes have on the way people in Central America live?

5. **Critical Thinking** What were some causes of unrest in Nicaragua and El Salvador in the 1970s and 1980s, some of which continue to this day?

Write About Geography

Write answers to the following questions.

1. The ancient Maya wrote in pictures instead of words. Write a short letter to a friend using pictures.

2. Choose a country in Central America to visit. Research the country in the library or on the Internet. Write what you would want to see, and why.

Group Activity

In your group, create 20 questions about this chapter. Write each question on an index card. Write the answers on a sheet of paper. Exchange cards with another group. See how many questions each group can answer correctly.

Gauchos herd animals in the Pampas, or grasslands, of Argentina. What would these workers be called in the American West?

Chapter 9 / South America

Words to Know

landlocked	surrounded by land
terrace	a long step cut into a slope to create level land for farming
aqueduct	a structure that carries water from one place to another
quipu	a knotted string used by the Inca to keep records
cacao	the plant from which chocolate is made
smuggle	to move goods in or out of a country illegally, often to avoid paying taxes
junta	a small group of military leaders who take power and rule a country by force

Places to Know

Andes Mountains

Amazon River Basin

Guiana Highlands

Brazilian Highlands

Pampas

Patagonia

Learning Objectives

• Describe the culture of the ancient Incas.

• Describe the economy of the Andean region.

• Explain the importance of the Amazon rain forest.

• Discuss the land, people, and music of Brazil.

• Explain how and why Argentina differs from other South American countries.

• Describe the pattern of military rule in South America.

The Land and Countries of South America

Remember
A rain forest is a dense forest
that grows in a moist area.

The continent of South America has many climate extremes. South America has the world's largest rain forest, the highest waterfall, and the longest mountain range found on land. It also has one of the longest rivers in the world, the Amazon, which carries more water than any other river. Each of these features marks one of South America's geographic regions.

Andes Mountains

This rugged chain of peaks stretches more than 5,000 miles. Many of the peaks are more than 22,000 feet tall. One mountain in the Andes, called Aconcagua, rises 22,834 feet above sea level.

Amazon River Basin

The Amazon River flows through this huge, low region. The climate is hot and wet, and dense rain forest covers the land.

Guiana Highlands

Rain forest covers these high hills. This region has a tropical climate and the world's highest waterfall, Angel Falls in Venezuela.

Brazilian Highlands

Gentle hills and high, flat areas mark this region. The Iguaçú Falls, a cluster of 275 waterfalls, is a famous landmark.

Pampas

The Pampas are flat and covered with grass, and the climate is fairly moist.

Patagonia

This is a region of high plateaus—cold, dry, windy, and bare of trees.

South America has 13 countries. Bolivia and Paraguay are **landlocked**, or surrounded by land. All the other countries border one of the two oceans or the Caribbean Sea.

You Decide

What problems might a landlocked country have?

No one knows how many people lived on this continent before the Europeans came. The number may have been as high as 30 million. These people spoke many different languages. Many of the native languages are still spoken throughout parts of South America.

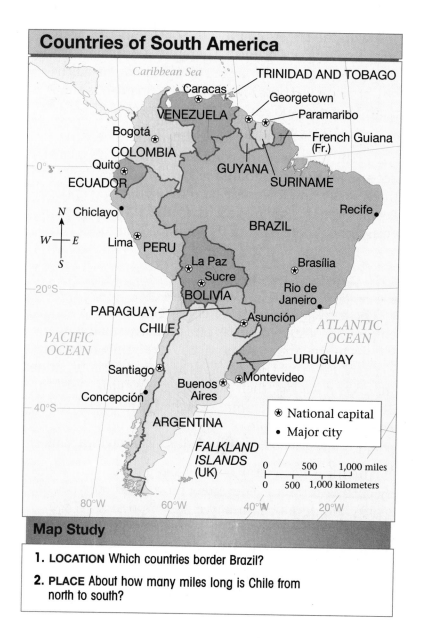

Countries of South America

Caribbean Sea

TRINIDAD AND TOBAGO

Caracas

Georgetown

VENEZUELA

Paramaribo

Bogotá

French Guiana
(Fr.)

COLOMBIA

Quito

GUYANA

SURINAME

ECUADOR

N Chiclayo

Recife

W—E

BRAZIL

Lima PERU

La Paz

Brasília

Sucre

BOLIVIA

Rio de
Janeiro

PARAGUAY

CHILE

Asunción

ATLANTIC
OCEAN

PACIFIC
OCEAN

URUGUAY

Santiago

Buenos
Aires

Montevideo

Concepción

✷ National capital
• Major city

ARGENTINA

FALKLAND
ISLANDS
(UK)

0   500   1,000 miles
0   500   1,000 kilometers

80°W   60°W   40°W   20°W

Map Study

1. LOCATION Which countries border Brazil?

2. PLACE About how many miles long is Chile from north to south?

Beginning in the 1500s, the continent was colonized by Europeans. Each country still reflects its colonial past. The French, British, and Dutch had small colonies in the northeastern part of the continent. English is now the main language spoken in Guyana, Dutch is the main language in Suriname, and French is the main language in French Guiana, which is still a colony of France.

Brazil, the largest country in South America, was once a colony of Portugal. Therefore, Portuguese is the main language spoken in Brazil. Spain colonized the rest of South America, which is why Spanish is the main language spoken on the continent.

Most of the people of South America live near the coast. The interior of the continent is lightly populated because jungles and mountains cover much of the land there. Roads and towns are hard to build in such places. People cannot easily make a living there. People have not even visited some parts of the Amazon rain forest yet.

The Ancient Incas

The Incas built South America's greatest native empire. They started out as one of many small native groups in the Andes. Around A.D. 1200, they began to make war on their neighbors. Then, in the 1400s, under three great leaders, their power began to grow. Within 30 years, the Incan empire stretched from present-day Ecuador to the middle of Chile. It lasted until 1532, when the Spaniards destroyed the Incan civilization.

The Incas knew how to farm steep mountain slopes by cutting **terraces**. They grew more than 60 types of plants and developed many kinds of potatoes. They tamed llamas, which are like small camels. They also tended other animals for food.

The Incas were great builders. They built stone **aqueducts** to bring water to their fields. Their long, fine roads connected their empire. They built temples and houses, and they made walls to hold the soil in place. The huge stones that they cut fit together perfectly. Their buildings still stand, which is amazing in a land where earthquakes are common.

Machu Picchu was one of the cities built by the Incas.

Incan society was tightly organized. Every person had a fixed place. At the top was the emperor, who was seen as a god. Beneath him were priests, generals, and members of the emperor's family. Below these were the common people, who had to serve in the army when called. They also had to work on building projects. The rest of the time they worked mainly as farmers. The government—the Inca, or emperor—made sure everyone had food, clothing, and shelter.

All land belonged to the emperor, but he gave it to families to work. Each piece of land was divided into three parts: one for the emperor, one for the gods, and one for the farmer. Most of the emperor's food was stored. In times of drought or crop failure, this food was given out to people. Government workers kept track of what farmers grew. They used a knotted string called a **quipu** to keep their records. Even today, some Andean Indians use quipus to keep track of their animal herds.

✓ Check Your Understanding

Write your answers in complete sentences.

1. What are the Pampas?

2. Why do South Americans speak so many languages?

3. Why did the Inca emperor store much of his crop?

Modern Life in the Andes

Today seven countries are located entirely or partly in the Andes: Venezuela, Colombia, Ecuador, Peru, Argentina, Bolivia, and Chile.

The Andes is a poor region. In its rural areas, some people are subsistence farmers, living mainly on potatoes, corn, and a grain called quinoa. Most of the people, however, farm cash crops on large plantations. On a plantation, only one crop is grown—it might be bananas, coffee, sugar cane, or **cacao**, the plant from which chocolate is made. The plantation owner chooses a crop that can be sold abroad.

Andean people use llamas like this one for many purposes, including carrying supplies and providing milk and wool.

A one-crop plantation economy tends to make a country poor. Crops sell for very little. The people must import expensive manufactured goods and even food. Nevertheless, colonists from Europe started the plantations, and for them the system worked. It gave their home countries cheap goods, and it made the colonists rich. Today the system works for those who own the plantations. Many of the owners are foreign companies that are making a lot of money and, therefore, have no reason to want change.

Some people in the Andes make their living by mining. The Andes are rich in minerals such as gold, tin, copper, and gems. Foreign companies own many of the mines and pay the working people low wages.

Venezuela is lucky enough to have oil. That makes it wealthier than five of the other six countries in the Andes. Ecuador and Peru have some oil and natural gas, too, but they have not tapped much of it yet.

Illegal drugs are a big business in the Andean region. One such drug is cocaine, which is made from the leaves of the coca plant. Coca grows wild in Bolivia and Peru, and the leaves can be harvested several times a year. Because of this, the crop provides a steady income.

The coca leaves are shipped to Colombia where the drug cocaine is made from them. Making and selling cocaine is against the law in Colombia. However, drug dealers often pay police and government officials not to interfere in the drug business. These criminals have guns and private armies.

From Colombia, people **smuggle** the drug to the United States or Europe. The governments of both Colombia and the United States want to stop the drug trade. This is difficult, because coca provides an income for the poor people of the Andes. Some experts say farmers will stop growing coca only when they can make a living growing something else.

$ Economics Fact

Colombia grows a lot of coffee, yet fresh coffee is hard to find there. That is because most coffee beans are exported.

Brazil

Brazil is the largest country in South America. More than half of the people of Brazil are of European and Asian descent. About 6 percent of the people are of pure African descent, and fewer than 1 percent are descendants of the native people. The rest are of mixed background.

Portuguese sailors came to Brazil in the 1500s to set up banana and sugar cane plantations. They brought enslaved Africans to do the work.

Celebrations

CARNAVAL

The soul of Brazil is the coastal city of Rio de Janeiro. It has more than 10 million people. It is home to a world-famous festival called Carnaval, which is part of a Catholic holiday.

Carnaval comes just before Lent, when Catholics are supposed to give up things they like. Carnaval is considered a last chance for people to have fun before Lent. The same holiday also is celebrated in other cities. Farther north, in New Orleans, Louisiana, the holiday is called Mardi Gras.

Lavish costumes and dancing mark the celebration of Carnaval in Brazil.

Critical Thinking Why would people have begun the celebration of Carnaval?

Slavery has since ended, and African culture is very much alive in Brazil. African religions, for example, have many followers. Most Brazilians would say that they are Catholics, but many of them mix some African religion into their Catholicism.

Brazil is the largest and most industrialized country in South America. Jobs can be found there in steel mills, car factories, coffee-processing plants, and other industries. São Paolo is the main industrial city, with a population of about 10 million people.

Brazil's capital is Brasília. This unusual city was planned and built by the government in power from 1945 to 1964. Since Brasília is a planned city, the streets are very orderly. Most buildings are sleek and modern.

The Amazon Rain Forest

In the center of South America, near the equator, is a huge lowland called the Amazon River Basin. It covers much of Brazil, as well as parts of Peru, Bolivia, Colombia, and Venezuela. Water flows along the eastern slope of the Andes Mountains and collects in valleys to form streams. These streams empty into rivers, which then flow into the Amazon. Together, the Amazon and the smaller connecting rivers travel more than 4,000 miles. The Amazon empties into the Atlantic Ocean at a spot near the equator.

Rain forest, thick with trees, vines, bushes, and other plants, covers most of the river basin. The air is hot and wet there. The insects carry deadly tropical diseases such as malaria. Native populations, such as the Yanomamo, have adapted to this environment, but few Europeans have settled there.

Thousands of species of animals, including this frog, live in the Brazilian rain forest.

The Amazon rain forest is home to more than 50,000 types of plants. Animals of all kinds are also plentiful. Anacondas, one of the world's largest snakes, live here. These nonpoisonous snakes can grow as long as 30 feet. Many kinds of lizards, fish, and insects also live in this rain forest. Some are found nowhere else on the Earth.

Yet the Amazon rain forest—like the one in Central America—is vanishing. People in Brazil and Peru are cutting the trees down. Lumber companies have clearcut many patches of the forest, destroying millions of acres. The governments of Peru and Brazil have tried to get these companies to plant new trees to replace the ones they have cut down. The governments have met with little success.

People have also cut down the forest in order to "clear the land." This is just what European settlers did to the forests of North America. They cut away trees and brush so they could grow crops.

This is not a good reason to cut down the trees, though, because the soil in the rain forest is not very good for farming. Only a thin layer of topsoil supports plant life. Once trees and brush have been removed, rain washes away this top layer of soil. Scientists worry about the loss of the rain forests and how this will affect the Earth's air and water.

✓ Check Your Understanding

Write your answers in complete sentences.

1. Name one way that Andean people make a living.

2. Why is Brasília unusual?

3. Why is clearing the rain forest for farming a poor idea?

GLOBAL ISSUES
Saving the Rain Forests

Rain forests are important to the whole world. Plants give off oxygen, and rain forests contain a lot of plants. The world's biggest rain forest is in the Amazon River Basin. It has been called "the lungs of the world."

Some industries are able to use the rain forest without destroying it. The rubber industry is one example. Wild rubber trees grow throughout the rain forest. Workers make thin cuts in the trees, and a milky liquid called latex flows out. The workers collect this latex in containers. The latex is shipped to factories, where it is turned into rubber. The rubber is then sold all over the world for use in making tires and other items.

The rain forest has many other products that may be useful. For example, medicines can be made from many of the plants. Some environmentalists believe that these products should be developed. People will not cut down the rain forest if they can make more money by letting it grow.

Answer the questions below.

1. How can industries use the rain forest without destroying it?

2. Why is the Amazon rain forest called "the lungs of the world"?

MAKE A DIFFERENCE
Most paper is made from trees. The less paper people use, the fewer trees need to be cut down from places such as rain forests. Keep track of how much paper you use in a day. Then work in a group to list how you could use less paper. Create a poster to hang in your school.

The Rhythm of Brazil's Music

Brazil has a rich musical history. Each of the many ethnic groups in the country has added something to Brazil's musical heritage. For the native peoples, music was an important part of their religious ceremonies. They used many kinds of drums and rattles. Rhythm was more important than melody in their music.

Brazilian music begins with these traditional rhythms. Instruments that create mainly rhythm are called percussion instruments. Such instruments are a key part of most modern Brazilian bands.

Catholic missionaries brought the music of the Church to Brazil. Melody was important in the music of the Catholic Church, and that influenced and changed the traditional music. Later, the Portuguese settlers came along with their folk music. They introduced the Italian accordion and Spanish guitar, which were popular in Portugal, into Brazilian music.

The greatest influence on Brazilian music, however, came from African peoples. They brought along the musical heritage of Angola, Central Africa, and the Sudan. African music has added excitement to the hot rhythms of Brazilian music and has given Brazilian music its energy.

Practically every style of music in Brazil has a dance that goes with it. The samba is the most common kind of dance music in Brazil—especially during Carnaval. Most samba bands use drums, metal rattles, and bells. A quieter form of samba, called bossa nova, spread to the United States. Now Brazilian music often uses electric instruments. One more recent style is called tropicalism. It blends Brazilian folk music with modern rock.

HISTORY FACT

Antonio Carlos Jobim's "Girl from Ipanema" is probably the best-known bossa nova song.

Argentina

Argentina is unlike the other countries in South America. First, it has fewer native peoples. The number of native peoples living there was never high, and most of those who did live there were murdered in wars with European settlers.

Second, Argentina has a broad European heritage. The first settlers were Spaniards, but immigrants from other European countries began coming to Argentina in the 1800s. In this way, Argentina is much like the United States and Canada. The people of Argentina have roots in Germany, Britain, Italy, and other parts of Europe.

Argentina is very urban and literate. About a third of Argentina's citizens live in Buenos Aires, which is a busy city with museums, art galleries, theaters, and dance companies. The literacy rate in Argentina is much higher than in other South American countries.

Like the United States, Argentina has cowboys. In Argentina, however, the cowboys are called gauchos. They herd cattle on the Pampas, the grassy northern plains.

During the 1930s, the Argentine people hoped that cattle would make them rich. However, things took a turn for the worse. In 1943, a military man, Colonel Juan Perón, seized control. He was a popular leader, but he managed the country poorly.

By the 1950s, Argentina's economy was very weak. Since then, this South American country has seen much political trouble.

Military Governments in South America

Argentina's troubles are not unusual. Other countries in South America and elsewhere have seen the same sort of trouble: The economy goes bad, and then the military takes over. Power ends up in the hands of a **junta**, which is a small group of colonels and generals. Paraguay, Brazil, Peru, Chile, and Bolivia have all been ruled by juntas at one time or another.

In Argentina, a junta seized power in 1976 and then moved to crush all those who fought or even complained about it. Some people were put in jail, some were killed, and some simply disappeared. The government waged war against its own citizens.

As many as 30,000 people fell victim to the Argentine junta. No one talked about what was going on, but everyone knew. Mothers of victims marched silently each week in a public place in Buenos Aires. The rest of the world saw their protests. Pressure increased from other countries. The United States stopped giving money to Argentina.

 **Geography Fact**

In Argentina, the Falkland Islands are called the Islas Malvinas.

Finally, the junta made the one mistake no military government can afford: They lost a war. The Argentine army invaded the Falkland Islands off the coast of Argentina. Britain and Argentina both claimed these islands as their own, but British forces pushed out the Argentine army. Afterward, the members of the junta had to resign from power. In 1983, new elections were held. Nevertheless, the military remains strong in Argentina—as it does throughout the rest of South America.

✓ **Check Your Understanding**

Write your answers in complete sentences.

1. How did Catholic missionaries influence Brazilian music?

2. Who was Juan Perón?

3. How did the Argentine junta lose power?

GEOGRAPHY IN YOUR LIFE
Reading Contour Maps

Contour maps show the elevation, or height, of a place. The closer the lines on a contour map, the steeper the area. If the lines are far apart, the land is flat. On a contour map, the elevation may be written on each line.

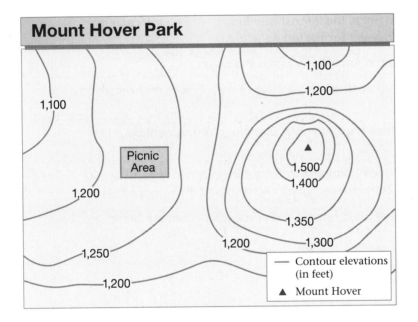

Mount Hover Park

1,100

1,200

1,100

Picnic Area

1,200

1,500

1,400

1,350

1,250

1,200

1,300

— Contour elevations (in feet)

▲ Mount Hover

Answer the questions below.

1. What do the lines on this map show?

2. Where is the highest place in this area?

CHALLENGE When might a contour map be useful?

Apply the Skill

You have to find a way up Hover Mountain from the picnic area. Trace this map. Then, draw what you think the easiest way up would be.

Summary

Six main geographic regions of South America are the Andes, the Amazon River Basin, the Brazilian Highlands, the Guiana Highlands, the Pampas, and Patagonia.

The Amazon River Basin holds the largest rain forest on the Earth and is an important source of oxygen for the whole world.

Most of the people in South America live near the coast.

The Incan empire covered most of the Andean region. The Incan civilization was destroyed in 1532.

The main Andean countries are Colombia, Ecuador, Peru, Argentina, Venezuela, Bolivia, and Chile.

Brazil is the largest and most industrialized country in South America. It was colonized by the Portuguese but has a sizable African population.

Military governments have ruled many South American countries from time to time.

aqueduct
cacao
landlocked
junta
smuggle

Vocabulary Review

Complete each sentence with a term from the list.

1. To _____ is to move goods in or out of a country illegally.

2. The plant from which chocolate is made is _____.

3. A structure that carries water is an _____.

4. A group of leaders who rules a country by force is a _____.

5. If a country is _____ it is surrounded by land.

Chapter Quiz

Write your answers in complete sentences.

1. Why is the Amazon rain forest important?
2. Why is Argentina unlike other South American countries?
3. Explain how a junta gains power.
4. **Critical Thinking** Why is the population of South America not spread evenly throughout the land?
5. **Critical Thinking** What are the disadvantages of having a one-crop plantation economy?

Write About Geography

Complete the following activities.

1. Write a summary of the way Incan society was organized.
2. Write descriptions of the six main geographic regions on cards. Exchange cards with a partner. Try to guess the names of the regions.

Group Activity

Your group is visiting one of the South American countries. Create five scrapbook pages that show what you see on your trip. Possibilities include using pictures, writing descriptions, and drawing menus.

The Caribbean contains hundreds of islands, including Jamaica. What might life be like on a Caribbean island?

Chapter 10

The Caribbean

Words to Know

archipelago	a chain of islands
inhabited	having people living on the land
coral	the stony outside skeletons of tiny sea animals; billions of such skeletons pile up to form underwater ridges called coral reefs
trade wind	a tropical wind that blows from the northeast and southeast toward the equator
commonwealth	a self-governing political unit that is part of a nation or states; a group of self-governing states
communism	an economic system in which the government owns all property and businesses
ally	a close partner
embargo	an order that forbids trade with a certain country

Places to Know

Cuba

Jamaica

Puerto Rico

The Bahamas

Haiti

Dominican Republic

Learning Objectives

- Identify the main islands and island groups in the Caribbean.
- Describe how the Caribbean islands were settled.
- Describe how the islands came to be colonies of European countries.
- Trace the ancestry of Caribbean islanders.
- Explain the importance of religion to Haitian culture.

The Caribbean Islands

The Caribbean Sea lies east of Central America, and in this sea are hundreds of islands. Most are part of one **archipelago**, or chain of islands, called the Antilles. This chain stretches from Mexico to South America in a 2,000-mile arc. These islands were formed by volcanoes. The largest islands are Cuba, Jamaica, Hispaniola, and Puerto Rico. Together, they make up the Greater Antilles. East of Puerto Rico are many smaller islands, including the Virgin Islands, Martinique, Barbados, Grenada, and Trinidad. These smaller islands make up the Lesser Antilles.

The Caribbean Islands

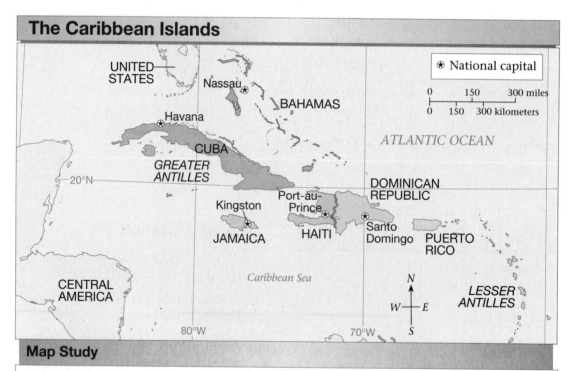

Map Study

1. **REGION** What is the national capital of Jamaica?

2. **LOCATION** Which group of Caribbean islands is closest to the United States?

The Bahamas are a group of islands north of the Antilles. Some of the 700 islands in this group are not even **inhabited** by humans. The Bahamas were created from **coral**, or the hard skeletons of billions of tiny sea animals. As these creatures die, their skeletons build up and form islands such as the Bahamas.

The climate of the Caribbean islands is tropical. Yet the islands are warm, not hot, because **trade winds** cool them down. These trade winds blow toward the southwest from the Atlantic Ocean. They pick up water as they come across the ocean. Between July and October, the trade winds bring storms. Sometimes, these storms turn into dangerous hurricanes with wind speeds of more than 75 miles per hour. Most of the time, the trade winds just make the islands comfortable. Fine beaches and a pleasant climate account for the main industry in the Caribbean—tourism.

Many islands in the Caribbean are independent countries. One island, Hispaniola, is divided into two countries: Haiti and the Dominican Republic. Puerto Rico is a territory of the United States. Some of the smaller islands are colonies of European countries such as Britain, France, and the Netherlands.

People started migrating to the Caribbean about 3,500 years ago. The first to come were the Ciboney people. Next came the Arawak Indians from South America. The Arawak nearly killed all of the Ciboney. A few hundred years later, another group of people, the Caribs, came from South America. The Europeans, who came last, named the region after the Caribs. By 1900, Europeans had killed almost all the native peoples.

Some native ways live on in this region. The Arawak and the Caribs, for example, brought cassava from South America. Along with yams and corn, this starchy root was their main source of food. These foods are still widely grown and eaten in the Caribbean.

Economics Fact

Hurricanes hurt the tourism industry. For example, in 1999, Hurricane Floyd's 140 m.p.h. winds battered the Bahamas. Tourists did not visit, and many islanders lost their jobs.

Explorers, Pirates, and Settlers

After Christopher Columbus landed in the Americas, many Spanish explorers followed in search of gold. Most of the gold was on the mainland, but before the Spaniards could explore, they needed to get ready. They also needed to rest after their long sea voyage. So they set up bases on the Caribbean islands, and from these bases, they attacked the peoples of the mainland.

Soon Spanish ships were hauling heavy loads of gold back to Europe. Pirates began to hide in the islands, attacking the Spanish ships and stealing their gold. The pirates are gone now, but smugglers have replaced them. Smugglers are drug dealers who move illegal drugs from South America through these islands to the United States.

The first colonies in the Caribbean were Spanish. By the 1600s, Britain, France, and the Netherlands were setting up colonies, too. These new colonists started growing sugar cane on the islands. Like the Spaniards, they enslaved Africans to work in their fields. The enslaved people, in turn, brought their beliefs, folk tales, and customs from Africa. They spoke many African languages at first but slowly developed new languages that they could all speak.

Sugar cane farming was hard work, and the enslaved people were underfed and mistreated. Enslaved Africans far outnumbered European colonists on the islands, though, and rebellions were common.

In the 1800s, it became illegal to import enslaved workers. After that, paid workers came from India, China, and other parts of Asia. These workers settled on the islands and added Asian customs and religions to the Caribbean way of life. For example, Trinidad has a community that practices Hinduism, a religion that comes from India.

Puerto Rico

The island of Puerto Rico started out as a Spanish colony. In 1898, Spain lost the Spanish-American War to the United States. As a result, Puerto Rico became a U.S. territory. Despite U.S. control, the culture of the island has been and remains Hispanic.

In 1952, Puerto Rico was given **commonwealth** status. This means that Puerto Ricans are U.S. citizens who have limited rights. For example, they have no voting representatives in Congress. On the other hand, Puerto Ricans pay no U.S. taxes and can elect their own government. They can also migrate freely to the U.S. mainland. Since the 1950s, many have done so looking for jobs. Many Puerto Ricans travel back and forth from the mainland to the island. This is because their extended families still live in Puerto Rico.

Today people do not have to leave Puerto Rico to find jobs. The Puerto Rican economy is booming. In the 1950s, the governor started a program to improve the economy. Companies from the mainland built hotels and started industries there. Puerto Rican factories now make medicines, clothes, electronic items, and many other goods.

Remember
A colony is owned and governed by another country.

HISTORY FACT

Some people want Puerto Rico to become the fifty-first state of the United States. Others want it to become an independent country.

✓ **Check Your Understanding**

Write your answers in complete sentences.

1. How did the Caribbean islands form?

2. What kind of work did the colonists in the Caribbean do on the islands?

3. How did Puerto Rico become a territory?

Cuba

Cuba's history has been a stormy one. After winning independence from Spain in the Spanish-American War, Cuba came under U.S. control, which lasted until 1934. A military dictator named Fulgencio Batista took over and opened up Cuba to U.S. businesses. Batista was especially friendly to a crime organization called the Mafia. Plenty of money flowed into Cuba through the Mafia. Havana became a city of nightclubs and gambling. A few Cubans grew rich. However, most of the people remained very poor.

After 25 years in power, Batista was overthrown in a rebellion led by a young lawyer named Fidel Castro. In 1959 Castro became the leader of Cuba.

Spotlight On

CUBA AND U.S. BASEBALL

When the Baltimore Orioles traveled to Cuba to play the Cuban national team in 1999, there was a storm of protest—and support. To some, the game was just a game. Some argued that even though the United States has a trade embargo against Cuba, that did not mean the teams could not meet. Playing baseball could have even led to more understanding between the countries.

The Cuban National team and the Baltimore Orioles take the field in their historic 1999 game.

To others, such as Cubans now living in Miami, the game was an outrage. "It's like taking part in the abuses that are going on there," said one angry Miami resident. Despite the mixed feelings, the Orioles flew to Havana and took the field. The Cubans won by a score of 3 to 2.

Critical Thinking Should this baseball game have taken place? Explain your point of view.

Castro turned Cuba into a Communist country. His government took control of all land and businesses. It began to provide free services, such as buses, health care, schools, and housing. Castro's government also clamped down on people's rights. The government decided where and how people could work and live. No one was permitted to speak against the government.

Many people fled Cuba in the 1960s. Some left because they were rich and wanted to keep their money. Others left because they hated **communism**. Communism is an economic system in which the government owns all property and businesses. Soon communities of Cuban immigrants sprang up in the United States—the largest one in Miami, Florida.

Before long, Castro's Cuba became an **ally** of the Soviet Union. This alliance made the U.S. government nervous. The Soviet Union and the United States were bitter enemies at the time. With Castro as an ally, the Soviet Union had a base of operations less than 90 miles from Florida.

In 1961, the Soviet Union began moving nuclear missiles onto the island. These missiles were capable of reaching cities in the United States. U.S. President John F. Kennedy demanded that the Soviet Union withdraw their missiles or else he would stop their ships. The Soviet Union agreed to remove the missiles. This event, which almost led to a nuclear war, was known as the Cuban Missile Crisis.

The U.S. government later tried to weaken Cuba with a trade **embargo**. That is, it asked that no one buy sugar—Cuba's main crop. The embargo could have led to Castro's downfall, but the Soviet Union agreed to buy Cuba's sugar crop every year. In 1991, however, the Soviet Union fell apart. Since then, Cuba's economy has suffered. Many Cubans are now dissatisfied with Castro. After more than 40 years, they want change—and some want to see better relations with the United States.

Haiti and the Dominican Republic

Haiti is the western third of the island of Hispaniola. It was the first nation in the Americas to be governed by people of African descent.

Haiti is on the western third of the island of Hispaniola. It was the first nation in the Americas to be governed by people of African descent. It began as a French colony, but in 1804, the enslaved people there rebelled against the French power and took control. Today, nearly everyone in Haiti is of African descent. Most people speak French or Creole patois, which is a language that formed when French was mixed with various West African languages.

Racial tension has always been a problem in Haiti. People with darker skin have fewer social and economic opportunities than those with lighter skin. About two-thirds of the people in Haiti live in rural areas and are subsistence farmers.

In 1957, François "Papa Doc" Duvalier became dictator of Haiti. His son, "Baby Doc" Duvalier, took over, and several years later, the people revolted. "Baby Doc" fled. Eventually, a freely elected president, Jean Bertrand Aristede, took control. Aristede did not serve for long, but the leaders who have succeeded him also have been freely elected.

At one time, Haiti had a booming tourist trade, but its racial tension and political trouble now keep tourists away. Even Haitians are leaving, trying to get away from the poverty and political problems. Some try to sail to the United States in small, leaky boats. Tragically, many of them do not make it.

The official religion in Haiti is Catholicism. Most Haitians also practice a form of spirit worship called Voodoo. They believe that all objects, whether alive or not, have a spirit.

The eastern part of Hispaniola is the Dominican Republic. This country is very different from Haiti. The land was settled by Spain and gained its independence in 1844.

This church and fountain are located in Altos de Chavon, Dominican Republic.

Spain continued to control the area for some time, however. Most of the people in this nation are mestizo. They speak Spanish and live mostly in rural areas. They make their living as subsistence farmers.

✓ Check Your Understanding

Write your answers in complete sentences.

1. How did Cuba change after Castro became leader?

2. Why did Cuba become an ally of the Soviet Union?

3. Why has tourism decreased in Haiti?

4. How is the Dominican Republic different from Haiti?

Summary

Most of the Caribbean islands are part of the Antilles, a chain of volcanic islands that stretches about 2,000 miles. The Bahamas are a chain of coral islands, not part of the Antilles.
The first islanders were the Ciboney, Arawak, and Carib peoples. Most Caribbean people today are descended from European colonists, Africans, native peoples, or all three.
Europeans from Spain, France, Great Britain, and the Netherlands colonized the Caribbean. They built sugar cane plantations, bringing enslaved people from Africa to do the work.
Puerto Rico is a U.S. territory with a stable government and a strong economy.
Cuba is the only Communist country in the Americas.
Haiti and the Dominican Republic are separate countries on the island of Hispaniola.

Vocabulary Review

Write *true* or *false*. If the underlined term is false, change it to make it true.

1. An island that is <u>inhabited</u> has people living on it.

2. Billions of <u>coral</u> skeletons pile up to form underwater ridges called coral reefs.

3. A chain of islands is a <u>trade wind</u>.

4. An <u>archipelago</u> is a tropical wind that blows from the northeast and southeast toward the equator.

5. A <u>commonwealth</u> is a close partner.

Chapter Quiz

Identify each country on the map with the letter
for each of the following countries.

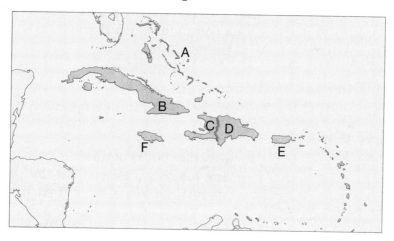

1. Haiti

2. The Bahamas

3. Puerto Rico

4. Cuba

5. Dominican Republic

6. Jamaica

Write About Geography

Complete the following activities.

1. You are on a Caribbean cruise. Visit three islands, and draw your route. Describe each island.

2. A U.S. baseball player is meeting a Cuban baseball player. Write a scene that tells what they might say.

Group Activity

It is 1961, and the Cuban Missile Crisis is happening. Write a newspaper article, act out a radio report, or do a television broadcast about this event.

Unit 3 **Review**

Comprehension Check

Answer each question in a complete sentence.

1. What peoples have affected Mexico's history?

2. Why has there been political unrest in Central America?

3. Describe the economy of the Andean region.

4. Why were the Caribbean islands home to pirates and invaders?

Building Your Skills

Answer each question in a complete sentence.

1. Where is the Central Plateau in Mexico?

2. What does a climate map show?

3. What do lines close together on a contour map mean?

4. Describe the physical geography of the Caribbean.

Where Is It?

Write the name of the place based on the information below.

1. The largest city in Mexico

2. Much of this country's economy is based on a canal

3. The longest mountain range in South America

4. The Caribbean island which is a commonwealth of the United States

Writing an Essay

Answer one of the following essay topics.

1. Describe both the short-term and long-term effects that the Spanish settlers had on Mexico.

2. Explain the effects of volcanoes and earthquakes on life in Central America.

3. Explain why so many countries in South America were under military rule.

4. Describe some of the different peoples of the Caribbean and how they came to be there.

Geography and You

The United States works to protect its resources such as forests. Should the United States work to protect the Costa Rican rain forest as well? Explain.

 **Unit 4** **Africa South of the Sahara**

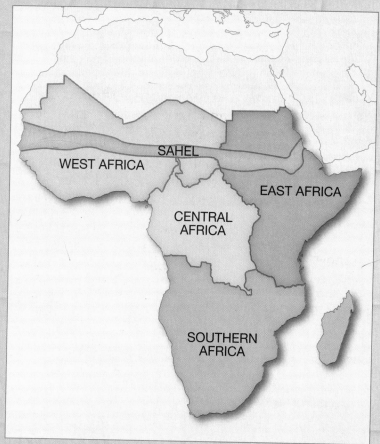

SAHEL

WEST AFRICA

EAST AFRICA

CENTRAL AFRICA

SOUTHERN AFRICA

South of the Sahel, the continent of Africa can be divided into four main regions. In what ways might each region be different?

TRAVEL LOG

Creating masks is one way that people express themselves and their culture. As you read this unit, find other examples of how people express themselves. Describe three of these ways.

African mask

Nigeria is West Africa's largest and most powerful country. What can you tell about Nigeria by looking at this photograph?

Words to Know

sub-Saharan	the region of Africa south of the Sahara
Sahel	a strip of grassland along the southern edge of the Sahara
savanna	a grassland region near the tropics
animism	a belief that many spirits live within the natural world
ritual	an activity that has a sacred meaning and is part of the practice of a religion
invader	an outsider who comes into an area to conquer or destroy it
mosque	an Islamic place of worship
proverb	a short saying that expresses the values or morals of a culture

Places to Know

Niger River

Nigeria

Senegal River

Ghana

Liberia

Sierra Leone

Learning Objectives

- Describe the physical geography and climate of West Africa.
- Describe the heritage of three ancient West African kingdoms: Ghana, Mali, and Songhai.
- Tell how the European slave trade affected West Africa.
- Describe the population, politics, and economy of modern Nigeria.
- Identify some typical social, religious, and storytelling traditions of West Africa.

A Look at Sub-Saharan Africa

Along the northern edge of Africa is a desert called the Sahara, which stretches from east to west across the whole continent. The Sahara is the world's largest desert. It divides Africa into a northern strip and a large southern part called **sub-Saharan** Africa, or the region of Africa south of the Sahara.

Along the southern edge of the Sahara is an area called the **Sahel.** Short grass covers the ground. There are few, if any, trees. The land farther south is called **savanna**, which has tall grass and is dotted with trees.

Geography Fact

Most of sub-Saharan Africa lies between two lines of latitude called the Tropic of Cancer and the Tropic of Capricorn.

Sub-Saharan Africa can be divided into four main regions—each with its own physical geography and climate. The regions are West Africa, Central Africa, East Africa, and southern Africa. There are 44 countries in sub-Saharan Africa. Most of them were European colonies before 1945.

In West Africa, the land is low and flat. The Niger River makes a big curve through the region. Near the coast, rain forest covers much of the land. The climate is hot and moist. In some areas of the rain forest, the trees grow 200 feet high. In other areas, farmers and loggers have cleared many of the trees. There are fewer and fewer untouched areas of the forest.

In the past, farmers in the rain forest and in the less humid forests would clear the land by burning. They would plant crops for a few years until the land wore out, and then they would move on. Those who raised cattle would burn the forest and wait for grass to grow for their cattle. After centuries of this, much of the original forest is a patchwork of farmland, grassland, abandoned farmland, and some old-growth forest.

As you head inland into Africa, the forest thins out and rain is scarcer. After a few hundred more miles, the country becomes more open. This is the beginning of the Sahel.

The Ancient Heritage of West Africa

Thousands of years ago, people who were the ancestors of today's West Africans settled along the Niger and Senegal rivers. They lived in scattered villages, each of which was made up of one extended family. Families were linked together as clans, and several clans made up one large ethnic group. The clan remains the basic social structure in West Africa today, especially in rural areas.

Remember
A clan is a group of families who trace their history to the same ancestor.

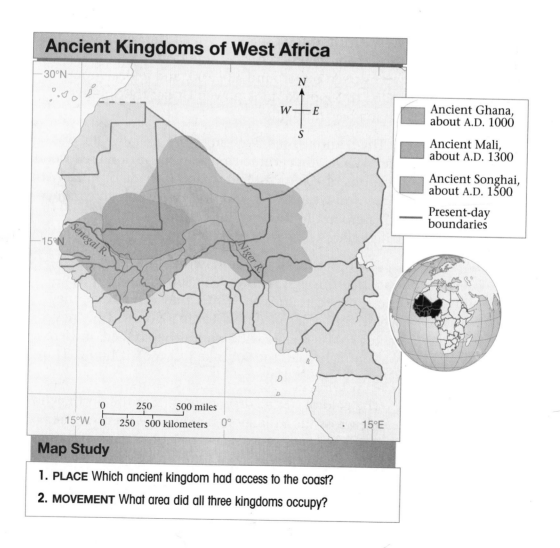

Ancient Kingdoms of West Africa

Ancient Ghana, about A.D. 1000

Ancient Mali, about A.D. 1300

Ancient Songhai, about A.D. 1500

Present-day boundaries

Senegal R.

Niger R.

0   250   500 miles
0   250   500 kilometers

15°W   0°   15°E

Map Study

1. **PLACE** Which ancient kingdom had access to the coast?

2. **MOVEMENT** What area did all three kingdoms occupy?

Religion was important to the West Africans. They believed that spirits lived in things, such as rocks and rivers, as well as in plants, animals, and people. Religious beliefs of this type are sometimes called **animism.** A religious **ritual**—including prayers, songs, and dances—was meant to influence the spirits. Even today, most West Africans, no matter which other faith they practice, still believe in animism.

The Kingdom of Ghana

Around A.D. 300, a kingdom called Ghana formed in West Africa. It took shape between the Niger River and the Sahara. The first rulers came from the north. They were driven out around A.D. 700, and a local group called the Soninke took power. Under the Soninke, Ghana began its rise.

The Soninke used two important metals. One was iron. While other ethnic groups in the region used wood weapons, the Soninke had weapons made of iron. With these iron weapons, the Soninke were able to conquer other groups. In this way, the Soninke—and their kingdom of Ghana—grew powerful.

The other metal was gold, which the Soninke obtained through trading. The Soninke would leave goods by a certain river. When they came back, they would find gold piled next to their goods. They never talked to the people with whom they traded. If there was enough gold, the Soninke just took it home. Thus, Ghana grew wealthy.

The gold of Ghana drew traders from the north, who came across the Sahara on camels. The West Africans had no salt, and these traders brought salt to exchange for gold. They also brought a new religion, Islam. The people of Ghana liked this new religion, and many of them became Muslims, or believers in Islam.

Much of the information we know today about ancient African kingdoms is gathered by studying found objects, such as this ancient African sculpture of a young queen.

The Kingdoms of Mali and Songhai

In the 1200s, Ghana fell to **invaders**, or outside conquerors. In its place rose Mali, an even greater empire. Mali was ruled by the Malinke (or Mandingo) nation, whose members were distant relatives of the Soninke. The Malinke emperors became Muslims and made Timbuktu their capital. Soon, Timbuktu became a famous center of Muslim learning, and people traveled thousands of miles to study there. Europeans heard legends about the great, golden city of Timbuktu. By the 1400s, a rival nation called the Songhai toppled the Malinke. Like the Malinke, the Songhai were Muslims, so they kept Timbuktu as a major city. The Songhai empire was just as grand as the kingdom of Mali, and it lasted about 150 years. It also fell to invaders—and a golden age came to an end in West Africa.

The Soninke, Malinke, and Songhai brought lasting changes to West Africa. The most important change, perhaps, was the introduction of Islam. Today, most West Africans are Muslims—and a **mosque** is a common sight. A mosque is a building that serves as an Islamic place of worship. Many West Africans speak Arabic, at least as a second language. They also follow the rules of Islam in the way they dress. They wear clothes that keep almost the whole body covered, and many keep their heads covered, as well.

However, that style of clothing is common to most West Africans, not just the followers of Islam. As part of the heritage of the ancient kingdoms, both men and women wear long gowns. These gowns are made of dyed cotton, with rich and bright colors and with bold stripes or patterns.

Today, the ancient kingdoms of the Soninke, Malinke, and Songhai are honored in West Africa. For centuries, however, they were forgotten because a great disaster came right after their days of glory—the European slave trade.

> ## $ Economics Fact
>
> When Mali king Mansa Musa traveled to Egypt, he took along 90 camels carrying gold. He gave away so much gold in Egypt that the price of gold was lowered for a decade.

The Slave Trade

The slave trade was connected to events on the other side of the world. In the 1600s, Europeans were colonizing the Americas and building plantations there. They brought enslaved people from Africa to do the work, as they knew African people were good farmers. Their skills would make the plantations prosper.

HISTORY FACT

No records tell exactly how many Africans were enslaved. Some people think the number may have been as high as 20 million.

Inland African ethnic groups caught people in wars and sold their captives to white slave traders on the coast. By the 1700s, some 60,000 Africans were being captured and sold every year. When the slave trade ended in the early 1800s, at least ten million Africans had been sold into slavery in America—and at least two million more had died on the way over.

The slave trade damaged Africa deeply. It caused kingdoms to fall, destroyed cities, and shattered clans and families. Slave traders often paid with guns. This made African ethnic groups that sold people into slavery powerful and wealthy. Even though they were settled people, some Africans gave up farming and began to make their living by becoming slave traders. Others gave up farming to save their lives—and became nomads, running from slavery.

After slavery ended in America, some former enslaved people returned to Africa. They settled along the Atlantic coast in their own country, which they called Liberia. Others settled in Sierra Leone, just north of Liberia. Both places are now independent countries.

✓ Check Your Understanding

Write your answers in complete sentences.

1. Why is there little old-growth forest in West Africa?

2. Who brought the religion of Islam to West Africa?

3. Who settled Liberia?

Modern Nigeria

Nigeria is the most powerful country in West Africa. Over 100 million people live there—more than 10 percent of Africa's entire population.

The Nigerians are divided, however, into more than 200 ethnic groups. The four main ones are the Hausa, the Fulani, the Yoruba, and the Ibo. These four groups comprise more than half the population. The Hausa and the Fulani believe in Islam and live mainly in the north. The Yoruba and the Ibo believe in Christianity, Islam, or animism and live mainly in the south.

This building in West Africa is a mosque, used by followers of Islam.

These groups have a history of disagreement and tension that goes back to at least the late 1800s, when the British colonized this area. Because some of the groups fought against—and others fought for—the British, bitter feelings were born at that time. After the British took over the area, the Ibo cooperated with them. Members of this group, therefore, got the best jobs—and more bad feelings were created among the four groups.

In 1960, Nigeria gained its independence. By then, however, the British had greatly influenced the country. Many Nigerians spoke English, and many had become faithful Christians. A Western system of government was in place, with a parliament and political parties.

The political parties had formed along ethnic lines. After independence, the Hausa and the Fulani won control of the government, but the Ibo controlled most businesses. In 1967, the Ibo tried to break away from Nigeria. They formed a country of their own called Biafra. However, Nigeria would not accept Biafra as an independent country, and a war broke out. About two million Ibo died in the war, most of them from disease and famine. After three years of fighting, Biafra gave up and rejoined Nigeria.

Since that time, the country has experienced ups and downs. Nigeria has oil. It is the source of much of the oil that the United States buys. The money from the sale of oil has brought rapid changes to Nigeria. People are flowing into the cities at a great rate. Lagos, the capital, has become a center of industry and trade. Factories in Lagos make such products as cloth and soap, and some put together car parts imported from abroad. In the 1980s, oil prices dropped—and all of Nigeria felt the jolt. Dependence on oil can be a mixed blessing, and some in Nigeria wonder whether it may be depending too much on oil.

Traditions of West Africa

Many West Africans feel strong ties to their own ethnic group. In Nigeria, for example, some people think of themselves as "Ibo" or "Yoruba" first. Only after that are they "Nigerian." Within the ethnic group, their loyalty is to their clan.

Clans can be very large in West Africa. A single Ibo clan, for example, may have as many as half a million people. Such a large clan has members who live in many different villages. Members gather from time to time for lively celebrations.

Most West African ethnic groups have unique customs. The Ewe of Ghana, for example, use drums as musical instruments and for sending messages. Strings stretched across a drum change its sound when played. Each sound has a meaning.

You Decide

How are you carrying on a tradition of your culture?

Celebrations

FESTIVAL OF THE YAMS

Yams are a vegetable similar to potatoes. They are an important food in West Africa. Many villages have festivals centering on yams. The festival happens once a year, just after the harvest. It lasts for several days.

First, villagers pray to the spirits of nature and give thanks for the harvest. Then, the village chief, dressed in fine robes, tells stories. Afterward, all the villagers bathe in the river, symbolizing a "fresh start." Finally, everyone enjoys dancing, music, and eating.

Critical Thinking The Festival of the Yams celebrates a crop harvest. What holidays in your culture celebrate harvests?

A chief carries a golden staff during a yam festival in the village of Akropong Akvapim in Ghana.

West African Folk Tales

West African cultures are well known for their storytelling and poetry. In the time of slavery, West Africans brought their tradition of storytelling to the Americas. Versions of their stories survive to this day. You may have heard some of the tales about Anansi the spider. This tiny hero is a trickster, who once fooled Nyame, the god of the sky. At that time, all the stories in the world belonged to Nyame. Through a clever trick, however, Anansi managed to get the tales for himself. That is why so many stories now exist about this Ashanti folk hero.

The Yoruba are well known for their **proverbs,** or short sayings expressing the values or morals of a culture. Riddles are popular among the Yoruba, too. Most riddles are meant to entertain or get people to think. Some are used to begin a storytelling event. The Yoruba also have many kinds of poems and songs. Some tell about everyday life in the community. Some are "praise songs," telling about gods, ancestors, or heroes.

The storytelling tradition goes back to the time of the ancient kingdoms of West Africa. In those days, the West Africans did not have written languages, and storytelling was a way of keeping records.

✓ Check Your Understanding

Write your answers in complete sentences.

1. Why do the main groups within Nigeria have a history of disagreement?

2. What are two uses for the "talking drums" of the Ewe of Ghana?

3. Why does the African tradition of storytelling go back to the days of the ancient kingdoms?

GEOGRAPHY IN YOUR LIFE
Understanding Time Zones

Time is not the same everywhere. This is because we measure time by the sun. As the Earth rotates, the sun shines in different places. The Earth makes a complete rotation of 360 degrees in 24 hours. Therefore, there are 24 time zones—one for each hour of the day. The International Date Line is in the Pacific Ocean. It is one day earlier east of this line than it is to the west.

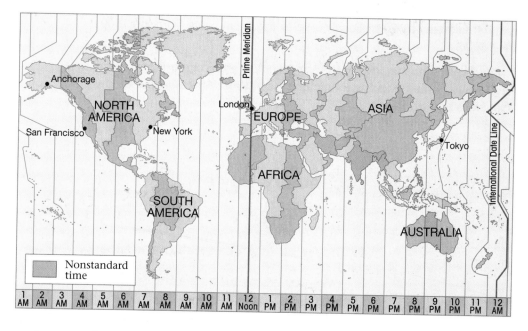

Answer the questions below.

1. Why are there 24 time zones?

2. When it is 9 A.M. in San Francisco, what time it is on the west coast of Africa?

   CHALLENGE If you want to televise a show in Tokyo so that it appears live in New York at 6 P.M., when should you turn on the cameras?

Apply the Skill

Think of three people you know who live in different parts of the country or the world. You plan to call each of them so they hear from you just after dinner. When should you call each one?

Summary

Africa below the Sahara is called sub-Saharan Africa. Sub-Saharan Africa can be divided into four regions: West Africa, Central Africa, East Africa, and southern Africa.

The Soninke, Malinke, and Songhai had powerful kingdoms in West Africa between the 700s and the 1500s. Timbuktu, capital of the Malinke empire and a major Songhai city, was once a great center of Muslim learning.

Africa lost as many as 20 million people to the slave trade from the 1500s to the 1800s.

For many West Africans, loyalty to their clan and ethnic group may come before loyalty to their country. Ethnic groups in West Africa have their own special skills and traditions.

Sahel
sub-Saharan
mosque
proverb
savanna

Vocabulary Review

Write a term from the list that matches each definition below.

1. The region of Africa south of the Sahara

2. A strip of grassland along the southern edge of the Sahara

3. A grassland region near the tropics

4. An Islamic place of worship

5. A short saying that expresses the values or morals of a culture

Chapter Quiz

Write your answers in complete sentences.

1. What was the first great kingdom in West Africa?

2. Which city became a famous center of Muslim learning?

3. Former enslaved Africans founded which countries?

4. **Critical Thinking** How did the slave trade change West Africa?

5. **Critical Thinking** Why did war break out after Nigeria became independent from Britain?

Write About Geography

Complete the following activities.

1. Use the vocabulary words in this chapter to create a crossword puzzle. Exchange puzzles with a classmate.

2. Reread the section about Anansi the spider. Write your own folk story with Anansi as the trickster hero.

Group Activity

Create a book of proverbs. Make up your own proverbs. Then write them in a book and illustrate the pages.

Beyond the Mali village of Djaloube is the Sahel. What can you tell about the climate in the area by looking at this photograph?

Chapter 12

The Sahel and Central Africa

Words to Know

desertification	a process by which dry grassland turns into desert
overpopulated	having more people in a given area than the resources can support
hydroelectric power	electricity made by machines that are operated by rushing river water
swamp	an area that has shallow standing water
tsetse fly	a bloodsucking African fly that often carries deadly parasites to humans, animals, and plants
ivory	a valuable white bone that comes mainly from elephant tusks

Places to Know

Zaire River

Congo

Democratic Republic of the Congo

Kinshasa

Shaba

Learning Objectives

- Trace the causes of desertification.
- Find the Sahel on a map, and describe the lifestyle of people who live there.
- Describe the climate and physical geography of Central Africa.
- Explain the importance of the Congo River.
- Name three serious tropical diseases of Africa.
- Describe the history and the current conditions of the Democratic Republic of the Congo.

The Growing Desert

The Sahel lies just south of the Sahara. It stretches across three regions of sub-Saharan Africa. It runs from the Atlantic coast almost to the Red Sea. Parts of Senegal, Gambia, Mali, Mauritania, Burkina Faso, Niger, Chad, and Sudan lie within the Sahel.

The word *Sahel* means "shore" or "border" in Arabic. Ancient Arabic traders thought of the Sahara as a sea of sand. The Sahel seemed to them a welcome "shore." The Sahel forms a border between the Sahara in the north and the savanna in sub-Saharan Africa. The Sahel is not as dry as the Sahara, but it is much drier than the savanna.

Farming in the Sahel is difficult. Even in good years, there is barely enough rain. Throughout history, this region has been hit by droughts. During these droughts, the grass thins out in the Sahel. The bare dirt turns to dust. Eventually, the land becomes desert. This process is called **desertification.**

The desert spreads nearer to a Sahel settlement.

Another cause of desertification is the way people use the land. For one thing, farmers overwork the soil. Because they cannot get enough food from one crop, they plant another as soon as that crop is harvested. Soil that never rests loses its nutrients. After a time, nothing will grow in the soil.

Many people in the Sahel keep cattle, sheep, or goats. These animals feed on the scattered clumps of grass. However, because there is so little of it, the animals eat the grass right down to the ground. Then, their hooves pound at the delicate root systems. As a result, the grass dies. This is called overgrazing.

Water wells add to the problem. Machines are used to dig very deep wells, which tap into water that lies far underground. Extra water allows a community to grow larger. In this way, wells add to desertification because they allow areas to become **overpopulated.**

Africa

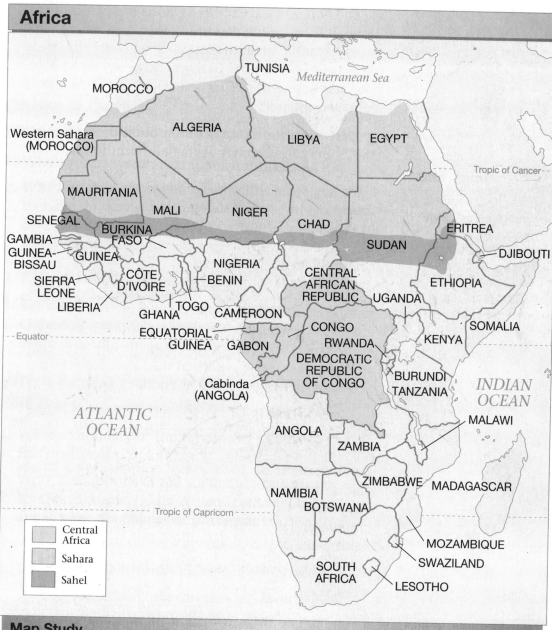

MOROCCO
TUNISIA
Mediterranean Sea
ALGERIA
LIBYA
EGYPT
Western Sahara (MOROCCO)
Tropic of Cancer
MAURITANIA
MALI
NIGER
CHAD
ERITREA
SENEGAL
BURKINA FASO
SUDAN
DJIBOUTI
GAMBIA
GUINEA-BISSAU
GUINEA
SIERRA LEONE
CÔTE D'IVOIRE
NIGERIA
BENIN
CENTRAL AFRICAN REPUBLIC
UGANDA
ETHIOPIA
LIBERIA
GHANA
TOGO
CAMEROON
Equator
EQUATORIAL GUINEA
GABON
CONGO
RWANDA
DEMOCRATIC REPUBLIC OF CONGO
BURUNDI
TANZANIA
KENYA
SOMALIA
Cabinda (ANGOLA)
ATLANTIC OCEAN
INDIAN OCEAN
ANGOLA
ZAMBIA
MALAWI
ZIMBABWE
MADAGASCAR
NAMIBIA
BOTSWANA
Tropic of Capricorn
MOZAMBIQUE
SWAZILAND
SOUTH AFRICA
LESOTHO

Central Africa
Sahara
Sahel

Map Study

1. REGION Which Central African countries does the equator run through?

2. LOCATION Which Central African country is landlocked?

The northern edge of the savanna is a part of the Sahel. It is becoming desert. In other areas where Sahel meets savanna, small trees shade the grasses. The trees' roots help keep the soil in place. However, because wood is a main source of fuel, people who live in this region cut down the trees.

Desertification is a problem around the world. In the 1880s, only 9.4 percent of the land on the Earth was desert. By the 1950s, 23.3 percent was desert. The Sahara is the largest desert in the world, and it is also the fastest spreading. In Niger, the desert has spread 60 miles in less than 20 years. Africa's population is growing—which will cause the desert to spread even faster, unless some action is taken.

The people who live in the Sahel could slow down the spread of the desert. They could, for example, plant fast-growing trees, such as the eucalyptus. They could keep smaller herds of animals. Large herds, however, are still seen as a sign of wealth in the Sahel. Some also keep large herds to avoid starvation.

Many people in the Sahel and savanna are herders who let their animals graze on open lands. Because herding does not always provide enough food for their families, many people also try farming. Trying to herd and farm at the same time creates a problem. In a dry land, herders have to keep moving. Otherwise, their animals will use up the grass. Farmers, on the other hand, have to stay in one place near their land.

In the Sahel, this problem often divides families. The women settle in a village, where they tend the crops. The men travel with the herds and return to the village when they can—but this may not be for weeks or months. Many African herders do not eat their cattle, sheep, or goats. Instead, they drink the animals' milk, or they drink small amounts of the animals' blood for protein.

Economics Fact

Sudan, an agricultural nation in the Sahel, is a poor country. It suffers from drought. Thirty percent of its population was unemployed in 1999.

The Tropics of Central Africa

Central Africa is very warm—the equator passes right through it. One part of this region receives more than 400 inches of rain each year. As a result, much of Central Africa is covered with tropical rain forest.

The rain feeds the Zaire, one of the world's longest rivers. In one place, this river forms the border between the countries of the Democratic Republic of the Congo and Congo, where it is called the Congo River. The river winds north, then turns west, then heads south, and finally empties into the Atlantic Ocean. It circles around a flat area called the Congo River Basin.

You Decide

Compare Central Africa to the tropics of South America. How are the two regions similar?

People living near the Congo River have long depended on the fish there as a source of food.

The Congo River system is the most important geographical feature of this region. It has long provided food in the form of fish, and throughout history people have used the river for travel.

People cannot travel the whole length of the river. In some places, the water rushes and crashes down rocky slopes. Such stretches of river are called rapids, which can overturn boats or damage them. Fast-moving river water is not all bad: It can be used to create electricity called **hydroelectric power.** The Democratic Republic of the Congo has built a big hydroelectric power plant on the Congo River.

Heavy rains wash nutrients out of the soil. For this reason, Central Africa is a poor place to grow crops. Despite this fact, many of the people in this region farm in rural areas. They raise mostly cassava and yams. In other areas, the people grow cash crops such as cacao, coffee, and palm trees. From palm trees comes palm oil, which people can use for cooking.

Remember
Cacao is the plant used to make chocolate.

Central Africa also has valuable minerals such as cobalt, copper, and diamonds. Cobalt is a very hard metal that is used to make tools for cutting and drilling. Mining these minerals provides jobs in Central Africa.

The rain forest is important to the region's economy. Rubber comes from the rain forest, and hardwood trees are cut down for lumber and other products.

✔ **Check Your Understanding**
Write your answers in complete sentences.

1. In what ways is Central Africa different from the Sahel?

2. Why are rivers important to the people of Central Africa?

3. How does heavy rain affect farming in this region?

Diseases of the Tropics

The climate of Central Africa contributes to health problems. Bacteria grow quickly in the heat and rain. Some bacteria break things down and make them rot. Insects are attracted to the rot and spread the bacteria, some of which cause diseases. The rain also creates **swamps**, where tiny, harmful life-forms grow. Many of these life-forms are parasites that cause diseases. Insects spread the parasites to people.

Three of the most dangerous tropical diseases in Africa are caused by parasites. These diseases are malaria, sleeping sickness, and river blindness. Malaria is a problem in most tropical areas of the world. The parasite that causes malaria is born in a swamp and is carried away by certain mosquitoes. When one of these mosquitoes bites someone, the parasite passes into the person's blood, where it multiples until the person becomes ill with fever and chills. In Africa, about one million children die of malaria each year. If malaria does not kill, it can make a person weak. People who get malaria can become sick off and on for the rest of their lives.

Sleeping sickness affects people, animals, and plants. Like malaria, it is caused by a parasite that is spread by an insect called the **tsetse fly**, which is a bit bigger than an ordinary house fly. Sleeping sickness usually causes death and has been known to kill whole herds of cattle—in which case, the people who depend on the cattle may starve to death.

A tiny worm causes river blindness. The worm lives in rivers, and an insect called the black fly spreads the worm to humans. Once inside a person, the worm multiplies, clusters at certain spots, and causes terrible itching. After a time, the person goes blind. River blindness is the most widespread of the three diseases.

Until the mid-1900s, diseases limited population growth in Central Africa. Since then, however, medicines have been created that fight tropical diseases. The medicines are costly—and in a poor region, many people cannot afford them.

African governments have spent a great deal of money trying to control the insects that spread diseases. Some of their solutions, however, have created new problems. For example, the governments have tried to kill tsetse flies with poisonous chemicals, but these chemicals are harmful to people. In some areas, people have burned the grasslands where the tsetse flies lay their eggs—but this leads to soil erosion. The flies also live on large, wild animals. Killing the wild animals destroys a source of food for the flies, but not everyone agrees that wild animals should be killed in order to destroy the flies.

Malaria can be controlled by draining swamps where mosquitoes breed. Getting rid of swamps in such a wet region costs a lot of money. As a result, the struggle against tropical diseases slows down economic growth in Central Africa.

The Democratic Republic of the Congo

Geography Fact

The Democratic Republic of the Congo is a different country from its geographic neighbor, Congo.

The Democratic Republic of the Congo, which until recently was called Zaire, is the largest country in Central Africa. This country is almost three times the size of Nigeria. It has about 48 million people—much less than Nigeria's population. Most of the people live in rural areas, where many work on plantations. The Democratic Republic of the Congo grows a lot of cotton and exports coffee and rubber.

The capital of this country is Kinshasa, located on the Congo River, about 300 miles from the Atlantic Ocean. Kinshasa has the look of a modern city. It has skyscrapers downtown, paved streets, and many big apartment buildings. People have electricity and running water.

Factories in the city make candles, soap, cloth, steel, and many other goods. A railroad moves goods to and from the coast.

The Shaba region, in the southeastern part of the country, also has some industrial plants. Shaba is a hilly area where copper is mined. The people of the Democratic Republic of the Congo were mining copper in this region long before European people arrived.

The country is home to about 250 ethnic groups, which have many different ways of life and speak many different languages. Most of these people are part of the same large language group—Bantu. This does not mean that they can communicate with one another. Two Bantu languages can be as different as English is from German.

In the cities, different ethnic groups live together. In rural areas, however, ethnic groups rarely mix. They may trade with one another, but they live in separate villages. People tend to marry within their own ethnic group. Some groups have a tradition of not getting along, and tension between such groups can lead to violence.

The Bambuti people are an unusual ethnic group in the Democratic Republic of the Congo. They live in the rain forest, along riverbanks. They are short—less than five feet tall. Bambutis are among the few people on the Earth who still live entirely by hunting and by gathering wild food. They hunt pigs, small antelope, and other animals of the forest. They use spears and bows and arrows, sometimes rubbing poisonous plants on their arrow tips. Storytelling and music are an important part of life for Bambutis.

More than half the population in Central Africa believes in animism. Some people are Christian. Many European countries sent Christian missionaries to the region during the 1800s. For this reason, the Christian influence is strong in Central Africa.

The Democratic Republic of the Congo became independent in 1960. Before that, it was colonized by Belgium and was called the Belgian Congo. This colony was a source of great wealth for Belgium. Belgian people took rubber, copper, diamonds, gold, palm oil, and **ivory** from their colony.

The Belgians were forced to leave in 1960. At that point, a civil war broke out. When it ended, an army general named Joseph Mobutu was in control. He changed the name of the country to Zaire. He gave native African names to all the cities. He also encouraged people to give themselves African names instead of European names. He changed his own name to Mobutu Sese Seko.

Mobutu held his country together for more than 30 years, but his government drew many complaints. Zaire had many resources, yet the country was very poor. In 1996, while Mobutu was out of the country, a group of rebels gained attention. Led by General Laurent Kabila, the rebels convinced the army and many citizens to join them. As a result, when Mobutu returned to Zaire in 1997, he was sent into exile by Kabila's forces.

Kabila declared himself president. He changed the name of the country to the Democratic Republic of the Congo. Today, the country is still very poor.

✓ **Check Your Understanding**

Write your answers in complete sentences.

1. What causes the three most dangerous tropical diseases in Africa?

2. Explain how ethnic groups get along in the Democratic Republic of the Congo.

3. Why do you think Joseph Mobutu changed the names of the country and the cities of the Belgian Congo?

GLOBAL ISSUES
Medical Epidemics

Every day, 5,000 people die of AIDS in sub-Saharan Africa. That number is shocking. It is also only part of the story. While AIDS is worst in Africa, this disease is a worldwide epidemic—a disease that spreads quickly.

The world has always faced epidemics. AIDS, though, may be the worst in human history. Groups from around the world are working to stop the disease and to help those who have it.

Governments and agencies are offering assistance. One such group is Doctors Without Borders. The group won the Nobel Prize for its volunteer work in treating the ill around the world. Other doctors are working hard to develop a vaccine against this disease. Dr. Seth Berkley, president of the International AIDS Vaccine Initiative, says, "Only a vaccine can stop the epidemic."

Answer the questions below.

1. What is a worldwide epidemic?

2. Why do you think Dr. Berkley thinks
a vaccine is necessary to stop the epidemic?

MAKE A DIFFERENCE
Put together a list of groups that help ill people and encourage teenagers to volunteer. Write a story for your school newspaper that tells about these chances to help. You might want to volunteer yourself.

Chapter

12 / Review

Summary

The Sahel is a region between the Sahara and the savanna. Droughts, overpopulation, poor land use, and overgrazing are causing the Sahel to become desert.
Tropical rain forest covers much of Central Africa.
The Congo River system is a major geographical feature of Central Africa.
Malaria, sleeping sickness, and river blindness are three widespread tropical diseases. These diseases have limited population and economic growth in Central Africa.
The Democratic Republic of the Congo was once a colony of Belgium, called the Belgian Congo, but it became an independent country in 1960.
The Bambutis are one of the Democratic Republic of the Congo's 250 ethnic groups and live entirely by hunting and gathering food in the rain forest.

desertification
hydroelectric power
swamp
overpopulated
ivory

Vocabulary Review

Complete each sentence with a term from the list.

1. A valuable white bone that comes mainly from elephant tusks is _____.

2. A _____ is an area that has shallow standing water.

3. An area is _____ when it has more people than its resources can support.

4. Electricity made by machines that are operated by rushing water is called _____.

5. A process by which dry grassland turns into desert is called _____.

Chapter Quiz

Write your answers in complete sentences.

1. What was the Democratic Republic of the Congo once called?

2. Which disease can the bite of a tsetse fly cause?

3. What is desertification?

4. **Critical Thinking** How does climate make Central Africa a difficult place for people to live?

5. **Critical Thinking** How is the lifestyle of Bambutis different from that of most other people?

Write About Geography

Complete the following activities.

1. You are visiting a family that makes its living from herding in the Sahel. In a letter home, describe what life is like for that family.

2. A community organization has just raised money to help Central Africa. Write how the money should be spent.

Group Activity

Have members of your group research a small country in Central Africa. Find out the population, the climate, and facts about the people and their lifestyle. Use the information to create a booklet about that country.

Musical instruments like this one played by a Sudanese man are common throughout the world. What kinds of musical instruments look similar to this?

Chapter 13 / East Africa

Words to Know

rift	a crack or separation in the Earth's crust, usually caused by forces deep beneath the surface
famine	a serious food shortage that causes many people to die of starvation
anthropologist	a scientist who studies the origins and development of human life and culture
nationalism	a strong feeling of loyalty to one's country
game reserve	a large area set aside for wild animals
endangered species	an animal in danger of dying out because its numbers are few

Places to Know

Great Rift Valley

Lake Victoria

Serengeti Plain

Mount Kilimanjaro

Learning Objectives

- Identify the countries and landforms of East Africa.
- Explain famine and malnutrition in Africa.
- Identify some common African customs.
- Explain the origins and importance of Swahili.
- Outline the history of colonialism in East Africa.
- Explain the purpose of game reserves.

The Region of East Africa

Djibouti is a small country on the horn of Africa. This part of Africa sticks out into the Indian Ocean. Three other countries are located on the horn: Ethiopia, Eritrea, and Somalia. Until recently, Eritrea was a province of Ethiopia. Only in 1993 did it win its independence. West of the horn lies the country of Sudan. Except for Ethiopia, all the countries on the horn border the Red Sea. Five countries south of the horn of Africa are part of East Africa, too. They are Kenya, Tanzania, Uganda, Rwanda, and Burundi.

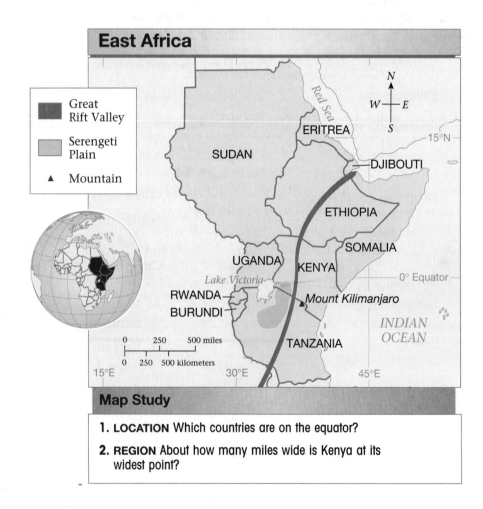

East Africa

Great Rift Valley

Serengeti Plain

▲ Mountain

SUDAN

Red Sea

ERITREA

DJIBOUTI

ETHIOPIA

SOMALIA

UGANDA

KENYA

Lake Victoria

RWANDA

BURUNDI

Mount Kilimanjaro

TANZANIA

INDIAN OCEAN

15°N

0° Equator

15°E

30°E

45°E

0   250   500 miles

0   250   500 kilometers

Map Study

1. **LOCATION** Which countries are on the equator?

2. **REGION** About how many miles wide is Kenya at its widest point?

East Africa's climate is very dry in the north but is less dry farther south. East Africa has gentle, rolling hills and steep mountains, some of which are volcanoes. The region also has flat, grassy plains, most of which are at high elevations. The equator runs through the middle of Kenya. Considering the latitude, this region should be hot. However, much of Kenya is at a high elevation and, therefore, cool.

East Africa has four famous landforms. One is the Great **Rift** Valley, which is a huge crack in the Earth's surface. Another is Lake Victoria—the world's third-largest lake. East of Lake Victoria is the Serengeti Plain—a flat grassland that is home to lions, giraffes, and many other wild animals. The fourth famous landmark is Mount Kilimanjaro. This snow-capped mountain is not part of a range but stands alone, rising nearly 20,000 feet above the plains.

War and Famine in the Northeast

The problem of hunger is widespread in Africa. The continent simply does not grow enough food for all of its people. Many children and adults suffer from malnutrition because their diet does not give them enough nutrients. Malnutrition can lead to many health problems, such as hair loss, abdominal swelling, and liver disease. The problem goes beyond malnutrition in some areas where there is **famine**, and people are starving to death. Some of the world's worst famines are taking place in northeastern Africa. In the 1980s, more than one million people there died of hunger. Famine remains severe in the region.

Why is there famine in Africa? One cause is population growth. In most of the continent, the food supply is growing—but the population is growing three or four times faster. In some places, the food supply is actually shrinking.

You Decide

What is the best way for other countries to help those starving in Africa?

Northeastern Africa is one such place where the food supply is shrinking. This area has all the problems of the Sahel. The desert is spreading and droughts are killing crops. However, northeastern Africa has another problem contributing to the famine—war.

Eritrea is independent now, but it struggled for independence for more than 20 years. Rebels in Ethiopia fought to overthrow their Communist government. The Communists in Ethiopia have fallen. However, Ethiopia remains unstable.

Ethiopia has also been fighting off and on with its neighbor Somalia. The two countries disagree about their border. In Somalia, where the central government fell apart in the early 1990s, various clans rule areas and are now at war with one another. In 1992, the United Nations sent soldiers to Somalia. This force included about 30,000 troops from the United States. They were trying to keep peace.

Remember
Refugees flee their homes because of war, political danger, famine, or economic hardship.

All this fighting has caused millions of people to flee their homes and become refugees. They cannot produce food. In the middle of a war, herders cannot care for their herds. Armed gangs take whatever food is grown. The United States and other developed countries have sent food to many African countries. However, little of this food reaches the war-torn areas. This is because soldiers either keep it for themselves or destroy the food so that their enemies cannot have it.

✓ **Check Your Understanding**
Write your answers in complete sentences.

1. What are the four major landforms in East Africa?

2. Why is hunger widespread in Africa?

3. How does war increase hunger?

GLOBAL ISSUES
World Famine

Every year, about 40 million people die from hunger or malnutrition. Famine is an extreme shortage of food. Malnutrition means not getting enough food to stay healthy. Famine has many causes. Some causes, such as drought or floods, are natural. Famine may also be caused by human problems. War and overpopulation are two of these.

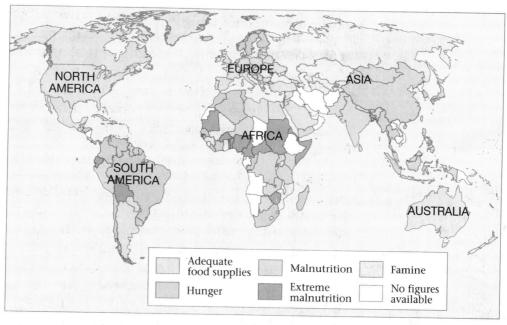

Adequate food supplies	Malnutrition	Famine
Hunger	Extreme malnutrition	No figures available

Answer the questions below.

1. If you wanted to be helpful in aiding the hungry in Africa, where would you send food?

2. Why do you think North America and Australia have adequate food supplies?

MAKE A DIFFERENCE
Write a letter to your local newspaper explaining the world famine situation. Include the names and addresses of two organizations to which people can send money.

The Great Rift Valley

Geography Fact

Some experts believe that East Africa is splitting away from the rest of the continent. Millions of years from now the Great Rift Valley may be an ocean.

The most striking landform in East Africa is the Great Rift Valley. Astronauts can see this giant crack from outer space. It is more than 4,000 miles long and runs from southern Africa to the Red Sea. In some places, the valley is 30 miles wide and 6,000 feet deep. The floor of the valley is mostly flat, but its walls can be steep.

The valley began to form millions of years ago. It is actually a series of cracks, or rifts. This may be a place where two tectonic plates are moving apart. Tectonic plates are large moveable pieces of the Earth's crust. As the plates move apart, the ground sinks. Because this continues to happen, the Great Rift Valley is still growing.

The walls of the Great Rift Valley contain many fossils. Fossils are the remains of plants and animals that died thousands or even millions of years ago. The Great Rift Valley attracts **anthropologists** from many nations. These scientists use physical clues, such as long-buried human bones, to study people from the distant past. Fossils and unearthed bones in the Great Rift Valley help anthropologists learn how human beings developed.

Kenya's Ethnic Groups

Over 28 million people live in Kenya. They belong to more than 40 ethnic groups. These groups have different languages or dialects and different customs and beliefs. The people live in separate villages and tend to live in different parts of the country. The Masai, for example, live in southern Kenya and northern Tanzania. The Turkana live in northwest Kenya. Luo villages are near Lake Victoria in the southwest. The Sambura live in the middle of the country.

Kenya's largest ethnic group, however, lives all throughout the country. These people are the Kikuyu. Of all the people in Kenya, the Kikuyu had the most contact with Europeans. As a result, they lost more of their land. Many of them ended up living in the cities. Today, about five million Kikuyu live in and around Nairobi, Kenya's capital. The Kikuyu have the most important jobs in the government. Kenya's first president, Jomo Kenyatta, was a member of this group.

Many Kenyans have adopted western customs. This is especially true in the cities. People dress in European-style clothes, live in modern apartments and houses, drive cars, and work in offices. Some ethnic groups in Kenya, however, are trying to hold onto their traditional ways. The Masai are one such people. The Masai herd cattle for a living. They measure wealth by heads of cattle, and they consider themselves to be the guardians of all the world's cattle. Masai men are known to be fierce fighters. By tradition, a Masai man trains for 15 years in the skills of war.

The old ways are sometimes hard to follow in a modern nation, however. In the past, for example, the Masai warred with other ethnic groups. This is no longer possible as the other groups are now their fellow Kenyan citizens. Some Masai men use their traditional skills to make money in the cities. For instance, they may work as guards.

Although they tend to live in different parts of the country, Kenya's ethnic groups get along fairly well. Some people even marry into other groups. In general, Kenyans, like most Africans, are more loyal to clan than to country. Government leaders in Kenya are trying to build up **nationalism**. They know that nationalism will strengthen the central government. They believe it will lead to even greater cooperation among the many different ethnic groups.

The Masai live in East Africa. They are some of the tallest people in the world.

Swahili: A Language of Trade

Most Kenyan people speak many languages. For example, those who live in Nairobi might speak English, French, and Portuguese in addition to their native language. Those who live in a rural village might speak a few of the local languages. For example, the Luo people speak Jaluo. A Luo farmer also might speak the languages of the Kikuyu and Luhya. This helps the farmer to communicate with neighboring villages.

There is one language that almost all Kenyans speak. It is called Swahili, which belongs to the Niger-Congo language group. The word *Swahili* is an Arabic word. It means "of the coast."

Before the 1500s, Arabic traders sailed regularly to East Africa. There they landed on the coast of Kenya and traded with Africans. Swahili, a blend of Arabic and Bantu, probably grew out of these communications.

Later, Portuguese traders started sailing to East Africa. They, too, traded with Africans along the coast, and many Portuguese words crept into Swahili. Even today, Swahili shows Portuguese influence. It contains words from Persian and Malay because Kenyans traded with what is today Iran and Malaysia.

Swahili is widely spoken in Africa. In some rural schools in East Africa, it is the only written language taught. In Tanzania, it is the official language.

As in ancient times, Swahili is an important language of business. Tourists and business travelers in Africa often learn some Swahili. It is the single most useful language for getting around in Africa.

GEOGRAPHER'S TOOL KIT
Using Language Maps

A language map shows what language groups are spoken in an area and where the speakers live. Africa has about 800 languages that fall into these four main groups. The Niger-Congo language group is the largest. It includes Swahili. Hausa is the most common language in the Afro-Asiatic group. The Khoisan languages use many consonant sounds.

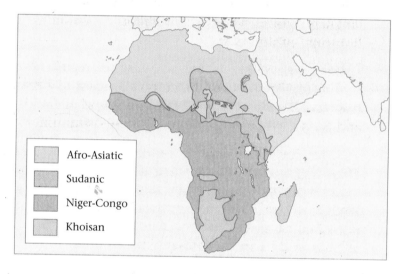

Afro-Asiatic

Sudanic

Niger-Congo

Khoisan

Answer the questions below.

1. What language group is most common in Africa?

2. What can you tell about the migration of the people who speak Afro-Asiatic from looking at this map?

CHALLENGE The number of languages in the world is shrinking. Why might this be happening?

Apply the Skill

Talk to five friends. Find out what languages their ancestors spoke. Then make a graph that shows how many people spoke each language.

Marriage Customs

When it comes to marriage, many East Africans—as do other Africans—follow the traditional customs of their ethnic groups. For example, boys and girls do not, as a rule, go out on dates. Marriage joins two families, not just two individuals. For a marriage to work, the families have to get along. The couple getting married may have little or no relationship before their wedding.

Many African cultures and religions practice polygamy, which means that men are permitted to have two or more wives. In sub-Saharan Africa, polygamy goes back long before Islam. Polygamy has begun to fade out in the cities, but it remains common among rural Africans.

Almost all African cultures have a custom called bridewealth. This is a payment that a man makes to the bride's family. Once wealth has changed hands, no one is likely to back out of the marriage agreement. Among some groups, bridewealth serves as a marriage certificate. Traditionally, a man pays bridewealth in gold, grain, sheep, goats, or other valuable goods. Cattle are the most common form of bridewealth for the Masai men of Kenya. City dwellers may pay in cash instead of goods.

Colonialism in East Africa

Arab traders came to East Africa for ivory, spices, and other goods. They also came to enslave people. They took thousands of Africans to the Arabian Peninsula each year. Some ended up as far away as India and China.

In the 1800s, the British halted the Arab slave trade. By then, however, the British themselves were busy colonizing the region. So were other Europeans. Germans, for example, settled the area now known as Tanzania.

The British set up the colony of Kenya. They began by building a railroad from the Indian Ocean to Lake Victoria. They brought 30,000 workers from India to lay the tracks. One place along the tracks was a center for trade between the Masai and the Kikuyu. This station became the city of Nairobi.

The train brought travelers across the Kenyan plains. Many of them were from the British middle class. In Kenya, they could become upper class by taking land from the Africans and building large tea and coffee plantations. The Africans also lost many basic rights to the British. For example, the British would not allow them to travel freely. The government ordered the Africans to pay taxes. Most Africans, however, could not pay these taxes in money, because in their culture there was no such thing as money. So the government forced the Africans to work for the British, and the Africans became little more than enslaved peoples in their own land.

Around 1951, a group of Africans in Kenya started a guerrilla army. They called themselves the Mau Mau. Most of the Mau Mau fighters were Kikuyu. For seven years, they waged war against British rule. In the first six years of warfare, 11,000 Mau Mau were killed. The group drew the rest of the world's attention to Kenya's problem. In the seventh year of warfare, the British at last agreed to share power. In 1963, Kenya became independent.

In colonial times, the British brought workers from India and Pakistan to Africa. Many of them stayed to set up stores or small farms. To their descendants, Africa is home. Many black Africans still think of the people of Asian descent as outsiders. Some want to prevent immigrants from owning land or taking jobs. In the country of Uganda, the prejudice against the Asian population led to violence. Asian peoples were driven out of that country in the 1970s.

East Africa's Game Reserves

A lion sleeps under a flame tree on the Serengeti Plain. Nearby, two more lions pace back and forth. Half-hidden in the tall grass are a pack of hyenas, picking at an antelope that the lions killed earlier. Suddenly, a truck pulls up. A game keeper pulls out her field glasses and looks around. Counting young lion cubs is part of her work in this East African **game reserve**. A game reserve is an area set aside for wild animals. Game reserves are meant to protect wildlife, and hunting within their boundaries is limited or forbidden.

The Serengeti Plain game reserve is home to giraffes and many other animals.

East Africa's reserves are needed because Africa has so many **endangered species** of wild animals. One endangered species is the mountain gorilla of Rwanda, Uganda, and the Democratic Republic of the Congo. Rhinoceroses, zebras, giraffes, and cheetahs are some of the many other species that roam freely on the game reserves. Wildlife is one of Africa's most valuable resources. Some of the wild animals that live in Africa do not live anywhere else on the Earth. Tourists travel from all over the world to see them.

People and wildlife do not always share the land easily. Wild animals trample farmers' fields and kill cattle. Elephant herds tear down trees and harm other native plants. Lions, elephants, and other large animals can pose a danger to people. Some people, in turn, can pose a danger to those animals. People who live on or near game reserves sometimes kill animals for money. This illegal killing is called poaching.

The governments of East Africa try to balance the needs of people with those of wildlife. Tanzania, for example, limits tourism. Yet Africa's population is growing. As the population grows, people may press to use more land. Preserving wildlife may then become more difficult.

✓ **Check Your Understanding**

Write your answers in complete sentences.

1. Why do scientists study the Great Rift Valley?

2. Why did many Kikuyu end up in the cities?

3. How did Swahili get its start?

4. What is the purpose of bridewealth?

5. How did the British make a living in Kenya?

Summary

Ethiopia, Eritrea, Somalia, and Djibouti are located in the horn of Africa. Uganda, Kenya, and Tanzania are three large countries south of the horn.
The Great Rift Valley, Lake Victoria, Mount Kilimanjaro, and the Serengeti Plain are four famous landforms of East Africa.
Drought, population growth, poor land use, and war are causing much famine in northeastern Africa.
Many African cultures practice polygamy, and nearly all follow the custom of giving bridewealth.
Swahili is the language of trade in East Africa. It is spoken throughout much of Africa.
Africa has many endangered species of wildlife, and game reserves protect wildlife in East Africa.

Vocabulary Review

Write *true* or *false*. If the statement is false, change the underlined term to make it true.

1. A serious food shortage that causes many people to die of starvation is a <u>famine</u>.

2. An <u>anthropologist</u> studies the origins and development of human life and culture.

3. A <u>rift</u> is a strong feeling of loyalty to one's country.

4. A large area set aside for wild animals is an <u>endangered species</u>.

5. A <u>game reserve</u> is an animal in danger of dying out because its numbers are few.

Chapter Quiz

Write your answers in complete sentences.

1. Which is the largest ethnic group in Kenya?

2. Cattle are very important in which culture?

3. What language do most Kenyans speak?

4. Critical Thinking In Africa, why is ethnic loyalty usually stronger than nationalism?

5. Critical Thinking How does war in northeastern Africa increase the problem of hunger in the area?

Write About Geography

Complete the following activities.

1. Write a poem based on one of the photographs in this chapter.

2. Much of the food given to Africa does not reach the people. Make a plan to ensure the food reaches people.

Group Activity

Plan a safari in Kenya. Look on the Internet for sites of companies offering safaris. Read what they offer and put together your own safari. Write where you will go, where you will stay, and what you will see.

Spectacular Victoria Falls is on the Zambezi River, bordering both Zambia and Zimbabwe. What uses could such a waterfall have?

Chapter 14 / Southern Africa

Words to Know

vegetation	the main plant life of an area
archaeologist	a scientist who studies items that people made long ago in order to learn about how they lived
apartheid	a system of laws developed in South Africa to keep racial groups separate
homeland	a special reserve in South Africa where many black South Africans were forced to move
sanction	a step taken by several nations acting together to punish another nation for breaking international laws
boycott	an attempt to change the actions of a company or country by refusing to buy its products
martial law	a state of emergency in which a government suspends citizens' rights and uses its army to control its people

Places to Know

South Africa

Namibia

Botswana

Zimbabwe

Kalahari Desert

Zambezi River

Learning Objectives

- Identify southern African resources.
- Explain how the Bantu migrations shaped many of Africa's native cultures.
- Describe the history of white rule in South Africa.
- Describe black nationalism as a movement.
- Identify some artistic traditions in southern Africa.

Southern Africa as a Region

South Africa is one of many countries in the region of southern Africa. It occupies the tip of the African continent. Countries north of South Africa are Namibia, Botswana, Zimbabwe, and Mozambique. Farther north are the countries of Malawi, Zambia, and Angola. All are considered to be part of southern Africa. The island nation of Madagascar is also considered to be part of southern Africa—as are two small countries surrounded by South Africa: Lesotho and Swaziland. Lesotho lies entirely within the borders of South Africa. Swaziland shares a short border with Mozambique.

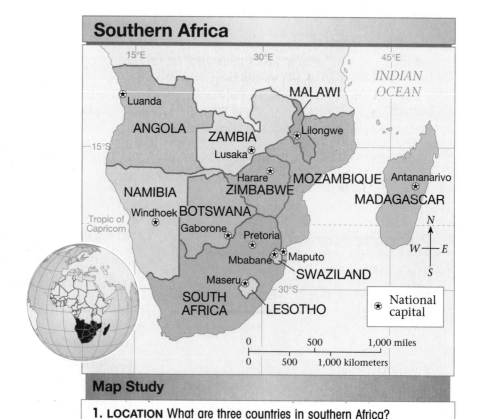

Southern Africa

Map Study

1. **LOCATION** What are three countries in southern Africa?
2. **REGION** Which ocean surrounds Madagascar?

As a region, southern Africa has many resources. It has gold, diamonds, copper, iron ore, lead, and zinc. There is oil under the seafloor off the southern coast. Much of the soil is rich.

There are two large deserts in the region—the Namib and the Kalahari. The eastern coast of southern Africa receives plenty of rain. In addition, five large rivers provide water. The Zambezi, Africa's fourth largest river, also provides hydroelectric power to the region.

South Africa is an industrialized country. Most of its people live in cities, such as Johannesburg, Cape Town, and Pretoria. The other countries of southern Africa are less developed. About 75 percent of their populations live in rural areas.

Ethnic Groups of Southern Africa

The smallest ethnic group of southern Africa is made up of the earliest known people in the area—the San and the Khoikhoi. Most of the San live in the Kalahari Desert. They follow an ancient way of life by hunting wild animals and by gathering wild plants. The other group of people, the Khoikhoi, are herders by tradition. The numbers of both groups are shrinking, and soon they may die out.

This Ndebele woman lives in Botshabelo, a republic of South Africa.

Black Africans make up the majority population of southern Africa. The ancestors of the black majority population were the Bantu, who drifted into the region many hundreds of years ago. The minority population is white. They are descended from European colonists, who began coming to the region in the 1600s and quickly took control.

In the late 1900s, however, the white people slowly lost power. Today, most of the white people of the region live in South Africa. They make up about 14 percent of the population. South Africa also has a large population of Asian immigrants, who came mostly from India.

The Bantu Migrations

Remember
Swahili, a common language in Africa, was formed from Bantu and Arabic.

The Bantu people originated far to the north, in West Africa, where they lived along the Niger River. Sometime after 500 B.C., they began to spread out and entered what is now the country of Sudan. Then, they drifted south. The Bantu migrations were very gradual and went on for about 2,000 years. Slowly, the Bantu spread throughout central, eastern, and southern Africa. At least ten major Bantu empires formed over the centuries.

In West Africa, the Bantu based their way of life on fishing. They lived in small settlements along the Niger River and traveled in boats. As they migrated, their way of life changed. They adapted to each new zone of climate and **vegetation**. On the northern savanna, they became herders. When they moved into the central African forests, they left their herds behind and became hunters and farmers. On the eastern plains and the southern savanna, they began to herd again.

As early as A.D. 400 to 500, the Bantu learned to work with iron. They developed this skill in the central African forests where they made charcoal from hardwood trees. The Bantu made axes, spears, and other tools of war, as well as tools needed for farming.

During their migrations, the Bantu merged with and passed on skills to groups they met. In South Africa, for example, the Zulus, the Xhosa, and the Sotho are descended from the Bantu. The same is true of the Shona and Ndebele, who live in Zimbabwe. In fact, nearly all of the black ethnic groups in southern Africa are descended from the Bantu. Today, these ethnic groups speak different languages, and each has its own customs and traditions.

The Ancient City of Great Zimbabwe

In the heart of Zimbabwe is an ancient Bantu city called Great Zimbabwe. Experts believe that most of the city was built in the eleventh century, but parts of the city were built perhaps 500 years earlier. The ruins are an impressive sight. Thick stones are piled high and form graceful curving walls. Stones are lined up perfectly. Some rows make a zigzag pattern, which was a symbol for their king. Clearly, the people of this city were master builders.

Great Zimbabwe was a trade center. Several thousand farmers lived around the city, where they brought their products and met traders from many places. For example, cowrie shells found in the ruins show that some traders came from the coast. Glass beads from Portugal have been found in the ruins, too. Did Portuguese traders travel to Great Zimbabwe? **Archaeologists** are still exploring this and other questions. An archaeologist is a scientist who studies items that people made long ago in order to learn about how they lived. One thing, however, is clear. The Bantu people had a civilization in this region before the Europeans arrived.

The walls of Great Zimbabwe have no mortar or cement to keep the stones in place. None was needed, because the stones were cut to fit together perfectly.

✓ Check Your Understanding

Write your answers in complete sentences.

1. In which southern African country do most people live in cities?

2. Who still lives in the Kalahari Desert?

3. From what group are most black ethnic groups in southern Africa descended?

4. Why did people travel to Great Zimbabwe in ancient days?

GEOGRAPHER'S TOOL KIT
Reading Vegetation Maps

When you look at a vegetation map, you see different colors. When you look at the key, you will see that every color means a different kind of vegetation. Grassland may be one color. Desert may be another. By looking at a vegetation map, you can get a good sense of the kind of vegetation that grows in a place.

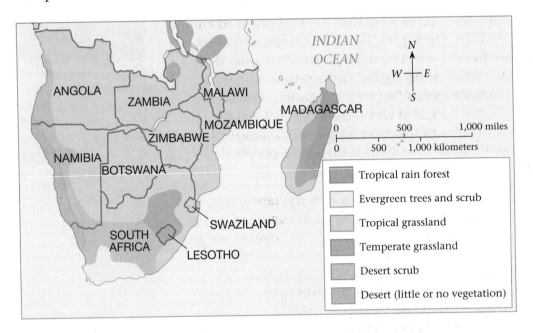

Answer the questions below.

1. Which country has the most desert?

2. What kinds of vegetation can you find in Botswana?

   CHALLENGE Which countries might be best for grazing cattle?

Apply the Skill

Think about what you know about your state. What grows in which places? Draw a vegetation map of your state. Find a published vegetation map. See how close you came to it.

European Colonization in South Africa

Europeans began to colonize South Africa about 350 years ago. At that time, they were setting up colonies all over Africa. Europeans did not think of most of these colonies as their home. They only thought of the colonies as places to make money. Most colonists stayed a few years and then went back to Europe. It was different, however, in the colony of South Africa, where European families thought of themselves as Africans, not Europeans.

Portuguese sailors were the first Europeans to land in South Africa. They gave the tip of the continent its name—the Cape of Good Hope. Dutch people settled the cape area in the 1650s. These people were called Boers, which means "farmers" in Dutch. Over time, their Dutch language was influenced by local African languages. Out of the mixture grew a language called Afrikaans. More than half of the white people in South Africa today speak Afrikaans.

The British came to the Cape in the late 1700s. They tried to end slavery, which the Boers practiced. So, in the 1830s, the Boers moved inland in covered wagons to get away from British rule. They battled the Zulu people who lived inland. The Zulus put up a fierce fight but lost. The British were pushing inland, too. They fought the Boers for control of South Africa. A three-year war between the British and the Boers ended in 1902. The Boers lost. During the war, more than 20,000 Boer women and children died in British prison camps. Bitter feelings about that war still divide white South Africans.

Today, the descendants of the Boers are called Afrikaners. In 1948, their political party won the national election. However, only white people were allowed to vote in that election. The Afrikaners remained in power for over 40 years.

The Afrikaners' National Party set up a system called **apartheid** in South Africa. This system forced white and nonwhite peoples to live separately. Under apartheid, a white person and a black person could not marry, could not go to the same schools, and could not mingle on buses. Black people were not allowed to hold skilled jobs. "Pass" laws prevented them from moving about freely. These laws forced every black person to carry a pass that showed where that person had permission to go. The pass laws made South Africa essentially a prison for the black population. Apartheid was applied not just to black people but to people of mixed race as well as people from India and Asia.

You Decide

Suppose you needed special permission to go anywhere except to school. How would you feel?

South Africa's Homelands

In 1959, the South African government created a separate **homeland** for each ethnic group. Transkei, for example, was a Xhosa homeland. All together, the homelands covered about 13 percent of the country. They were in poor, rural areas, with few resources. Most people who lived in a homeland tried to make their living as farmers or herders. Many could not make a living at all and supported their family by traveling to work in South Africa outside of their homeland.

A law passed in 1970 forced all black people to become citizens of a homeland. At that time, millions of black people lived outside the homeland regions. Many had never been to a homeland and had never intended to live in one. Nonetheless, they had to have a homeland stamped on their pass.

The South African government then declared four of the homelands to be independent countries. The people who lived there were forced to give up their South African citizenship. No other countries, however, recognized them as real countries. The world saw the homelands as part of the apartheid policy.

People around the world began calling for **sanctions** against South Africa because of apartheid. In the 1980s, the United States joined the nations that had imposed sanctions limiting trade with South Africa. Many people also organized their own **boycotts**, refusing to buy goods from companies that did business with South Africa.

Sanctions and boycotts put pressure on South Africa. F. W. de Klerk was elected president of South Africa in 1989. He knew that change was coming to South Africa whether white people wanted it or not. He argued for allowing some change in order to prevent violence in the future.

Under de Klerk, the laws that set up apartheid began to be abolished. The pass laws were withdrawn. Black people and white people could stay in the same hotels, live in the same neighborhoods, and ride the same buses. A new constitution was adopted in 1993 that gave black people the right to vote. The next year, the homelands were eliminated, and the era of apartheid ended.

Black Nationalism and the ANC

In 1912, black leaders in South Africa formed the African National Congress (ANC) for the purpose of supporting black nationalism. Black nationalism is a political movement. It calls on black people to put aside ethnic differences and act as one people.

In 1960, the ANC and the Pan African Congress (PAC) called for a peaceful protest against the pass laws. This event took place in Sharpeville, a part of Johannesburg. Police fired on the protesters, killing about 70 people, and the government declared **martial law.** The police were given almost total power over the citizens. The ANC was outlawed but continued its work in secret, gaining sympathy around the world for its cause. In 1989, South Africa's president met with ANC leaders. The next year, the ban on the group was lifted.

In 1994, South Africa held elections in which black people voted for the first time. The ANC won this election. Nelson Mandela, one of the ANC's most important leaders, became the president of the country. In five years, Mandela and the ANC accomplished much for South Africa. One of the toughest goals was to create a sense of unity among its citizens.

In June of 1999, Thabo Mbeki succeeded Nelson Mandela as South Africa's second black president. Most believe that Mbeki, who worked with Mandela since 1961, will continue with the policies that Mandela began.

Spotlight On

NELSON MANDELA

Nelson Mandela is one of the leaders of the ANC. He was born in 1918 in the Transkei. Neither of his parents had the chance to go school. Mandela, however, wanted to help change his country. He went to the University of South Africa and became a lawyer.

In 1944, he joined the ANC. As a member of this group, he fought legal battles against white rule in South Africa. He was arrested and charged with treason in 1962. Some white leaders claimed he was planning to overthrow the government. Several other ANC members were also charged with crimes.

Mandela was tried and sent to prison, where he remained for 28 years. He was released from prison in 1990 and immediately took his place as one of his country's major political leaders. In 1994, he was elected president of South Africa.

Critical Thinking Why do you think the people of South Africa elected Nelson Mandela to be president?

Nelson Mandela and wife Graca Machel

The Arts in Southern Africa

Music and dance are important in the traditional cultures of southern Africa. They are part of many religious rituals and are used by traditional healers. Southern Africans also enjoy music and dancing simply as arts and entertainment. Wedding celebrations always have music and dancing. Villages hold dance competitions. Professional dance groups perform in the cities, and some dance groups tour other countries.

Southern Africa has exciting popular music. Both rhythm and melody are important in this music. The Western world knows some of the popular music of southern Africa. Groups such as Ladysmith Black Mambazo from South Africa and Bhundu Boys from Zimbabwe tour the world.

The visual arts are also important. In Zimbabwe, for example, Shona artists work in stone. They make graceful, modern sculptures—often of animals. Unlike Benin bronzes and Côte d'Ivoire masks, which are rooted in ancient tradition, Shona sculpture is only 30 years old.

✓ Check Your Understanding

Write your answers in complete sentences.

1. Why do some descendants of the Boers, or Afrikaners, still have bitter feelings toward the British?

2. Describe what the homelands were like.

3. What event led the South African government to declare martial law in 1960?

4. What is one way that southern Africans use music?

Summary

South Africa is one country in southern Africa. Others include Zimbabwe, Angola, and Mozambique. South Africa is wealthy, urban, and industrialized, but other countries in the region are rural and less developed.

Southern Africa has rich mineral resources, good soil, and five rivers.

The San and Khoikhoi were the first people in southern Africa, but their numbers are now few. Most of the black people in southern Africa are descendants of the Bantu, and the white minority is descended mostly from European colonists.

South Africa's policy of apartheid became official in 1948. By the time of Nelson Mandela's election as president in 1994, it had fully ended.

boycott

archaeologist

vegetation

apartheid

sanction

Vocabulary Review

Write a term from the list that matches each definition below.

1. A system of laws developed in South Africa to keep racial groups separate

2. An attempt to change the actions of a company or country by refusing to buy its products

3. A step taken by several nations acting together to punish another nation for breaking international laws

4. A scientist who studies items that people made long ago in order to learn about how they lived

5. The main plant life of an area

Chapter Quiz

Write your answers in complete sentences.

1. Name two deserts in southern Africa.

2. Who were the first people to live in southern Africa?

3. Name a famous leader of the African National Congress.

4. Critical Thinking What was the purpose of the homelands?

5. Critical Thinking Why did South Africa abolish the system known as apartheid?

Write About Geography

Complete the following activities.

1. Trace a map of Africa. Draw the approximate route the Bantu took in their great migration. Explain the route in a short essay.

2. Choose an event that occurs in this chapter. Write a news article that explains what happened.

Group Activity

It is 1990. You are a group of ANC members trying to tell the world about your struggle. Design a campaign to get your message across. The campaign may include writing letters, designing posters, and giving interviews.

Unit 4 Review

Comprehension Check
Write answers to the following questions.

1. What changes did trade bring to the ancient kingdoms of West Africa?

2. Why is the tsetse fly a problem across much of Africa?

3. Why do many African governments encourage nationalism?

4. How did the Bantu people influence Africa?

Building Your Skills
Answer each question in a complete sentence.

1. Why is the time different in different parts of the world?

2. Describe the shape of the Sahel.

3. What can you tell from a language map?

4. What do the different colors mean on a vegetation map?

Where Is It?
Write the name of the place based on the information below.

1. A country founded by former enslaved peoples

2. It was once called Zaire

3. A huge crack in the Earth's surface where anthropologists find fossils to study

4. The southern African country with the most urban population

Writing an Essay
Answer one of the following essay topics.

1. Explain why there is often tension among the ethnic groups of Nigeria.

2. Discuss the causes of desertification near the Sahel.

3. Describe how Kenya became independent.

4. Describe the system of apartheid in South Africa.

Geography and You

Africa consists of many countries. Nationalism is sometimes a challenge because of this. How do Americans show nationalism? Would these ways work in Africa? Explain.

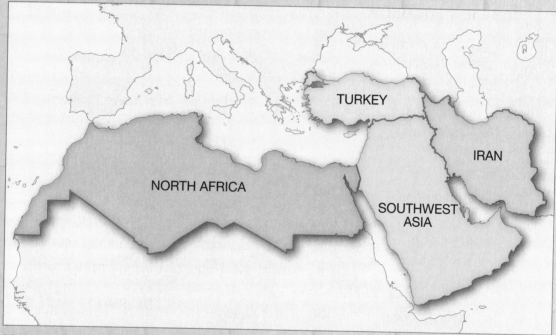

Little rain falls in this part of the world. How might that affect the way people live?

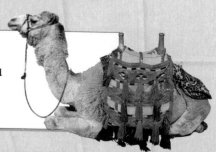

TRAVEL LOG

Describe the various people in this region as you learn about them. Explain how they are similar and how they are different.

Camel found in the Middle East

Women dress in traditional clothing on the streets of Morocco. How is this clothing suitable for life in this dry, desert land?

Words to Know

monarchy	a government run by a single ruler, usually a king or queen, who inherits the position
republic	a government in which laws are made by a small group of citizens elected by the people
erg	a huge sand dune that shifts over time
oasis	an area in a desert where water springs are found
pharaoh	the ruler of ancient Egypt
hieroglyphic	related to a system of writing in which pictures called hieroglyphs stand for ideas
arable	suitable for use as farmland

Places to Know

Morocco

Algeria

Tunisia

Libya

Egypt

Sahara

Learning Objectives

- Identify the Maghreb and describe its history.
- Describe the importance of the Sahara in North Africa.
- Identify some contributions and achievements of the ancient Egyptians.
- Describe the importance of the Nile River in world history and in Egyptian culture.
- Explain the importance of the Suez Canal for Egypt and for world trade.

The Countries of North Africa

There are five countries in North Africa: Morocco, Algeria, Tunisia, Libya, and Egypt. Two thousand years ago, the region that makes up Morocco, Algeria, Tunisia, and Libya was a Roman province called Africa. After A.D. 700, all of North Africa became one huge empire. The land from Morocco through Libya was called the Maghreb, which means "the west" in Arabic. Several later empires that were centered in Morocco also controlled most of the Maghreb and parts of Spain.

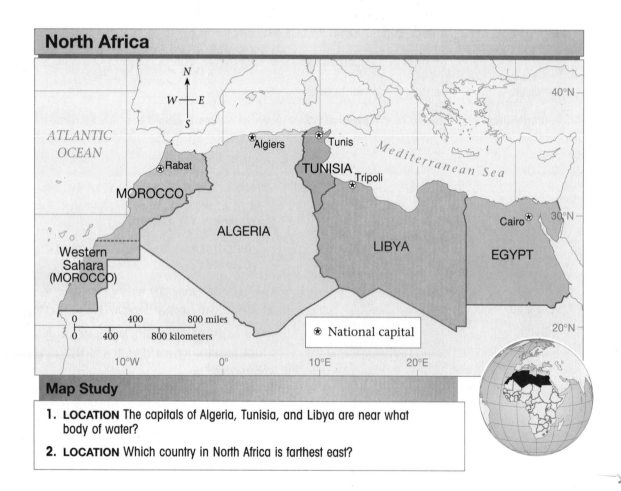

North Africa

Map Study

1. **LOCATION** The capitals of Algeria, Tunisia, and Libya are near what body of water?

2. **LOCATION** Which country in North Africa is farthest east?

In the 1800s and 1900s, European countries colonized North Africa. France controlled what is now Morocco, Algeria, and Tunisia. Italy took control of what is now Libya. The people of North Africa struggled against the Europeans. From those struggles grew four modern countries. Libya became an independent country in 1951. Morocco and Tunisia became independent in 1956. Algeria fought an eight-year war against France and finally won its independence in 1961.

History sets Egypt apart from the other countries of North Africa. In ancient times, it was a powerful empire. Later, it was conquered by the Roman empire, then by Arab peoples and then by the Turkish empire. Egypt became a separate country in the early 1800s. However, the British government controlled it. Not until 1936 did Egypt become truly independent.

Today, Morocco is a **monarchy** and is ruled by a king. Algeria, Tunisia, and Egypt are **republics**, with elected presidents. Libya is ruled by a military junta, which is headed by a dictator.

The People of North Africa

The original people of the Maghreb were the Berbers. After A.D. 700, however, Arab peoples traveled west from the Middle East to North Africa. As traders, missionaries, and conquerors, they brought the religion of Islam and mixed with the local people. Ever since, Arabic has been the main language of North Africa. Islam has also been the main religion. Today, the population of North Africa, from Morocco through Libya, is a mixture of the Berber and Arab peoples.

Remember
Islam is a religion that began in Arabia in the seventh century.

Most of the Egyptian people, by contrast, are descended from the Hamitic people. The Hamitic people settled along the Nile River thousands of years ago. Egyptians speak Arabic and practice Islam.

Even today, some Berber people are nomadic herders, who live in tents and move from place to place. Traditionally, the women of this nomadic group make cloth from goat hair and sew tents out of this cloth. The men elect the tribal leader, who decides when and where the group will migrate.

The Berbers keep goats, sheep, cattle, or camels. These nomadic people live mainly off the milk and dairy products from their animals. They also collect dates from wild palm trees.

Camels are especially important to the nomadic lifestyle because camels are well adapted to desert life. They can live for weeks without water and shut their noses to keep out sand during a windstorm. They can also walk across soft sand because their feet are padded.

Nomadic herders and their camels are well adapted to life in the desert.

About half of the people of North Africa live in cities. Most of the others are settled farmers. Most farmers grow cereals, such as wheat and barley, and fruits, such as grapes and oranges.

You Decide

Why do you think half of the population of North Africa lives in cities?

The Sahara

North Africa has the world's largest desert—the Sahara. It covers more than three million square miles. The Sahara is almost as large as the United States. It stretches through every country in North Africa, covering 80 percent of Algeria and Libya. In Libya, large parts of the desert are covered with loose sand. Wind blows the sand into hills called dunes. Huge dunes that shift over time are called **ergs**.

Most of the Sahara is hard and rocky. A few parts are even mountainous and catch some rainfall. Other parts of the desert are dotted with **oases**. These are places where water comes up from deep springs. An oasis may have a patch of grass and a few palm trees. The nomadic herders move from oasis to oasis out of necessity. Still, large parts of the desert in Algeria and Libya are completely uninhabited.

In Morocco, the Atlas Mountains stretch between the coast and the northern edge of the Sahara. They block rain-bearing winds from reaching farther south. These peaks rise as high as 13,600 feet. Small rivers flow out of the mountains. Some of the rivers flow north to the Mediterranean Sea. Farmers use the water from these rivers to irrigate their fields. Some of the rivers flow south, where they vanish in the desert.

✓ Check Your Understanding

Write your answers in complete sentences.

1. What was the Maghreb?

2. What is the main religion of North Africa?

3. Why are oases important to herders?

GEOGRAPHER'S TOOL KIT
Reading Economic Maps

An economic map gives you information about the wealth of a region. Such a map shows where and what resources are taken from the Earth. It will also show where and how people make their living.

Economic Map of North Africa

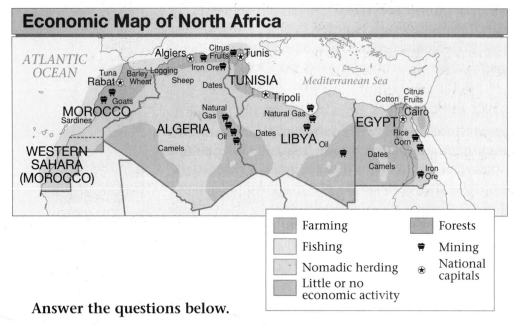

Legend:
- Farming
- Fishing
- Nomadic herding
- Little or no economic activity
- Forests
- Mining
- National capitals

Answer the questions below.

1. Which economic activity in Algeria has the most land area devoted to it?

2. Which countries have mining?

   CHALLENGE Why do people farm where they do in Egypt?

The Nile River: Past and Present

The main geographic feature in Egypt is the Nile River. It is the longest river in the world. It starts at Lake Victoria in East Africa and flows more than 4,000 miles to the Mediterranean Sea.

One of the world's first civilizations bloomed along the Nile River around 3100 B.C. People settled along the Nile because it was easy to farm there. Once a year, the Nile flooded its banks, spreading rich, new soil and providing water for irrigation.

In ancient Egypt, priests were powerful. The head priest developed into a **pharaoh**, or king. The ancient Egyptian people thought of their pharaohs as gods. Pharaohs ruled Egypt for about 3,000 years.

The ancient Egyptians built huge pyramids as tombs for their pharaohs. They built large temples, too. Many of these buildings still stand. The Egyptians also invented **hieroglyphic** writing. Their writings tell us much about their laws, religion, and daily life.

Geography Fact

The Great Pyramids at Giza are only a few miles from the skyscrapers of Cairo.

The Egyptians developed a 365-day calendar. They based it on the Nile floods, which came every year at about the same time. The Egyptian calendar had 12 months—each 30 days long. At the end of the year came five extra days that were set aside as feast days for the gods. These extra days completed the 365-day year. The modern Western calendar is based on this ancient Egyptian calendar.

In some ways, life along the Nile has not changed. The river still provides water for farmers. Boats still use the river as a highway. Egyptians still build houses out of clay from the riverbed. Farmers even use certain tools based on those used in ancient times.

In Egypt, many farmers still water their crops by hand using the shaduf. This form of irrigation has been in use for more than 3,000 years.

One such tool is the shaduf, which consists, in part, of a wooden beam set up next to the river. From one end of the beam hangs a bucket, from the other end a weight. The farmer dips the bucket in the water. The weight makes the bucket easy to lift. The farmer then empties the bucket into an irrigation ditch.

Thanks to the shaduf, the farmer does not have to haul water by hand. Still, irrigating a field this way is hard work. Farmers who can afford to buy water pumps gladly do so.

In some ways, however, life in the Nile River Valley has changed. Many big changes came after the Aswan High Dam was built about 500 miles upriver from its delta in 1971. The dam provides electricity and regulates the flow of the Nile.

Before 1971, farmers planted only once a year, right after the yearly flood. The floods no longer occur because the dam controls the Nile waters and allows the farmers to irrigate their fields year round. In addition, because the climate is warm all year, farmers can plant two or three times a year.

However, the dam has negative effects, too. Every year, floods used to bring new, rich soil, which was like a natural fertilizer. Now, farmers must buy fertilizer, which costs money and takes extra work to mix into the soil.

The floods also brought fast-moving water, which flushed the river clean. Now, the water in the Nile moves slowly, allowing a certain type of snail to live and grow in the irrigation channels. Snails of this type carry a parasite that causes a disease called bilharziasis, also called schistosomiasis.

The disease can be treated, but the treatment costs money. Most Egyptian farmers are poor and cannot afford this treatment. Bilharziasis is now a major health problem in Egypt.

Modern Egypt

Cairo is Egypt's capital. About ten percent of Egyptian people live in or near Cairo, the largest city in Africa. Cairo is growing very quickly. In this city, horses share the streets with cars. Some neighborhoods have tall apartment buildings, and some have mud huts. Many people in Cairo cannot find housing at all. Several hundred thousand people, in fact, live in an old cemetery, which the Egyptians call the City of the Dead.

The government owns and runs about 80 percent of the industry in Egypt. Yet, up to one out of every four workers in Cairo has no job.

In the Egyptian city of Cairo, carts and horses share the road with new cars.

Many more are underemployed. That is, they are trained for a job other than the one they have. For example, many taxi cab drivers in Cairo have university degrees. Meanwhile, prices of goods and services are rising 25 to 30 percent a year.

Egypt has the most productive farms in North Africa. Less than 5 percent of the land in Egypt is **arable**, however. The most important crop is cotton, which people cannot eat. Egypt has about 67 million people to feed. About a million more are added every seven months. This means that the country must import food. Yet Egypt needs money to pay for its imported food.

Egypt earns this money from three sources. One of the sources is exports. Egypt sells oil, cotton, and cotton products to other countries. Another source of money is tourism. Thousands of people visit Egypt each year to see the remains of the ancient civilization. A third important source of money is the Suez Canal.

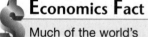

Economics Fact

Much of the world's oil travels through the Suez Canal on tankers.

The Suez Canal was opened in 1869 to connect the Red Sea and Mediterranean Sea. Before the canal was built, ships had to travel around Africa to get from Europe to East Asia. The Suez Canal reduced this journey by more than 4,000 miles. A French company built the canal. At first, France and Britain jointly owned it. Egypt took control of the canal in 1956. Now, ships must pay Egypt for the right to use the canal.

✓ Check Your Understanding

Write your answers in complete sentences.

1. Why did the ancient Egyptian people build pyramids?

2. How is life along the Nile the same today as it was in ancient times?

3. Name one way that Egypt earns money to import food.

GEOGRAPHY IN YOUR LIFE
Analyzing Photographs

When you read a photograph, you look for clues that tell you about the picture. You can read the caption. If there are people in the photograph, you can look at their clothing and what they are doing. You can look at the background. Is the land hilly? Can you see buildings? Remember that the photograph can only show a small part of the scene. When you look, think about what may not be shown.

A bus rides by a sphinx in Cairo, Egypt.

Use the photograph to answer the questions.

1. What things are ancient?

2. What things are modern?

CHALLENGE What does this photograph say about the history and culture of Cairo?

Apply the Skill

Look in the newspaper. Find a photograph that tells a story. Paste the photograph to a sheet of paper. Write what you can learn from the photograph.

Chapter

15 Review

Summary

Morocco, Algeria, Tunisia, Libya, and Egypt are the five countries of North Africa.
Three main physical features of North Africa are the Sahara, the Atlas Mountains, and the Nile River.
Arab and Berber peoples mixed and formed the main culture across Libya and the Maghreb. Arabic and Berber are the main languages of North Africa, and Islam is the main religion.
One of the world's oldest civilizations was centered in Egypt.
The Nile River is Egypt's most important agricultural resource.
The Aswan High Dam has helped farmers produce more food, but it has had some negative effects, too.
Cairo is the largest city in Africa.

arable
oasis
erg
hieroglyphic
pharoah

Vocabulary Review

Complete each sentence with a term from the list.

1. The name for an ancient Egyptian ruler is _____ .

2. If land is suitable for use as farmland, it is _____ .

3. A huge sand dune that shifts over time is a(n) _____ .

4. An area in a desert where water springs are found is a(n) _____ .

5. Writing in which pictures stand for ideas is _____ writing.

Chapter Quiz

Write your answers in complete sentences.

1. What are the five countries of North Africa?

2. Why did ancient Egyptians settle along the Nile River?

3. What tool do some Egyptian farmers use to help irrigate their crops?

4. **Critical Thinking** In what way does the Suez Canal help Egypt's economy?

5. **Critical Thinking** What changes has the Aswan High Dam brought to the Nile River Valley?

Write About Geography

Complete the following activities.

1. Create your own system of hieroglyphic writing. Write a note to a friend using it. Include the code.

2. What would life as an African nomad be like? Write a diary entry for a day spent in the Sahara.

Group Activity

Create a picture book for children about North Africa. Use pictures in this book and others for ideas. Show both past and present North Africa. Make sure you include enough information so that children will understand the region.

Both the mosque and the rugs in this photograph are typical of this region. What similarities do they share?

The Middle East: Southwest Asia

Chapter 16

Words to Know

pilgrimage	a trip to a place that has special religious importance
fertile	capable of producing a great deal
socialism	a political system in which the government controls farms and businesses
monotheism	the belief that there is only one god
Holocaust	the mass murder of Jewish and other people by Nazi forces
civilian	a person who is not a soldier
terrorism	violence directed against civilians in order to put pressure on governments
intifada	an organized rebellion by the people of Palestine against Israel

Places to Know

Arabian Peninsula

Fertile Crescent

Iraq

Syria

Saudi Arabia

Israel

Learning Objectives

- Explain why oil and water are valuable resources in this region.
- Tell how Islam affects daily life in the Middle East.
- Describe the ancient civilizations of the Fertile Crescent.
- Describe how the country of Israel came into being.
- Explain why the people of Israel and their Arabic neighbors do not get along.

Oil and Water

The Middle East is a region defined by history and politics. It stretches from Africa across the Arabian Peninsula into Asia.

The Middle East has a dry climate. Most of the Arabian Peninsula, in fact, is covered by desert. In the Middle East, fresh water is a precious resource because it is scarce. The area has plenty of oil, however.

The Middle East

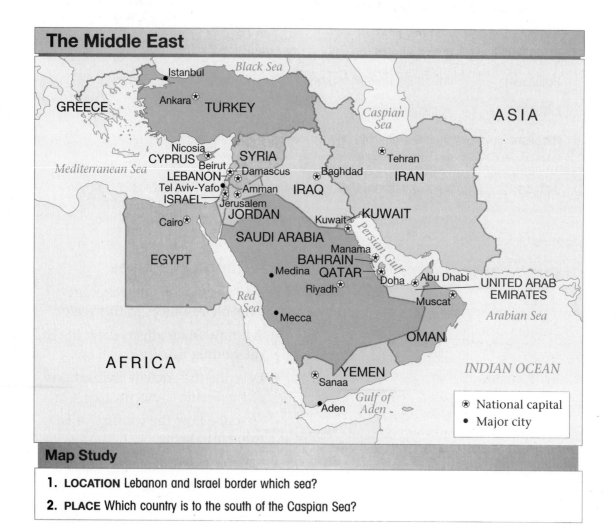

Map Study

1. **LOCATION** Lebanon and Israel border which sea?

2. **PLACE** Which country is to the south of the Caspian Sea?

About 65 percent of the world's oil is found in North Africa and the Middle East. Drilling for this oil began in the 1930s. Since then, oil has brought great wealth to some countries in the region.

Oil has also brought economic power to the region as a whole. In 1960, five countries came together to form OPEC, or the Organization of Petroleum Exporting Countries. Membership grew to 13 countries. Eight of these countries are in North Africa and the Middle East. Ecuador withdrew its membership from OPEC in 1992. Gabon joined, but it also withdrew in 1995.

Decisions made by the OPEC countries can affect the price of oil. For example, they can decide how much oil to produce. When they produce less, the price of oil goes up.

Oil has helped with the water shortage in the Middle East. Some countries, such as Saudi Arabia, have used their oil wealth to build desalination plants, which remove salt from water. Desalination plants turn seawater into fresh drinking water.

$ Economics Fact

The current member countries of OPEC are Algeria, Libya, Nigeria, Qatar, Indonesia, Saudi Arabia, Iran, Iraq, Venezuela, Kuwait, and the United Arab Emirates.

Islam

To many people, the most important feature of the Middle East is not oil but religion. Islam began on the Arabian Peninsula, and it is still centered there.

Islam began around A.D. 600. According to the Islamic faith, God sent the angel Gabriel to a man named Muhammad, an ordinary camel driver who lived in the city of Mecca. Muhammad was told that he was God's chosen prophet, or messenger. From that day forth, Muhammad preached the word of God as he received it. These messages were written in the Koran, the sacred book of Islam.

In Mecca, Muhammad preached that only one God exists. Mecca, however, was full of idols, or images that people worshiped. The people of Mecca made money from the visitors who came to worship these idols. So Muhammad's message was bad for business, and the people of Mecca plotted to kill him.

In A.D. 622, Muhammad moved from Mecca to the town of Medina. This move by Muhammad is called the hijra and marks the first year of the Islamic calendar. In Medina, Muhammad found many followers, who are called Muslims, and Medina became the first Islamic community. Eight years later, Muhammad conquered Mecca, destroying idols and declaring Mecca holy. To this day, only Muslims are allowed into Mecca.

The basic beliefs of Islam are that there is only one God and that Muhammad is his messenger. In Arabic, God is called Allah. The word *Islam* means surrender. The word *Muslim* means one who surrenders to God. All Muslims are considered equal and part of the large community of believers.

Islam is based on five duties called the Five Pillars of Islam. The first duty is to state the faith. The second is to say prayers. Praying involves speaking certain verses from the Koran while facing certain directions at certain times. The third duty is to give alms, or money, to the poor. Alms must equal 2.5 percent of a person's wealth. The fourth duty is to fast, or go without food and drink. Fasting takes place during Ramadan, the ninth month of the Islamic calendar. During Ramadan, Muslims must not eat or drink anything from dawn to dusk. The last duty is to make a **pilgrimage**, or a trip to a place that has special religious importance. In Islam, that place is Mecca. Every Muslim must try to make the pilgrimage at least once.

After Islam began in A.D. 622, it spread quickly. Within 40 years, the Muslim world was an Arab empire. By 750, this empire stretched from Spain to Afghanistan.

The sacred book of Islam, called the Koran, is written in Arabic. The page in this photo is from a thirteenth-century Koran.

Life in a Muslim Society

Islam deals with all aspects of life. For example, the teachings of Islam forbid pork and alcohol. Islam has rules about women's clothing, stating that faces and hands must be covered and clothing must not show off the shape of the body. Islam also has rules about marriage, stating clearly who can marry whom. It has rules about inheritance, declaring exactly how wealth should be divided after someone has died. Islam forbids gambling and does not allow interest to be charged on loans. It says what crimes must be punished and how. These rules come from the Koran, as well as from hadith—the sayings and customs of Muhammad. Islamic laws, taken as a whole, are called the sharia.

Muslims must wash before their daily prayers. They can say prayers anywhere as long as they are facing Mecca. On Fridays, observant Muslims go to the mosque for the noon prayer. There is no priest in the mosque. One person leads, but all the people say the same prayers.

Muslims can say prayers anywhere as long as they are facing Mecca.

Women and men pray separately. In fact, most activities for women and men are separate in Islamic society. In general, men and women who are not close relatives must not socialize—and in strict Islamic societies, they must not even see each other. Homes in countries in which Islam is followed often have a private area for women into which male outsiders cannot set foot.

Muslim men are allowed to have more than one wife at a time, as long as the women are treated equally. A Muslim woman can only be married to one man. Women typically marry at a young age—15 or younger. Marriages are arranged often by families.

The Koran sets values for Islamic society. Children must respect their parents. Kindness, generosity, honesty, and tolerance are valued. In theory, all Muslims are supposed to be equal.

The Desert Kingdoms

A desert of fine, golden sand covers most of the Arabian Peninsula. Saudi Arabia is, by far, the biggest country on the peninsula. Kuwait is in the northeast. Bahrain, Qatar, and the United Arab Emirates stretch along the eastern coast. Yemen and Oman border the Indian Ocean at the southern end of the peninsula.

The original people of this peninsula were the Bedouins, who were Arabic-speaking nomadic herders and raiders. Fewer than 300,000 Arab people are nomadic Bedouins today. On the peninsula, many of the Arab people take pride in their Bedouin heritage. Many of their values come out of Bedouin culture—for example, loyalty, courage, and generosity. Among the Bedouins, hospitality—that is, treating guests well—is considered a duty.

Remember
A clan is a group of families that trace their history to the same ancestor.

The Bedouins were organized into clans. The leader of a clan was called the sheikh and was chosen for his strength and wisdom. His son might or might not become sheikh. Today, the heads of powerful Arabic clans are still called sheikhs. The most powerful sheikh is the ruler of the country. In some countries, including Saudi Arabia, the ruler is called a king. In other countries, the ruler is called an emir.

Saudi Arabia is the richest Arabic country because it produces the most oil. It brings in workers from Yemen, Jordan, Pakistan, the Philippines, and other, poorer countries. By working in Saudi Arabia, these laborers are able to support their families back home. Oil-rich countries like Saudi Arabia also give loans to other Arabic countries.

With oil money, the kingdoms have built large, modern cities. Arab men in long white robes are a common sight in these cities. They wear a keffiyah, or a head cloth, which is held in place with a rope band. The keffiyah protects against sun and wind.

Ancient Middle East

North of the Arabian Peninsula are two big rivers that flow southeast into the Persian Gulf. These rivers are the Tigris and the Euphrates, which bring water to the dry region around them. Like the Nile, they also bring rich, new soil every year. The land between the rivers is, therefore, very **fertile**. This is why this area has long been called the Fertile Crescent.

Historians say civilization began in the Fertile Crescent in the ancient land of Mesopotamia. The cities of Sumer rose near the mouths of the Tigris and Euphrates rivers around 3500 B.C.

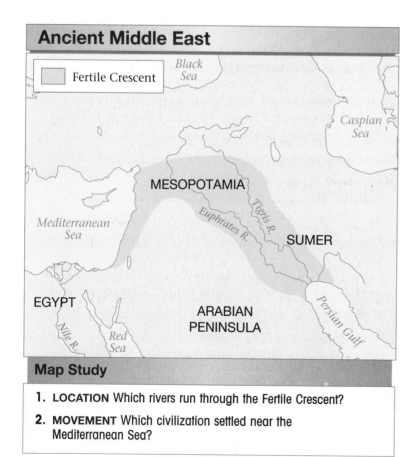

Ancient Middle East

Fertile Crescent

Black Sea
Caspian Sea
MESOPOTAMIA
Mediterranean Sea
Euphrates R.
Tigris R.
SUMER
EGYPT
ARABIAN PENINSULA
Persian Gulf
Nile R.
Red Sea

Map Study

1. **LOCATION** Which rivers run through the Fertile Crescent?

2. **MOVEMENT** Which civilization settled near the Mediterranean Sea?

Sumerians invented the wheel, the plow, and the sail. They developed geometry and arithmetic. They had a written language called cuneiform. Sumerian buildings were made of clay, so most of them have crumbled. However, elements of Sumerian building styles—such as domes and arches—can still be seen in the area.

At the north end of the Fertile Crescent lived the Phoenicians, who sailed the Mediterranean and founded many coastal cities. In their travels and conquests, the Phoenicians spread cultural achievements from the Middle East. The most important cultural achievement was their alphabet, which had 22 symbols that stood for sounds. Right now, you are looking at letters that grew out of the Phoenician alphabet.

Shortly after Islam began, the center of the Arabic empire moved to the Fertile Crescent. The first great Arabic capital was Damascus, which today is the capital of the country called Syria.

In A.D. 750, a new family took control of the Arabic empire. They built a new city called Bahgdad. Today, this city is capital of the country of Iraq.

Iraq and Syria

In the early 2000s, Iraq and Syria were both ruled by a political party called the Ba'ath, whose names means "rebirth." The Ba'ath Party is not based on religion but on two other ideas. One is Arabic nationalism, or the idea that there should be one united Arabic country. The other is **socialism**, or a political system in which the government controls farms and businesses.

The Ba'ath Party took power by force in both Syria and Iraq. Islam is important to the people of Iraq and Syria, although the governments do not strongly emphasize religion.

In 1980, Iraq was the most powerful nation in the Arabic world. Then, it waged an eight-year war against Iran. More than one million people died, and both countries were weakened.

When that war was over, Iraq invaded its neighbor Kuwait. This invasion led to the Gulf War of 1991, in which Western and Arabic countries forced Iraq out of Kuwait. In just a few weeks, Western military forces destroyed most of Iraq's industries. The war left many Iraqi people without food or clean drinking water, and diseases spread.

This war did special damage to the environment as well. More than ten million gallons of oil poured into the Persian Gulf. Some say people in Iraq opened up oil pumps off the coast and let oil flow into the Gulf on purpose. Some people say that the bombs dropped during the war broke oil pumps and caused the spills. In any case, fish, birds, and other wildlife died in great numbers. At the end of the war, Iraqi soldiers set fire to hundreds of oil wells, and the fires burned for months. Greasy smoke filled the air, and weather was affected as far away as Europe.

You Decide

Why might smoke in the air affect the weather?

Still, for many years after the war, the Ba'ath Party remained in control. Today, only Syria is ruled by the Ba'ath Party.

Water might be a source of possible future conflict in this region. The Euphrates River, for example, flows through Turkey, Syria, and Iraq. All three countries need the water from this river. When one country takes water from the river, less is left for the countries downstream. On the Euphrates, Turkey recently built a dam that prevents the normal flow of water to Syria and Iraq. Disagreements over water are now simmering in the Fertile Crescent.

Saudi Arabia

Saudi Arabia is a land of heat, dryness, and sand. It is the largest country in the Middle East, but more than half of the country is desert. The Rub'al Khali, called the Great Sandy Desert, occupies much of the southeast part of the country.

Saudi Arabia is a traditional, Islamic country. It is a kingdom ruled by members of the royal Saud family. The Sauds are part of an ancient dynasty. They have governed in the area, on and off, since the fifteenth century. The king rules with the advice of a council whose members he appoints. Law is based on the sharia, the law of Islam.

Before oil was discovered in 1938, Saudi Arabia was largely home to herders and nomads. It was a nation limited by its lack of water. Today, the country is estimated to have one-fourth of all the oil reserves in the world. Since 1938, the country has transformed itself using oil money. Saudi Arabia has invested in roads, airports, industry, and plants to desalinate water.

Oil has allowed Saudi Arabia to provide generous benefits for its citizens. Schooling is free, although no child is required to go. The government also pays for medicine and medical care. As the world's need for oil continues, the country of Saudi Arabia will continue to prosper.

✓ Check Your Understanding

Write your answers in complete sentences.

1. How does oil help to solve water problems in the area?

2. What are the basic beliefs of Islam?

3. What is the Fertile Crescent?

Israel

Modern Israel was founded in 1948. It is the only non-Islamic country in the Middle East. About 95 percent of the people in Israel are of Jewish heritage. Most of the rest of the people are of Arabic descent. The main language of Israel is Hebrew, although many Jewish people also speak Yiddish and English.

The religion practiced by Jewish people is called Judaism, which began at least 5,000 years ago, when Jewish people were called Hebrews. Judaism was the first religion based on **monotheism**. That is, the Hebrews believe that there is only one god. Islam and Christianity also are monotheistic religions.

Celebrations

PASSOVER

Many Jewish holidays celebrate events in history. Passover is one such holiday. It is in memory of the Exodus, the Hebrews' escape from ancient Egypt. Thus, Passover celebrates the idea of freedom.

Jewish people gather to celebrate the holiday of Passover with a Seder in Israel.

On the first night (and sometimes the second) of Passover, Jewish people serve a ritual meal called a Seder. At the beginning of the Seder, the story of Passover is told. Several foods are eaten that stand for parts of the story. For example, there is matzoh— a flat bread made without yeast. Matzoh is a reminder that the Hebrews left Egypt before their bread could rise.

The Seder includes many songs and prayers. The overall spirit of the feast is joyful rather than solemn. Some Jewish people celebrate seven days of Passover, and some celebrate eight.

Critical Thinking Why do you think the overall spirit of Passover is joyful rather than solemn?

The sacred writings of Judaism are called the Torah. Social justice has always been an important value in Judaism. The Jewish people believe that god is just and that people who want to serve god must therefore try to make a just society on the Earth.

Geography Fact

Jerusalem, now the capital of Israel, is a holy city for Jewish, Christian, and Muslim peoples alike.

The Hebrews settled in a land called Palestine. Later, they migrated to Egypt, where they were enslaved. Moses, their greatest prophet, led the Hebrews out of their slavery. The journey out of Egypt and slavery was called the Exodus. It is a key event in Jewish history. During the Exodus, god gave Moses the Ten Commandments, which are basic to Judaism, as well as to Christianity and Islam.

The town of Bethlehem is honored in Judaism as the birthplace of David, the King of Israel. In Christianity, the town is honored as the birthplace of Jesus.

When the Hebrews returned to Palestine, they formed the kingdom of Israel. This kingdom existed off and on from 1025 B.C. until A.D. 70, when the Romans ended it. The Jews were then scattered throughout the world.

Modern Israel is an industrialized, urban country. It is also a democracy. The Israeli people are generally prosperous and well educated. In Israel, both men and women are required to serve in the armed forces when they turn 18.

Although most Israelis live in cities, agriculture is important to the country. Israel has had some success overcoming desertification. The Israelis have planted trees and have used advanced irrigation systems to create new farmland. Israelis grow and export many crops, such as tomatoes, grapefruit, potatoes, wheat, and cotton.

The Arab-Israeli Conflict

Israel has been in conflict with its Arabic neighbors since it was founded in 1948. The conflict is rooted in history. Over the centuries, the Jewish people have been a persecuted minority in many lands. In the 1800s, some Jewish people sensed a growing danger to themselves in Europe. They decided that they could never be safe until they had their own homeland, or Zion. They were called Zionists. Zionism encouraged Jewish immigration to Palestine, where ancient Israel had been.

Palestine, however, was occupied mainly by Arabic people. Arabic nationalism was on the rise. Arabs throughout the Middle East were fighting their Turkish rulers and were trying to push Europeans out of their lands. Various Arab groups wanted their own independent countries. In 1917, Britain declared that it would support a Jewish country in Palestine. The idea of Britain deciding what should happen in Palestine angered the Arab populace. Conflict began to grow between the Arabs and the Jewish immigrants.

During World War II, the Zionists' worst fears came true. Nazi Germany killed about six million Jewish and other peoples in Europe. This event has become known as the **Holocaust**. The war created thousands of desperate Jewish refugees. Many Jewish people headed for Palestine when Western countries would no longer give them refuge.

You Decide

Israel is a small country surrounded by enemies. Why do you think it would be concerned about where its borders are drawn?

Both Jewish and Arabic peoples claimed Palestine. The United Nations decided to divide Palestine. One part would be Jewish Israel. The other would be Arabic Palestine. The Jewish people agreed to this plan. Modern Israel was established, and the people became known as Israelis. The Arabs did not agree with the partition and attacked the Israelis. The Israelis, however, won the first war.

Israel claimed some of Arab Palestine. Some of it ended up as part of Jordan. Many Arabs who had lived in Palestine became refugees. These people are now known as the Palestinians.

Wars between the Israelis and different Arabic countries broke out again in 1956, 1967, and 1973. Israel captured more land in the second war and lost some in the third. Meanwhile, Palestinians waged another kind of war. Small groups of Palestinians attacked Jewish **civilians**. Palestinians and their allies called this guerrilla warfare. The Israelis and their allies, however, called it **terrorism**. A leader in this war against Israel was the Palestine Liberation Organization, or PLO.

In 1978, Israel and Egypt signed the Camp David agreement. Under this agreement, Israel gave some land back to Egypt in exchange for peace. Although the agreement has angered other Arabic countries, Egypt and Israel have remained at peace.

The Israelis still control much of the rest of the land that they captured during the wars with the Arabs. Violence is common between Jewish settlers who moved to these areas and the Palestinians who already live there.

In the late 1980s, Palestinian opposition to Israel became an organized rebellion called the **intifada**. Arab and Israeli leaders have held peace talks. Palestinians were represented at these talks. In the 1990s, Israel agreed to turn over to the Palestinians the territory it captured from Jordan in 1967, the West Bank, and the territory it captured from Egypt in 1967, the Gaza Strip. The process is sure to be a slow one, but hope remains that Israelis and Palestinians can remain at peace.

The Arts in the Middle East

Arabic art is rooted in Bedouin culture and has been shaped by Islam. From long ago, the Bedouins have prided themselves on their poetry, which has a musical quality. The Koran uses the musical language of Arabic poetry and is rich with images. Reading aloud from the Koran is considered an art and is done in a special musical voice not used for any other book.

Arabs view handwriting as a fine art, too. Quotations from the Koran are often written in an elegant style called calligraphy. Calligraphy also decorates buildings and vases.

Israeli art is a product of Jewish tradition from around the world. Immigrants brought their dance, art, and music to Israel and shaped the arts there. Israel is also well known for its classical and progressive instrumental music.

✓ **Check Your Understanding**

Write your answers in complete sentences.

1. What central idea do Islam and Judaism have in common?

2. What was the PLO founded to do?

3. How does Bedouin tradition influence Arabic art?

Summary

The Middle East is a region that runs from Egypt through the Arabian Peninsula to Turkey and Iran.
Fresh water is scarce in the Middle East, but oil is plentiful.
Islam is the main religion of every Middle Eastern country, except Israel.
The ancient Sumerian and Phoenician civilizations were in the Fertile Crescent, and Syria and Iraq are two modern countries in this area.
Modern Israel was founded in 1948 as a Jewish state.
Jewish and Arabic peoples came into conflict because both wanted to make Palestine their home.

Vocabulary Review

Write *true* or *false*. If the statement is false, change the underlined term to make it true.

1. Land is <u>fertile</u> if it is capable of producing a great deal.

2. <u>Zionism</u> is the belief that there is only one god.

3. A person who is not a soldier is a <u>civilian</u>.

4. A political system in which the government controls farms and businesses is called <u>terrorism</u>.

5. An organized rebellion by Palestinians against Israel is the <u>Holocaust</u>.

Chapter Quiz

Write your answers in complete sentences.

1. What was Muhammad's journey from Mecca to Medina called?

2. Judaism was the first religion based on what idea?

3. The Ba'ath Party controlled which Middle Eastern countries?

4. **Critical Thinking** Why is oil so important to Middle Eastern countries?

5. **Critical Thinking** What are three ways in which Islam has affected the culture of the Middle East?

Write About Geography

Complete the following activities.

1. Find pictures of the Arabic architecture in this book. Design a house in that style.

2. Write a summary of the history of Israel.

Group Activity

Your country has just discovered enormous oil reserves. You have enough money to rebuild society. Each person in the group can take an area of society, such as education, and decide how to improve it.

Istanbul is the largest city in Turkey. It is located along the straits that join the Black Sea with the Aegean Sea. What can you tell about Turkey from this photograph?

Chapter 17

The Middle East: Turkey and Iran

Words to Know

secular	not having to do with religion
dynasty	a series of rulers who belong to the same family
fundamentalist	a person who believes that the basic beliefs of a religion should be followed exactly
theocracy	a country whose government is run by religious leaders
epic	a long poem or story
minaret	a tower of a mosque

Places to Know

Turkey

Anatolia

Kurdistan

Republic of Armenia

Istanbul

Iran

Learning Objectives

- Explain how modern Turkey developed out of the Ottoman Empire.
- Identify the relationship between modern Iran and ancient Persia.
- Compare the religion and politics of Iran and Turkey.
- Describe how Shiism is different from Sunnite Islam.
- Name some admired Persian poets.
- Identify some typical features of Islamic art and architecture.

Turkey and the Turkish People

Turkey lies between Europe and Asia. A small part of it is in Europe, and the rest is in Asia. The Asian part of Turkey is called Anatolia.

About one-third of the population of Turkey lives in rural communities. Turkey's big cities are growing quickly. Turkish is the main language in the country. A minority group who are called the Kurds, however, speaks its own language and forms about 20 percent of Turkey's population. The Kurds live in southeastern Turkey and across the border in Iraq, Iran, and Syria. The Kurds call the whole area where they live Kurdistan. Many of them would like this area to be an independent country.

The Armenian people are another minority group in Turkey. They are Christians who have been persecuted by the Turkish, Kurdish, and other Islamic groups surrounding them. During World War I, the Turkish government killed almost a million Armenians. Many of the survivors fled. Most Armenians now live in the Republic of Armenia, north of Turkey.

The Turkish people did not start out in Turkey. Their original home was in the plains north of Afghanistan. Sometime in the eleventh century, waves of Turkish people began moving out of Central Asia. They conquered and ruled many places over the centuries. Turkish empires arose in Iran, then in Egypt, and later in India. The Turks became Muslims, like the people they conquered. One group of Turks drifted into Anatolia. Their leader was named Othman, from whose name comes the word "Ottoman." In the 1300s, the power of the Ottoman Turks began to grow. In 1453, they conquered Constantinople and ended the 1,000-year-old Christian Byzantine empire. They renamed the city Istanbul and made it their own capital.

At its height, the Ottoman Empire stretched from Eastern Europe to the Maghreb. The head of this huge empire was known as the sultan. He called himself the caliph as well. That title means "head of the Muslim world." He listened to advice from learned religious men but took orders from no one. He had complete power to do as he pleased.

The Ottomans, however, did not change with the times. They ignored science and developed little modern technology. By 1900, their empire was weak.

Remember

The Maghreb was part of North Africa. It included the countries of Morocco, Algeria, Tunisia, and Libya.

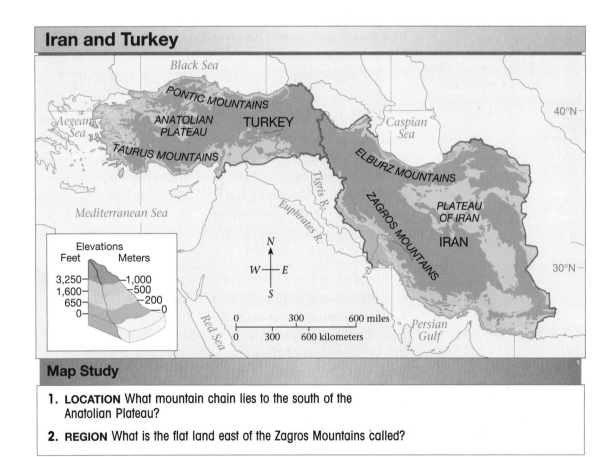

Iran and Turkey

Map Study

1. **LOCATION** What mountain chain lies to the south of the Anatolian Plateau?

2. **REGION** What is the flat land east of the Zagros Mountains called?

Ataturk's Revolution in Turkey

In World War I, the Ottomans lost most of their lands, and the sultan's power passed to a group known as the Young Turks. One of the Young Turks was a man named Mustafa Kemal, who organized the remains of the empire into a Turkish state. Modern Turkey was born. In 1923, Mustafa Kemal became Turkey's president. He gave himself the last name of Ataturk, which means "Father of Turks."

Ataturk was determined to make Turkey part of the modern world. He blamed Islam for his country's lack of progress. He turned Turkey into a **secular** state— that is, he separated the government from religion. Ataturk set up a new system of law based on ideas from the West instead of from Islam. He took power away from religious leaders. Turkish people were still allowed to practice their religion—but within limits.

In the new country, polygamy was made illegal. Women were given many rights. They could vote, enter public life, and walk around without veils. Western-style clothes were encouraged. In fact, some traditional clothes were made illegal. For example, the round, high red hat called a fez was outlawed. To Ataturk, the fez was not part of the new culture he envisioned for Turkey.

Ataturk's government set up a public school system. It built roads and hospitals and industries. Even the written language was changed. Turkish is now written with Roman letters rather than Arabic, using basically the same alphabet that English does. The culture of Turkey became much more like that of Western Europe.

Ataturk died in 1938. After his death, the modernization of Turkey slowed down. Islam regained some of its strength. Today, more than 90 percent of the Turkish people practice Islam, but Turkey remains a secular state.

Kemal Ataturk remains a popular hero in Turkey.

GLOBAL ISSUES
Natural Disasters

In 45 seconds in 1999, life changed in northwestern Turkey. After a huge earthquake, more than 13,000 people were dead. At least 200,000 people were homeless. The earthquake flattened town after town.

Throughout history, people have faced natural disasters. Some have to do with the weather. Hurricanes and blizzards are two of these. Other natural disasters, such as earthquakes, are caused by disruptions in the Earth.

In ancient days, some people believed that their gods punished them with natural disasters. They had no warning when a disaster would strike. Today, scientists can predict some disasters so people can leave the area. They can help decrease the effects of others. For example, buildings can be built to resist earthquakes. Also, today when disasters strike there is help from groups such as the Red Cross.

Answer the questions below.

1. Name a natural disaster that has to do with weather.

2. Why might a natural disaster be more devastating in a poor area than a rich area?

MAKE A DIFFERENCE
The Red Cross helps out anywhere disaster strikes. Find out from your local Red Cross office what you can do as a volunteer. You could also ask what areas of the world need help and work to raise funds for victims of disasters in those areas.

Iran

East of Turkey lies the country of Iran. It is located in the heart of the ancient Persian empire, which developed and spread across the Middle East about 2,500 years ago. The empire and its culture continued to exist throughout history. It was ruled by invaders at times, including the Greeks, Romans, Arabs, and Turks. At other times, it was ruled by various Persian **dynasties**.

Persian people are now the main—but not the only—ethnic group within Iran. They make up more than half the population. Their language, Farsi, written in the Arabic script, is spoken throughout the country. The Azerbaijanis represent about 16 percent of the population and speak a Turkish language.

Celebrations

PERSIAN NEW YEAR

One of the biggest holidays in Iran is Now-Ruz—the New Day—celebrated in March. This holiday began long before Islam came to Iran. One ritual of Now-Ruz involves building a fire, which people jump over. As they jump, all the bad luck that they have collected during the past year burns away—and they can start fresh.

People in Iran celebrate the Persian New Year in March.

This ritual is probably left over from an ancient Persian religion called Zoroastrianism. This ancient religion taught that two great forces rule the world—one good, one evil. Good is associated with fire and light, and evil with darkness. Good and evil are locked in a never-ending struggle. A small minority in Iran still practices this religion.

Critical Thinking Why is spring an appropriate season to celebrate this holiday?

Iran is populated by Kurds and Arabs, as well as other ethnic groups such as the Luri, Bakhtiari, Baluchi, and Qashqai. Most of these groups have their own languages, and some—such as the Kurds—have struggled for independence from Iran. Some of the smaller ethnic groups, such as the Baluchi, are still nomads. In the 1960s, the Iranian government tried to make all the nomadic people settle down and become farmers, but it met with limited success.

Whatever their background, nearly all Iranians are Muslims, and modern Iran is controlled by its religious leaders. Women must dress according to Islamic laws or face punishment. Many women wear a chador, a long garment that covers the head and can be used as a veil. A chador can be any color and may have flowery designs. The most religious Iranian women, however, favor a plain, black chador. They say the purpose of a chador is to keep a woman covered modestly, not to make her pretty or attractive.

In one way, however, Iran is different from other Islamic countries. In Iran, Shiite Muslims far outnumber Sunnites. About 95 percent of the population belong to this branch of Islam. Iran is the only nation in which Shiism is the official religion.

You Decide

Why would groups such as the Kurds want independence from Iran?

✓ **Check Your Understanding**

Write your answers in compete sentences.

1. Who are the Kurds?

2. Why was the Ottoman Empire weak by 1900?

3. Who was Mustafa Kemal?

4. How is Iran different from other Islamic countries?

Sunnism and Shiism

Sunnism and Shiism are the two main branches of Islam. The split began right after the prophet Muhammad died. Muslims disagreed about how to choose a new caliph.

One group believed that the new leader should be elected by the whole Muslim community. They said that any good, wise man could be a candidate. They supported Abu Bakr, the prophet's father-in-law. The members of this group became the Sunnites.

The other group believed that Muhammad had chosen his own successor, and it was his son-in-law Ali. They said Muhammad had passed a special religious power to Ali. Ali had thus become the Imam, a holy man who could not make a mistake. Ali's followers came to be known as Shiites. Shiites believe there is always an Imam in the world. Ali, they say, was the first. His son Husayn was next, and the religious power has continued to pass down in Ali's family. Shiites believe no one knows who today's Imam is. Someday, they believe, the Imam will reveal himself again.

Ali's son Husayn was murdered in A.D. 680 by rival Muslims. Shiites remember this event every year in a ritual play. Shiites also make pilgrimages to where the murder of Husayn took place.

> ### HISTORY FACT
>
> Shiites think of the Imam as a perfect man who cannot make a mistake. Sunnites believe that no living human is perfect.

The Pahlavi Years

In the 1920s, Iran moved away from Islam. The changes began under a king named Reza Shah Pahlavi and continued under his son, the second Reza Shah. The first Reza Shah admired Ataturk and wanted to copy him. He tried to weaken religious leaders in Iran. He built public, nonreligious schools, as well as roads, hospitals, and factories. He also passed laws allowing women to enter public life.

After World War II, oil was discovered in Iran. Money began flowing into the country. Western companies opened offices in Iran. Cities grew rapidly, and bars, nightclubs, and theaters opened. Iran became more like the West. The traditional way of life began to crumble, even in the villages.

Many Iranians did not like these changes. They considered the government corrupt. They felt that the West had colonized Iran. They believed the Shah had betrayed his country for money. Certainly, the Shah had become one of the world's richest men. He held onto power with the help of his secret police. He had his opponents jailed and tortured.

About six million people live in Tehran, the capital of Iran.

The Islamic Revolution in Iran

In 1979, millions of people poured into the streets of Iranian cities and demanded the downfall of the Shah. Before long, the Shah fled the country. One of his main enemies, Ruhollah Khomeini, was living in France at the time. Khomeini was an ayatollah, a Shiite religious leader. The Shah had driven him out of Iran years earlier, but Khomeini came back to Iran after the Shah left. Most Iranians accepted Khomeini as the leader of the revolution.

Remember
The sharia governs marriage, divorce, property rights, contracts, crimes, and punishments.

Khomeini's strongest followers were Muslim **fundamentalists**, who interpreted religious laws very strictly. Khomeini's followers started a new political party that took control of Iran. This party set up a **theocracy**, which is a government controlled by religious leaders. The new government threw out all laws based on European ideas. Iranian laws are now based on the sharia, the laws of Islam.

The new Iranian leaders worked to rid their country of Western culture. Western-style clothes were forbidden. Western movies, television programs, books, and music were limited or forbidden. Because the United States was the greatest supporter of the Shah, the Iranian government considered the United States an enemy.

The Iranian revolution was brought about by the people, but not everyone was happy with it. Thousands of Iranians left the country. Iran lost many doctors, teachers, and other professionals. With the Iran-Iraq war, Iran lost still more people. Many of its young men died.

When Khomeini died in 1989, Iran's economy was in bad shape, and Iran had few allies. Today its new leaders wish to improve Iran's relations with the rest of the world. They are also working to repair Iran's economy. Still, they have no wish to entirely weaken the role of Islam in Iranian life.

People gather to support Ayatollah Ruhollah Khomeini

Persian Literature

Iran has a long literary history. Most of its literature is poetry. The first great Persian poet was Firdausi, who lived in the tenth century. At that time, Arabic was considered the language of culture. Firdausi, however, chose to write in Persian. He wrote an **epic** poem. An epic is a long poem or story that celebrates a hero.

Firdausi's epic poem was called the *Shah-nameh*. It tells the story of the Iranian people. The *Shah-nameh* starts with the creation of the world and ends at the dawn of Islam. The poem is filled with kings, heroes, monsters, magicians, and giants drawn from folklore. Today, adults tell children stories from the *Shah-nameh*.

The most beloved Persian poet is Hafiz, who wrote only short poems—never longer than a page. Each of his poems expresses a strong feeling, such as love or joy. All of Hafiz's works can fit into one small book. Iranians sometimes use his poems to tell fortunes.

Many Persian poets were deeply religious men called sufis. Sufis believed they could sometimes speak to God. They often wrote love poems about God. One great sufi poet was Rumi, whose poems were filled with extraordinary images. His masterpiece is called "Masnavi." It is packed with stories that express sufi ideas.

Persian poetry of the past was very formal. A poem had to follow certain rhythms and had to rhyme in certain ways. Modern Iranian poets usually write what they call "New Verse." Poems in this style may not rhyme, and the rhythm may change from line to line. Modern Persian poets often write about politics and personal feelings.

Islamic Art and Architecture

Islamic art emphasizes decoration. The decoration is generally on some useful item, such as a vase. The item is decorated with a complicated pattern that is always balanced and orderly. Usually, it has brilliant colors and tiny details. The carpets of the Turkish and Iranian people are especially famous as works of Islamic art.

Islamic painters generally avoid trying to copy nature, probably because Islam warns strongly against the worship of idols. In Turkey and Iran, Muslim artists paint illustrations for books such as the *Shah-nameh*. Artists use single-hair brushes to create these finely detailed illustrations.

Architecture is an outstanding Islamic art form. It was developed not by Arabs but by the people whom they conquered. Some of the finest Islamic architecture is found in Turkey and Iran.

Every mosque has certain features. Each has a large empty space inside, where the community can pray together on Fridays. It also has a needlelike tower called a **minaret**, from the top of which someone calls worshipers to daily prayers. The mihrab, a hollow in the wall facing Mecca, lets worshipers know which direction to face when they pray. Almost every mosque has a domed roof, arched doorways and windows, and walls and ceilings covered with mosaics. The designs on a mosque are like those on other Islamic art objects—complicated, orderly, and detailed.

✓ Check Your Understanding

Write your answers in complete sentences.

1. How do Shiite and Sunnite beliefs differ?

2. How did the Pahlavi rulers change Iran?

3. Why do Islamic painters usually not paint nature?

GEOGRAPHER'S TOOL KIT
Using Charts

One of the best ways to understand information is to organize facts on a chart. Charts can show you how important ideas connect to one another.

Here is how to use a chart.

- Read the title on the chart.
- Look at the labels on the side and the top or bottom.
- Look at the information in the chart.
- Analyze what the information shows.

Iran and Turkey

Country	Population	Male Life Expectancy	Female Life Expectancy	Household Income
Iran	61,531,000	66.1	68.7	$19,536.00
Turkey	64,567,000	69.5	74.4	$4,294.00

Source: *Encyclopedia Brittanica,* 2000

Answer the questions below.

1. Which country has the larger population?

2. How much longer do men in Turkey generally live than men in Iran?

CHALLENGE Which country do you think has a better quality of life for its people? Why do you think so?

Apply the Skill

Create a chart like this that compares two other countries. The two countries you choose should be on the same continent. Use an almanac or the Internet to do your research.

Summary

Turkish people began migrating out of Central Asia around A.D. 1000.
The Ottoman Turks built a large and powerful empire that lasted roughly from the 1400s to the 1800s.
Kemal Ataturk created the modern, secular nation of Turkey.
Iran is located where the ancient Persian Empire was centered.
In 1979, an Islamic revolution toppled a corrupt government in Iran and moved Iran away from Western culture.
Sunnism and Shiism are the main branches of Islam.
Mosques are the most important examples of Islamic architecture. Every mosque has a minaret and a mihrab.

epic
secular
theocracy
dynasty
minaret

Vocabulary Review

Write a term from the list that matches each definition below.

1. A series of rulers who belong to the same family

2. A tower of a mosque

3. A country whose government is run by a religious leader

4. A long poem or story that celebrates a hero

5. Not having to do with religion

Chapter Quiz

Write your answers in complete sentences.

1. What are the main geographic features of Iran and Turkey?

2. What title did the Shiites give to their new leader?

3. What features are included in a mosque?

4. **Critical Thinking** How was Ataturk's response to Western culture different from Khomeini's response?

5. **Critical Thinking** How did Shiism begin?

Write About Geography

Complete the following activities.

1. Write a conversation between a follower of the Shah and a follower of Khomeini. Have each explain his or her beliefs.

2. You have just been caught in the 1999 earthquake in Turkey. Write what you experience.

Group Activity

Write an epic poem in your group. Decide on the general story. Then give each person a section to write. Put the sections together. Read the poem to the class.

Unit 5 **Review**

Comprehension Check

Write answers to the following questions.

1. How is Egypt different from the countries of the Maghreb?

2. Who are the Palestinians?

3. Why did Islam split into the Shiite and Sunnite branches?

4. What did Ataturk do to make Turkey a more western society?

Building Your Skills

Answer each question in a complete sentence.

1. What does an economic map show?

2. Which is larger, Israel or Syria?

3. How do you use a chart?

Where Is It?

Write the name of the place based on the information below.

1. The world's largest desert

2. The Arabic country that produces the most oil

3. The largest city in Turkey

Writing an Essay

Answer one of the following essay topics.

1. Explain the importance of the Nile River both in history and today.

2. Explain the Arab-Israeli conflict.

3. Describe how Iran changed during the Pahlavi years and then how it changed during Khomeini's reign.

Geography and You

Desert and sand has meant nomadic lives for many people in the Middle East. Oil has brought wealth to this region. How have geographical features in the area in which you live affected your life?

Unit 6 ▶ Western Europe

SCANDINAVIA

BRITISH ISLES

CENTRAL WESTERN
EUROPE

SOUTHERN EUROPE

Look at the location of Scandinavia and Southern Europe. How might the location of those two areas determine how life differs for the people living there?

TRAVEL LOG

You are on a trip to Europe. As you learn about each country, write a conversation you might have with a friend about that country. In your conversations, explain what makes each country different.

London telephone booth

About 20 percent of Ireland's land is used for crops. Most of the rest is suited for grazing. What climate would be good for raising animals?

Chapter 18 — The British Isles

Words to Know

moor	a rolling plain covered with grasses and small shrubs
bog	a wet, spongy area
cottage industry	a small-scale manufacturing operation in which people make goods by hand in their own homes
Industrial Revolution	a period of rapid industrialization in many Western countries that began in the 1700s
wage	money paid to workers
trade union	an organization of workers who are in the same industry; a labor union
strike	to stop work, as a group, until certain demands are met

Places to Know

England
Scotland
Wales
Great Britain
Republic of Ireland
Northern Ireland

Learning Objectives

- Identify the political units of the British Isles.
- Explain the causes and consequences of the Industrial Revolution.
- Tell how the British Empire shaped British society.
- Tell how the ancient Celts influenced culture in Ireland.
- Explain the political troubles in Northern Ireland.

Countries of the British Isles

Some Britons do not think of themselves as Europeans. To them, Europe means the European continent—the mainland. They live on the British Isles, which include two main islands and many smaller ones. The largest island is divided into three countries—England, Scotland, and Wales. Each country has its own government. Together, the three countries are called Great Britain.

Across the Irish Sea is the next largest island, which is divided into two countries. One is the Republic of Ireland. The other is Northern Ireland. The Republic of Ireland is an independent country. Britain controls Northern Ireland. Great Britain, Northern Ireland, and many tiny islands nearby make up the United Kingdom.

The smaller islands include the Shetlands, which are located about 125 miles north of Scotland. In the past, the people of these cold, windswept islands lived mostly by farming or fishing. Then oil was discovered near the Shetlands, beneath the North Sea. Because Britain owned these islands, it could claim some of the oil.

The British Isles have a good climate for farming. The surrounding sea brings steady rainfall. The ocean keeps temperature fairly even. Winter snows are light in southern England. Compared with other places at the same latitude, Britain's climate is mild.

The northern area of Scotland, called the Highlands, is a windy, rainy area, known for its uneven mountains and lakes. Most of the Highlands, though, consist of **moors**, which are rolling plains covered with grasses and low shrubs. On the moors are **bogs**—wet, spongy areas.

Bogs are also a feature of the lowlands of Ireland. When plants in bogs die and do not decompose, they form peat. Peat can be burned for fuel. One 370-square mile group of peat bogs in Ireland is mined for use in power stations.

Most people of the British Isles speak English, but they speak many different dialects of the language. In Scotland, Ireland, and Wales, some people speak varieties of Gaelic. This was the language of the Celtic groups who invaded the British Isles about 2,300 years ago. In the Republic of Ireland, people are encouraged to learn Gaelic. Elsewhere, however, Gaelic is dying out.

About 64 million people live in the British Isles. Close to 75 percent of them live in urban areas. The largest city is London, which is in southern England. It is located near the mouth of the Thames River, England's most important waterway. Two other important cities are Birmingham and Manchester, which are located in the middle of the country. They are large industrial centers.

London, the capital of England, is the largest city in southern England.

Western Europe

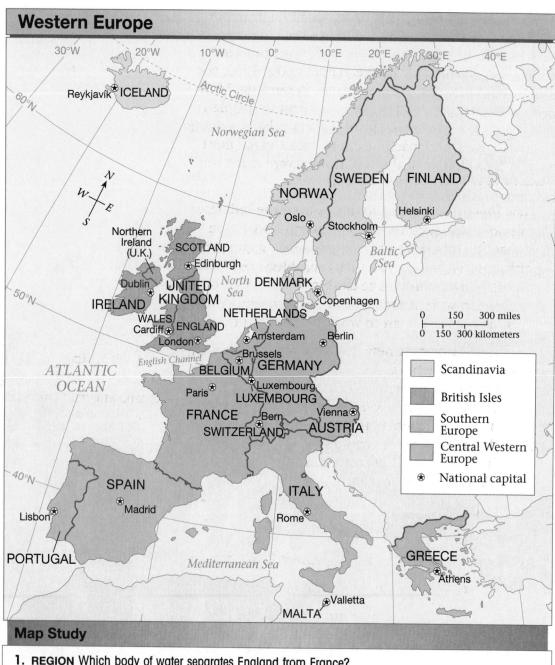

The Oldest Industrial Nation

Roughly between 1750 and 1850, England went through a remarkable change. Before about 1750, the economy of the country was based on farming. Most manufactured goods were made by hand in people's homes. This way of making things was called a **cottage industry**. By 1850, machines in factories made most goods. This change in the way things were made was called the **Industrial Revolution**.

New inventions helped to bring about the Industrial Revolution. One such invention was the power loom. This machine was driven by the power of running water. Wealthy people bought these new machines and built factories. Weavers who made cloth at home could not compete with such factories. Most of them shut down their businesses and went to work in the factories.

The most important new machine was probably the steam engine, which was invented in 1769 by James Watt. Steam engines were used to power ships and trains. A network of railroads developed in England. Trains could haul heavy materials such as coal and iron ore. Steel-making factories could now be built. Cities grew up around these industrial areas. By 1850, half of the population of England lived in large urban areas.

> **You Decide**
>
> Can a country become industrialized without a good transportation system? Why or why not?

✓ Check Your Understanding

Write your answers in complete sentences.

1. What are the three countries of Great Britain?

2. Why do some people in the British Isles speak Gaelic?

3. Why was the steam engine important to the Industrial Revolution?

A New Class System

The Industrial Revolution changed the social structure of England. In earlier times, most English people were either large landowners or landless farmers. The Industrial Revolution created a new "working class"—people who worked for **wages** in mines and factories. This new class of workers labored in noisy, crowded, unhealthy places. Many had to live in slums. They worked up to 12 hours a day, 6 days a week. The machines they used were dangerous. About 10 percent of the workers were children.

The Industrial Revolution in England changed the way goods were made.

The Industrial Revolution also created a new and growing middle class. People were needed to work in banks and offices. Engineers and technicians were needed to design and fix the new machines. All of these workers could work and hope to earn higher pay. New jobs also opened up for teachers, doctors, and others.

Meanwhile, the working class fought to improve their living and working conditions. In the 1830s, workers began to form **trade unions**. Workers found they were more powerful when they banded together into these unions. If factory owners refused the workers' demands, the workers could go on **strike** and stop working. Sometimes, other unions would go on strike to show support. Factory owners would then be forced to make deals with their workers. Slowly, unions raised workers' wages and shortened their working hours.

Trade unions became very powerful in Britain. By the 1900s, many trade union leaders supported socialism to some degree. A new political party called the Labour Party was formed to represent workers. The Labour Party took control of the government for some time. It passed laws and started programs that changed British society. One of these programs provides low-cost medical care to all citizens. Another provides money to workers who have lost their jobs or cannot work due to age, illness, or injury. Because the Labour Party forced the government to buy coal, steel, and railway companies, the government now controls these major industries.

Remember
Socialism is a political system in which the government controls farms and businesses.

Britain is no longer at the forefront of industrial nations. In some ways, it has suffered from being the world's oldest industrial nation. Its factories, railroads, and other equipment have grown old. It has used up some of its mineral resources, such as tin and lead. It has lost many markets to newer industrialized countries, such as Japan and the United States. Above all, however, Britain has suffered from the loss of its empire.

Sunset on the British Empire

At the time of the Industrial Revolution, Britain had colonies all over the world. Britons used to say, "The sun never sets on the British Empire." They were right. British colonies existed in Asia, Africa, the Caribbean, the Americas, and the South Pacific. The colonies supplied Britain with cheap raw materials, and they bought finished goods made in Britain. The colonies helped Britain deal with its growing population, too, as many Britons moved, or were sent, to the colonies.

Eventually, however, some of the colonists decided to break away from Britain and start new countries. The United States was founded in this way. Elsewhere, colonized people fought for independence. Britain sent soldiers to try to keep control of such colonies as India, Burma, and Kenya. Britain also guarded against other European nations that wanted some of its colonies.

One such nation was Germany, which Britain fought in two great wars. Most of the world became involved in these wars. The first war—World War I—lasted from 1914 to 1918. The second war—World War II—raged from 1939 to 1945. Germany lost both times, but the wars weakened Britain as well.

Between 1948 and 1960, Britain was forced to grant independence to most of its colonies. As its empire crumbled, however, Britain agreed to accept immigrants from these colonies. Many people moved to Britain looking for economic opportunities. As a result, Britain is now home to over two million immigrants from its former colonies. These immigrants have come from India and Pakistan, from the Caribbean, and from various parts of Africa. London and other cities have large ethnic neighborhoods. The new immigrants face a lot of prejudice. Despite this prejudice, Britain has become a multicultural society.

Geography Fact

Malta, which is made up of six islands (only three of which are inhabited), was a British colony until 1964. Most of the people there speak Maltese, a West Arabic dialect with some Italian words.

The Celts

The people of Ireland are descended from a nomadic people, the ancient Celts. The Celts originally lived in Eastern Europe. They were driven west by other nomadic groups and by the Romans. Most of the Celts migrated to the British Isles. Some of them moved into Britain, and others settled in Ireland.

About 30,000 Celtic sites have been unearthed in Ireland, including ancient homesteads and stone forts. Lovely objects made of gold and other metals have been found in these sites. The Celts were expert metalworkers. Poets, storytellers, bards, and musicians held important places in Celtic society. A bard is a singing poet. Much of the folklore of these people has survived into modern times.

Celebrations

NATIONAL EISTEDDFOD OF WALES

A group of Celts also migrated to Wales. The Welsh, like the Irish, are proud of their Celtic roots. The people of Wales have special meetings, called eisteddfodau. There, they speak Welsh, a form of Gaelic.

The National Eisteddfod is the largest of these meetings. It is a celebration of Welsh culture. It features contests in music, dance, arts, and crafts, but the grandest contest is in poetry reading. The people who enter this poetry contest are bards who wear long white robes and headdresses. As in ancient times, bards have an important place in Welsh society.

Critical Thinking Why do you think bards have an important place in Welsh society?

Welsh people remember their Celtic roots at the National Eisteddfod.

By A.D. 400, part of Britain was a Roman colony. Rome was a Christian empire. In A.D. 431, a young priest named Patrick began converting the Irish Celts to Christianity. Patrick had grown up in Britain. He was captured by pirates at age 16 and sold into slavery in Ireland. After six years as a slave, he escaped and became a priest. He devoted the rest of his life to converting Ireland to Christianity. Today, Irish people all over the world still celebrate Saint Patrick's Day on March 17.

By A.D. 600, Ireland was considered a Christian land. Christian monasteries were built throughout the country. Today, the island of Ireland is still predominantly Christian. Most of the people in the Republic of Ireland are Catholic.

In the 600s, Irish monks created a written Celtic language using the Roman alphabet. They wrote down Celtic stories, legends, and history. They also wrote Bible stories in Celtic. The monks painted the manuscripts by hand, illustrating their texts with Celtic designs from ancient metalwork. The most famous one is the Book of Kells, which was completed in A.D. 810.

A page from the Book of Kells

Politics of Northern Ireland

English people invaded Ireland about 1,000 years ago. They have tried to rule the island ever since. Today, Britain controls only a small part of Ireland called Northern Ireland.

In the 1500s, the king of England broke away from the Roman Catholic Church. He turned England into a Protestant nation. The Irish, however, remained firm Catholics even though the entire island of Ireland was ruled by Britain at the time. Relations between the Irish and the English had never been good, but this new religious difference only made matters worse.

The Irish grew more rebellious so English monarchs tried a new way to control them. The monarchs encouraged English and Scottish families to move to Ireland. The English kings helped these families become landowners and gave them a great deal of political power.

The Irish, however, kept fighting. In 1920, the British were forced to divide Ireland. The largest part—the southern portion—became the independent Republic of Ireland. There, at least 95 percent of the people are Roman Catholic. Northern Ireland, however, remained under British control. Only a third of the people there are Catholic. The rest are Protestant.

The Catholics of Northern Ireland are descended from the ancient Celts. They are generally poorer than the Protestants. The Protestants are descended from Scottish and English immigrants. The Protestants control most of the wealth. For example, Protestants own most factories in Northern Ireland. Catholics living in Northern Ireland can have trouble getting good jobs and housing.

Catholics in Northern Ireland want to become independent from the United Kingdom. They want to join the Republic of Ireland. This would make the Protestants a minority. Therefore, Protestants in Northern Ireland want to keep living under British rule.

After Ireland was divided, some Catholics formed the Irish Republican Army (IRA). Some members of this secret army wage war against Protestants and British soldiers. IRA terrorists have also been active in England—especially in London. In 1998, a peace agreement was reached between British and Irish governments and the divided groups in Northern Ireland. However, the peace process has been slow because of political problems. In addition, small terrorist groups on both sides have not obeyed the agreement.

You Decide

Why would the Protestants of Northern Ireland fear becoming a minority? What could happen to them in a united Ireland?

Heroes of Fiction

English legends and literature have given the world many memorable characters. One such character is a legendary outlaw called Robin Hood, who supposedly lived in the late 1100s. Two real kings were a part of the Robin Hood story: Richard the First and his brother John. Robin Hood and his men robbed the rich and gave to the poor. Many writers have retold the story of this dashing outlaw and his Merry Men.

Perhaps England's greatest writer was the poet and playwright William Shakespeare, who lived from 1564 to 1616. Shakespeare created many famous fictional characters. Many lines from his plays have become well-known sayings. In the play *Romeo and Juliet,* Shakespeare created two of the world's most famous lovers. To this day, Romeo and Juliet stand for the idea of intense, reckless, unhappy love.

Another famous fictional hero of English literature is Sherlock Holmes. A writer named Arthur Conan Doyle invented this odd and brilliant detective in the 1800s. Many writers have followed in Doyle's footsteps, attempting to create their own odd and brilliant detectives. Two examples of these detectives are Miss Marple and Hercule Poirot, created by the English writer Agatha Christie. Although Christie died in 1976, her novels remain popular. They have been translated into dozens of languages and are read by millions every year.

✓ Check Your Understanding

Write your answers in complete sentences.

1. Why is Britain no longer the leader of industrial nations?

2. Why does Britain have many immigrants?

3. Why do Irish people honor St. Patrick?

4. Name an important English writer.

GEOGRAPHY IN YOUR LIFE
Reading City Tourist Maps

If you have ever visited a new city, state, or country, you have probably seen a tourist map. These maps highlight the attractions that tourists most want to see. To use these maps, first look over the entire map. Next, look at the places highlighted. Choose the ones you want to visit. Then, map a course to visit these sites.

Edinburgh Town Center

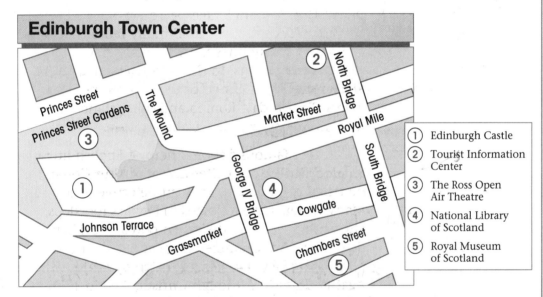

1. Edinburgh Castle
2. Tourist Information Center
3. The Ross Open Air Theatre
4. National Library of Scotland
5. Royal Museum of Scotland

Answer the questions below.

1. What attraction is on the corner of George IV Bridge and Cowgate?

2. What would be the best way to walk from the Tourist Information Center to the Royal Museum of Scotland?

   CHALLENGE What can you tell about Edinburgh from looking at this map and its attractions?

Apply the Skill

Create your own walking tour of Edinburgh's Town Center. Trace or redraw the map onto another sheet of paper. Then, draw your walking route on the map. Visit about three sites. Describe your route in a paragraph.

Summary

England, Scotland, and Wales make up Great Britain. Great Britain, Northern Ireland, and many small islands form the United Kingdom. The Republic of Ireland is an independent country.
Most Britons speak English. Some Irish, Welsh, and Scottish people speak forms of Gaelic—but mainly as a second language.
The Industrial Revolution brought economic growth to England. It also created a working class and a middle class, and it led to the rise of the Labour Party.
The British Empire came to an end after World War II. Many people from the former colonies moved to Britain.
Most Irish people are descended from the ancient Celts. Celtic folklore, music, and art are important parts of modern Irish culture.
Religious differences and economic injustice have led to violent conflict in Northern Ireland.

cottage industry
Industrial Revolution
strike
trade union
wage

Vocabulary Review

Complete each sentence with a term from the list.

1. Money paid to workers is called a _____ .

2. The _____ was a period of rapid industrialization in many countries.

3. A small-scale manufacturing operation in which people make goods by hand in their homes is called a _____ .

4. To _____ is to stop work as a group.

5. A _____ is made up of workers who are in the same industry.

Chapter Quiz

Write your answers in complete sentences.

1. Why does modern England have many different ethnic groups?

2. What is the title of the Celtic work Irish monks completed in A.D. 810?

3. What is the name of the organization that waged war against British control in Northern Ireland?

4. **Critical Thinking** What are some of the differences between Northern Ireland and the Republic of Ireland?

5. **Critical Thinking** How did British workers gain more rights and political power?

Write About Geography

Complete the following activities.

1. Look at the Book of Kells on page 266. Draw your own illustrated page using a saying that inspires you.

2. Write a short essay that compares what England was like before and after the Industrial Revolution.

Group Activity

Write your own play based on the Robin Hood story. Set it in the present day. Write in parts for every group member. Practice your play and then present it to a group of younger students.

These long narrow bays called fjords are common in Scandinavia. How would these landforms affect the way people live here?

Words to Know

fjord	a long, narrow bay surrounded by cliffs
radioactive	giving off the kind of energy used in nuclear bombs and power plants
welfare state	a country in which government money is used to provide people with social services
pension	money paid regularly to a person who has retired or grown too old to work
saga	a long, detailed story or account of an event
mythology	the study of traditional stories known as myths

Places to Know

Sweden

Denmark

Finland

Iceland

Norway

Greenland

Learning Objectives

- Describe the role of the sea in the Scandinavian way of life.
- Explain the early history and culture of Scandinavia.
- Explain the social welfare system in Scandinavian countries.
- Describe Norse sagas and mythology.

The Land and the People

Sweden is located in Scandinavia, a region in Northern Europe. The other countries of Scandinavia are Denmark, Finland, Iceland, and Norway. The island of Greenland, which lies west of Iceland, belongs to Denmark but has its own government. Greenland is closer to North America than to Europe.

A large part of Scandinavia lies within the Arctic Circle, or the area north of 66.5 degrees N latitude. Seasons in the Arctic Circle are extreme. During the winter, this region gets little or no sunlight. The nights are long, the days are very short, and it is extremely cold. In summer, the days are long and the nights are short. The climate is never hot.

About 20,000 years ago, Northern Europe was covered by glaciers. As they moved slowly south, they scraped away the topsoil. That is why Scandinavia has little good farmland today. The glaciers also cut deep ruts into the Earth. After the ice melted, these ruts became valleys and lakes.

Sleds and skis are a common form of transport in this snowy region.

One typical Scandinavian landform is called a **fjord**. A fjord is a long, narrow bay surrounded by cliffs. Fjords are found all along the coast of Norway. Many fjords contain rocky islands, called skerries. Skerries block rough sea waves. In most fjords, therefore, the water is very calm.

Most Scandinavians are ethnically related. Most Danes, Swedes, and Norwegians are descended from Germanic people who migrated north and settled on the Scandinavian Peninsula long ago. Their languages are related, too.

Finland has a different history. The Finns originally came from Asia. Their language is not related to any European language except Hungarian. Their ancestors, in fact, may have been related to the Turks.

However, Finnish culture has been influenced by that of its neighbor, Sweden. For example, like the Swedes, most Finns are Protestant Christians.

About 40,000 Samis live in the Arctic areas of Northern Europe and Russia. These people are also known as Lapps. They form the largest ethnic minority in Scandinavia. They may be descended from people who were there before the Germans and Finns arrived.

Scandinavia

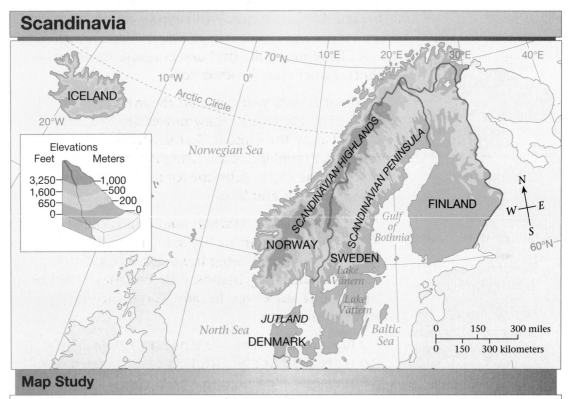

Map Study

1. **LOCATION** Which place has the most hills in Scandinavia?
2. **PLACE** What is the largest lake labeled on the map?

Finish this Page!

The Samis are nomadic reindeer herders by tradition. In the late 1980s, however, **radioactive** pollution from a nuclear power plant accident made most reindeer meat unsafe to eat and their milk unsafe to drink. As a result, the Samis have been forced to give up their herds and their nomadic lifestyle.

The country of Iceland is not connected to the European mainland. It consists of one main island and many smaller ones. The islands of Iceland were formed by underwater volcanoes. Today, volcanic activity provides geothermal power in Iceland. Iceland's capital, Reykjavik, has a geothermal heating system, as do many other Icelandic towns. Water from underground hot springs is piped into homes and businesses to keep them warm.

Celebrations

MIDSUMMER

Midnight is only half an hour away now. It is Midsummer's Eve. Families are gathered on porches to wait for the sun to set. Almost everyone in Sweden has the day off because today is Midsummer.

Midsummer is a holiday celebrated throughout Scandinavia. It takes place on June 24. This holiday is a time for friends and family to get together. Often, they share a simple meal outdoors. They may have boiled, unpeeled potatoes. They may enjoy herrings, small fish from the North Sea. In some places, people decorate their homes with summer flowers.

Family and friends celebrate Midsummer.

Critical Thinking How does your community mark the beginning of summer?

Life by the Sea

The sea has long been important to the people of Scandinavia. For one, Scandinavians are never far from the water because they live on islands and peninsulas. Many prefer to live along the coast. The weather is warmer there because an ocean current, called the North Atlantic Drift, keeps the coast warm.

Scandinavians need the resources that the sea provides because the rocky soil and the cold inland climate make farming difficult. Scandinavians depended mainly on fishing before they developed industry. In Iceland, fishing is still an important part of the economy. Fish and fish products make up about 80 percent of Iceland's exports.

Thanks to the fishing tradition, a big shipbuilding industry has developed in Scandinavia. Shipbuilding provides many jobs in Norway, Sweden, and Finland. In the past, the ships were built of wood taken from the forests that cover much of Scandinavia. Today, most ships are made of steel. Trees, however, still are an important part of the region's economy. They are used to make paper and other wood products.

Shipbuilding led naturally to another industry— shipping. Norway has one of the world's largest fleets of cargo ships. Many Norwegians work on these ships.

The sea also gives Norway its most valuable resource: oil. Norway shares the oil of the North Sea with Great Britain. Oil is now one of Norway's main exports.

Geography Fact

The North Atlantic Drift starts in the Caribbean, flows northeast across the Atlantic, and sweeps along Norway. It keeps most harbors free of ice, even in winter.

✓ Check Your Understanding

Write your answers in complete sentences.

1. How do glaciers from long ago affect Scandinavia today?

2. Who are the Samis?

3. What is the North Atlantic Drift?

The Scandinavian Welfare System

The Scandinavian countries have strong economies and stable governments. Their political system is a special form of socialism. In Scandinavia, property and business remain in private hands. The governments, however, collect very high taxes. They use this money to provide many social services to their citizens. Countries run on such a system are called **welfare states**.

In Sweden, for example, low-cost medical care is available to everyone. A visit to any doctor costs just $10 to $15. People can visit a dentist free of charge until the age of 19. After that, they pay only a small fee. Education is also free. The Swedish government even pays for good students' college education.

When people lose their jobs, the government pays them enough to live on until they find new ones. The same benefits are paid to people who cannot work or have never found a job. Unemployed union workers in Sweden may get up to 90 percent of their normal pay. Those who are working get at least five weeks of vacation each year. The longer they have worked, the more vacation time they get. The government gives a full **pension** to people when they leave work at age 65.

The government also pays most child-care costs. Nearly all children in Sweden, for example, go to child-care centers at age one. Parents who stay home with their children get government help for the first year.

Everyone benefits from the welfare state, but not everyone is pleased with it. Some people do not want to pay half of their income or more in taxes to the government. They would rather decide for themselves how to spend the money they earn. Some feel they are working hard to support people who will not work. Recently, immigrants have been coming to Scandinavia. These immigrants get the same benefits as citizens born in Scandinavia. Some Scandinavians resent this.

$ Economics Fact

After retirement, most Swedish people receive annual pensions of about 60 percent of their average earnings during their 15 highest-paid years.

GLOBAL ISSUES
World Literacy

Literacy is the ability to read and write. Literacy and development often go together. Subsistence farmers do not need to read or write to work. In developed industrialized countries, however, most jobs require some literacy.

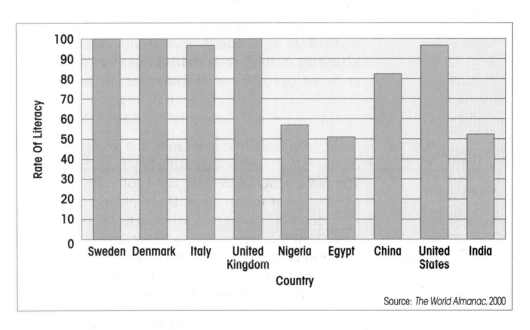

Source: *The World Almanac, 2000*

Answer the questions below.

1. How developed would you say the Scandinavian countries are?

2. What factors other than the economy may affect literacy?

MAKE A DIFFERENCE
You can help a person who is struggling to learn to read. There are many programs in which volunteers tutor others. Check with your school district to find out when and where you can help.

Telling Tales

The Vikings, also known as Norsemen, loved to tell tales of great adventures. They told stories about their ancestors, ancient German chieftains. Some of the events really happened, but fanciful details were added. These tales came to be known as the Norse **sagas**. Originally, the sagas were memorized and sung aloud. They were written down between A.D. 1000 and 1300.

Viking **mythology** is found in the Norse sagas. Mythology is the study of traditional stories known as myths. According to the Vikings, the lands of the gods and goddesses surrounded the human world.

Spotlight On

THE VIKINGS

Early Scandinavians were called Vikings. They lived in timber homesteads throughout Sweden, Norway, and Denmark. In the ninth and tenth centuries, Vikings were feared throughout Western Europe. They would raid, or steal, other people's goods.

The Vikings were not just raiders, however. They were traders and explorers as well. Viking traders sailed south to North Africa, Turkey, and Jerusalem. They also crossed Eastern Europe into the lands that are now Russia. Viking explorers also landed in North America—500 years before Columbus did. Around A.D. 1050, however, Viking power began to fade.

The Viking helmet was a symbol of strength.

Critical Thinking Why do you think the Vikings did their raiding in the winter?

Beyond these superior beings lived even more powerful beings called giants. The gods and the giants were always at war. The Vikings believed the world would end someday. The giants would beat the gods in a final battle and then destroy everything.

The Vikings thought the gods and goddesses lived in a castle called Valhalla. The king of the gods was a one-eyed magician named Odin, or Woden. He had lost his eye stealing poetry from the giants. His wife was named Frigga, or Fria. His son, Thor, was the god of storms.

Scandinavia has a rich tradition of folklore and fairy tales, too. These tales are filled with trolls, elves, and other strange creatures. "East of the Sun and West of the Moon" is one well-known Scandinavian folk tale. The nineteenth-century Danish writer Hans Christian Andersen created new fairy tales in the style of the old ones. He wrote some of the best-loved children's stories of the Western world.

> **HISTORY FACT**
>
> In English, three days of the week take their names from Norse gods. Wednesday started out as "Woden's Day." Thursday has the name of Thor. Friday is named after Fria.

✓ Check Your Understanding

Write your answers in complete sentences.

1. Why is Sweden called a welfare state?

2. Why do some Scandinavians resent immigrants?

3. What is Valhalla?

4. Who is Hans Christian Andersen?

Summary

Sweden, Norway, Denmark, Finland, and Iceland are the five countries of Scandinavia.
The sea plays a major role in Scandinavian life. Fishing, shipping, and shipbuilding are major industries.
Early Scandinavians, called Vikings, ruled much of Northern Europe from the ninth to the eleventh centuries.
In Scandinavian countries, the government collects high taxes but provides many social services.
Viking history and mythology form the basis for Norse sagas, an important contribution to Western literature.

Vocabulary Review

Write *true* or *false*. If the statement is false, change the underlined term to make it true.

1. <u>Mythology</u> is a long, detailed story or account of an event.

2. A <u>fjord</u> is a long, narrow bay surrounded by cliffs.

3. A <u>welfare state</u> is a country in which government money is used to provide people with social services.

4. <u>Radioactive</u> means giving off the kind of energy used in nuclear bombs and power plants.

5. Money paid regularly to a person who has retired is a <u>saga</u>.

Chapter Quiz

Write your answers in complete sentences.

1. What are the five countries that make up Scandinavia?

2. Explain how the Scandinavians depend on the sea.

3. Describe what you are likely to hear in a Norse saga.

4. Critical Thinking How is Iceland different from its Scandinavian neighbors?

5. Critical Thinking What are the benefits of a welfare state?

Write About Geography

Complete the following activities.

1. Would you like to live under the Swedish welfare system? Write reasons to support your opinion.

2. Choose a city or area in Scandinavia to visit. Find out more about it. Write what you want to see and why.

Group Activity

Have each member of your group write five questions about this chapter. Within your group, choose the best twenty questions, and make a test. Exchange tests with another group. See if you can answer their questions.

The Alps are the highest mountains in Europe. They are also a popular tourist destination. How might these mountains have affected history and culture in Europe?

Chapter 20 / Central Western Europe

Words to Know

dike	a barrier built to hold back seawater
Reformation	the sixteenth-century religious movement that began the Protestant branch of Christianity
capitalism	an economic system in which land, factories, and businesses are privately owned and run for profit
cold war	a sharp conflict between countries without actual war
reunification	to come together again after being divided
currency	the type of money used in any particular country

Places to Know

Austria

Belgium

France

Germany

Luxembourg

Liechtenstein

The Netherlands

Switzerland

Learning Objectives

- Tell how the Alps affected the movement of people across Europe in the past.

- Explain how the Protestant religions are different from Roman Catholicism.

- Explain why Germany is considered an economic and political leader in Europe.

- Describe the role of Paris as a cultural center.

- Explain how the Economic Union (EU) is moving Europe toward greater unity.

The Countries of Central Western Europe

The countries in this region include Austria, Belgium, France, Germany, Luxembourg, Liechtenstein, the Netherlands, and Switzerland. Rotterdam, in the Netherlands, is the world's biggest and busiest port. It forms the main gateway into and out of Central Western Europe. All eight of the countries in this region are very active in world trade. They have productive farms and factories, so they have much to sell.

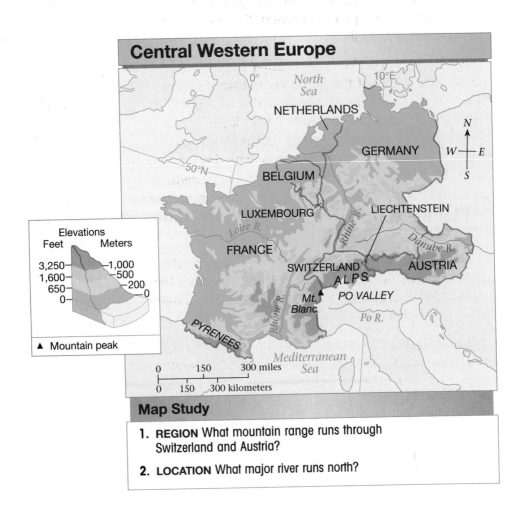

Central Western Europe

Map Study

1. **REGION** What mountain range runs through Switzerland and Austria?

2. **LOCATION** What major river runs north?

Europe's rivers form a network for moving goods from one place to another. The Rhine flows north through Switzerland, France, Germany, and the Netherlands. A canal connects it to the Rhône, which flows south to the Mediterranean Sea. The Rhine is connected to the Danube, which flows through seven countries to the Black Sea. Highways and railways complete the transportation system.

The main languages of Central Western Europe are German and French. English is also spoken. Many people speak more than one language. Switzerland has four official languages: French, Swiss German, Italian, and Romansh.

Much of Central Western Europe is a low plain. About 40 percent of the lands are below sea level. At one time, these lands were marshy. The Dutch built a system of earthen **dikes** to hold back the seawater. They also built drainage canals. Using windmills for power, they pumped out the water. The dry land could then be farmed. Today, electric pumps have replaced most of the windmills. However, the dikes must always be kept in good repair. Keeping the sea back remains a constant job.

In France and Germany, the plains slope gently upward. Farmers grow grapes, wheat, barley, and other grains. The coal and iron ore found there help make this a highly industrialized region.

Farther south, the plains end at a looming chain of mountains called the Alps. These are Europe's tallest mountains. The Alps stretch from southeastern France to western Austria. Mont Blanc, Europe's tallest peak, is located in the French Alps. Other mountain chains branch down from the Alps into southern Europe. A separate range, the Pyrenees, forms part of the border between France and Spain.

You Decide

In small countries where trade is important, people often speak more than one language. Why do you think this is the case?

The Alps

Throughout history, the Alps have served as a barrier to movement. People migrating north or south—as well as invading armies—tended to slow down when they reached the Alps. As a result, separate cultures developed on each side of this range. In the south, the Romans and Greeks dominated. In the north, Celtic and Germanic tribes filled the plains.

Life in the Alps today reflects the region's physical geography. For instance, Switzerland has more than 3,000 miles of railroads crisscrossing the country. The trains run on narrow tracks and can travel the steep, rugged mountains. Many railroad tunnels cut through the Alps.

People cannot do much farming in the Alps. There is too much rock and too little topsoil. Alpine dwellers, therefore, have always herded goats and sheep. Dairy products form a main part of the Alpine diet.

Level land is scarce in the Alps. Therefore, houses tend to be small. Houses also have steep, peaked roofs, which let snow slide off. Flat roofs might collapse under the weight of winter snow.

✓ Check Your Understanding

Write your answers in complete sentences.

1. Why are the countries of Central Western Europe active in world trade?

2. What are the main languages of Central Western Europe?

3. Why are Alpine dwellers mostly goat and sheep herders?

GEOGRAPHER'S TOOL KIT
Understanding Culture Maps

Cultural maps give information about the people who live in an area. These maps may have information on religions, languages, occupations, or age groups. To read these maps, first look at the title. Then, look at the key. Match the items listed in the key to the map to understand the information on the map.

Major Religions of Western Europe

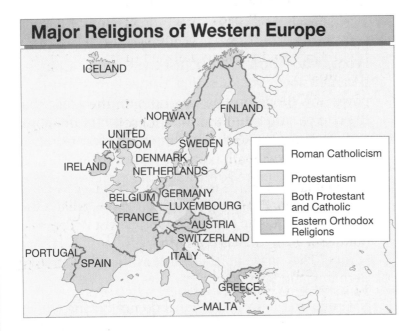

Key:
- Roman Catholicism
- Protestantism
- Both Protestant and Catholic
- Eastern Orthodox Religions

Answer the questions below.

1. What are the two most common religions in Western Europe?

2. What religion are most northern Europeans likely to practice?

CHALLENGE Northern Ireland is controlled by Britain. How does the map show this?

Apply the Skill

Use this map to write a short essay. Explain which religions are in which areas of Western Europe.

The Protestant Reformation

At the start of the sixteenth century, nearly everyone in Europe belonged to the Roman Catholic Church. Some people, however, felt that the Church had grown too interested in money.

In 1517, a German monk named Martin Luther wrote down his complaints and listed them in public. Suddenly, he found himself leading a religious rebellion. His followers soon included many German kings and princes.

Revolts against the Catholic Church began in other places. The whole upheaval was called the **Reformation**. People who "protested" against the Catholic Church became known as Protestants. Under Protestantism, power was thought to belong more to the people than the church. After the Reformation, much of the power and wealth of the Catholic Church moved to kings and the upper classes in the new Protestant areas. This helped lead to more governments chosen by the people.

Today, there are over 400 million Protestants in the world. The Catholic Church claims almost twice as many followers, but Protestants are strong in parts of Western Europe. They make up about half of the population in Germany and Switzerland.

Unlike Catholics, Protestants do not belong to one church. They have no overall leader but are divided into many religious groups, called denominations. For example, Lutherans, Presbyterians, Baptists, Unitarians, and Methodists are all Protestants. These denominations have somewhat different ideas, but they also share some general beliefs.

HISTORY FACT

Martin Luther was born in 1483 in Saxony, Germany. He was 34 when he listed his protests in public. He died in 1546.

Germany: Economic Powerhouse

Germany was one of the first industrialized countries. By 1900, it was competing with Britain and the United States. It was also a center of culture. Germans made great contributions to art, music, philosophy, and science.

World War II, however, left Germany a broken country. Its cities were leveled, and its people were starving. The winners of the war had divided Germany into two countries. West Germany joined the Western world as a democratic country. Its economy was based on **capitalism**. East Germany came under the control of the Soviet Union. A Communist government took over. The city of Berlin was also divided into East and West Berlin.

Celebrations

THE SALZBURG FESTIVAL

Europe has been home to many great composers. Perhaps the most well known one was Wolfgang Amadeus Mozart. Mozart was an Austrian composer born in 1756. He lived only 35 years, but he started composing music at the age of four. Even though his life was short, he created more than 600 musical works—many of them considered masterpieces.

The home in Salzburg where Mozart was born is now a museum. Every summer since 1920, the city of Salzburg celebrates Mozart's music. The Salzburg Festival brings to the city more than 150,000 visitors. At the festival, there are concerts, plays, and operas.

Critical Thinking How do festivals—such as, the Salzburg Festival—affect the local economy?

A puppeteer performs at the Salzburg Festival.

The two Germanys became a point of friction in the **cold war**, which was a tense competition between the United States and the Soviet Union. This rivalry was called a "cold" war because the two sides never battled each other directly. Each side tried to prove it had the better system.

East Germany did not do well. Its people grew poor. Its rulers used prisons and police to keep order. Many people tried to escape, which made communism look bad. The Soviets built a wall around East Berlin in 1961. The whole city was turned into a sort of prison. The Berlin Wall became a symbol for the cold war.

West Germany, by contrast, did well after the war. It used loans from the United States to rebuild quickly. Its standard of living rose to a high level. The country became an industrial power. It produced steel, automobiles, machinery, electronics, chemicals, and many other products.

In 1990, the cold war ended. East and West Germany joined together and became one country again. This **reunification** worried some people. They feared that a united Germany would build up its military. They worried that Germany might bully its neighbors as it had in the past.

So far, however, reunification has only caused trouble for Germany itself. This is because eastern Germany is much less developed than western Germany. Eastern German factories tend to be old and broken down. Many of the people there do not have jobs. Because western Germany has provided costly economic aid help to the eastern Germans, the German economy as a whole has been weakened.

Before reunification, West Germany had a shortage of factory workers. The country, therefore, welcomed workers, who were called guest workers, from Southern Europe and the Middle East.

Geography Fact

Germany has more than 80 million people. Its population is larger than that of any other country in Western Europe.

Germans cheer as the Berlin Wall falls.

Today, they are still living in Germany and remain an important part of the labor force. Now, the country has a large population of unemployed Germans, who are competing with the guest workers for jobs. Some Germans resent this situation and have begun to listen to people who preach racism and hatred. Attacks against guest workers have been on the rise.

✓ Check Your Understanding

Write your answers in complete sentences.

1. Why did Martin Luther rebel?

2. Why was Germany divided after World War II?

3. In what way has reunification hurt West Germany?

Paris: Fashion, Food, and Art

In English, the words *chic* and *vogue* mean "stylish" or "fashionable." That both words are French is no coincidence. Paris is not just the capital of France, but it is also the world capital for style and fashion.

Many people go to Paris to buy such items as clothes, jewelry, and perfume. Most of the world's best-known fashion designers work in this city. Every year, the designers hold fashion shows in Paris. Clothing manufacturers come to see what is about to become chic.

The French have also raised cooking to a high art. Cuisine, the French word for "kitchen," has come to stand for "fine food" in English. Paris has many famous cooking schools. The most respected one is the Cordon Bleu, which means "blue ribbon." Going to this school is considered to be a great honor.

Classic French cuisine developed in the 1600s. French chefs learned to use spices and herbs in complicated ways. They invented hundreds of delicate sauces made with ingredients such as cream, butter, eggs, wine, and fancy vinegar. Recently, the French have developed a new style of cooking that uses more fresh vegetables and fewer fats. In both classic and new French cooking, a meal must appeal to all of the senses. The look and texture of food matter as much as the flavor.

Paris also is well known for its art. In the 1800s, a style called impressionism was born in Paris. Artists such as Renoir, Monet, and Degas were among the first to work in this new style. Before impressionism, only certain subjects were thought proper for painters, who were supposed to show "important" scenes from literature, history, or religion. Painters did most of their work in studios and tried to make their paintings look like photographs.

The impressionist artists broke all the rules, however. They painted natural or everyday scenes and worked outdoors. Instead of worrying about carefully finished paintings, they tried to catch their first "impressions" of fleeting light and color. Instead of mixing colors, some impressionist artists experimented with dabs of bright, unmixed color on their canvases.

This Claude Monet painting was created in the impressionist style.

The impressionist artists renewed Paris's status as the center of the art world. Artists flocked there to study and to show their work. The impressionist artists also made "breaking the rules" a popular artistic idea. Dozens of new movements arose, each one breaking more rules. Most great European artists of the twentieth century spent at least some time in Paris. Today, Paris is no longer the capital of new art, but it is still home to many artists. It has good museums, which show many kinds of art. In fact, the Louvre in Paris is considered one of the world's greatest art museums.

Moving Toward European Unity

The countries of Europe are independent, but their economies are intertwined. Railroads, highways, and waterways run across borders. The countries have long depended on one another's goods and resources. New developments keep making travel in this region easier. For example, there is the Chunnel, which is a 31-mile-long tunnel that was dug beneath the English Channel. People can travel by high-speed train from England to France through the Chunnel. Improved transportation brings the European countries closer together.

In 1957, several European governments set up an organization called the Common Market to strengthen their economies. Member nations could trade freely. They did not have to pay fees for exporting and importing goods to each other. They could lend money to each other to develop new industries.

The Common Market developed into a strong economic force. Working as a group, European countries could compete with such economic powers as Japan and the United States.

In the 1980s, the Common Market was renamed the European Community (EC) and had 12 member nations. The EC still encouraged free trade, but it went further. It encouraged political unity among the member nations.

Today the EC is called the European Union, or EU. There are currently 15 member nations of the EU. In addition to promoting unity, the EU has been working to unify the monetary system. In the past, each country had its own **currency**, or type of money. In Germany, for example, people used deutsche marks to buy goods. In France, they used francs. When Germans wished to buy goods in France, they needed to change deutsche marks into francs. Having one currency for all EU nations, therefore, makes trade much easier. In 1999, the euro became the official currency of 11 member nations of the EU. It replaced each of their national currencies. Plans are underway to have all EU members use the euro in the near future.

Some citizens of EU countries, however, oppose such unity. They are afraid of losing their own national identity. Other Europeans worry about inequalities among EU members. In making decisions within the EU, for example, a small country like Belgium may not have as strong a voice as a large country like Germany.

✓ **Check Your Understanding**
Write your answers in complete sentences.

1. How did the impressionist artists break the rules?

2. What does the Common Market do?

3. Why does having one currency help the EU nations?

GEOGRAPHY IN YOUR LIFE
Reading Floor Plans

If you visit the Louvre, a museum in Paris, you will use a floor plan like the one below. A floor plan shows what attractions are in a building and where they are located. To use a floor plan, first look at the attractions available on each floor. Then, decide what you want to see. Finally, plan the route you want to take to visit the attractions.

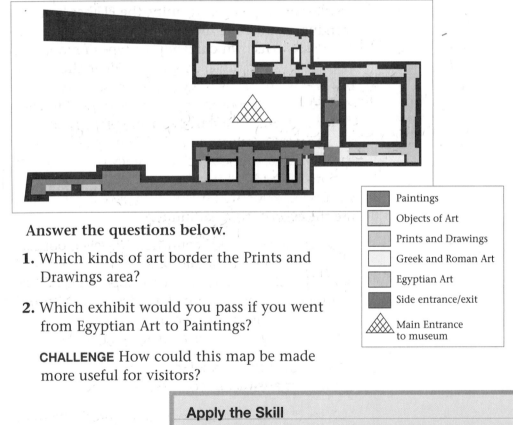

■	Paintings
■	Objects of Art
■	Prints and Drawings
□	Greek and Roman Art
■	Egyptian Art
■	Side entrance/exit
◬	Main Entrance to museum

Answer the questions below.

1. Which kinds of art border the Prints and Drawings area?

2. Which exhibit would you pass if you went from Egyptian Art to Paintings?

CHALLENGE How could this map be made more useful for visitors?

Apply the Skill

Create a floor plan of your school. The map should show people where different rooms and halls are located. You may want to label key places such as the gymnasium and the cafeteria.

Summary

The main countries of Central Western Europe are Germany, France, the Netherlands, Belgium, Luxembourg, Liechtenstein, Switzerland, and Austria. The region is highly industrialized and developed.

Much of the land in Belgium and the Netherlands is below sea level. A great plain stretches across northern Germany and France. The highest mountains in Europe are the Alps, which stretch from France to Austria.

Germany was divided into two countries after World War II and became one country again in 1990.

Impressionism, an important art style, began in France in the 1800s.

The European Union (EU) works to improve economic cooperation among its 15 member nations. It is now uniting Europe politically as well as economically.

capitalism

currency

Reformation

dike

reunification

Vocabulary Review

Write a term from the list that matches each definition below.

1. A barrier built to hold back seawater

2. The sixteenth-century religious movement which began the Protestant branch of Christianity

3. To come together after being divided

4. The type of money used in any particular country

5. A system in which land, factories, and businesses are privately owned and run for profit

Chapter Quiz

Write your answers in complete sentences.

1. What is an important waterway in Central Western Europe?

2. What group of French artists often worked outdoors instead of in a studio?

3. What allows people to travel quickly between England and France?

4. **Critical Thinking** Compare Germany before and after reunification.

5. **Critical Thinking** Why are some people against European unity?

Write About Geography

Complete the following activities.

1. Choose three countries from Central Western Europe. Make a chart that compares their languages, religion, and geography.

2. Write a speech explaining why your small European country should or should not join the European Union.

Group Activity

Each group member lives in a different Central Western European country. Each person writes a journal entry about what happened during one day in that country. An entry could describe an event that happened, a job that was performed, the scenery, or the day's cuisine. Put the journals in a book.

Portugal's warm climate attracts tourists to its seaside resorts. What other advantages are there to living near water?

Chapter 21 / Southern Europe

Words to Know

pesticide   a chemical used to kill insects or other pests

marine   having to do with the sea

philosopher   a thinker who seeks knowledge and wisdom

Renaissance   a creative period in European history, lasting roughly from 1400 to 1600 and marked by widespread interest in exploration, invention, and the arts

fascism   a form of government headed by a dictator who supports private property but strictly controls industry and workers

Places to Know

Greece

Italy

Portugal

Spain

Andorra

Learning Objectives

- Describe the economy of Southern Europe.
- Identify what the ancient Greeks and Romans contributed to modern Western culture.
- Describe the structure and history of the Roman Catholic Church.
- Tell why industrialization has come late to Southern Europe.
- Describe the history of democracy in Spain.

Countries of the Mediterranean

Geography Fact

The Apennines, which run through Italy, are a branch of the Alps. So are the Dinaric Alps, which run south into Greece. Together with the Alps, these ranges make up the Alpine System.

There are five major countries in Southern Europe. They are Greece, Italy, Portugal, Spain, and the tiny country of Andorra, which lies between Spain and France.

These countries share a warm, dry climate. Temperatures do not vary much from winter to summer. This type of climate is called Mediterranean because it is found along the whole coast of the Mediterranean Sea. Although Portugal borders on the Atlantic, it also has a Mediterranean climate.

Thousands of islands are scattered across the Mediterranean Sea. The largest ones are Sicily and Sardinia, which are part of Italy. Another large island is Malta. Greece has about 2,000 islands, including Crete and Rhodes. Only about 170 of the Greek islands are inhabited, however.

Compared to countries such as Germany and France, Southern Europe is poor. Southern Europe is less industrialized than Western Europe. Although its farms are less productive, more people work in agriculture in Southern Europe. However, they use less advanced technology than in Western Europe. Southern Europe has poor, rocky soil, which adds to the farmers' problems. In some places, people have been farming the same land for so long that they have used up the nutrients. Many people make their living by fishing. Yet, chemicals and other **pesticides** have been threatening the **marine** life of the Mediterranean Sea. Tourism is another important business in Greece, Italy, and Spain.

Directly north of Greece is a region called Eastern Europe. Greece is not considered part of this region because it was closely connected to Italy in ancient times. The Romans of Italy borrowed and developed Greek culture as they built an empire stretching from Spain through Greece into Asia.

Spain and Portugal are called Latin countries because they were so strongly influenced by Rome. They had their years of glory centuries after Rome had its. Both Spain and Portugal were great seafaring nations from the 1400s to the 1700s. Those years were remembered in the West as "the Age of Discovery." The Spanish conquered and settled much of the Americas. Portuguese sailors explored Africa and settled in South America.

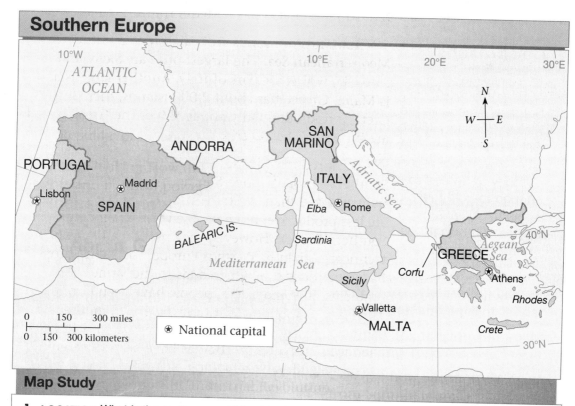

Southern Europe

Map Study

1. **LOCATION** What is the southernmost island in Southern Europe?
2. **PLACE** What country borders the Aegean Sea?

Gifts From Ancient Times

The civilizations of ancient Greece and Rome formed the basis of modern Western culture. The ancient Greeks created some of the world's finest temples, public buildings, and sculptures. Their main gifts to the modern West were stories and ideas. The Greeks created countless myths, or stories about their gods and goddesses. *The Iliad* and *The Odyssey*, two epic Greek poems, are still read throughout the world.

Celebrations

THE OLYMPIC GAMES

South of Athens lie the Pelopponesian Plains. Here, in 776 B.C., the first Olympic Games took place. The ancient Greek cities were more or less constantly at war, but they all agreed to stop fighting long enough to hold these games. Athletes, poets, musicians, and spectators gathered at a sacred place called Olympia.

The first time they gathered, there was only one event: a 210-yard race. After that, Greeks held Olympic Games every four years and added more events.

The first modern games were held in Athens, Greece in 1896. Now, the Olympics are held every four years in a different city around the world. They celebrate human strength and skill. They also stand for the idea that peaceful competition is better than violence.

Cathy Freeman, an Olympic track and field athlete, holds the Olympic Torch at the Opening Ceremony of the 2000 Olympics in Sydney, Australia.

Critical Thinking In what ways are the modern Olympics like the ancient games?

Drama began in ancient Greece. It grew out of certain Greek religious rituals, which were acted out on stage and then developed into plays. Some of these dramas, or plays, were tragedies, which told of sad and terrible events. Some of the plays were comedies, which had happy endings.

Greek **philosophers** wondered about many things, including nature. Out of their questions and ideas came much of modern science. The idea that natural forces rather than spirits cause disease came from Greek philosophers. Modern medicine is built on this idea.

Democracy first developed in certain Greek cities. There, citizens elected their own leaders. Greek democracy was not perfect. Greeks enslaved others and did not allow women or poor people to vote. Still, the Greeks were the inventors of the idea of democracy.

The Romans contributed much to modern, Western culture, too. They were great builders, and some of their roads and bridges still stand. They improved the science of plumbing. Roman aqueducts carried fresh water hundreds of miles, and Roman baths were legendary. Rome's main contribution to modern life was its system of law. The laws that the Romans made kept their complicated empire running smoothly. This system of law was logical, sensible, and fair. For example, the democratic idea that the law applies equally to all citizens comes to us from Roman law. The legal system of every Western country is based, at least in part, on Roman law.

✓ Check Your Understanding
Write your answers in complete sentences.

1. Which country are Sicily and Sardinia a part of?

2. Why are Spain and Portugal called Latin countries?

3. What are *The Iliad* and *The Odyssey*?

4. Where did democracy first develop?

Roman Catholicism and the Vatican

Almost everyone in Italy, Portugal, and Spain belongs to the Roman Catholic faith. In Southern Europe, only Greece is not a Catholic country. Worldwide, the Roman Catholic Church has 900 million members—more followers than any other Christian faith. More than 90 percent of the people in Luxembourg, France, and Belgium are Roman Catholics.

Vatican City is the headquarters of Catholicism. This city lies completely within Rome, the capital of Italy. Politically, however, Vatican City is not part of Italy. It is an independent state—the smallest one in Europe. In fact, it takes up only 0.17 square miles. Vatican City is governed by the Pope, the head of the Roman Catholic Church, and by the officials that he appoints. Vatican City has one of the oldest governments in the world. It has its own currency and post office. It even has its own army. Yet, there are only about 1,000 citizens in this independent state.

The Basilica of St. Peter is the main structure in Vatican City. It was built in the fourth century and is the world's oldest Christian church. During the **Renaissance**, the Catholic Church provided money to support great artists. One of these famous artists was Michelangelo, who painted religious scenes on the ceiling of the Sistine Chapel at the Vatican.

The Catholic Church is centered in Rome because 2,000 years ago the Middle East was part of the Roman Empire. In the fourth century, the ruler of Rome made Christianity the official religion of his empire. Most cities in the empire had churches, but they all agreed that the Church of Rome was the most important. The bishop of Rome became known as the Pope, or "father," of all Christians.

People from all over the world visit the Basilica of St. Peter in Vatican City.

Around that time, the Roman Empire was divided into two parts. Rome remained the capital of the Western Empire. Constantinople became the capital of the Eastern Empire. The church at Constantinople slowly pulled away from the one in Rome. By the eleventh century, the two churches had different rituals and different calendars. They also disagreed about the role of the Pope.

In 1054, the split became complete. Christians of the East called their church orthodox, which means "the right way." Followers of the Roman church continued to call their church catholic, which means "for everybody." Most Greeks belong to the Eastern Orthodox Church.

From Farm to Factory

$ Economics Fact

Italy has become more industrialized. In the late 1990s, some of Italy's top exports were production machinery, clothing, and motor vehicles.

The Industrial Revolution of the eighteenth and nineteenth centuries left Southern Europe nearly untouched. Physical geography had something to do with this. Southern Europe is mountainous. Roads and railways are hard to build, and few of the rivers can be used as waterways. Without a good transportation system, industrialization is difficult.

There were other problems, too. Spain, for example, had iron ore, but its coal was of poor quality. Therefore, it lacked some of the resources needed to make steel.

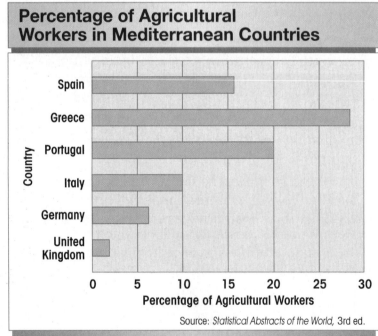

Percentage of Agricultural Workers in Mediterranean Countries

Source: *Statistical Abstracts of the World,* 3rd ed.

Graph Study

1. **REGION** Which country has the highest percentage of agricultural workers?

2. **INTERACTION** About what percentage of workers in Portugal work in agriculture?

Italy was divided into many small independent states that would not cooperate with each other. Until 1829, Greece was part of the Ottoman Empire. The Turkish people did not allow Greece to develop a modern economy.

When World War II began, the economy of Southern Europe was still based on farming. After the war ended, countries in this region worked hard to develop industries. Italy and Spain took advantage of their rushing rivers to build hydroelectric plants, and both countries found oil and gas within their borders. Spain is now a leading builder of ships and ship engines. Italy makes cars and chemicals. Both countries produce steel, textiles, and shoes. Greece and Portugal still lag in manufacturing. Greece, however, does have an important shipping industry and is building other factories.

In short, Southern Europe is now going through its own industrial revolution. As a result, people are leaving rural areas such as southern Italy and southern Spain, looking for jobs in the cities. Some have left the Mediterranean area altogether to work in places such as Germany and Scandinavia.

The trend from farm to factory has brought many social changes. For example, large, extended families are breaking up. Small families are more common.

You Decide

Only the older people are left in some small villages of Southern Europe. The young people have left to find jobs in the cities. How do you think this affects the region's culture?

Democracy in Spain

Spain became a Christian kingdom around 1500. That monarchy lasted almost 450 years. In 1931, the king stepped down to let Spain become a democratic republic. However, Spanish General Francisco Franco would not accept democracy and destroyed the new government in a savage civil war. Franco took over as dictator of Spain in 1939. He ruled for the next 36 years.

Franco's political party, called the Falange, believed in **fascism**. Under Franco, the Falange was Spain's only legal political party, and Roman Catholicism the only religion. Although Spain has several regions with their own languages, under Franco these languages were banned. Everyone had to speak the Castilian Spanish dialect. Workers were not allowed to form trade unions or go on strike. Franco's government controlled newspapers and other media. Anyone who criticized Franco was punished.

Franco's fascism made Spain an outcast nation for many years. The victors in World War II had suffered too much in fighting fascist governments like Franco's. Therefore, they were unwilling to help Spain after the war.

Franco wanted Spain to return to a monarchy after his death. He chose the new king: Juan Carlos, grandson of the last Spanish king. When Franco died in 1975, King Juan Carlos did something surprising. He supported democracy. Two years after Franco's death, Juan Carlos oversaw fair elections. Franco's followers won only 8 percent of the vote.

Juan Carlos remains popular among Spaniards. By his own choice, he has little or no official power. He serves only as a symbol for the nation. The elected parliament and prime minister are the real rulers. Spaniards can now express their differences in any language they choose. Spain has finally achieved democracy.

✓ **Check Your Understanding**
Write your answers in complete sentences.

1. What is Vatican City?

2. Why did the Orthodox and Roman Catholic churches split?

3. How is the industrialization of Southern Europe changing where people live?

When people think of the Mediterranean coast, they often picture clean beaches and blue water. In real life, scenes like this are fast disappearing. Rivers flowing into the Mediterranean Sea are carrying pesticides and industrial wastes. Southern European countries are dumping garbage and sewage into the water. Oil tankers on the Mediterranean Sea have also spilled raw petroleum on the surface of the water.

Because the Mediterranean Sea is closed in nearly all the way around, pollution that goes into the sea tends to stay there. The pollution is also threatening the fishing industry. Some species of marine life have disappeared. Many others are diseased. People who eat fish caught in the Mediterranean can become ill.

In theory, the problem can be solved. Wastes can be cleaned in sewage treatment plants. Dumping of garbage can be limited. To solve the pollution problem, the many countries that border the Mediterranean will have to cooperate—which will not be easy.

Answer the questions below.

1. Why do you think countries have such a hard time cooperating to solve a common problem?

2. What is one way that the governments of the area could cooperate to reduce pollution?

MAKE A DIFFERENCE
Most of us throw away more than we realize. That garbage ends up in landfills. For a week, keep a list of everything you throw away. After a week, look at your list. Circle what you could recycle, reduce, or reuse.

Summary
Spain, Portugal, Italy, Greece, and Andorra are the main countries of Southern Europe.
Southern Europe has a Mediterranean climate: warm and dry with little change in temperature from winter to summer. The economy of Southern Europe is based mainly on farming, fishing, and tourism. Recently, however, the region has become more industrialized.
The heritage of ancient Greece includes art, mythology, drama, and literature. The Greeks laid the basis for modern science and developed the idea of democracy.
The ancient Romans built great roads, highways, aqueducts, and plumbing systems. All modern legal systems in the West are based at least partly on Roman law.
The Roman Catholic Church is a highly structured Christian church with over 900 million members.
Spain moved peacefully from a fascist system to a democratic one in 1975.

marine
philosopher
fascism
pesticide
Renaissance

Vocabulary Review

Complete each sentence with a term from the list.

1. A chemical used to kill insects or other pests is a _____ .

2. Sewage in the Mediterranean Sea threatens _____ life.

3. A creative period in European history is the _____ .

4. A form of government headed by a dictator who supports private property but strictly controls industry and workers is _____ .

5. A thinker who seeks knowledge and wisdom is a _____ .

Chapter Quiz

Write your answers in complete sentences.

1. What is a Mediterranean climate?

2. Is Southern Europe more or less industrialized than the countries north of the Alps?

3. When did most industries in Southern Europe develop?

4. Critical Thinking How has ancient Greece influenced modern western culture?

5. Critical Thinking Why was Southern Europe slow to become industrialized?

Write About Geography

Complete the following activities.

1. Create a poster designed to show the contributions of ancient Greece and Rome to life today.

2. Write a short essay that discusses how the Olympic Games support the idea of peaceful competition.

Group Activity

Create a cultural map of Southern Europe. First, trace a map of Southern Europe. Then, decide what you want to include. Use colors or symbols to show cultural differences such as languages, religions, and occupations.

Unit 6 Review

Comprehension Check
Answer each question in a complete sentence.

1. How did the Industrial Revolution change the social structure of England?

2. What is a welfare state?

3. How has Germany been affected by its reunification?

4. How has the European Union affected the economy of Western Europe?

Building Your Skills
Answer each question in a complete sentence.

1. What is the best way to use a tourist map?

2. Describe where Scandinavia is in Europe.

3. What are some things you might find on a cultural map?

4. What sea do most of the countries of southern Europe border?

Where Is It?
Write the name of the place based on the information below.

1. The island in the British Isles claimed by two countries

2. The country in Scandinavia whose people came from Asia and whose language is related to Hungarian

3. The country that was reunited in 1990

4. The country where democracy first developed

Writing an Essay
Answer one of the following essay topics.

1. Explain why the Industrial Revolution occurred.

2. Explain why the sea is so important in Scandinavia.

3. Describe the changes that occurred in Germany in the twentieth century.

4. Explain how the economy of southern Europe became more industrialized.

Geography and You

What are the economic, political and cultural similarities between the European Union and the United States? What are the differences?

Unit 7 ▶ Russia and Eastern Europe

EASTERN EUROPE

RUSSIA

FORMER SOVIET STATES

Russia is the largest country in the world. What might be some of the challenges of governing such a large area?

TRAVEL LOG

Take note of the art you see in each chapter of this unit. Write your reactions to each piece of art. What similarities do the works of art have in this region? How is each unique?

Ukrainian hand-painted egg

This photograph shows the inside of the largest department store in Moscow. This building was once used to trade goods. What would life be like if you had to trade goods rather than buy them?

Chapter 22 · Russia

Words to Know

permafrost	permanently frozen layer of soil just beneath the Earth's surface
steppe	land that is dry, flat, and covered with grass
estate	a large area of land or property usually owned by one person or family
serf	a peasant who cannot legally leave the land on which he or she works
collective farm	a large farm run by a group of people working together under government supervision
glasnost	a policy that allows open discussion about Soviet life and politics
perestroika	a policy that allows the rebuilding of the Soviet economy
coup	the sudden violent overthrow of top government leaders by another group of leaders

Places to Know

Russia

Siberia

Ural Mountains

Moscow

St. Petersburg

Learning Objectives

- Describe the physical geography and climate of Russia.

- Describe Siberia and its role in Russian culture.

- Explain why communism failed in the Soviet Union.

- Outline the history of the Russian Orthodox Church.

- Describe Russia's heritage.

A Country in Two Continents

Russia is the biggest country in the world. The entire United States could fit into Russia with room left over for Western Europe. From north to south, Russia covers about 2,800 miles. From east to west, it covers more than 5,600 miles. Russia stretches across 11 time zones. People on the western border are waking up as people at the eastern edge are having dinner.

The most outstanding landform of this region is a huge, low plain. This plain is divided by the Ural Mountains, which run north and south.

The Ural Mountains are little more than high, gentle hills. They have never served as much of a barrier to movement. Even so, they are important to Russia's geography. The Urals divide the region into two parts. Russia west of the Urals is considered part of Europe. Russia east of the Urals is considered part of Asia. The larger eastern part is called Siberia.

In its far north, Russia has a polar climate. This part of the country borders the Arctic Ocean, which is full of ice most of the time. The weather is bitterly cold throughout most of the year—too cold for trees and most other plants to grow. The soil is usually frozen. In fact, a layer just beneath the surface stays frozen all year round. This layer, called **permafrost**, never melts. However, the ground above the permafrost melts in the summer. When it does, the moisture has nowhere to go. It just sits on the ground, making the soil soft.

Most of Russia has a continental climate—that is, the seasons are sharply different. Summers are warm but short. Winters are long and very cold. This zone gets just enough rain to support vast forests. In the north, most of the trees are evergreens. Farther south, broad-leafed trees, such as elms and maples, are common.

A small part of southern Russia lies in a very dry zone. The winters are bitter, but the summers are long and hot. There is only enough rain to support grass, not trees. This area is part of the **steppes**, a vast grassland.

Climate has greatly affected Russian life. As you know, ports are important to the development of trade. Most of Russia's ocean ports, however, are icebound in the winter. Lack of ports has limited Russia's contacts with the world and has restricted Russian trade and economic growth. Throughout history, Russian leaders have expanded their country in order to gain control of warm-water ports.

Siberia

If Siberia were an independent country, it would be the world's largest. It is about twice the size of European Russia. Yet it has less than a third as many people because of its harsh climate. Cold winters and short summers make farming difficult in Siberia. The enormous forests make grazing all but impossible. Warm housing is expensive to build. The Yakuts, a people of central Siberia, wear six layers of woolen clothing to keep warm. Their houses have triple window panes. They often leave their car engines running, or else the engines might freeze or crack.

Ever since the 1700s, Russian leaders have used Siberia as a prison. Between 1929 and 1953, millions of prisoners were sent to the heart of this vast land. Some were criminals, but many were political prisoners—that is, they were punished for their political ideas. Siberian "prisons" did not need walls or fences. Prisoners could not escape. There was simply nowhere to go.

Siberia is rich with resources such as coal, oil, tin, iron, diamonds, and many other minerals. For the past century, governments in Russia have been trying to develop this region and use it as more than just a prison.

HISTORY FACT

In 1905, the Trans-Siberian Railroad was completed. It runs 5,778 miles, from European Russia to the Pacific coast.

Great rivers such as the Ob, the Yenisey, and the Lena flow north across Siberia. Some of the world's largest hydroelectric plants have been built on these rivers. Dozens more are being constructed.

During World War II, many Russian factories were moved to Siberia, where they could not be bombed by Russia's enemy, Nazi Germany. After the war, the government in Russia continued to develop these industries. Siberia now has steel mills, chemical factories, and some of Russia's top science centers.

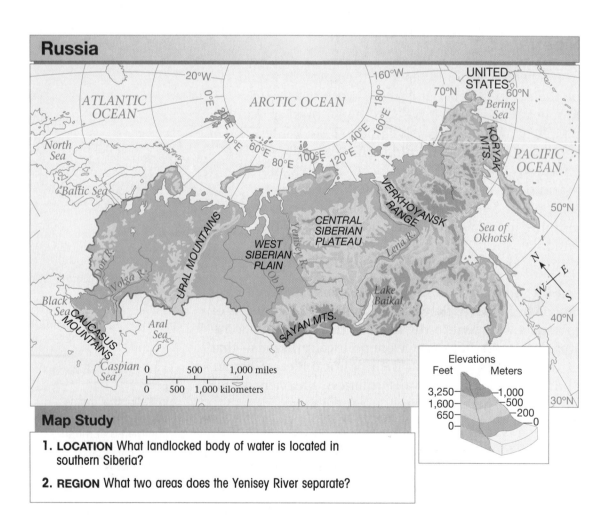

Russia

Map Study

1. **LOCATION** What landlocked body of water is located in southern Siberia?

2. **REGION** What two areas does the Yenisey River separate?

Early Russia

Long ago, the forests of Russia were home to scattered bands of Slavic people. In the 700s and 800s, Vikings from Scandinavia began moving south through these lands. Legend has it that certain Slavic groups invited the Vikings to be their rulers. These Vikings united the Slavic groups, and in the process the Vikings took on Slavic ways. Some experts say the word *Russian* comes from Rurik, the name of a Viking prince. Others say it comes from Rukhs-as, the name of a Slavic group.

The first Russian kingdom rose in the late 800s. It was centered in Kiev, a city on the Dnieper River. Mongol groups from the east, however, destroyed Kiev and other Russian cities in A.D. 1238. They ruled Russia for about 250 years. As the Mongols grew weak, another Russian city—Muscovy, now called Moscow—began to grow powerful. The Russians of Moscow overthrew the Mongols in 1480. One Russian prince, Ivan the Third, called himself czar, a Russian version of the Latin word Caesar, meaning "emperor." From that time on, the Russians of Moscow began to build an empire. By the 1800s, the Russian czar ruled an empire that stretched from the Arctic Ocean to the Black Sea. In just 70 years, the czar added all of Siberia to his empire. As the Russian empire grew, many non-Slavic people found themselves living within its borders. The Yakuts of Siberia are just one example. Most of the people of Russia, however, were—and still are—Slavic.

✔ Check Your Understanding

Write your answers in complete sentences.

1. How has climate affected Russian life?

2. Why did Siberian prisons need no fences?

3. Why did Moscow become the center of Russia?

GEOGRAPHY IN YOUR LIFE
Reading Weather Maps

When you look at a weather map, first look at the key to see what the symbols mean. Temperature is often shown by color. A line with arrows represents a cold front—and cold weather. Half circles represent a warm front—and warm weather. The arrows and half circles show which way the cold or warm air is heading.

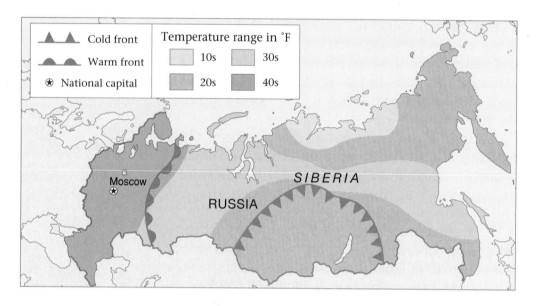

Answer the questions below.

1. About how warm is the city of Moscow?

2. Is the weather warmer near the capital or near Siberia?

   CHALLENGE Can the people living south of Russia expect warmer or colder weather to come?

Apply the Skill

Look at the weather map of your state in the newspaper. Discuss with classmates what the weather map tells you.

The Workers' State

In 1917, a Communist revolution took place in Russia. Communism is the name of a political and economic system. Communists believe that workers should own the means of production—land, buildings, machines, and technology.

Communist thinkers believe that under their system, governments and borders will disappear, and workers will rule. Until that day, however, they believe the government should own and run everything for the common good. They also say a Communist political party should run the government. These ideas were developed by the German philosopher Karl Marx. In Germany, however, communism never made much progress. It was in Russia that the world's first Communist revolution took place.

Before the revolution, Russia was organized into huge **estates** that were owned by nobles with titles like "Count" and "Prince." Most of the people in Russia were **serfs**, who were tied by law to the land. Serfs could not leave the estate where they lived. If the owner of the estate sold his property to someone else, the serfs were sold as well.

In the 1800s, some educated army officers and students in Russia began to complain about these injustices. The czar had many of these people killed or sent to Siberia. Still, protests grew.

In 1917, revolts broke out and the czar was overthrown. Nine months later, a Communist government took power. The Communists had to fight armies raised by the nobles and paid for by capitalist nations of the West. After winning, the Communists changed the name of Russia to the Union of Soviet Socialist Republics, or U.S.S.R. Most people called it the Soviet Union.

HISTORY FACT

Catherine the Great was one of Russia's most powerful rulers. When the serfs revolted in the 1770s, they were crushed by her army.

The Communists ended private ownership of land. They started **collective farms** on which farmers worked for the government. Soviet leaders wanted to quickly turn their country into an industrial power. They built many factories and started making cars, airplanes, tractors, and other heavy machinery.

Soviet Communists believed in taking care of the basic needs of all of the citizens. The Communists built a grand system of public transportation. They built schools and made education available to everyone. They also made health care and housing available to everyone. Housing, however, was built as cheaply and quickly as possible. Style and luxury were not considered important—or even desirable.

Soviet leaders were afraid of enemies abroad. After all, Western nations had tried to defeat them in the revolution. Later, in World War II, Russia was invaded by Germany and suffered more casualties than any other nation—about 30 million. For these reasons, the Soviet Union developed its weapon program and built one of the strongest armies in the world.

Soviet leaders also feared enemies at home. Between 1929 and 1953, a dictator named Joseph Stalin ruled the Soviet Union. He organized a secret police force called the Committee of State Security, or KGB. Under Stalin, anyone who spoke against the government was arrested. Stalin's policies and the KGB were responsible for the deaths of some 20 million Soviet citizens.

Communism in Russia began with the 1917 revolution.

The New Russian Revolution

By the 1980s, the economy of the Soviet Union was failing. Workers were reluctant to work hard, because the system did not reward their efforts. To make matters worse, the Soviets went to war in Afghanistan. As the war in this tiny nation dragged on, many people lost confidence in the Soviet government.

In 1985, a new leader named Mikhail Gorbachev came to power. He tried to change the Soviet system. His policies included **glasnost**, which means "openness" in Russian. For the first time in years, people were free to say what they thought without fear of punishment. Another policy was **perestroika**, which means "restructuring." Under this policy, people could start private businesses.

As the system opened up, many non-Russian ethnic groups within the Soviet Union grew restless. Violence broke out in some of the individual republics. New leaders appeared, demanding faster change. Old leaders insisted on slower change. Some Communists refused to accept any of Gorbachev's policies.

In August 1991, a handful of Communist Party leaders tried to overthrow Gorbachev. The Soviet people, however, rallied behind Gorbachev and other similar leaders. Thousands of people poured into the streets of Moscow to protest this **coup**.

One of these new leaders was Boris Yeltsin, who would soon become the first democratically elected president of Russia. Yeltsin climbed on a tank in front of a government building and ordered the army to arrest the leaders of the coup. The army obeyed Yeltsin, and the coup failed.

Remember
Democracies are representative governments elected by the people.

Gorbachev continued as official leader of the Soviet Union and the Communist Party. Within a year, however, the Communist Party lost control over the government and the people. One by one, each of the republics, including Russia, declared their independence from the Communist Party and the Soviet Union. A new Commonwealth of Independent States replaced the old Soviet Union. However, Lithuania, Latvia, and Estonia did not join the new organization. In December 1991, with no political party or union to lead, Gorbachev stepped down from power.

Economics Fact

In 1998, Russia's economy was in severe crisis. It began to rebound the next year, but the country's economy is still weak.

So far, political changes in the former Soviet states have only made the economic problems worse. Russia has asked the world for financial help. The United States and some Western European countries have provided some money and may provide more. However, Western leaders have questions about the political struggles in the new states. For example, who will control the atomic bombs and other weapons that the Soviets built?

Spotlight On

ST. PETERSBURG

It has been called Russia's crown jewel. Without a doubt, St. Petersburg is one of the most beautiful cities in Europe, a city of graceful palaces and grand cathedrals. The city is a cultural center for Russia. It is still home to Russia's world-famous ballet dancers and an inspiration to Russian writers.

The dome of St. Isaac's Cathedral, shown in the center of this photograph, is a landmark in St. Petersburg.

The Russian czar Peter the Great ordered workers to begin constructing the city in 1703. It was an expensive order. Almost 100,000 people died of cold and hunger during its construction. In 1712 the city became the capital of Russia, which it remained for two centuries.

The name of the city has changed throughout Russian history. Peter the Great named the city for his patron saint. During World War I, the Germanic name was changed to Petrograd. When Soviet leader Vladimir Lenin died in 1924, the name changed to Leningrad. In 1991, even before Russia became its own country, the city became St. Petersburg once more.

Critical Thinking Why do you think the city was renamed St. Petersburg instead of given a new name?

The Russian Orthodox Church

Communists believe that the only world is the one you can touch. Religion, they think, is largely a trick that focuses workers' attention on life after death instead of on everyday life. The Soviet government tried to discourage religion. To some extent it succeeded: About 60 percent of Russia's population today practice no religion at all. About 25 percent, however, still belong to the Russian Orthodox Church. Now that communism has fallen, Russian churches are opening up again.

The first Christian missionaries drifted into Eastern Europe in the 700s or 800s. Because the Slavs had no written language, the Christian monks invented one and used it to write a Slavic Bible. The alphabet they invented is called Cyrillic, after Saint Cyril, one of the monks. Russian is still written in this alphabet.

In A.D. 988, Prince Vladimir of Kiev became a Christian and ordered all his subjects to become Christians, too. Russians followed the teachings of the Orthodox Church in Constantinople, the capital of the Byzantine Empire. For centuries, Russians looked to Constantinople, or "New Rome," as a religious center.

Then, in the 1400s, Muslim Turks conquered Constantinople and overran much of Eastern Europe. Most Orthodox Christians came under Muslim rule. Only Russia remained independent and powerful. Many Russians felt that the Orthodox Christian world had now moved to Russia. They called Moscow "the Third Rome."

The Russian Orthodox Church became an independent church, closely tied to the idea of a Russian nation. Russian writers and thinkers began to use phrases such as "holy Russia." In fact, some felt Russia now had a sacred job—to protect and nurture the Orthodox Church.

Orthodox Christians often hang icons in their homes and churches to promote religious teachings.

Champions of Sports

Under communism, sports were given special importance. Soviet leaders thought that strong athletes proved the superiority of communism. In Soviet society, successful athletes were given special benefits, such as larger apartments. The government paid for athletes' training. Coaches tried to find young children who were likely to become great ice skaters, gymnasts, runners, or other sports stars.

The athletes were trained for international competition such as the Olympics. Often, children were separated from their families for years while they trained. Because of their efforts, the Soviet Union was always a top medal winner in the Olympics. Now that the Soviet Union has broken up, individual states are responsible for training their athletes.

A Cultural Treasure House

According to Communist policy, art had to serve the political goals of the party. Artists were ordered to paint scenes from real life and to always portray workers as heroes. This type of art was called socialist realism.

Yet the Soviets were surrounded by a rich artistic heritage. In fact, Soviet leaders met in a medieval fort called the Kremlin. Within the walls of the Kremlin are fine examples of Russian architecture from czarist times, including palaces and churches. Many of the churches have domes shaped like onions that come to a point. Some of the church walls are covered from floor to ceiling with bright paintings of religious subjects.

Music and literature flourished in Russia before 1917. The works of Russian composers are admired around the world. Peter Tchaikovsky, for example, is a well-known Russian composer.

Construction was begun on St. Basil's Cathedral in Moscow in 1555 and completed in 1679.

Some of the world's finest novels were written by Russian writers, such as Leo Tolstoy and Fyodor Dostoyevski. Modern writers have a large audience in Russia, too. Popular Russian poets, for example, draw crowds of 50,000 and more to their readings.

Another important Russian art form is classical ballet. This elegant style of dancing developed in Italy and France. It was brought to Russia in the early 1700s, a period when Russian royalty took great interest in the culture of Western Europe.

The first dancers were serfs. In 1738, the czar's court set up a ballet school to train dancers. For 200 years, this school attracted some of Europe's best teachers. The Imperial Ballet eventually became the Kirov Ballet Company.

The Soviet government supported ballet. Both the Kirov Ballet and Moscow's Bolshoi Ballet gained in strength during the Soviet era. Both are still very much alive today.

✓ Check Your Understanding

Write your answers in complete sentences.

1. What was a serf in Russia?

2. Explain the policy of perestroika.

3. Describe the Communist view of religion.

4. What would you see inside the Kremlin?

Summary

Russia is the largest country in the world. A large central plain spreads over western Russia. The Ural Mountains separate the European plain from the Siberian plain, which is in Asia.
The first Russian kingdom, Kiev, developed during the 800s.
In 1917, the Russian czar was overthrown, and a new Communist government was formed. This was the start of the Soviet Union.
Communism brought industry, technology, and education to Russia. However, the Communist government limited people's freedoms. In 1991, the Soviet Union fell apart.
Historically, most Russians have belonged to the Russian Orthodox Church, and about 25 percent of the Russian people still belong to it.
The Russian artistic heritage includes elaborate church architecture, widely read novels, and well-known classical ballet.

Vocabulary Review

Write *true* or *false*. If a statement is false, change the underlined term to make it true.

1. A policy that allows open discussion about Soviet life and politics is called <u>perestroika</u>.

2. The sudden violent overthrow of top government leaders by another group of leaders is called a <u>coup</u>.

3. A peasant who cannot legally leave the land on which he or she works is a <u>serf</u>.

4. An <u>estate</u> is a large farm run by a group of people working together under government supervision.

5. A permanently frozen layer of soil just beneath the Earth's surface is called <u>permafrost</u>.

Chapter Quiz

Write your answers in complete sentences.

1. What is the name of Gorbachev's policy that was supposed to mend Russia's economy?

2. Who was the first czar of Russia?

3. Why did the Soviet Union develop one of the strongest armies in the world?

4. **Critical Thinking** Why does Russia suffer from a shortage of warm-weather ports?

5. **Critical Thinking** Why did Russians call Moscow the "Third Rome"?

Write About Geography

Complete the following activities.

1. In Soviet art, workers were heroes. Write a short story or draw a picture in which a worker is the hero.

2. Create a poster that explains how Russia moved from communism to democracy.

Group Activity

Russia has had a dramatic history. With your group, create a performance that explains, through short scenes, the important events in Russian history.

The land in Eastern Europe, such as this area in Lithuania, is good for farming. Yet more people hold service or industry jobs than jobs in farming. Why do you think this is?

Chapter 23

Some Former Soviet States

Words to Know

bureaucracy	any organization made up of appointed officials organized into many ranks
capital good	a manufactured product—such as steel, tractors, or factory machinery—used to produce other products
consumer good	a product that satisfies people's wants or needs
privatization	the act of private companies taking over farms, factories, and other businesses
chernozem	a rich, black soil, which is common in cool or dry climates
cease-fire	an agreement to stop fighting

Places to Know

Baltic States

Baltic Sea

Belarus

Ukraine

Moldova

Caucasus Mountains

Transcaucasian States

Learning Objectives

- Tell how the republics of the former Soviet Union are changing economically.

- Describe the three newly independent Baltic states.

- Describe the culture and economy of Belarus, Ukraine, and Moldova.

- Describe the three former Soviet states in the Caucasus Mountains.

- Identify characteristic folk dances of some former Soviet states.

The Breakup of the Soviet Union

The Soviet Union was made up of 15 separate republics, or states. By December 1991, the Soviet Union no longer existed. All of the states that were part of the Soviet Union became independent, self-governing countries. You will read about nine of the former Soviet states in this chapter. Immediately following the breakup of the Soviet Union, 12 of these countries formed the Commonwealth of Independent States.

Former Republics of the Soviet Union

Name of Republic	Year Gained Independence	Location
Estonia Latvia Lithuania	September 6, 1991 September 6, 1991 September 6, 1991	Baltic Europe
Belarus Moldova Ukraine	August 25, 1991 August 27, 1991 December 1, 1991	Eastern Europe
Russia	August 24, 1991	Europe and Asia
Georgia Azerbaijan Armenia	April 9, 1991 August 30, 1991 September 23, 1991	Transcaucasian Asia
Kyrgyzstan Uzbekistan Tajikistan Turkmenistan Kazakhstan	August 31, 1991 August 31, 1991 September 9, 1991 October 27, 1991 December 16, 1991	Central Asia

Chart Study

1. How many countries in Eastern Europe gained their independence in 1991?

2. Which former republic was first to gain independence?

The purpose of the Commonwealth was to establish common rules for all of its member states in such areas as economic policy, foreign relations, and the military. However, from the beginning, the Commonwealth's member countries disagreed about many things. The Commonwealth still exists today, but its power over its members' states is reduced.

Remember
A commonwealth is a group of self-governing states.

Independent Republics

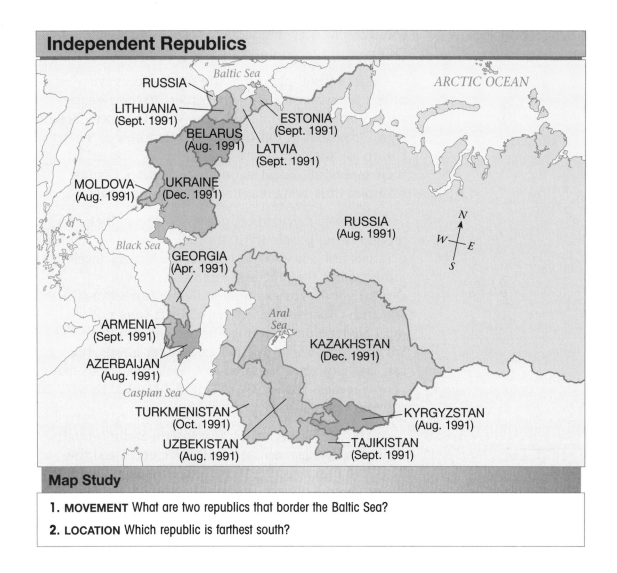

Map Study

1. **MOVEMENT** What are two republics that border the Baltic Sea?

2. **LOCATION** Which republic is farthest south?

From Communism to Capitalism

You Decide

What might be some benefits of central planning?

Communism changed the structure of society throughout Soviet-controlled lands. Under communism, the state owned everything, including factories, businesses, shops, banks, and land. All decisions were made by a small group of people in Moscow called the Central Committee. These people were the top leaders of the Communist Party. Not only did they make laws and set policies, but they also made economic decisions. For example, they decided what each farm should grow. This type of decision making was called central planning.

Under central planning, the top leaders gave orders to assistants, who gave orders to their helpers and so on, down to the workers. When workers faced a problem, they could not solve it themselves. They had to ask their supervisors what to do, who asked their supervisors—and so on, up to the top. Central planning thus created a huge, slow **bureaucracy**.

A centrally planned economy, however, does not produce what people want. It produces what the central planners feel is needed. Therefore, the Soviets developed industry, but they focused mainly on producing **capital goods**. For example, they made a lot of steel and heavy machinery. These products were not what most Soviet citizens wanted or needed. People in the Soviet Union began to crave **consumer goods**, such as cars and clothing. A shortage of consumer goods made people restless in the Soviet Union. Many of these shortages persist today.

In the 1930s, Soviet dictator Joseph Stalin brought agriculture under central control. He organized the land into big collective farms and even bigger state farms. The collective farms, run by groups of villagers, were controlled indirectly by the government.

The state farms were run directly by the government. Communist Party officials told farmers what to plant and how to farm. Orders came from the leaders in Moscow, who knew little or nothing about local soil, water, and other conditions. As a result, their ideas often did not work. Yet when farms produced poorly, the farmers were punished.

At first, many farmers protested and refused to grow anything at all. Millions of people in the 1930s in the Soviet Union starved as a result. Stalin responded by having millions of farmers killed or sent to Siberia.

In the end, Stalin did bring all farms under central control. Unfortunately, the state farms did poorly, and the collective farms did only a little better. Workers on the collective farms, however, were allowed to work tiny, private garden plots. They could sell whatever they managed to grow in their spare time. These little gardens became the most productive farms in the Soviet Union. Although these gardens took up less than 1 percent of the land, they produced about 25 percent of all farm products.

Now that Soviet communism has ended, many leaders favor **privatization**. They are urging private companies to take over all of the farms, factories, and other businesses. However, after three generations of communism, this has been hard to do. People who grew up under communism may not like central planning, but they are used to it. Few of these people have the skills needed to start and run their own businesses. These skills cannot be developed overnight. At present, therefore, some form of central planning continues in most of the former Soviet republics.

Economics Fact

By 1990, the Soviet Union had almost 30,000 collective farms and more than 18,000 state farms.

The Baltic States

Estonia, Latvia, and Lithuania are located at the edge of the Baltic Sea. Because of the sea, the region has a milder climate than Russia does. The Baltic ports do not freeze and are open for trade all year round.

The Baltic states were some of the most developed areas of the Soviet Union. All three states have a well-educated work force. Nearly half of the people live in cities rather than rural areas.

In A.D. 1200, a German military-religious group, the Teutonic Knights, conquered Estonia and Latvia and ruled for 200 years. Later, at various times, Sweden and Denmark each ruled these countries. In 1940, the Soviet Union took over these independent Baltic countries. After that, many Russians settled in the Baltic states. In Latvia, Russians and Belarussians make up about 39 percent of the population. Russians form a large minority in Estonia, too. Under the Soviets, everyone had to learn Russian. As a result, Russian is widely spoken.

Latvia has almost no natural resources, so it imports raw materials from other former Soviet republics. With these raw materials, Latvia manufactures products to sell. Latvia produces steel, ships, cement, fertilizer, and textiles, among other things. At one time, it was known as the "workshop" of the Soviet Union. After independence, Latvian manufacturers began to look for markets in the West. So far, however, they have not been able to compete fully with other European countries.

Estonia is near Finland. The Estonians are ethnically related to the Finns. During the Soviet era, many Western products were brought into Estonia through Finland. Compared to other states that once belonged to the Soviet Union, Estonia has a high standard of living. Estonia's cities, with their ancient stone buildings, are considered quite beautiful.

Ancient stone buildings of Estonia help make this country one of the most beautiful in the former Soviet Union.

Estonia has a good deal of industry and is also strong in agriculture. Grain, vegetables, and livestock are the main farm products.

During the 1300s, Lithuania was one of the most powerful states in central Europe. It included what is today Belarus and much of Ukraine. Later, however, it became part of Poland. Even today, about 7 percent of the people in Lithuania are Polish. Most religious Lithuanians belong to the Roman Catholic Church, brought to this area by Polish people.

Russia began taking Lithuanian land in the 1600s and took it over completely in 1940. A nationalist movement arose in Lithuania, however. In 1990, Lithuania became the first republic to declare its independence from the Soviet Union, although the Soviets did not grant freedom until 1991. Today the country has industries that include shipbuilding, and manufacturing. It must, however, import oil and other energy resources.

You Decide

The Baltic states would like to become members of the European Union (EU). How do you think this would affect their cultures?

White Russia, Little Russia, and Moldova

South of the Baltic states are the republics of Belarus, Ukraine, and Moldova. Russians, Ukrainians, and Belarussians are all Slavic peoples. Their customs and languages are not quite the same, but they are similar. Ukraine, in fact, has sometimes been called "Little Russia." Kiev, the capital of the first Russian kingdom, is a city in Ukraine. The Belarussians, too, are closely related to the Russians. In Russian, "belo" means "white." Belarussian means "white Russian."

Traditionally, Belarus and Ukraine have been agricultural. Potatoes, beets, and other root crops grow well in Belarus. In fact, Belarus is sometimes known as the "land of potatoes." It also has important industrial centers, such as Minsk, where factories produce machines, tools, and other goods.

Farms are common in the countryside of western Ukraine.

Ukraine is the third largest of the 15 republics. Next to Russia, it has the highest population. Ukrainian farmers grow mainly wheat and other grains. During the Soviet era, Ukraine was known as the "breadbasket" of the Soviet Union. Russia depended on Ukrainian wheat. It also depended on Ukrainian industries. About 25 percent of the Soviet Union's industrial goods were produced in Ukraine.

Ukraine was able to industrialize rapidly because of its rich resources, such as oil, natural gas, and iron. Ukraine also provided hydroelectric power to the Soviet Union. The Soviets were not eager to accept Ukrainian independence. Today, Russia is cut off from Ukrainian grain. As a result, Russia faces dangerous food shortages.

The steppes found in southern Russia actually begin in Ukraine. The steppes stretch from the Carpathian Mountains in western Ukraine through Russia and into Siberia and Mongolia in the east. Wild grasses grow so thickly on these plains that early Slavic settlers could not keep the land cleared. They used the land mainly to graze livestock. Because of the dry climate, the grasses here decay slowly when they die. The decaying grasses create a rich, dark soil called **chernozem**. This type of soil is what makes Ukrainian farmland so productive.

West of Ukraine is the republic of Moldova. Romanians settled Moldova many centuries ago. Between 1415 and 1991, however, it was ruled mainly by Turks and by Russians. After World War I, Moldova joined Romania briefly. However, Russia regained control of the territory in 1944. Even so, most Moldovans consider themselves Romanian. Their main language is Romanian. Moldova also has fairly large populations of Ukrainians and Russians. These groups worried when Moldova declared its independence from the Soviet Union in 1991. They feared that Moldova would become part of Romania again. So far, this has not happened.

Remember

Steppes are dry flatlands with few trees but lots of tall, wild grass.

HISTORY FACT

According to legend, Prince Dragos of Transylvania founded Moldova in the fourteenth century. He named the country after a local mountain stream.

✓ Check Your Understanding

Write your answers in complete sentences.

1. When did the Soviet Union cease to exist?

2. What are the differences between state farms and collective farms?

3. Why is chernozem important to Ukraine?

GLOBAL ISSUES
Chernobyl

In 1983, the building of a nuclear power plant was completed in Chernobyl, Ukraine. Its purpose was to provide electricity to the region. Three years later, an explosion in the plant killed 32 people and allowed radioactive material to escape.

That was only the beginning of the disaster. Winds blew the radioactive material from Chernobyl north to Scandinavia. As you learned in Chapter 19, radioactive pollution harmed the reindeer population of Scandinavia. In parts of Ukraine and Belarus, radioactive pollution sank into the soil and ruined farmland. Cows ate plants harmed by this pollution, which spoiled their milk, and people became ill from this milk. Radiation polluted the rivers, too, and affected the fish.

Nearly 200,000 people were forced to leave the area around Chernobyl. Some farm communities in that area are deserted to this day. The people fled so quickly that they left their belongings behind. Some people who did not get away quickly enough are still sick today. Ukraine is still struggling to recover from the disaster at Chernobyl. This land may not be safe to use for thousands of years. Dealing with this hazard will continue to drain the Ukrainian economy.

Answer the questions below.

1. What happened in Chernobyl in 1986?

2. Why was the explosion of Chernobyl so disastrous?

MAKE A DIFFERENCE
Conserving energy can mean fewer power plants are necessary. Check your home to see which lights, computers, and appliances are on. Where can you save energy?

The Transcaucasian States

Along the southwest corner of Russia are the steep Caucasus Mountains. They stretch between the Black Sea and the Caspian Sea. Rural villagers in the Caucasus Mountains region tend to live long, healthy lives. Many, in fact, live more than 100 years. The villagers think hard work and diet are responsible for their long lives.

Three republics lie in this mountainous area: Georgia, Armenia, and Azerbaijan. Even in Soviet times, Russian culture did not affect these republics much. They have historically been influenced more by Turkey and Iran. Most of the people in this region are not Slavic like the people are in Russia.

In the Caucasus Mountains, many people live a long life.

Throughout history, Georgians have been known as strong warriors and able hunters. The main ethnic group in Georgia is the Kartvelians. Minority groups in Georgia include Turks, Greeks, Armenians, Ossets, and Kurds. Some of these minority groups are Islamic. Most Georgians worship in the Georgian Orthodox Church, which is similar to the Russian Orthodox Church.

Georgia has fine farmland, with orchards of cherries, apricots, grapes, and other fruit. The land also supports grain and dairy farms. Many rural people still make their living as traditional herders.

Ancient Armenia was the first kingdom to make Christianity its official religion in A.D. 314. At that time, Armenia was larger than it is today and covered lands that are now part of Turkey and Iran. When the Turkish empire took control of these lands, thousands of Armenians fled the area to other parts of the world. Many ended up in the country now called Armenia.

Education is important to Armenians. The country has a large pool of trained, educated workers. It is well known for its Physics Institute and other science centers. In Soviet times, Armenia trained many of the Soviet Union's doctors, engineers, and astronomers.

An ongoing conflict with Azerbaijan has caused problems for Armenia. The two countries have long been divided by religion. The people of Azerbaijan are mainly Muslims. The Armenians are mainly Christians. Each country has an ethnic minority from the other country. Each minority complains of being treated unfairly. In the early 1990s, the countries warred over an area called Nogoro-Karabakh. Stalin gave this land to Azerbaijan, but most of the people there are Armenians. Both countries now claim the area. Yet a **cease-fire** declared in 1994 has held. A cease-fire is an agreement to stop fighting.

Armenia was weakened both by the war with Azerbaijan and by a devastating earthquake in 1988. However, by 1995, the economy was again growing.

Geography Fact

The Caspian Sea, with an area of 143,000 square miles, is the largest inland body of water in the world.

Azerbaijan lies between Armenia and the Caspian Sea. Most of the people in Azerbaijan are Azeris, who are a Turkish people with strong historical ties to Persia, today's Iran. Azeris are well known for their crafts, such as carpet weaving, metalworking, wood carving, and jewelry making. Azeri artists use styles similar to those seen in Turkey and Iran.

Folk Dances

Folk dances express the culture of a people. In Soviet times, the government encouraged the republics to express their differences through their folk dances. Today, costumes and style of movement show from which republic a dance comes. Each type of dance has a specific purpose. Some dances tell stories. Some tell the audience about a period of history.

In Ukraine, male dancers sometimes wear Cossack costumes. The Cossacks rebelled against Polish rule and set up the first Ukrainian state. They developed into legendary fighters. The dancers are a reminder of the Cossacks' warrior tradition.

The Soviet Union supported folk dance companies throughout the republics.

Georgian folk dances are meant to show courage and strength. The men wear traditional, dark, knee-length coats and capes. They show off their long, metal knives. They wear soft, high boots and dance on the knuckles of their toes.

✓ Check Your Understanding

Write your answers in complete sentences.

1. Why has Armenia's economy been weak?

2. Why do Ukrainian dancers wear Cossack costumes?

3. Name the three republics of the Transcaucasian States.

Summary

In the Soviet Union, the government owned and ran all factories, farms, and businesses. Economic decisions were made by a small group of central planners in Moscow.
Most of the former Soviet states are moving toward privatization.
The Baltic states of Lithuania, Estonia, and Latvia are located on the Baltic Sea.
Russians, Ukrainians, and Belarussians are Slavic peoples.
The states of Georgia, Armenia, and Azerbaijan are located in the Caucasus Mountains. Azerbaijan is mainly Islamic. The other countries in the Caucasus region are mainly Christian.
The former Soviet Union encouraged folk dances, which remain unique to each region.

bureaucracy

capital good

consumer good

chernozem

privatization

Vocabulary Review

Write a term from the list that matches each definition below.

1. A rich, black soil, which is common in cool or dry climates

2. Any organization made up of appointed officials organized into ranks

3. A product that satisfies people's wants or needs

4. The act of private companies taking over farms, factories, and other businesses

5. A manufactured product used to produce other products

Chapter Quiz

Write your answers in complete sentences.

1. What economic movement in the former Soviet states is leading to private ownership of farms and factories?

2. Which republic was the first official Christian kingdom?

3. What is a major crop of Ukraine?

4. **Critical Thinking** Why was the Soviet economy slow and inefficient?

5. **Critical Thinking** How does folk dancing express the culture of a people?

Write About Geography

Complete the following activities.

1. It is 1991. Write a speech explaining why your Soviet state should become an independent, noncommunist country.

2. You own a shop selling shoes. Write what the shop was like under central planning, and how it has changed now that your country is independent.

Group Activity

Create a proposal to persuade businesses to locate in the former Soviet countries. Every group member can write a section of the proposal. You might consider resources, available workers, or a low cost of living. Share the proposal with the class.

Since the fall of communism, Prague, the capital of the Czech Republic, has become a popular tourist destination. Why would the fall of communism lead to more tourism?

Chapter 24

Other Nations of Eastern Europe

Words to Know

Balkanization	breaking up into small groups that fight each other
neutral	not supporting either side in a disagreement or struggle
solidarity	a complete coming together
velvet revolution	a revolution without bloodshed
ethnic cleansing	a policy in which members of one ethnic group drive away or kill members of other ethnic groups
acid rain	rain water that carries large amounts of chemicals

Places to Know

Czech Republic

Poland

Hungary

Slovenia

Croatia

Serbia

Learning Objectives

- Describe the physical and cultural geography of Eastern Europe.
- Explain how physical geography and location have led to political problems in Eastern Europe.
- Describe the revolution against communism in Eastern Europe.
- Explain environmental damage in Eastern Europe.
- Describe the folk dancing of Eastern Europe.

The Land and the People

Prague is the capital of the Czech Republic, a country in the heart of Eastern Europe. The term *Eastern Europe* usually refers to the region that lies east of Germany, west of the former Soviet Union, and north of Greece. The countries of Eastern Europe are Poland, Slovakia, the Czech Republic, Hungary, Slovenia, Romania, Croatia, Yugoslavia, Bulgaria, Bosnia-Herzegovina, Macedonia, and Albania.

The northern part of this region is marked by a great, flat plain. In the middle of the region is the Carpathian Mountains. These mountains curl halfway around a smaller plain, the Hungarian Basin. In the southern part of the region is the mountainous Balkan Peninsula. The Danube River flows mainly east through the middle of Eastern Europe and empties into the Black Sea. The Danube is one of the most important waterways in Europe.

The landforms of Eastern Europe have greatly affected its history and culture. In the north, where the land is flat, it was easier for people to spread out. Therefore, they had more contact with their neighbors. Languages and customs tended to blend together.

Today, the country of Poland takes up most of this flat, northern area. Most of the people in Poland have much the same ethnic background and share much the same culture. They are a Slavic people. One problem with flat land is that it is easy to invade. Throughout history, Poland has been attacked many times—from the west, east, and south. The borders of Poland have shifted often.

In the rugged mountains of the Balkan Peninsula, travel was never easy. Even now, this area has poor transportation systems. Roads are rough. Laying railway lines throughout the region has proven difficult.

> ## HISTORY FACT
>
> The Danube River has inspired many poets, artists, and composers. Johann Strauss wrote a famous waltz called "On the Beautiful Blue Danube."

The Countries of Eastern Europe

Baltic Sea

LITHUANIA

RUSSIA

BELARUS

GERMANY

POLAND

⊛ Warsaw

⊛ Prague

CZECH REPUBLIC

SLOVAKIA

UKRAINE

⊛ Bratislava

AUSTRIA

⊛ Budapest

MOLDOVA

SLOVENIA

HUNGARY

⊛ Ljubljana

ROMANIA

CROATIA ⊛ Zagreb

BOSNIA-HERZEGOVINA

⊛ Belgrade

⊛ Bucharest

Black Sea

Sarajevo ⊛

YUGOSLAVIA

BULGARIA

ITALY

Adriatic Sea

⊛ Sofia

⊛ Skopje

Tirana ⊛

MACEDONIA

ALBANIA

GREECE

TURKEY

| ⊛ National capital |

Map Study

1. **PLACE** What is the capital of Poland?

2. **REGION** In early 1993, Czechoslovakia was broken into two countries. Which two countries shown on the map do you think formerly made up Czechoslovakia?

Long ago, rural villages were very isolated. People would not see or hear from their neighbors for long periods of time, if ever. Therefore, cultural differences developed. Slavic groups, who spread south, split into smaller groups. Four such groups are the Serbs, Croats, Czechs, and Slovenes.

Pockets of different ethnic groups are sprinkled throughout the Balkans. Their differences often are a source of trouble. The term **Balkanization** was invented for this region. It means breaking up into small groups that fight each other. This describes exactly what has happened in the Balkans throughout history. Even today, some of the world's most bitter fighting is taking place in this region.

Eastern Europe always has been squeezed between two or more cultures that do not get along. More than 2,000 years ago, the conflict was between the Romans of the south and the nomadic groups of the north and east. The edge of the Roman Empire ended in the Balkans, in the area now called Romania. The people of this country are descended from the ancient Romans. Their language is related to Italian, Spanish, and French.

In the tenth century, warlike groups called the Magyars moved out of Asia. They fought their way across the Balkans to the Hungarian Basin. They settled there and became peaceful farmers. The Magyars called themselves the people of the On-Ogur, which means "Ten Arrows." Today, their land is called Hungary, which comes from On-oguria.

Remember
The Eastern Orthodox Church includes both the Greek and Russian Orthodox churches.

In the Middle Ages, Eastern Europe lay between Christians in the west and Muslims in the east. Armies of Christians and Muslims marched through the Balkans attacking each other. Today, many Muslims live in Bosnia, Albania, and Bulgaria. Hungary and Poland are mainly Catholic. Other countries are Orthodox Christian, a legacy of the ancient Byzantine empire.

GEOGRAPHER'S TOOL KIT
Comparing Historical Maps

A historical map shows human geography at a time in history. Comparing historical maps of the same area at different times shows how the human geography has changed. For example, country borders may be different. To compare historical maps, look at the titles. Notice what time period each map covers. Look for differences between the maps.

Poland, 1918–1945

German control (1939)
Soviet control (1945)
German control (1945)
- - - Border of Poland from 1918–1939

Modern Poland

Answer the questions below.

1. Which countries claimed part of Poland in 1945?

2. Was Poland larger during 1918–1939 or today?

   CHALLENGE What do these maps suggest about the history of Poland?

Apply the Skill

Find maps of another part of the world after major change, such as Africa in 1900 and today. Compare the maps. Write how the area's human geography has changed.

The Soviet Shadow

During World War II, Nazi Germany conquered Eastern Europe. As the war went on, however, Soviet armies slowly drove the German armies out of the area. When the war ended, Eastern Europe was under Soviet control.

Officially, the various countries of this region gained their independence. In each country, however, a Communist party took power. Most of these parties took their orders from the Soviet Union's Communist party. Only Albania and Yugoslavia remained truly independent. Albania simply cut itself off from the rest of Europe. It let hardly anyone in or out. It grew its own food, and had almost no trade with foreign countries. Yugoslavia had a strong Communist leader named Tito, whom the Soviet Union left alone.

Several rebellions against Moscow's rule broke out in Eastern Europe. In 1956, Hungary revolted, declaring itself **neutral** in the cold war between the Soviet Union and the West. The Soviets rushed 200,000 soldiers and 2,500 tanks into Budapest, the capital of Hungary, and stopped the revolt.

Then, there was the "Prague Spring." This movement took place in Czechoslovakia in 1968. The country's Communist party wanted a more democratic form of government. It tried to give the people certain freedoms, such as freedom of speech. The Soviets sent troops into Czechoslovakia in 1968, and about 100 people were killed. To avoid more bloodshed, the leaders of Czechoslovakia stepped down and let the Soviet Union appoint new leaders for the country.

The 45 years of Soviet control made its mark on Eastern Europe. Fear and bureaucracy became part of the culture. In some countries, such as Hungary, people found some ways around the system. In many places, however, resentment over Soviet control grew deeper.

The Solidarity Movement

In 1980, another nation in Eastern Europe, Poland, rebelled against Soviet control. The new rebellion began at the shipyards in Gdańsk. Poland has the world's biggest shipbuilding industry, and the Gdańsk shipyards employ thousands of workers.

Many of these workers were not happy with their wages and working conditions. Yet they could not go on strike or form a union because these acts were forbidden by Polish law. In August 1980, the workers in Gdańsk broke the law. Led by a young electrician named Lech Walesa, they went on strike. The workers then formed Solidarnosc, or "Solidarity trade union." The word **solidarity** means a complete coming together.

Poland's leaders promptly declared Solidarnosc illegal and jailed some of the union leaders. Workers protested, but the government broke up their demonstrations. Polish workers continued to hold union meetings secretly. The Solidarity movement began to inspire people all across Eastern Europe.

In 1988, Mikhail Gorbachev, the Soviet ruler, set new policies for Soviet control of this region. Each country would have the right to find its own path to socialism. He then started pulling Soviet troops out of Eastern European countries.

The next four years brought revolutionary changes to Eastern Europe. Citizens protested against their Communist governments. What each country ended up finding was its own path away from socialism. The Romanians, for example, fought bloody battles in 1989 to overthrow their brutal dictator, Nicolae Ceausescu. Romanians killed Ceausescu and his wife, which aired on live television. The country's army then fought on the side of the people against Ceausescu's well-armed secret police.

A student celebrates the velvet revolution in 1989. She is holding a picture of Väclav Havel, the Czech Republic's first president after communism.

You Decide

The breakup of Czechoslovakia has been called the "velvet divorce." What do you think the word *velvet* suggests?

Czechoslovakia, in 1989, put a peaceful end to communism with its **velvet revolution.** Communism was simply declared dead. A period of change began. During this period, however, Czechoslovakia broke apart. The country's two main ethnic groups—Czechs and Slovaks—could not get along. They formed independent nations: the Czech Republic and Slovakia.

✓ Check Your Understanding

Write your answers in complete sentences.

1. Why has Poland been easy to invade?

2. What was the "Prague Spring"?

3. How did the rebellion in Poland begin?

Majorities and Minorities

Every country in Eastern Europe has a main ethnic group. No ethnic group, however, lies entirely within the borders of a single country. No country is without several ethnic, cultural, or religious minorities.

Most Hungarians, for example, live in Hungary. However, Romania has a large Hungarian minority group. Serbia is populated mainly by Serbs. Yet, in the southern province of Kosovo, most people are Albanian.

Some minorities in Europe have no countries of their own. The Jewish population is one such minority. Today, Hungary has the largest Jewish community in Eastern Europe. However, the community numbers only 65,000 people.

Celebrations

ASSUMPTION DAY

Polish Catholics honor Assumption Day each August. It is one of Poland's most important religious holidays. On this holiday, thousands of people make their way to the sacred town of Czestochowa. A famous painting hangs in Jasna Gora, a monastery in Czestochowa. This painting is over 500 years old. It shows the baby Jesus in the arms of Mary, his mother. Their faces are blackened by age, because the painting is so old. For this reason, it is called the Black Madonna.

During the Soviet era, many Polish Catholics considered their religion to be a statement against communism, which had outlawed religion. The festival of the Black Madonna became a political statement. People sang protest songs as well as hymns.

Critical Thinking Why did Polish Catholics consider the festival a political protest during the Soviet era?

The Black Madonna of Czestochowa

During World War II, Jews in Warsaw were rounded up by the Nazis and forced to live in a certain part of the city.

Before World War II, Poland had 3.4 million Jewish people. Nazi forces murdered about three million of them. Most of the other Jewish people emigrated from Poland. Today, fewer than 13,000 Jewish people remain in Poland.

Gypsies are another minority group in Eastern Europe. Most of them live in Romania. Gypsies also live in Hungary, Slovakia, and many other countries. The Gypsies are nomads—but today they are urban nomads, perhaps the only ones in the world. They make their living from various trades in the cities but are always on the move. The first Gypsy people probably came from India. Their language, Romany, is related to Sanskrit, the ancient language of India. In World War II, the Nazi forces put about 500,000 Gypsies to death in concentration camps. A concentration camp is a place where people, as prisoners of war, are held.

Conflicts in the Former Yugoslavia

Ethnic differences have led to great trouble in what was—from the period after World War I to the early 1990s—called Yugoslavia. This country broke apart when its Communist government weakened. Between 1991 and 1992, the republics of Croatia, Slovenia, Macedonia, and Bosnia-Herzegovina declared independence. Only Serbia and Montenegro remained in Yugoslavia.

Serbian leaders wanted all Serbs to live within one country. These leaders were trying to expand Serbia. Serbian forces invaded Croatia, where they joined local Serb military groups. The Serbs also started a policy called **ethnic cleansing**. This policy is the killing or driving away of other ethnic groups from areas where Serbs were living. For example, the Serbian military invaded the province of Kosovo. In spite of intervention by the United States and many Western European allies, about 850,000 Albanians fled. Eventually, the Serbian forces retreated. Some Albanians returned to Kosovo.

Croats started ethnic-cleansing programs as well. Serbs also encouraged the Serbian minority in Bosnia-Herzegovina to revolt. This led to a fierce war in Bosnia. The warring groups were Serbs, Muslims, and Croats. The Bosnian Serbs had most of the weapons. Many Bosnian Muslims were killed or herded into concentration camps. After several years of fighting, a 1995 peace accord ended the war in Bosnia.

Geography Fact

Bosnia and Herzegovina are two territories that joined together to form one republic. Bosnia is in the north. Herzegovina is in the south.

Ethnic Groups in the Former Yugoslavia, 1992

Legend:
- Albanians
- Bulgarians
- Croats
- Hungarians
- Macedonians
- Montenegrins
- Muslims
- Serbs
- Slovenes
- No Majority

Map Study

1. **REGION** Which ethnic groups live in Serbia?
2. **REGION** Which ethnic groups live in Slovenia?

A Damaged Environment

Eastern Europe is one of the most polluted areas in the world. This came about because Communist governments were eager to develop industry. Power plants and factories burned mainly brown coal, a fuel that pollutes highly. Industries dumped toxic wastes where they could soak right into the ground.

Most of the rivers, soil, and groundwater in Eastern Europe have been poisoned by toxic waste. In fact, nearly all of the water in Romania and Poland is dangerous to drink.

The forests in this region are almost gone. Experts believe that much of this damage can never be undone. One type of pollution, **acid rain**, is damaging stone structures, such as old buildings. It damages forests and waterways as well.

The pollution is not just a nuisance but a menace. In southern Poland, half the children have damaged sight or hearing. In Budapest, people go to a lung clinic to breathe oxygen for 15 minutes at a time. One out of every 17 deaths in Hungary is now related to pollution, according to the government.

Citizens have formed groups to struggle with these environmental problems. The Polish Ecological Club, for example, works with Solidarnosc. In Hungary, there is the Danube Circle. Germany, Sweden, and other European countries have offered to help pay for the cleanup of the polluted areas. People in these countries know that pollution does not stop at borders. The pollution of Eastern Europe is a problem for other parts of Europe as well.

Folk Art in Eastern Europe

The people of Eastern Europe have lively traditions of folk art. The folk music of this region is especially rich. Folk musicians play accordions, flutes, pipes, violins, and other string instruments. In Hungary and Romania, the Gypsy influence adds a flavor that is both festive and sad. Most of the folk music styles go with certain folk dances. Folk dancers—especially in the Balkans—wear colorful clothing.

Music, group dancing, and festive outfits add excitement to such celebrations as Romanian village weddings. These all-day parties are announced long in advance by horsemen riding through the village. On the wedding day, friends shave off the groom's beard to mark the change in his life. Other friends spend the whole morning braiding the bride's hair. At midnight, there is a special dance for the bride.

The classical music of Eastern Europe draws upon its folk music. For example, the Hungarian composer and musician Franz Liszt was inspired by both Romanian and Hungarian folk music. So was his countryman Bela Bartok. The Czech composer Antonin Dvorak drew upon the rhythms and melodies of Czech folk music. The Polish composer Frédéric Chopin took inspiration from Polish folk music. Many of Chopin's great piano works were based on Polish dances such as the mazurka.

✓ Check Your Understanding

Write your answers in complete sentences.

1. Where do most Gypsies live?

2. What led to the fierce war in Bosnia?

3. Why have people in other parts of Europe offered to help pay for pollution cleanup in Eastern Europe?

Summary

Eastern Europe is the region north of Greece, east of Germany, and west of the former Soviet Union.
Poland occupies the large northern plains. It is a Slavic and Catholic nation.
Many small ethnic groups occupy the Balkan Peninsula.
Eastern Europe has been invaded and crossed by many armies, and borders have changed there many times.
After World War II, most of Eastern Europe came under the control of the Soviet Union.
Between 1980 and 1992, communism ended in Eastern Europe.
The former Yugoslavia has been the scene of fierce conflict between Serbs, Croats, and Bosnian Muslims since the fall of communism.
The Communist governments in Eastern Europe contributed to serious environmental damage.

ethnic cleansing

neutral

acid rain

velvet revolution

Balkanization

Vocabulary Review

Complete each sentence with a term from the list.

1. A revolution without any bloodshed is a _____ .

2. If a country is _____ , it is not supporting either side in a disagreement or struggle.

3. _____ is a term that describes the breaking up into small groups that fight each other.

4. Rain water that carries large amounts of chemicals is called _____ .

5. A policy in which members of one ethnic group drive away or kill members of other ethnic groups is _____ .

Chapter Quiz

Write your answers in complete sentences.

1. After World War II, what were the only two Eastern European countries that the Soviet Union did not control?

2. Name some groups who have carried out a policy of ethnic cleansing.

3. What was the Solidarity movement?

4. **Critical Thinking** How has physical geography affected the culture and history of Eastern Europe?

5. **Critical Thinking** How did politics contribute to Eastern Europe's environmental problems?

Write About Geography

Complete the following activities.

1. You are a Polish worker who has just heard Lech Walesa call for a strike. Write a letter that details your reactions.

2. Write a speech that tells why people should support an effort to clean up pollution in Eastern Europe.

Group Activity

How much do people know about Eastern Europe? Write a short list of true or false questions about this region. Have each group member ask five people the questions. Total the correct answers for each question.

Unit 7 Review

Comprehension Check
Answer each question in a complete sentence.

1. In what two continents is Russia located?

2. What was central planning?

3. Why was the Polish government against the Solidarity trade union?

4. What are some examples of environmental damage in Eastern Europe?

Building Your Skills
Answer each question in a complete sentence.

1. How can a weather map show what kind of weather might be coming to an area?

2. What is the largest independent republic in what was the Soviet Union?

3. What can comparing historical maps tell you?

Where Is It?
Write the name of the place based on the information below.

1. The area of Russia that was often used as a prison

2 Once known as the "breadbasket" of the Soviet Union

3. When it was still joined with Slovakia, this country was known as Czechoslovakia

Writing an Essay
Answer one of the following essay topics.

1. Why did communism take root in Russia?

2. Why is there still some central planning in former Soviet states?

3. Why has there been so much war among people in the countries in Eastern Europe?

Geography and You

The Soviet Union controlled many of the countries of Eastern Europe. What do you think it was like for those countries to gain freedom after so many years of dependence?

Unit 8 ▷ Central and East Asia

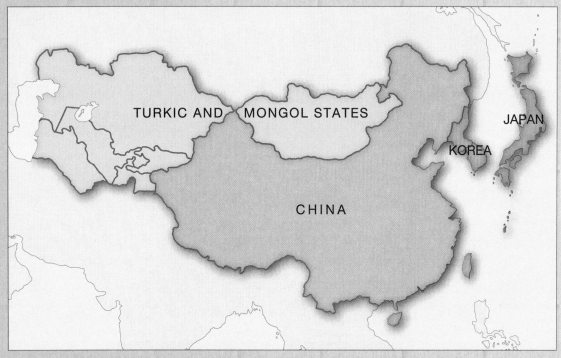

The countries of Central and East Asia vary in size and shape. What kind of main landforms are Japan and Korea?

TRAVEL LOG

The lotus flower is a symbol of Asia. As you read about the countries in this unit, choose a symbol for each one. Write why you think each represents the country and its people.

Lotus flower

This family lives in a small village in Mongolia. How does their home show the Mongol people's nomadic past?

Chapter 25 / The Turkic and Mongol States

Words to Know

loot	to seize and carry away goods
satellite	a country that is independent in name but is actually controlled by a bigger, more powerful country
strategic	important to carrying out a war or for defending against attack
tungsten	a metal used in lightbulbs
yurt	a movable round tent covered in felt or animal skins

Places to Know

Uzbekistan

Turkmenistan

Tajikistan

Kyrgyzstan

Kazakhstan

Mongolia

Learning Objectives

- Describe the physical geography of Central Asia.
- Identify the main ethnic groups in Central Asia.
- Tell about the Mongol empire and its impact on history.
- Explain how communism has changed Mongolia.
- Describe the cotton-based economy of the former republics of Soviet Central Asia.
- Identify the conflicting forces for change in the former republics of Soviet Central Asia.

The Land and the People

Geography Fact

The tallest peak in the Pamirs is 24,590 feet high. There are also many other peaks in this range that are more than 20,000 feet tall.

Remember
The steppes region begins in southern Russia.

Uzbekistan is one of the countries located in the steppes of Central Asia. This vast grassland has two main areas. In the west is a low, flat basin. In the east is a hilly plateau. Both areas are windswept and very dry. The western steppes surround the Kara-Kum (black sand) and Kyzyl Kum (red sand) deserts. The eastern steppes border on the Gobi Desert. The Altay, the Tien Shan, and the Pamir mountain ranges separate the two areas. Broad valleys run between them.

Over the centuries, the steppes have been home to countless groups of nomadic herders. Most of these nomads were Turkic or Mongol. The two groups are ethnically related, and both speak languages in the Ural-Altaic language family. The Turkic people of Central Asia now live mostly in the western steppes. As their name implies, they are related to the people who founded what is today called Turkey. The Mongol people live in the eastern steppes.

The western steppes were part of the Soviet Union from the 1920s to 1992. Before that time, the whole region was known simply as Turkestan. The Soviet leader Joseph Stalin carved the region into five republics: Turkmenistan, Uzbekistan, Tajikistan, Kyrgyzstan, and Kazakhstan. When the Soviet Union fell apart in 1991, each of the five republics became independent countries. They now contain about 50 million people. Most of them are Sunnite Muslims.

Tajikistan stands out from the other countries in the region. The Tajik people are neither Turkic nor Mongol but are related to the people of Iran. The Tajiks speak a dialect of Farsi, the main language of Iran. They are descended from Persians, who ruled the area about 2,500 years ago. The Tajiks have never been nomadic. Over the years, however, they have taken on some of the characteristics of their Turkic and Mongol neighbors.

Most Mongol people live in the country of Mongolia. This large, landlocked nation was long ruled by China. It became independent in 1921. After that, it was controlled—but never owned—by the Soviet Union until that nation's collapse in 1991. Mongolia then moved toward becoming a democracy. About two and a half million people live in Mongolia. Some Mongols also live north of the border, in Siberia. Some live farther south, in China. Traditionally, the majority of Mongols are Buddhists.

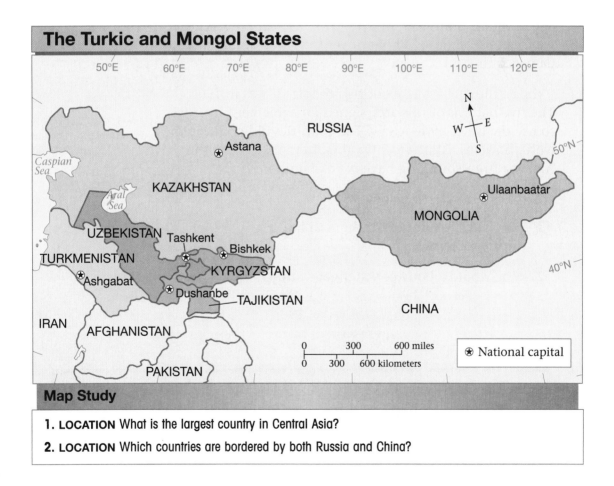

The Turkic and Mongol States

Map Study

1. **LOCATION** What is the largest country in Central Asia?

2. **LOCATION** Which countries are bordered by both Russia and China?

GLOBAL ISSUES
Saving the Aral Sea

The Aral Sea is a body of water that lies between Kazakhstan and Uzbekistan. It is fed by two rivers, the Syr Darya and the Amu Darya. In 1960, the Aral was the world's fourth largest sea. The Soviets, however, drew water from the rivers to irrigate their new cotton farms.

With less water, the Aral Sea began to shrink. As it shrank, it grew more salty. Freshwater fish living in the sea began to die. Ships were stranded on the salty deserts that were once seashores. Salt blew over the lands nearby and damaged the soil.

Today, the Aral Sea is about half the size it was in 1960. The five nations of this area signed an agreement in 1992 to use the water more wisely. The countries did not keep their word, however. More recently, the attempts to keep the Aral Sea from shrinking have been abandoned.

Answer the questions below.

1. Why did the saltiness of the Aral Sea cause problems?

2. Why would a body of water get saltier?

MAKE A DIFFERENCE

Contact your local water authority. Ask them to send information on how to save water. Make a list of their suggestions, and put a check next to the ways you save water now. Then, circle two new ways you can try to save water from now on.

The Mongol Empire

Mongolia lies east of Kazakhstan. Today, Mongolia plays almost no role in world affairs. Yet in the 1200s, it was the heart of the biggest land empire ever seen.

The Mongols first appeared in history around the year 900. They were just one of the many small bands of nomadic herders and hunters of the steppes. Their skill at horseback riding and archery made them renowned warriors. Sometimes, they raided towns and farms in China. More often, they fought each other, because they did not yet think of themselves as one people.

Then, in 1162, the Mongol leader Genghis Khan was born. He proved himself a master politician and warrior. By 1205, he had united all the Mongol groups under his rule. He was ready to lead his armies against others in the world. He conquered much of China, Russia, Persia, and the Arabic empire.

After his death in 1227, his sons and grandsons continued his conquests. The Mongol empire reached its height under Genghis Khan's grandson, Kublai Khan. The empire stretched from Southeast Asia to Europe. By that time, however, the empire was divided into four parts, each ruled by a different grandson of Genghis Khan.

Officially, Kublai Khan headed the whole empire. In practice, however, he was "just" the emperor of China. Mongol power faded under his rule. In 1368, the Mongols were driven out of China. By 1502, they controlled only Mongolia. In 1691, Mongolia became a province of China.

The Mongols were famously savage in battles. Cities that fought against them were utterly destroyed and all of the occupants were killed. Cities that surrendered to them without a fight were merely **looted**. To loot is to seize and carry away goods.

> ## HISTORY FACT
>
> Genghis Khan's real name was Temujin. The name Genghis, meaning "ocean," was given to him later. It referred to his vast power. Khan is a title that means "Chief."

After their conquests, however, the Mongols became fair rulers. Kublai Khan accepted Chinese ways and even used traditional Chinese forms of government. He rebuilt China's canals and supported the arts and sciences. The Mongols who ruled the Persians and Arabs converted to their religion, Islam. Under Mongol rule, Persian culture flourished.

World trade opened up under Mongol rule since people could travel safely through the vast area under Mongol control. Thus, during this era, people from China, Persia, India, the Middle East, and Europe had the chance to meet and exchange ideas.

Spotlight On

THE SILK ROAD

Silk is a light, strong cloth woven from threads made by silkworms. The Chinese people discovered how to make this cloth at least 4,600 years ago. They kept the process secret. People who wanted silk had to go to China. In ancient Rome, silk was highly valued. Many traders made the long and difficult journey to China.

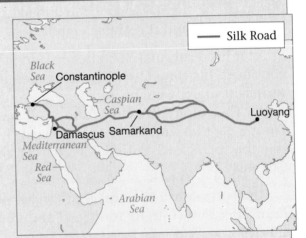

Over time, a regular route developed. It was called the Silk Road. It ran from the Mediterranean coast through Persia and Central Asia into China. Trading posts along the route grew into lively cities.

Religions such as Islam and Buddhism moved east along the Silk Road. Inventions such as gunpowder and the printing press moved west. The Silk Road was probably at its busiest in the days of the Mongol empire. Yet, after the 1500s, sea travel became popular. Trade along the Silk Road died out.

Critical Thinking Why was the Silk Road important to the world?

Communist Rule in Mongolia

Mongolia gained its independence from China in 1921 with help from the Soviet Union. Three years later, Mongolia's Communist party took power. The Mongolian people looked to the Soviet Union for protection. In exchange for giving this protection, the Soviet Union made Mongolia a **satellite** country. A satellite is a country that is independent in name but is actually controlled by a bigger, more powerful country.

The Soviets were interested in Mongolia for **strategic** reasons. The Soviets had never trusted China. In 1958, a split developed between the Soviet Union and China. War seemed possible. Mongolia was considered strategic because it was located between the Soviet Union and China. Controlling Mongolia, therefore, allowed the Soviet Union better protection from, and access to, China. Whenever war seemed likely between the Soviet Union and China, Soviet troops moved into Mongolia, right up to China's border.

Until the Communist revolution, most Mongolians were Buddhists. Their religion originated in Tibet, a nation now ruled by China. Mongolia had large monasteries, such as the Gandan Lamasery in the capital city of Ulan Bator. The Communists shut down most of the monasteries. However, Gandan Lamasery was left open as a museum. Over 100,000 monks had lived there in the past, but only about 100 monks are living there today.

✓ **Check Your Understanding**

Write your answers in complete sentences.

1. What two nomadic groups are from Central Asia?

2. Why did trade open up under Mongol rule?

3. What is a satellite country?

Mongolia Today

Communist rule changed Mongolia in many ways. The Communist government replaced family-owned herds with big herding collectives. It also started collective farms to grow wheat and other crops.

The Communist government also began to mine Mongolia's natural resources, such as coal, copper, gold, tin, and **tungsten**, which is a metal used in lightbulbs. Today, Mongolia exports these minerals. The Communist government also built factories, which now produce textiles, leather, cement, and chemicals. These new industries have led to the growth of cities. In modern Mongolia, about 42 percent of the population lives in urban areas.

This type of house is called a yurt.

Most Mongolians lived a nomadic life in the past. Families followed their herds of sheep, goats, and other livestock from pasture to pasture. They used horses and camels for transportation. They lived in a type of movable house called a **yurt**, with walls of felt or animal skins stretched over a wooden frame.

Livestock is still very important to the economy of Mongolia. Animals provide milk and dairy products. The milk from female horses, or mares, is used to make a drink called koumis. The raw material for Mongolia's textile and leather industries comes from livestock.

Few Mongolians are nomadic anymore. In winter, they herd their animals into barns and feed them hay from a state farm. Yurts are still common in rural Mongolia and even in the suburbs of big cities. Today's yurts, however, are fixed in place. Most of them have stoves, and some are even equipped with electric lights.

After the Soviet Union collapsed, people in Mongolia held demonstrations and demanded change. In 1992, elections were held for the new parliament. The Communists won the most seats. The next election, in 1996, placed a non-Communist government in power for the first time since 1921.

Democratic rule is still new to the country. The leaders of Mongolia are privatizing the economy. They also are making reforms that include more cultural and religious freedoms.

Celebrations

THE NATIONAL NAADAM

Every July 11, Mongolians celebrate a National Naadam, or public festival, to celebrate the Mongolian Revolution—the nation's independence from China in 1921. The National Naadam features contests in traditional Mongolian sports. The most important events are archery, horse racing, and wrestling.

Mongolia's National Nadaam celebrates the revolution in which the country gained independence from China in 1921.

Both men and women compete in horseback riding and archery. In some of the archery contests, the athletes have to shoot from horseback. Now, as in the past, Mongolians learn to ride as children. In the National Naadam, the featured race is the one for boys between 7 and 12 years of age.

The wrestling contests are open only to men. The wrestlers wear tight vests, colorful briefs, and heavy boots. Each one tries to topple the other. The first to touch the ground with anything but his feet loses.

Critical Thinking Why do you think Mongolian children learn skills from the past, such as archery and horseback riding?

A Cotton-Based Economy

Like the Mongolian peoples, the Turkic peoples of the western steppes used to be nomadic herders. This way of life ended after the Soviet government took control of their lands. The Soviet government wanted to make the region more productive and saw that the soil was rich enough to farm. Only water was lacking. So the Soviets built irrigation works that brought water from distant rivers.

The republics of Soviet Central Asia soon became major producers of cotton. In fact, they supplied most of the cotton used in the Soviet Union. The cotton was grown on collective farms much like the ones in Russia.

Cotton is the main cash crop of the Central Asian republics.

These collectives used modern farm machinery to plow, plant, and harvest. Cotton brought in so much money that it was called "white gold."

Unfortunately, the Soviets used harmful chemicals to kill pests and protect against plant diseases. Cotton farming thus led to pollution. The new irrigation systems also harmed the environment.

When the Soviet Union broke up, the economies of the republics of Soviet Central Asia suffered. The republics had traded within the Soviet empire. These links fell apart. The countries also had trouble changing the way they worked. Some people resisted the new ways. They were used to industry and farming run by the state. Now, the businesses were privately owned. Some who ran these businesses had little experience running companies. Kyrgyzstan, for example, produced about half the goods and services in 1995 than it did in 1990.

These republics are recovering, though. Many have large reserves of resources such as gold and oil. They have made deals with foreign companies to mine these resources. Also, private farmers are settling in. Their farms are doing better. The future looks brighter in these former states of the Soviet Union.

A Region at a Crossroads

The former republics of Soviet Central Asia are changing. The biggest question has to do with Islam. During the Soviet era, the government discouraged religion throughout the country. No money was given to mosques or religious teachers in Soviet Central Asia, or anywhere in the U.S.S.R. All students had to study communism in school. Factories did not give workers "prayer breaks." Few Soviet Muslims could get time or permission to make the pilgrimage to Mecca.

Now that independence has come to the Central Asian republics, Islam is an increasing force. Mosques are opening up. Muslims can go to Mecca again. Communists still hold power in some places, however, such as Tajikistan. In 1992, Islamic and democratic groups joined forces in Tajikistan to fight the Communist government. They did not gain power, but this struggle goes on.

Meanwhile, Iran and Turkey are competing for influence over the Muslims of this region. Iran would like to see the republics become Islamic states. If this happens, Islam will be the official religion. All laws will be based on Islam.

Turkey favors the idea of a secular, democratic state and emphasizes Turkic culture as a unifying force. In fact, some people in this region would like to see the Turkic republics join together. They favor one unified Turkic state in Central Asia.

Instead of joining together, however, some of the republics may break further apart, because these republics have restless minority groups. Uzbekistan, for example, has a Tajik minority. Tajikistan has an Uzbek minority. In Kazakhstan, the Russians actually outnumber the ethnic Kazakhs. Conflicts between such groups may lead to some shifting of borders in these countries. Truly, Central Asia is a region at a crossroads.

Geography Fact

A cultural center has been set up in Jeinav, Uzbekistan, to revive Arabic traditions. About 200,000 people of Arabian descent live in this area.

✓ Check Your Understanding

Write your answers in complete sentences.

1. How did Communist rule change Mongolia?

2. Why did the economies of the Central Asian republics suffer after the Soviet Union breakup?

3. Why has independence in Central Asia meant that Islam is an increasing force?

GEOGRAPHER'S TOOL KIT
Using Timelines

A timeline lists important events in the order that they happened. To read a timeline, first read the title. Then, look at the left and right ends of the line. They will tell you how much time the timeline covers. Next, look at the important events shown on the timeline. The line will be divided into equal units of time, or intervals.

Government of Kazakhstan, 1917–1994

1917
Russian Revolution puts an end to imperial rule.
Kazakh leaders establish Kazakh government by Russia.

1991
Kazakhstan declares independence from U.S.S.R.

1900   1910   1920   1930   1940   1950   1960   1970   1980   1990   2000

1922
U.S.S.R. founded.
Kazakhstan becomes self-ruling Soviet Socialist Republic.

1928
Soviets replace Kazakh leaders with Soviet leaders.

1994
First free elections held since independence.

Answer the questions below.

1. Who ruled Kazakhstan until the Russian Revolution in 1917?

2. In what year did Kazakhstan break from the U.S.S.R.?

CHALLENGE Why would the event in 1928 upset the Kazakhs?

Apply the Skill

Create a timeline of the past year. On a sheet of paper, write at least five notable events that occurred in your life. Then, put them in order. Finally, create a timeline.

Summary

Steppes and deserts cover most of Central Asia. Mountains divide the region into two parts.
Most Central Asians are Turkic or Mongol. Tajiks, who are ethnically Persian, live in the region as well.
Five republics lie in the western steppes: Turkmenistan, Uzbekistan, Tajikistan, Kyrgyzstan, and Kazakhstan.
Mongolia is on a plateau in the eastern steppes.
Traditionally, the Turkic and Mongol peoples were nomadic herders, but Communist governments put an end to this way of life.
The Mongols ruled the biggest land empire in history in the 1200s and 1300s.
Cotton is the main cash crop of Central Asia.
Islam is a rising force in the former republics of Soviet Central Asia.

yurt
tungsten
satellite
strategic
loot

Vocabulary Review

Write a term from the list that matches each definition below.

1. A metal used in lightbulbs

2. To seize and carry away goods

3. A country that is independent in name but is actually controlled by a bigger, more powerful country

4. A movable, round tent covered in felt or animal skins

5. Important to carrying out a war

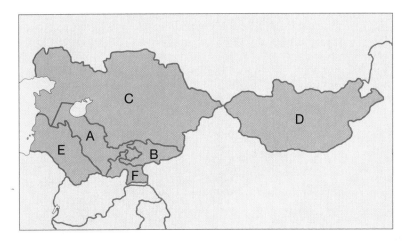

Chapter Quiz

Write the correct letter for each place.

1. Kazakhstan   **3.** Turkmenistan   **5.** Kyrgyzstan

2. Uzbekistan   **4.** Tajikistan   **6.** Mongolia

Write About Geography

Complete the following activities.

1. Draw an advertisement for the Silk Road. Explain the exchange of goods and ideas along the road.

2. Write an essay in which you compare religion in Central Asia before and after the republics gained independence from Communist governments.

Group Activity

Think about the leaders you have read about in this chapter. List the traits of a good leader. Discuss the lists with the group. Then, make a master list.

The Great Wall of China was built to protect the country's northern border. What kind of protection would the wall provide?

Chapter 26 / China

Words to Know

seismograph	a device for measuring earthquakes
classless society	a society in which no group of people has more wealth, power, or status than any other
class struggle	the struggle between the upper class and the lower class
invest	to spend money for something, such as a business, that may return a profit
jade	a hard stone that is usually green

Places to Know

Himalayas

Gobi Desert

Huang He

Chang River

Taiwan

Hong Kong

Learning Objectives

- Describe the physical geography of China.

- Identify important inventions and engineering achievements of ancient China.

- Describe Confucianism and its influence on Chinese history and society.

- Explain how communism has affected China's culture and economy.

- Explain the differences between the People's Republic of China and the Republic of China.

The Land and the People

Remember
Russia is the world's largest
country in size.

HISTORY FACT

The Gobi has some of
the world's richest
fossil beds. Scientists
have found dinosaur
eggs here that were
laid about 70 or 80
million years ago.

China is an East Asian country that has the world's largest population—about 1.2 billion people. Roughly one-fifth of all the people on the Earth are Chinese. Yet in land size, China ranks only third. Most of its people live in the eastern third of the country, where low plains, gentle hills, and broad river valleys offer good farmland. The rest of the country is filled with deserts and mountains, which can hardly be farmed at all. The Himalayas—the world's tallest mountains—loom in the southwest. The Gobi, a desert, covers much of northern China.

China has two great rivers, the Huang He and the Chang Jiang. These rivers have been used for both transportation and irrigation since ancient times. The Huang He is known to Westerners as the Yellow River. Chinese civilization began along its banks. The Chang Jiang, known to Westerners as the Yangtze, is the world's third-longest river. It is 3,950 miles long.

The Huang He has flooded about 1,500 times in recorded history. It floods easily because it carries so much silt down from the mountains. Thus, the riverbed keeps rising, which pushes the water level higher. The Chinese have built dikes to contain the river. Yet the river bottom keeps rising, so the builders have to keep building the dikes higher. In some places, the Huang He is 12 feet higher than the land on either side. Many times, floods have ruined crops and caused famines in China. In the 1930s, four million people died of hunger after such floods.

The crowded eastern part of China is called the heartland. It is considered the heart of China and of Chinese culture. This region stretches from the border of Vietnam to the Central Asian steppes. The heartland can be divided into three main areas: North China, South China, and the Sichuan Basin.

North China has always been the center of political power. It has China's richest soil, but its climate is cold and dry. South China has long been the center of China's economic power. It has less fertile soil, but the climate is mild and humid. Rice, tea, cotton, and citrus fruits grow well there. The Sichuan Basin lies in the southwest. It has good farmland and it also has valuable minerals. China's other provinces lie north and west of the heartland.

$ Economics Fact

Beijing, the main city in North China, is the nation's capital. Shanghai, one of the world's biggest cities, is in South China. Guangzhou, once known as Canton, is another important port.

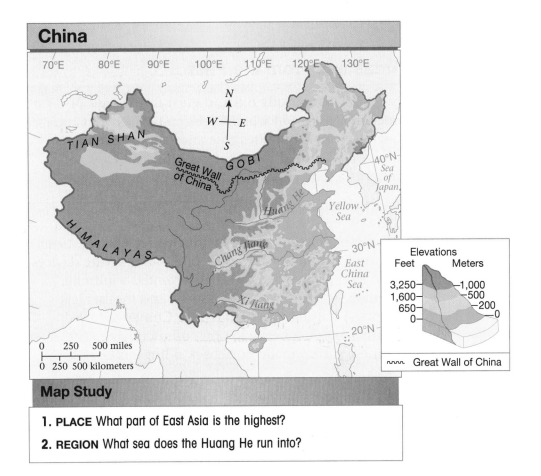

China

Map Study

1. **PLACE** What part of East Asia is the highest?

2. **REGION** What sea does the Huang He run into?

About 94 percent of China's people belong to an ethnic group called Han Chinese. They take their name from the Han dynasty, which ruled China from 202 B.C. to A.D. 220. China also has about 60 ethnic minority groups—such as Tibetans, Mongols, and Uighurs—but they make up only 6 percent of the population.

The Han Chinese people speak many different dialects. The written language, however, is the same for all dialects because Chinese is written in characters, not letters. A character stands for an idea rather than a sound. Two people may pronounce a character quite differently, but they get the same meaning from it.

Treasures From the Past

China was already old and great in the days of ancient Greece. Yet when Greek culture faded, China's kept growing. Dynasties rose and fell, but each one built on what had come before. Modern China thus inherits a long and brilliant legacy.

The Chinese knew how to cast bronze and iron 3,000 years ago. By then, they had already invented silk cloth, crossbows, and bendable metal armor. Later, during the Han dynasty, they built labor-saving devices such as the wheelbarrow. They invented windmills, sundials, water-powered hammers, and mechanical clocks. A harness invented by the Chinese allowed a horse to pull a heavy load without choking. The Chinese stirrup made horseback riding easier.

The Golden Age of China came during the Tan and Song dynasties. In this era, which lasted roughly from A.D. 600 to 1200, the Chinese invented gunpowder, printing, and the compass. Earlier, they had also invented paper and the first **seismograph**, a device for measuring earthquakes. The West learned of these inventions later, after the Mongols had opened up world trade.

The ancient Chinese built some of history's most dramatic structures, such as the Great Wall, begun by the first emperor of China in the third century B.C. The emperor wanted to build the wall to keep out the warring nomads of Central Asia. The wall, which is still standing, was strengthened and built up in the 1500s and 1600s.

Another great structure is the Grand Canal, built in the seventh century. It is the world's longest canal—about 1,000 miles. It connects the Chang River to the cities of the north. It did much to improve trade and travel in China. Today, after 1,300 years, most of it is still in use.

Geography Fact

The Great Wall of China is 1,500 miles long, 12 feet wide, and as high as 40 feet tall in places.

The Teachings of Confucius

Few figures have influenced China as much as Confucius. This great teacher and philosopher was born about 551 B.C. He lived in a time when the ruling dynasty of China was crumbling. All around him, Confucius saw war, crime, and injustice. Confucius decided to work out the basis for a peaceful, orderly society. He claimed that he was just describing how people had behaved in the past. In fact, he was developing a new moral code. His students wrote down his sayings in a collection called the Analects, which provides a guide to good behavior.

Confucius put the family at the center of life. He saw five key relationships in society as a whole. One key relationship was that between a ruler and his subjects. Another relationship was that between a father and his son. Yet another relationship was that between an elder brother and a younger brother. The other two key relationships were between a husband and his wife, and between two friends.

Respect for elders is a Confucian ideal upheld in modern China.

In each relationship, Confucius said, one side is higher and one is lower. Both sides have duties. A son, for example, must honor and obey his father, while a father must teach and protect his son. Confucius saw the father-son relationship as the model for all five relationships.

He also taught that only "perfect gentlemen" should hold high positions of power. Anyone, however, could become such a gentleman through study and effort. He felt education, not birth, made a person noble.

In the Han dynasty, the teachings of Confucius became the basis for the Chinese government. Han rulers set up a bureaucracy to run China. To enter the bureaucracy, people had to study Confucian teachings and pass an exam. Scholars became the ruling class in China.

Some Confucian ideas remain a part of Chinese life today. The family is still important, as well as respect for elders. The Chinese still believe that people can improve themselves through effort and study. They still stress "correct" attitudes and behavior. However, communism has lessened the importance of Confucius to modern China.

✓ **Check Your Understanding**

Write your answers in complete sentences.

1. Why does the Huang He flood easily?

2. In what part of China is political power centered?

3. How did the West learn of Chinese inventions such as paper and gunpowder?

4. What did Confucius put at the center of life?

Communism Comes to China

In 1911, a revolution overthrew the Chinese emperor. In the years that followed, two parties competed for power. One was the Guomindang, or Nationalist Party, led by Chiang Kai-shek. This party favored capitalism and Confucian values. The other was the Chinese Communist Party, led by Mao Zedong. This power struggle led to a bloody civil war.

In 1934, Chiang Kai-shek tried to eliminate the Communist army. However, the Communists headed what became known as their famous Long March. About 100,000 people—mostly teenagers—started on this 6,000-mile walk to safety. More than 80,000 of them died along the way. Yet the Long March was a success, because the Communists spread their ideas as they marched. After the Long March, they began winning Chinese peasants over to their side.

In 1949, Mao and his army entered Beijing, the capital of China. Mao and his followers set up the People's Republic of China as a new Communist nation. Mao had three main goals. He wanted to end hunger and poverty in China. He wanted to build a self-sufficient economy. He wanted to create a **classless society**. Mao thought crime and violence came out of **class struggle**, or the struggle between the upper and the lower class. He felt it was the struggle between those who had more and those who had less. If there were no classes, there could be no class struggle. Mao wanted a society in which everyone was equal.

You Decide

In what way were Mao Zedong's ideas the opposite of those taught by Confucius?

The Communists did improve the Chinese economy. They built dams on the Huang He that brought the flooding under control. Famine was no longer a common problem in China. China has no extreme poverty and no homeless people.

The Communists could not end class struggle completely, however. In 1965, Mao Zedong said that the Communists themselves had become a new upper class. He called on people to overthrow Communists who had become selfish and greedy. Thus began China's Cultural Revolution. Millions of educated people lost their jobs. Many people were jailed, and some were even killed. The economy was ruined.

After Mao's death in 1975, Deng Xiaoping took charge. Deng Xiaoping did not care about a classless society. He just wanted the economy to work. He invited foreign countries to **invest** money in China. To invest is to spend money for something, such as a business, that may return a profit. Chinese people were allowed to start small businesses and work for their own profit.

China Today

Today, most of the farms in China are worked by single families. These families lease land from the government. The families have to grow and sell a certain amount of food to the government at a fixed price. If they can raise more food, they are free to sell the extra food to anyone else for whatever price they can get. This is called the Responsibility System. Under this system, China grows more than enough food for its people.

The leaders of China also give factory managers freedom to make their own decisions now. This, too, has helped the economy run more smoothly. China's industries are growing about 7 percent every year. This is about six times as fast as industries are growing in the United States.

Deng even allowed some freedom of speech at first. Yet in 1989, Chinese students held demonstrations to demand democracy. Deng, however, wanted to make it clear that China remained under the strict rule of the Chinese Communist Party. He ordered the army to crush the demonstrations. Thousands of students were killed or hurt.

With the breakup of the Soviet Union, China became the only major Communist country. In 1993, Jiang Zemin became president. Under his control China's economy has kept growing. Despite some protests against China's human rights policies, the United States opened trade with China in 2000.

In 1989, thousands of Chinese students protested against communism at Tiananmen Square in Beijing.

Medicine in China

China has a system of traditional medicine very different from that of the West. This system of medicine is based on a belief in qi, a life energy. Chinese doctors say that qi is made up of two opposite forces: yin and yang. When yin and yang are in balance, qi flows freely through a person's body. The person is healthy. When the forces are out of balance, qi slows down. The person gets ill.

Chinese healers restore the balance with herbal medicines. Acupuncture is also widely used in China. With acupuncture, needles are pushed into certain parts of the body to relieve pain and treat illness.

In China, the Communist government built many hospitals and health-care centers where both Western and traditional Chinese medicines are used. To care for its vast rural population, the government has trained "barefoot doctors." These health-care workers treat minor illnesses and give physicians time to deal with more serious medical problems.

The One-Child Family

The Chinese people have long valued large families. That is one reason why the country has more than a billion people. The government knows that it must control population growth. Since the 1970s, therefore, China has encouraged the country's system of one-child families. The government offers a reward to families that agree to have only one child. Families that have more than one child have to pay heavy fines. This program has cut China's birth rate in half.

Unfortunately, the Communists have not been able to change the fact that most Chinese parents prefer to have boys. Traditionally, only boys carry on the family line. If a one-child family has a girl, the family line ends. Sometimes, the government makes exceptions to its one-child rule. If the first child is a girl, a family may be allowed to have another child.

Chinese Arts

Chinese civilization has produced many forms of art. Bronze pottery and sculptures were cast by Chinese artists more than 3,000 years ago. Chinese artists also developed pottery to a high art. Between the 900s and 1200s, they perfected porcelain, an especially fine, thin type of baked clay pottery. In the West, fine pottery has come to be known simply as china.

Chinese sculptors often worked in **jade**, a hard stone that is usually green and that chips and scratches easily. Even today, jade carving is a fine craft in China. The Chinese people see calligraphy as the finest of arts. The brushstrokes developed for calligraphy were also used in Chinese landscape paintings. Calligraphy and landscape paintings have often gone together.

A Chinese artist made this cloisonné vase by baking enamel onto metal.

Under communism, such traditional Chinese arts have suffered. The Chinese Communists have demanded that art express political ideas. Modern Chinese artists create posters showing workers as heroes. They use bold colors and a realistic style.

Chinese dance companies perform ballets based on the theme of class struggle. Chinese operas perform stories that tell about the revolution. Since the 1980s, however, many Chinese artists have been returning to more traditional styles of art.

Spotlight On

CHINESE CALLIGRAPHY

The characters used in Chinese writing are pictures in themselves. The Chinese language does not have an alphabet. Instead, words are written with images.

This system of writing is ancient. The first Chinese calligraphy dates from the eighteenth century B.C. The inventor of Chinese writing, Ts'ang Chieh, used the natural world to create pictures. The sun, for example, was shown with a circle. As the language developed, the images grew more sophisticated.

Throughout the centuries, all well-educated Chinese people were trained in calligraphy. Creating fine calligraphy with brush and ink was not just writing. It was also a spiritual and artistic activity. It still is today. A calligrapher may spend hours getting into the proper mood. Then he or she may create a whole page of calligraphy in a few seconds. Calligraphers try for balance and harmony in their work. The Chinese believe calligraphy shows the spiritual level of the writer.

Critical Thinking How does Chinese calligraphy differ from English writing?

Chinese calligraphy is considered a spiritual activity. Calligraphers try for balance and harmony in their work.

Taiwan

Remember
Martial law is a state of emergency in which a government suspends citizens' rights and uses its army to control its people.

In 1949, Chiang Kai-shek and his army fled the Communists. They went to Taiwan, an island in the East China Sea. About two million anti-Communist refugees also made the move. Taiwan called itself the Republic of China. It was a capitalist country ruled by the political party, Guomindang. No other political party was allowed to form. The country was put under martial law.

The Republic of China claimed to be the real China. It promised to reconquer the mainland soon. The United States and Japan recognized this government. They poured money into Taiwan and helped to develop its economy.

An artist paints Taiwan's skyline. Although the country is small, Taiwan is one of the wealthiest in Asia.

Then, in the 1970s, the United States changed its policy. It decided to recognize the People's Republic of China—on the mainland—as the real China. Soon, Japan and other countries also accepted the People's Republic of China. Taiwan became "the other China." The shock of this move led to changes in Taiwan. Martial law was lifted. The country began moving toward democracy.

Today, Taiwan is a highly urban, industrial country. It makes everything from CD players to cars. Its middle class is growing. It has a well-equipped army. Though small in size, it is one of Asia's most powerful countries.

Hong Kong

Hong Kong is a city on the southern coast of China. It is one of the world's busiest capitalist centers. For years, Hong Kong was a British colony. The British only leased the land. In 1997, the lease ran out. The People's Republic of China took over Hong Kong.

The change in government has weakened Hong Kong's economy. Even the Chinese government's agreement to make no changes in Hong Kong for 50 years has helped little. Many wealthy Chinese business people have left Hong Kong for places like Canada and the United States.

✓ **Check Your Understanding**

Write your answers in complete sentences.

1. What was the Cultural Revolution?

2. Why does China encourage one-child families?

3. Why did some Chinese people migrate to Taiwan in 1949?

Summary

China is a large country in East Asia. It has a population of about 1.2 billion people.
China has an ancient civilization and has often led the world in culture and technology. Chinese people invented silk cloth, paper, printing, the seismograph, and the compass.
Chinese society and government were once based on Confucianism.
In 1949, China became a Communist nation called the People's Republic of China. The leader Mao Zedong was determined to build a classless society. Yet, China's new leaders are more interested in making the economy work.
Highly valued arts in China include calligraphy, landscape painting, and jade carving.
The Republic of China is a capitalist nation on the island of Taiwan.
Hong Kong is an international business center. It became part of the People's Republic of China in 1997.

classless society

invest

jade

seismograph

class struggle

Vocabulary Review

Write a term from the list that matches each definition below.

1. A hard stone that is usually green

2. A society in which no group of people has more wealth, power, or status than any other group

3. The struggle between the upper class and the lower class

4. A device for measuring earthquakes

5. To spend money for something, such as a business, that may return a profit

Chapter Quiz
Write your answers in complete sentences.

1. What type of society was Mao Zedong determined to build in China?

2. What is the name of the philosophy that guides behavior in five key social relationships?

3. Where did anti-Communist nationalists settle after the 1949 revolution?

4. **Critical Thinking** How has its written language helped to keep China united?

5. **Critical Thinking** How has communism changed life for Chinese peasants? Give one example.

Write About Geography
Complete the following activities.

1. Reread the section about Chinese inventions. Choose one and describe how it is used today.

2. Think about how China has changed. Write what you think China will be like in the future.

Group Activity
Confucianism sets out a code for living. Within your group, create your own code for classroom conduct. Have each person work on a rule. Edit each other's work and put the rules together to form the code.

This wooden gateway serves as the symbolic entrance to a historic Buddhist temple complex. Japanese art, architecture, and religion reflects themes from nature. What are some natural elements found in this photograph?

Chapter 27 Japan

Words to Know

tsunami	a huge sea wave caused by an underwater earthquake or volcanic eruption
shrine	a sacred place or structure where people go to pray
meditation	quiet, focused thought
nirvana	in Buddhism, the condition of having reached enlightenment
noh	a form of traditional Japanese theater that uses minimal stage settings
kabuki	a form of popular Japanese theater that uses elaborate stage settings

Places to Know

Hokkaido

Honshu

Shikoku

Kyushu

Tokyo

Hiroshima

Nagasaki

Learning Objectives

- Describe the geography of Japan.
- Explain why Japan depends on foreign trade.
- Describe Japan's two main religions, Shinto and Buddhism.
- Explain Japan's role in World War II, and tell how the war affected Japan's economy.
- Describe a typical Japanese home.
- Describe some typical Japanese arts.

A Land of Limited Resources

HISTORY FACT

Japan is sometimes called "the land of the rising sun." Japan is the Japanese pronunciation of Ciponga, the ancient Chinese name for this land. Ciponga meant "land from which the sun rises."

Remember
Earthquakes and volcanoes have seriously affected Latin America, as well.

Japan is an island nation in the Pacific Ocean. It is a little more than 100 miles from the Asian mainland. About 4,000 mountainous islands make up this country. The four largest islands are Hokkaido, Honshu, Shikoku, and Kyushu. About 80 percent of the people of Japan live on Honshu, where Tokyo, the capital, is located. Also on the island of Honshu is Mount Fuji, a snow-capped volcano that was once considered sacred by Japanese people.

Japan has more than 190 volcanoes, about 30 of which are still active. The volcanoes create many hot springs, which Japanese people use as resorts. The Japanese also use steam from the hot springs to heat schools and other public buildings.

Earthquakes are a major problem in Japan. One earthquake that struck in 1923 killed more than 100,000 people. Japan also gets frequent **tsunamis**. Tsunamis are huge, destructive waves caused by an undersea earthquake or volcanic eruption.

Rugged mountains cover more than 80 percent of the land in Japan. Therefore, many areas are too steep to farm. Nevertheless, Japanese people have created farmland by cutting terraces into some hillsides. They have also created new farmland by draining marshes. Rice is the main crop.

Japan also gets much of its food from the sea. In fact, their fishing industry leads the world. Cod, halibut, tuna, salmon, and many other types of fish are caught off the coasts of Japan. Seaweed and shellfish are actually raised by "sea farmers." Between what it gets from the land and the sea, Japan manages to produce most of its own food. Seafood and rice are the main staples in the Japanese diet.

The sea has shaped Japanese culture in other ways. Long ago, the sea kept Japan isolated from outside influences. As a result, most Japanese people today belong to the same ethnic group. In fact, ethnic minorities make up less than 1 percent of Japan's population. The Japanese have a strong national identity and discourage immigration from other countries.

The Ainu are one of Japan's ethnic minorities. They live mainly on the island of Hokkaido. Archaeologists believe that the Ainu were the first people to live in Japan. Immigrants from China later pushed them north.

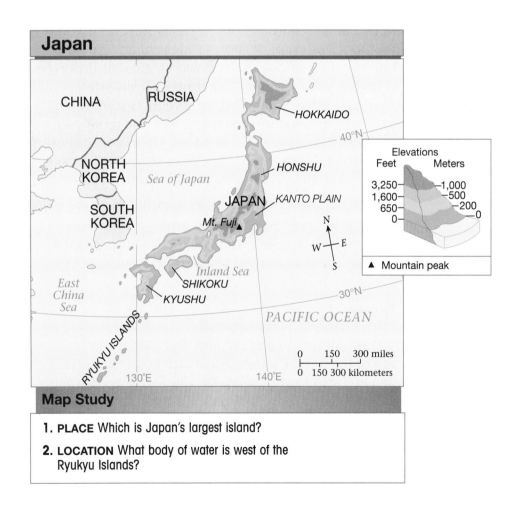

Japan

Map Study

1. **PLACE** Which is Japan's largest island?

2. **LOCATION** What body of water is west of the Ryukyu Islands?

Only about 15,000 Ainu survive today. The Ainu look different from other Japanese people. They have darker skin, and the men wear heavy beards. They practice a religion in which bears are very important. Their language is related to no other known language on the Earth.

About 125 million people live in Japan. The country is about the size of California, yet it has more than half as many people as the whole United States. Most of these people are crowded onto the lowlands, and almost 80 percent of them live in cities. Thus, Japan is one of the world's most crowded nations.

Geography Fact

Only 14 percent of the land in Japan can be used in agriculture.

Japan also is one of the world's most highly industrialized countries. Yet, it has almost no natural resources. For example, it has little coal and no oil or iron. What Japan does have, however, are skilled workers. Japan buys the raw materials it needs from other countries. It then manufactures products from these materials, sells them abroad, and uses the money to buy more raw materials. Therefore, Japan depends on international trade more than most countries. Because it sells more than it buys, Japan is a wealthy nation.

Cars are Japan's leading export. Other Japanese products include steel, iron, scientific instruments, electronics equipment, and chemicals. Most people in Japan are employed in industry and business.

Shinto

Shinto is an ancient religion that guides the Japanese way of life. It is practiced widely in Japan. It centers on a belief in kami. Originally, kami were gods and goddesses who lived in trees, mountains, and storms. Over time, however, kami came to mean a sacred power that is part of all things, living and nonliving. The word Shinto means "the way of the gods."

Shinto is not a formal religion with firm rules. It is more like a set of attitudes and values. In the Shinto view, people are born good. If they practice the way of kami, they will continue to be good.

Shinto has no founder and no sacred texts. It took shape gradually over the course of Japan's early history. In the eighth century, however, two important books were written that tell about the view. They are the *Kojiki* and the *Nihongi*. Both are collections of Japanese folk stories, ancient customs, history, and geography. They describe ancient Shinto practices.

Followers of Shinto often pray at **shrines**. A Shinto shrine is usually a simple wooden structure, which has a place for people to wash their hands before praying. People may pray for good health, good fortune, or protection from enemies. Every year, each shrine hosts various public festivals. Many of these festivals have something to do with planting, growing, or harvesting crops. Ceremonies such as weddings may also take place at a Shinto shrine.

Buddhism

Buddhism came to Japan in the sixth century. It did not compete with Shinto as it sought to address different matters. Both religions flourished side by side. Today, most Japanese people practice both Buddhism and Shinto.

Buddhism began around 550 B.C. in India. It spread south to Sri Lanka and east through China to Japan, Korea, and Southeast Asia. It was founded by an Indian prince named Siddhartha Gautama who dedicated his life to exploring one question: Why is there suffering? Searching for the answer brought Siddhartha to a state of wisdom called enlightenment. Afterward, he was known as the Buddha or "enlightened one."

The Temple of the Golden Pavilion is one of Japan's most famous buildings.

Buddhism teaches that living is suffering. It also teaches that people are reborn many times into lives of suffering. People suffer because they desire, or feel attached to, the things of this world. They can escape suffering by putting a stop to their desire and attachment.

Buddhism presents a way to reach this difficult goal. The Buddhist path includes clear thinking, good conduct, honorable work, and **meditation**. In Buddhism, meditation means focusing on one thing and keeping the mind still.

By following this path, Buddhists hope to reach enlightenment. Those who succeed become part of a world beyond thought called **nirvana**. Those who fail are born into a new body after they die and must live another life of suffering. According to Buddhism, people keep being reborn until they become enlightened.

Japan has many Buddhist temples, where priests perform religious rituals. Statues of Buddha are common. One branch of Japanese Buddhism, however, does not use images and rituals. It is called Zen Buddhism and emphasizes simple living, hard work, meditation, and study with an enlightened teacher.

✓ **Check Your Understanding**

Write your answers in complete sentences.

1. How did Japan become a highly industrialized country without having many natural resources?

2. What is kami?

3. What does Buddhism teach?

Japan's Foreign Policies

In the 1600s, Japan closed its borders to outsiders. It wanted to keep Western influences, such as Christianity, out of the country. In 1853, however, the United States demanded that Japan start trading with other countries. A fleet of U.S. warships delivered the message. Japan was too weak to refuse.

Shocked by its own weakness, Japan began to arm itself. By 1894, it had the strongest military force in Asia. Japan fought China for control of Korea and won. Ten years later, it beat Russia in a short war. In the 1930s, a group of military leaders came to power in Japan and decided to build a colonial empire. Japan was industrializing quickly. It needed natural resources. Japan's military took control of Manchuria, the northeast corner of China.

Shortly after this, World War II began. In 1941, Japan attacked the U.S. Navy at Pearl Harbor, in the Hawaiian Islands. This action drew both nations into the war, mainly against each other.

At first, Japan scored stunning victories. By 1942, its empire stretched from China to Myanmar (formerly Burma). Japan's conquests included Korea, the Philippines, Indonesia, and most of the small islands of the South Pacific. The Japanese government ruled harshly, however. The people they conquered feared and hated them.

It all began to change, however. The United States and its allies began to use submarines to cut Japan off from the land it controlled. Without resources, Japan's economy began to fail. Meanwhile, the United States had perfected a new weapon in 1945—the atomic bomb. Two of these bombs were dropped on Japan. The cities of Hiroshima and Nagasaki were leveled. Over 120,000 people died. Many more were damaged by radiation. These terrible bombings forced Japan to surrender.

You Decide

Japan is the only country that has suffered a nuclear attack. How do you think this may have affected Japanese attitudes toward war?

The war left Japan's cities in ruins. Its ruling military class fell from power. The United States forced Japan to adopt a new constitution, which forbids Japan to keep a military force or to make war. Japan still has an emperor, but its real power lies in the hands of a democratically elected parliament. The head of government is the prime minister. The party that wins the most seats in parliament gets to name the prime minister.

An Economic Miracle

Economics Fact

Japan suffered its worst recession, or economic downturn, in 1998. Not since World War II had Japan's economy been so troubled.

After the war, the United States wanted a strong capitalist ally in East Asia. Therefore, it began to help Japan rebuild its economy. Having no military proved to be an advantage for Japan. The country could spend all of the extra money building factories and buying new equipment.

Out of the new factories came a flood of inexpensive, low-quality goods such as toys and cameras. As it captured markets throughout the world, Japan began to raise the quality and price of its goods. Its products now have a reputation for quality. Japan also has some of the world's most advanced technology.

Loyalty and hard work are traditional Japanese values. They make for a disciplined workforce. Workers in Japan rarely come to work late or go home early. Many of them must be forced to take vacations. Quitting one corporation to work for another is not done generally, although it is becoming more common.

The loyalty works both ways. Japanese corporations rarely lay off employees. Traditionally, once people are hired by a corporation, they are hired for life. Traditions such as these have helped Japan build the world's second-largest economy.

Large business groups or corporations control the Japanese economy. The Liberal Democratic Party represents their interests. This party has won every election since the war. As a result, the Japanese government works closely with big business. For example, government money is used to help develop new products. The government taxes manufactured goods from other countries. This means that foreign companies cannot compete in Japan, because the taxes make their products too expensive.

Education for Success

The Japanese people value education. After all, their economy depends on highly trained workers. Teachers are well paid and have high status. Nearly 95 percent of young people complete high school. About 40 percent go on to college. Other industrialized countries, such as the United States, have a much lower rate of college attendance.

Getting into college is very difficult. Young people in Japan must compete for limited openings. College entrance exams are tough. So are high-school entrance exams. The competition to get into good high schools is strong. Even in grade school, therefore, Japanese children are under pressure to study hard and do well.

A Japanese Home

A typical Japanese home is small. When Japanese people enter a home, they take off their shoes and change into slippers. Keeping the floor clean is important, because people traditionally sit on the floor on cushions or on straw mats called tatami.

Most Japanese homes mix traditional and modern features. For example, you will probably find computers in the home. Yet, the bedrooms will probably have no beds. People usually sleep on a kind of mattress called a futon, which is spread on the floor. A traditional Japanese living room has a nook or inset space, where a few carefully chosen items are arranged in an artistic display.

Japan's cities are crowded and large. People have to travel long distances to get to work. Many people work in the city but live in a distant suburb. Many Japanese businesspeople stay in the city during the week and go home only on weekends.

Traveling businesspeople stay in their hotel rooms such as these in Osaka, Japan. Japan is one of the most crowded countries in the world.

The Position of Women

In 1947, Japan's government gave women the same rights as men. This included the right to vote. By law, therefore, Japanese men and women are equal. In practice, the situation is quite different. Ancient Japanese traditions give women a less important role in society than men, and these traditions remain strong. Most leaders in business and government are men. Women generally are supposed to take care of the home and the children. Household finances are included in their duties. A husband typically turns over his entire paycheck to his wife. It is then her responsibility to manage the money.

In light of these traditions, it may seem odd that about half of all workers in Japan are women. However, women workers earn much less money than men. Many women only work part time. Some do not receive pensions or other benefits.

It is more difficult for women to get into colleges than it is for men, even if their exam scores are high. Often, women who do earn college degrees do not get professional jobs. Instead, they end up working as clerks, waitresses, or secretaries. Even professional women such as engineers, accountants, and architects often work only until they get married.

On a Tokyo street, two women walk—one wears a kimono and the other a suit.

The Arts in Japan

Japanese religions have affected the arts of Japan. From Shinto comes a deep feeling for nature. From Buddhism—especially Zen Buddhism—comes a high admiration for simplicity. Japanese arts stress simplicity and natural beauty. Traditional architects design simple, graceful buildings that fit into a natural setting. They use such building materials as wood and bamboo. At one time, windows were made of paper instead of glass.

Nature is often the subject of Japanese poetry. One kind of Japanese poem is the haiku, which has exactly 17 syllables and just three lines. The first and third lines have five syllables each, and the second line has seven syllables.

The Japanese have perfected the art of making woodblock prints. Many of these prints show scenes from nature, such as ocean waves or Mount Fuji. To make a woodblock print, the artist carves a design into a block of wood. The wood is then inked and stamped onto a sheet of paper or cloth.

Flower arranging is another popular activity. As an art, it is called ikebana. This art emphasizes shapes and lines more than color. Flowers, leaves, stems, and other materials are used as symbols.

In Japan, gardening is considered an art. Japanese gardens express Buddhist ideals. The gardens are calm and peaceful places where people can meditate. Plants, ponds, rocks, and bridges are arranged to create balanced, beautiful views. Patterns are irregular, as in nature.

Japan has two traditional forms of theater. **Noh** drama developed in the 1300s and has changed little since then. A noh play has little action and is performed on a stage that is nearly bare. Generally, there are only two main actors. The story is chanted by a chorus of men and expresses Buddhist ideas. **Kabuki**, by contrast, is popular entertainment. The stage is crowded with color and action. The actors wear elaborate costumes and sing and dance as they act out popular stories of love, war, and adventure.

Kabuki theater presents stories of love, war, and adventure.

✓ Check Your Understanding

Write your answers in complete sentences.

1. What forced Japan to surrender in World War II?

2. Describe a typical Japanese home.

3. What are two forms of Japanese theater?

GEOGRAPHER'S TOOL KIT
Understanding Line Graphs

A line graph shows trends, or changes, over time. To read a line graph, first read the title. That tells the subject of the graph. Then, look at the bottom, which shows the time period that is covered. The left side of the graph tells what is changing. The line on the graph will show you the changes over time.

Japan: Goods and Services Produced, 1950–1990

Answer the questions below.

1. What trend does this graph show?

2. What decade shows the least increase in the amount of goods and services produced?

CHALLENGE Based on Japan's history, why do you think the output of goods and services was so much lower in 1950?

Apply the Skill

Create a line graph that tells how many hours you slept each night for the past two weeks. Can you tell any trends from looking at your graph?

Summary

Japan is made up of about 4,000 mountainous islands. Honshu is the main island of Japan. Three other large islands are Hokkaido, Shikoku, and Kyushu.
Japan has few natural resources, yet it is highly industrialized. It buys raw materials from other countries and exports finished goods.
In Japan, most people practice both Buddhism and Shinto.
The United States defeated Japan in World War II. To end the war, the United States dropped two atomic bombs on Japan.
Big business, organized into large corporations, has great political power in Japan.
A high regard for education has given Japan a skilled work force.
Japan's constitution gives equal rights to women by law. Tradition, however, gives women a lesser role in public life.

meditation
shrine
noh
tsunami
nirvana

Vocabulary Review

Complete each sentence with a term from the list.

1. The condition of having reached enlightenment is called _____ in Buddhism.

2. A _____ is a sacred place or structure where people go to pray.

3. A huge sea wave caused by an undersea earthquake or volcanic eruption is a _____.

4. Quiet, focused thought is called _____.

5. A form of traditional Japanese theater that uses minimal stage settings is known as _____ theater.

Chapter Quiz

Write your answers in complete sentences.

1. What is the most populated island of Japan?

2. What is the name of the philosophy that teaches that desire causes suffering?

3. What is a three-line poem that has exactly 17 syllables?

4. **Critical Thinking** What difficulties might a Japanese woman face?

5. **Critical Thinking** Why has Japanese industry been so successful?

Write About Geography

Complete the following activities.

1. Write an essay that explores how the physical geography of Japan affects life there.

2. Compare daily life in Japan with daily life for people where you live.

Group Activity

Haiku is a three-line poem with five syllables on the first line, seven syllables on the second line, and five syllables on the third line. Have each group member write at least one haiku. Remember that haiku is often based on nature. Put the poems into a book. One group member should design a cover.

More than 10 million people live in Seoul, the capital of South Korea. In what ways does living in a highly populated city affect everyday life?

Chapter 28 Korea

Words to Know

occupied	controlled by a foreign military force
truce	a temporary agreement to stop fighting
demilitarized zone	an area where no military forces are allowed
sweatshop	a factory that pays very low wages to laborers who work long hours in crowded conditions

Places to Know

Seoul

North Korea

South Korea

38th parallel

Pyongyang

Learning Objectives

- Explain how physical geography has shaped Korean culture.

- Tell how Korea came to be split into two separate countries.

- Compare the political and economic structures of North Korea and South Korea.

- Explain how South Korea's family structure is changing.

- Describe tae kwan do, Korea's national martial art.

A Rugged Peninsula

The Korean Peninsula is in northeast Asia between the Yellow Sea and the Sea of Japan. The Yalu and the Tumen rivers separate it from China, its northern neighbor. It shares a short border with Russia's Siberia—about 20 miles. To the southeast, across the Korean Strait, lies the Japanese island of Kyushu. There are two countries on the Korean Peninsula: North Korea and South Korea.

Korea has a varied climate. The north is dry and has long, cold winters. The south benefits from warm ocean currents. Summers in the south are mild and moist. Winters are cold, but they are short.

Geography Fact

Seoul is the fourth-largest city in the world. Seoul is the capital of South Korea.

Korea's main agricultural crop is rice. Most of the good farmland is in the south. The north, however, has more mineral resources, including coal and iron. Korea has a long coastline, but it provides few good harbors for large ships.

About 70 percent of the Korean Peninsula is covered with mountains. These mountains are low but steep. Because of the mountains, cultural differences have developed among the Korean peoples. For example, there are six different dialects of the Korean language.

Yet physical geography has also protected Korea. The mountains slowed armies coming from the north. Armies coming from any other direction had to approach by sea. Korea managed to keep out invaders for most of its long history.

Korean civilization goes back more than 2,000 years. Over the centuries, it has been strongly influenced by Chinese culture. For example, Buddhism came to Korea through China. Koreans borrowed building ideas from the Chinese. Steep roofs, red tiles, and upturned corners are features of buildings in both countries.

However, Korean culture is strong and unique. The language, for example, is written with letters, not characters, as is Chinese. Koreans perfected the lovely blue-green pottery glaze known as celadon. Traces of Korea's ancient animist religion can still be seen in its customs. Christian missionaries have influenced Korean culture, too. In fact, Christianity is Korea's main religion.

Remember
Animism is a belief that many spirits live within the natural world.

A Divided Nation

Korea became one country in A.D. 668. Although it was attacked many times and **occupied** twice, it remained unified until 1910. In that year, it was conquered by Japan and became a colony. The Japanese government tried to do away with Korean culture. Koreans were forced to use Japanese names and to speak only Japanese. They also were used as enslaved laborers.

During World War II, Soviet and U.S. troops drove the Japanese out of Korea. Soviet troops came in from the north. The United States moved in soldiers from the south. The two armies met at 38 degrees north latitude, a line now known as the 38th parallel.

Unfortunately, Korea became a battleground during the cold war. The Soviet Union wanted Korea to become a Communist nation. The United States wanted it to become a capitalist democracy. Because neither side could overcome the other, Korea was divided into two separate countries in 1948. One was North Korea, or the Democratic People's Republic of Korea. The other was South Korea, or the Republic of Korea. The 38th parallel marks the approximate border between them.

In 1950, North Korea tried to reunite the peninsula with force by invading South Korea. The United Nations sent in 400,000 troops to defend South Korea. Most of these soldiers were from the United States. Communist China supplied troops to help North Korea. The Korean War lasted three years and cost more than 5 million lives.

In 1953, both sides agreed to a **truce.** When the fighting stopped, neither side had gained an inch. A strip of land along the 38th parallel became a **demilitarized zone** or DMZ. All military forces agreed to pull their troops back from this area. To this day, however, both keep large forces near the DMZ. A real peace treaty has never been signed. Officially, the two Koreas are still at war.

North Korea is a strict Communist nation. It is also one of the world's most isolated countries. It has few dealings with any other country, especially since the collapse of the Soviet Union. Few people are allowed in or out, so little is known about North Korea except what the government reports. The government says that Pyongyang, the capital, is a city of 2.5 million people. North Korea was ruled for almost 50 years by one man, Kim Il Sung. He was succeeded by his son, Kim Jong Il.

South Korea has a strong capitalist economy, but it is politically unstable. A military dictator who ruled the country for 18 years was killed in 1979. The general who took over was forced out of office by riots. The current president of South Korea is Kim Dae Sung. The government has kept many of its critics in jail for years. Many of its leaders since 1979 have been corrupt.

You Decide

Most Koreans would like North Korea and South Korea to be united. Why do you think this is?

There are strong signs of a thaw between the two countries, though. In 2000, for the first time, the two Korean presidents met. Even more surprising, the leaders agreed to work to unite their countries.

Millions of Koreans have relatives across the border whom they have not seen since 1950. In August of 2000, 200 family members from North and South Korea met. "It took 50 years for me to travel such a short distance," said one North Korean man as he arrived to meet his sister.

The path to reuniting the two countries will not be easy. South Korea watched West Germany pay a high price to rejoin East Germany. Yet there is hope. In the 2000 Olympics, athletes from North and South Korea marched together. It may be a view of the future.

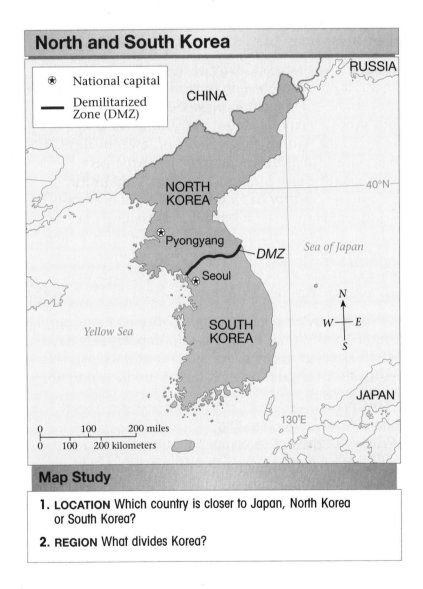

North and South Korea

⊛ National capital

━━ Demilitarized Zone (DMZ)

RUSSIA

CHINA

NORTH KOREA

40°N

⊛ Pyongyang

DMZ

Sea of Japan

⊛ Seoul

Yellow Sea

SOUTH KOREA

N
W—E
S

JAPAN

130°E

0   100   200 miles
0   100   200 kilometers

Map Study

1. **LOCATION** Which country is closer to Japan, North Korea or South Korea?

2. **REGION** What divides Korea?

One Little Tiger

After the Korean War, South Korea rebuilt its cities and small factories with help from the United States. Today, South Korea has one of the world's fastest-growing economies. For this reason it is known as one of Asia's four "little tigers." The other "little tigers" are Hong Kong, Taiwan, and Singapore. The nickname sets them apart from Asia's economic dragon—Japan.

South Korea makes many of the same products as Japan. It produces steel, iron, electronic goods, and cars. It also manufactures plywood, textiles, clothes, and shoes. It exports almost everything it makes. South Korea's goods are generally of lower quality than Japan's, but they tend to be less expensive. Thus, South Korea is doing what Japan did in the 1950s. The country has found markets all over the world and is now the twelfth-largest trading nation. It has a growing middle class. Its people enjoy a high standard of living compared to most Asian countries. South Koreans work hard for their success, however. On average, they work 55 hours a week.

North Korea is a highly industrialized nation, too. Unlike South Korea, it exports and imports very little. North Korea grows its own food and uses its own raw materials for its industries. It makes products only for North Koreans.

$ Economics Fact

North Korea has been struggling with a famine since 1995. Some of the causes of the famine are flooding, droughts, and shortages of fuel and machines.

✓ **Check Your Understanding**

Write your answers in complete sentences.

1. Why is Korea a Christian country?

2. Why did Korea become a battleground during the cold war?

3. How is South Korea like Japan in its economy?

GEOGRAPHY IN YOUR LIFE
Reading Transportation Maps

Public transportation helps cut down on traffic jams and pollution. Many cities have trains that move through underground tunnels, called subways. A subway system usually has many lines. Trains running along each line stop at various stations. A subway map shows the different lines and stations.

Seoul Subway System

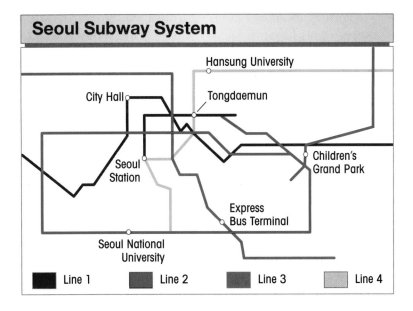

Hansung University

City Hall

Tongdaemun

Seoul Station

Children's Grand Park

Express Bus Terminal

Seoul National University

Line 1   Line 2   Line 3   Line 4

Answer the questions below.

1. Which line leads to the bus terminal?

2. What is the most direct route from Seoul Station to Seoul National University?

CHALLENGE Why do you think an industrial center like Seoul needs a subway system?

Apply the Skill

Choose a place to travel. Find a transportation map for that city. Write directions for using transportation from one place to another in that city.

A Changing Family Structure

Korean society has changed a great deal since the Korean War. In 1950, half of the population worked in agriculture. Many Koreans lived in isolated mountain villages, and quite a few had never been outside their villages. In those days, sons traditionally did not leave home when they married. Instead, they brought their wives into the household. A typical Korean home had three or four generations living under the same roof.

Family life was heavily influenced by Confucian values and ideas. Koreans valued sons. They also valued age. The eldest men were the most respected. Women traditionally played a minor role both in the family and in Korean society.

In the crowded cities, the pattern of family living has changed. There is not enough room for large families to live together. Single adults often have their own apartments. Young couples live in their own homes, away from the rest of the family.

As Korea has industrialized, women have gone to work in great numbers. Women make up most of the workforce in the **sweatshops**. A sweatshop is a crowded factory that pays low wages. Korea has been able to make affordable goods for export mainly because of these low wages. Korea's economy would not be where it is today without these low-paid workers.

Still, Korean families have not given up traditional Confucian values. Adult children visit their parents often. It is still common for young people to be introduced to each other through a matchmaker. Koreans also consider it their duty to take care of the graves of their ancestors. On one holiday, family members weed the grave sites of their ancestors and plant flowers or shrubs.

Women working at an electric company in South Korea.

Korean Martial Arts

The martial arts are techniques for hand-to-hand fighting. Buddhist monks developed the first of these arts in India more than 15 centuries ago. As Buddhism spread to China and Japan, so did the martial arts. Gradually, they branched into many different styles. Kung fu, aikido, Shaolin temple boxing, tai chi chuan, judo, kendo, and karate are a few of these styles.

Karate is probably the most famous martial art. It is a way of fighting without weapons. Karate masters use their hands, feet, and other parts of their bodies. They depend on speed, grace, inner calm, and strength of mind.

These students are practicing tae kwon do, the Korean martial art.

Tae kwon do, which means "methods of smashing with the hands and destroying with the feet," is a Korean form of karate. This martial art was perfected during the Silla dynasty, Korea's "golden age." The Silla dynasty lasted from A.D. 668 to 918. In this era, Korean warriors were sent to China to learn Buddhist fighting techniques. These warriors developed these techniques into tae kwon do.

When Japan took over Korea in 1910, Koreans were not allowed to express their own culture. Japanese martial arts replaced Korean ones. After 1945, Koreans wanted to re-introduce their martial arts. Tae kwon do found a place of honor as a national art. Tae kwon do competitions are now held in Korea and all over the world.

HISTORY FACT

Tae kwon do uses fast, striking movements—mainly kicks, jumps, and punches. A tae kwon do master can kick forward, to the side, or backward.

Tae kwon do students wear a loose-fitting, two-piece uniform made of thick, white cloth. The jacket folds together in front. It has no buttons, but it is held shut with a colored belt. The color of the belt shows the student's rank. Beginners wear white belts. As they improve, they move on to yellow, green, blue, red, or brown belts. Finally, they get black belts. Then, they are no longer students but masters.

Students compete with others of their rank. When students begin practice, they bow to the teacher to show respect. Then they bow to their partner. Like all martial arts, tae kwon do stresses spiritual strength and calm. Meditation helps students get into this state of mind. It helps them find a spiritual energy, which they can use to conquer their opposites.

✓ Check Your Understanding

Write your answers in complete sentences.

1. How has the role of women changed in Korea?

2. What are martial arts?

3. Why was tae kwon do little practiced in Korea from 1910–1945?

GLOBAL ISSUES
Saving the Dolphins

Dolphins often swim where tuna do. Fishermen follow the dolphins to help them find tuna. Some fishermen use drift nets. These nets drift over a huge area of ocean—as much as forty miles. The nets catch everything in their path. That can include dolphins and other animals that are killed by the nets. As much as 40 to 50 percent of the catch in drift nets is wasted. Since 1959, about 7 million dolphins have been killed this way.

In the 1970s, activists began a campaign to stop drift-net fishing. Today, many tuna fish cans have a dolphin-safe label. That means that dolphins were not killed to catch the tuna. Instead, fishermen used a different method of fishing.

Korea's fishermen, along with those from Japan and Taiwan, have been known for using drift nets. In 1997, the Republic of Korea agreed to cut its use of drift nets by half. More and more, countries are realizing that the decisions they make affect the entire world.

Answer the questions below.

1. Why do fishermen follow dolphins to catch tuna?

2. Why do you think Korea agreed to reduce its use of drift nets?

MAKE A DIFFERENCE
Not all tuna is dolphin safe. Go to your local grocery store. Check for dolphin-safe labels. Report back to your class about what you find.

Summary

Korea is a mountainous peninsula in East Asia. Korea has a distinct culture of its own. Yet Korea has been strongly influenced by China and was a colony of Japan from 1910 until World War II.
After World War II, Korea was occupied by both Soviet and U.S. troops. As a result, Korea was divided into two separate countries.
The 38th parallel marks the border between North Korea and South Korea.
North Korea is a strict and isolated Communist country. South Korea is a capitalist country with a rapidly growing economy. Both North Korea and South Korea are highly industrialized.

Vocabulary Review

Write *true* or *false*. If the statement is false, change the underlined term to make it true.

1. If an area is <u>occupied</u>, then it is controlled by a foreign military force.

2. A temporary agreement to stop fighting is a <u>sweatshop</u>.

3. An area where no military forces are allowed is a <u>demilitarized</u> <u>zone</u>.

4. A laborer who works long hours for low wages in a crowded factory probably works in a <u>truce</u>.

Chapter Quiz

Write your answers in complete sentences.

1. What is the capital of North Korea?

2. What is the strip of land between North Korea and South Korea, where no soldiers may be stationed known as?

3. Why is South Korea known as one of Asia's "little tigers"?

4. **Critical Thinking** What caused Korea to split into the countries of North Korea and South Korea?

5. **Critical Thinking** How has Korea's location and physical geography affected its history and culture?

Write About Geography

Complete the following activities.

1. You have lived in isolated North Korea and are just visiting the United States. Write what surprises you.

2. Create a timeline of the Korean War. Your timeline should begin in 1945 and end in 2000.

Group Activity

One half of your group are North Korean and South Korean Olympic athletes who are marching together. The other half of your group are reporters who interview the Olympians and write articles about them. The athletes can edit the articles.

Unit 8 Review

Comprehension Check
Answer each question in a complete sentence.

1. How did Genghis Khan affect world history?

2. Who was Mao Zedong?

3. How was Japan affected by World War II?

4. How are North Korea and South Korea different?

Building Your Skills
Answer each question in a complete sentence.

1. How can you tell how much time is covered in a timeline?

2. Where is Taiwan?

3. When would you use a line graph?

4. What does a city transportation map show?

Where Is It?
Write the name of the place based on the information below.

1. The largest former republic of Soviet Central Asia

2. The world's tallest mountains

3. The island where 80 percent of Japanese people live

4. The country in the Korean Peninsula controlled by Communists

Writing an Essay
Answer one of the following essay topics.

1. How did the Communists change life in Central Asia?

2. Did Mao Zedong manage to create a classless society in China? Explain your answer.

3. How did Japan become a world economic power?

4. Describe how North Korea and South Korea became separate countries.

Geography and You

China is among the largest countries in the world and is the country with the most people. The United States, which is smaller and has fewer people, is a greater world power. Why do you think this is?

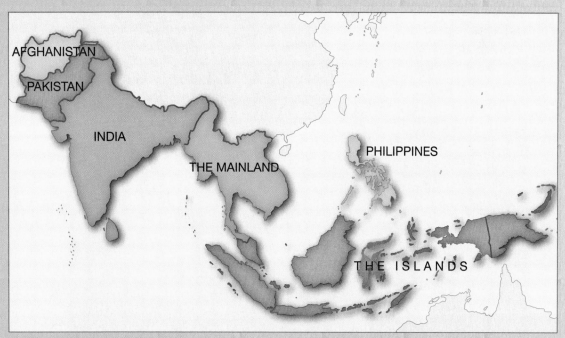

AFGHANISTAN

PAKISTAN

INDIA

THE MAINLAND

PHILIPPINES

THE ISLANDS

All of the countries in the region of South and Southeast Asia, except one, have at least one border that touches water. Which is the one country that is landlocked?

TRAVEL LOG

The sitar is one of the most well-known instruments in India. As you travel through South and Southeast Asia, write about three other things that people should know about this region.

Indian instrument, the sitar

These Jaipur women are wearing saris, the national Indian dress. Why might they be carrying jars?

Words to Know

subcontinent	a large portion of a continent that is geographically isolated from the rest of the continent
monsoon	a seasonal wind that creates a strong pattern of wet and dry seasons in parts of Asia
reincarnation	rebirth into a new body or physical form in this world
incarnation	the particular physical form that a spirit takes in this world
karma	a fate or destiny shaped by one's past actions in this lifetime or in a previous lifetime
caste	a fixed social class into which one is born and from which one cannot move

Places to Know

Mumbai

Hindu Kush

Thar Desert

Deccan Plateau

Indus River

Ganges River

Learning Objectives

- Describe India's climate and major landforms.
- Trace the sources of India's culture.
- Describe Hinduism and its role in India's culture.
- Explain how the British colony of India was divided after independence and eventually became three countries.
- Tell how most people in India live and work.

The Indian Subcontinent

Bombay, now called Mumbai, is located in a part of southern Asia called the Indian **subcontinent**. This part of Asia is cut off from the rest of the region by mountains and jungles. India is the largest country on the subcontinent. Bangladesh, Bhutan, Nepal, and Pakistan are also on the subcontinent. Northwest of Pakistan is Afghanistan, which separates the Indian subcontinent from Central Asia.

The Himalayas form the northern border of the subcontinent. They are the tallest mountains in the world and stretch about 1,500 miles. The Himalayas create a barrier that has rarely been crossed except by airline. The rugged Hindu Kush in Afghanistan are mountains that are almost as tall, but they have been crossed regularly. Armies have poured through its narrow gaps—the best-known of which is Khyber Pass.

South of the Himalayas is a large, open plain. It covers most of northern India, part of Pakistan, and all of Bangladesh. Three important rivers flow out of the Himalayas and through this plain: the Indus, the Ganges, and the Brahmaputra.

The climate of the Indian subcontinent varies quite a bit. The northern mountains have a dry climate, much like that of Central Asia. In the northwest is a barren region called the Thar Desert. The plains of the northeast are mild and moist. Much of India is heavily affected by **monsoons**. These are seasonal winds that change direction regularly, twice a year. Between May and October, the monsoons blow from the ocean toward land. Beginning around July, monsoons bring warm weather and heavy rains—as much as 15 inches a month. Between October and May, the monsoons blow the other way—from the land out to sea. During these months, the winds bring cooler, dry weather from Central Asia.

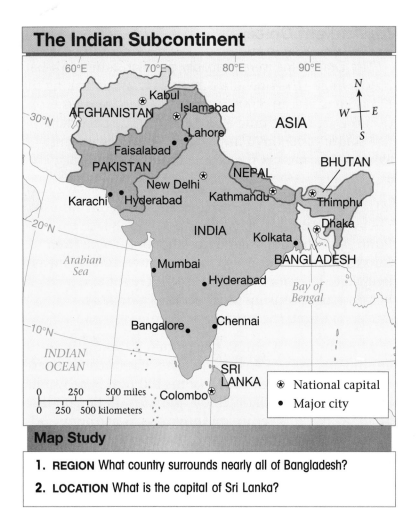

The Indian Subcontinent

60°E 70°E 80°E 90°E

30°N

Kabul
AFGHANISTAN Islamabad
Lahore
Faisalabad
PAKISTAN
New Delhi
Karachi Hyderabad Kathmandu

ASIA

NEPAL BHUTAN
Thimphu

N
W — E
S

20°N

Arabian
Sea

INDIA Kolkata

Dhaka

BANGLADESH

Mumbai
Hyderabad

Bay of
Bengal

10°N

Bangalore Chennai

INDIAN
OCEAN

0   250   500 miles
0   250   500 kilometers

SRI
LANKA
Colombo

⊛ National capital
• Major city

Map Study

1. **REGION** What country surrounds nearly all of Bangladesh?
2. **LOCATION** What is the capital of Sri Lanka?

The major landform in central India is the Deccan Plateau. It has low hills and shallow valleys. Three small mountain ranges line its edges.

The culture of India has many layers. More than 200 languages are spoken in the country. At least 24 of them are spoken by more than one million people. There are 25 states in India, each with its own official language or languages. Hindi is the official national language, but only 30 percent of the people speak it. Bengali, Tamil, Urdu, and English are important languages, too.

An Ancient Culture

The Dravidians were probably the first settlers in what is now India. The Dravidians built a civilization along the Indus River at least 5,000 years ago. Aryan invaders took over the area some time after 1500 B.C. The Dravidians fled south to the tip of India, where their descendants—almost 25 percent of the people in India—live today.

The Taj Mahal

The Aryans borrowed some ideas from the Dravidians, mixed them with their own, and developed Hinduism. The Aryans also brought the Sanskrit language to India. Most of India's modern languages come from Sanskrit. Many Hindu texts were written in this ancient language. Therefore, Sanskrit is still taught and read but no longer spoken. Most people in India are descended from the Aryans.

Muslims from Central Asia started attacking India around A.D. 1000. Previous invaders had become a part of Hindu society, but the Muslims did not. North India became a patchwork of Hindu and Muslim kingdoms. Then, in the 1500s, Turko-Mongol warriors conquered most of the subcontinent and started what was called the Mogul empire. For the next 200 years, Muslim Moguls ruled a mostly Hindu nation. Today, pockets of people living in the north of India are related to the Turks and Mongols of Central Asia.

Muslims added much to the culture of India. Their support made Urdu a major language. The Taj Mahal, a tomb of a Mogul queen, is often called the world's most beautiful building. Muslims remain a large, separate minority in modern India.

The next outsiders to rule India were the British, starting in the 1700s. As a result of their rule, English is still the language of business throughout the country. The laws and government of India are modeled on those of Britain. The British also created the world's most extensive railroad system in India.

Hinduism

About 82 percent of the people of India call themselves Hindus. Unlike some other religions, Hinduism had no precise beginning and no founder. It has no single holy book, but many sacred texts. The *Vedas*, for example, are four ancient books of hymns. The *Upanishads*, written around 600 B.C., discuss Hindu philosophy. Hindu beliefs and practices vary widely. Hindus worship thousands of gods. Each Hindu is free to choose his or her favorite. All Hindus, however, share certain broad ideas.

Hindus believe that every living creature has a soul, and that every soul is part of a larger spirit. According to the Hindus, when people die, their souls are reborn into new bodies in a process called **reincarnation**. Each time people are reincarnated, they move up or down in the social order, depending on how they have lived. Good beggars may become kings, and bad kings may become beggars.

The goal of life for a Hindu is to escape this endless cycle of rebirth. Reaching this goal, however, takes many lifetimes. In the end, one reaches a state called nirvana, wherein the soul becomes part of one great soul, known as Brahman.

Brahman is everlasting and unchanging. Brahman has many **incarnations**. These incarnations are the gods of Hinduism. For example, there is Vishnu the Preserver, who has appeared in the world as the hero Rama and the god Krishna.

According to Hinduism, everything that a person does influences what will eventually happen to that person. This is called the law of **karma**. Everything that a person does in this life will also add to his or her karma for the next life. Living right will move people closer to nirvana.

Shiva is the god of destruction. Yet, he is also the "seed of life," bringing new creations to life.

The Hindu Way of Life

Hinduism is more than a religion. It is a way of life. A Hindu's whole day is filled with religious rituals. Ordinary activities such as eating, bathing, and brushing teeth are rituals. Birth, marriage, death, and other important life events also have rituals.

Spotlight On

THE *MAHABHARATA* AND THE *RAMAYANA*

The *Mahabharata* is an epic Hindu poem—the longest poem ever written. It tells the story of a war between two tribes. In this war, the god Krishna fights as a human, helping a hero called Prince Arjuna.

This painting shows a scene from the epic Hindu poem the Mahabharata.

The *Mahabharata* is not just a story but a religious text. In the middle of the poem is a long conversation between Krishna and Arjuna. In this conversation, Krishna explains the meaning of life according to Hinduism. This conversation is the *Bhagavad Gita*, a book in itself.

The *Ramayana* is another epic religious poem filled with stories. It follows the adventures of Rama and his wife Sita, who are presented as the perfect man and woman. By their behavior, Rama and Sita show children what kind of persons they should become. In the main adventure, Rama—with the help of Hanuman, the monkey king—saves Sita from an evil king.

Most classical plays and dances in the Hindu world are based on stories from these poems.

Critical Thinking How are the *Mahabharata* and the *Ramayana* different?

The Hindu way of life is held in place by a strict **caste** system. Hinduism teaches that every person is born into a caste and cannot leave it until he or she dies. After death, a person may be reborn into a higher or lower caste depending on his or her karma. The caste system is thus like a ladder. Through reincarnation, individuals can climb the ladder. Only from the top rung can they reach nirvana.

Early Hinduism recognized four castes. At the top were priests, or Brahmins. Below them were kings and warriors. Lower were landowners and merchants. At the bottom were workers. Below the bottom was a group called the Untouchables, who had no caste at all. Originally, these were probably the Dravidian people whom the Aryans had conquered.

Over the centuries, the four castes were divided into thousands of subcastes called jatis. Many jatis are tied to particular jobs. A shoemaker may be of one jati while a barber is of another, for example.

A person may not marry or socialize outside his or her caste. Each person must wear the clothes that mark his or her caste. A person of one caste must speak to people of other castes in certain ways. A person of one caste cannot eat food prepared by people of other castes.

Only by remaining dutiful to their caste can people rise to another caste in the next life. Those who complain or struggle against the system will only sink to a lower caste. Thus, the caste system encourages people to accept their place in life. The caste system has brought order to India, but it has also prevented social change and progress toward equality.

In modern India, laws have been passed to weaken the caste system. For example, Untouchables now have the right to own property, which they did not have in the past. However, the caste system remains strong, especially in villages. Marriages between castes are rare, and Untouchables are still treated poorly.

HISTORY FACT

Rivers are sacred to Hindus, and the Ganges is the most sacred of all. Millions of people bathe in its holy waters during a festival called the Kumbh Mela.

This Brahman temple sits on a lake in India.

Other Religions in India

Remember
Buddhism was founded by an Indian prince named Siddhartha Gautama.

Hinduism has many branches, and some of these branches have grown into whole new religions. Buddhism, for example, began in the sixth century B.C. as a movement to reform Hinduism. The Buddha accepted the Hindu ideas of reincarnation, karma, and nirvana. He dismissed most Hindu rituals. He also rejected the caste system. He said that everyone could reach nirvana in one lifetime, if they followed the path he taught.

The Mauryan dynasty of early India—from 321 B.C. to 181 B.C.—supported Buddhism. By A.D. 600, Buddhism had become a major religion of east Asia. In India, however, Hinduism was replacing Buddhism. Today, only 1 percent of the people of India practice Buddhism.

The Sikhs branched out from Hinduism in the 1500s. Sikhs believe in reincarnation and nirvana but have no priests or caste system. Each person needs a personal teacher or guru in order to reach nirvana.

In the 1600s, the Sikhs had to defend themselves against the Moguls. As a result, they became very warlike. They have been known for their military values ever since. In modern India, Sikhs have clashed bitterly with Hindus. Some Sikhs demand an independent country in northern India. In 1984, Sikh terrorists killed India's president, Indira Gandhi.

Muslims make up about 11 percent of the Indian population—about 90 million people. That makes India the fifth-largest Islamic country in the world. Muslims and Hindus have a long history of conflict in India. The trouble is partly rooted in history. The Muslims invaded India and looted Hindu cities for six centuries.

The conflict goes beyond history, however. Two religions could hardly be more different than Hinduism and Islam. Islam, for example, insists that there is only one god. Hindus, however, worship many gods. Islam holds everyone to be equal, but Hinduism puts everyone in a caste. Muslims eat beef but not pork. Hindus will eat pork, but they consider cows sacred.

✓ **Check Your Understanding**
Write your answers in complete sentences.

1. How is India affected by monsoons?

2. Where do many descendants of the Dravidians live?

3. Why are caste systems important in the Hindu way of life?

Three Nations From One Colony

The British first came into India when the British East India Company set up trading posts along the coast. By the 1700s, the company controlled trade in India. Soon, this private company was running India like a government and hired Indian soldiers, or sepoys, to protect its businesses. In 1857, the sepoys rebelled, the British government stepped in, and India became an official British colony.

Within a generation, the people of India formed the Congress Party to seek independence from Britain. In the 1920s, the great Hindu leader Mahatma Gandhi became the head of this political party. Gandhi preached complete nonviolence. As millions joined Gandhi's movement, India became impossible to govern.

The Congress Party was not the only group seeking independence. Another was the Muslim League, led by Mohammed Ali Jinnah. This group wanted a separate country for the Muslims of the subcontinent.

By 1947, the British knew they had to give up their colony. They decided to divide the subcontinent into two countries. One would be India, a country with a Hindu majority. The other would be Pakistan, a Muslim nation. As soon as the new borders became official, Hindus rushed out of Pakistan into India. Muslims went into Pakistan. Riots occurred throughout the subcontinent. As many as 500,000 people were killed. Within about 6 months, roughly 13 million people had moved within the region.

Pakistan originally had two parts. One was east of India, and one was west of it. Over a thousand miles separated the two parts, yet they were supposed to be one Muslim nation. In 1970, East Pakistan declared itself independent. West Pakistan tried to crush the rebellion, but it failed. In 1971, East Pakistan officially became Bangladesh.

You Decide

Bangladesh has more people per square mile than any other country in the world. What kinds of problems does a crowded country have?

Earning a Living

In India, at least 650 million people live in small villages. Most of these people work as farmers. More than one-third of these farmers own no land. They work someone else's land in exchange for a share of the crops. Many Indian farmers still use wooden plows pulled by oxen or buffalo.

In recent years, the government has helped farmers to form cooperatives. These organized groups of farmers can borrow enough money to buy farm machinery. Thus, cooperatives have helped to improve living conditions for many farmers. India's food production is now growing faster than its population.

Jawaharlal Nehru, India's first leader, wanted to build up India's industries. Today, India is following the path that Nehru laid out. Even though it has a huge rural population, India is a highly industrialized country. India makes everything from cars to toothpaste. It supplies all the consumer goods used by its citizens. It trains more engineers and scientists than any nation except the United States and Russia. It has nuclear power plants and nuclear bombs. Industrialization in India has led to rapidly growing cities. Unfortunately, millions of people in these crowded and overgrown cities can barely make a living.

Housing and Health

A typical village house in India has mud-brick walls, one room, and no windows. People go indoors mainly to sleep. The rest of the time, they live outdoors. Good housing is a problem for the people of India. In the cities of India, the problem worsens: Some people live in fine, large houses, while millions live in large slums. Many people are homeless and live on the streets.

Economics Fact

Cows are important to India's economy. Killing cows is forbidden in most of India.

Clean water is in short supply in India. People may have to use the same water for cleaning, drinking, and carrying away human waste. In such conditions, cholera, typhoid, and other diseases spread quickly.

Malnutrition also adds to the health problems in India. Few of the people who live on farms eat three meals a day. People weakened by hunger are less able to fight off disease. In recent years, India has trained many doctors and built health clinics all over the country. Medical care has improved, but this has led to rapid population growth. By 2010, India is expected to have more than one billion people.

One way to measure health standards is to look at life expectancy. This is the average length of time that people are expected to live. People who get enough food and medical care tend to live longer. In India in 1947, the life expectancy rate was only about 28 years old. Today, the rate in India is about 62 for men and 64 for women. In more developed countries, where most people have enough food and medical care, the rates are higher.

Clothing and Foods

In India, the sari is the national dress for women. It is a piece of cloth about six yards long, wrapped around the body. Most city men wear Western clothes, but rural villagers usually wear a dhoti. This is a long strip of cloth that is wrapped around the waist and tucked in to form pants. Because India has such warm weather, light-colored, cotton clothes are common.

The people of India generally do not eat much meat. Many are vegetarians. Rice and lentils, a kind of dried, flat pea, are staple foods. Chapatti is the most common type of bread. These flat, round loaves of wheat bread are cooked on a griddle.

Each region of India has its own style of cooking. In general, curries are representative of the cuisine in the north. A curry is a dish made with a blend of spices such as cumin and coriander. The cooking of southern India uses fewer spices but more hot pepper.

Dance and Music

The tradition of classical dancing is highly developed in India. Each region has its own styles. Kathak dancing, for example, is popular in the north. Kathak dancers wear ankle bracelets that make noise when they dance. The dancers stamp their feet to match the rhythms of the music. Kathakali is a dramatic, classical dance style from Kerela, a state in southwestern India. Kathakali dancers act out stories from the great Hindu epic poems, such as the *Ramayana*.

The classical music of India began developing at least 3,000 years ago. The music is usually performed by a small group. The instruments always include small hand drums and often include a stringed instrument such as a sitar.

Movies are India's main popular art. India makes about 800 films a year. Most large villages have their own movie theaters.

✓ **Check Your Understanding**
Write your answers in complete sentences.

1. Why was the Congress Party formed?

2. How do most villagers in India make a living?

3. How old is the classical music of India?

Summary

The major countries of the subcontinent are India, Pakistan, Bangladesh, Bhuton, and Nepal. The main landforms of the Indian subcontinent are the Himalayas and Hindu Kush, the northern plains, and the Deccan Plateau. The main rivers are the Indus, Ganges, and Brahmaputra.
The classical culture of India began with the Aryans, who came to India around 1500 B.C.
Muslim invaders and British colonists each added to the culture of India.
Hinduism is the main religion in India. Other important religions include Buddhism, Sikhism, and Islam.
India's caste system is supported by Hinduism. The system puts everyone in a closed group with a fixed rank in society. Today, all Indians have equal rights by law. In practice, however, the caste system remains strong.
Most of the people of India live in villages and work as farmers.

caste
monsoon
subcontinent
incarnation
karma

Vocabulary Review

Write a term from the list that matches each definition below.

1. In Hinduism, a fate or destiny shaped by one's past activities

2. The particular physical forms that a spirit takes in this world

3. A fixed social class into which one is born and from which one cannot move

4. A large portion of a continent that is geographically isolated from the rest of the continent

5. A seasonal wind that creates a strong pattern of wet and dry seasons in parts of Asia

Chapter Quiz

Write your answers in complete sentences.

1. Why has India had little direct contact with China?

2. What is the main landform in central India?

3. What religion grew out of the culture of the ancient Aryans?

4. **Critical Thinking** What features of modern India come from the British?

5. **Critical Thinking** How are Hinduism and Buddhism similar?

Write About Geography

Complete the following activities.

1. Write an essay discussing how having more than 200 languages might affect the lives of people in India.

2. Learn more about Gandhi's nonviolent methods in the library and on the Internet. How did he use these methods to help gain India's independence? Explain your findings in a short essay.

Group Activity

India is a popular tourist stop. Create a group guidebook of India. Give each member of the group a section of the book to design. Include sights, restaurants, and lodging. Look in the library and on the Internet for more information and ideas.

Pakistan is a country of great natural beauty. What can be seen in the photograph that would make farming here difficult?

Words to Know

Taliban	the group of Sunnite Muslims who instituted Islamic fundamentalist rule in Afghanistan
dowry	money or goods that a bride brings to a marriage
buffer state	a small country that separates two large countries and prevents a conflict between them
mujahideen	warriors who fight for Islam

Places to Know

Punjab

Sind

Baluchistan

North-West Frontier Province

Northern Areas

Kashmir

Learning Objectives

- Describe the physical geography of Pakistan and Afghanistan.
- Name the main ethnic groups and languages of Pakistan and Afghanistan.
- Describe everyday life in Pakistan and Afghanistan.
- Explain how Islam affects family life in Pakistan and Afghanistan.
- Trace the role of storytelling in Pakistan and Afghanistan.
- Explain the warfare in Afghanistan since the late 1970s.

A Dry, Rocky Land

Remember
The Hindu Kush are a geographic feature of northern India, as well.

Geography Fact

The border between Afghanistan and Pakistan was drawn by the British in 1893. Many of the same groups of people live on both sides. As a result, this border has never been strictly observed.

In the northwestern corner of the subcontinent of India are the countries of Pakistan and Afghanistan. Much of this land is mountainous and dry. The Hindu Kush run through northern Pakistan and into Afghanistan. Lack of rainfall makes farming difficult in this region. Only about 13 percent of Afghanistan and 26 percent of Pakistan can be farmed. Even so, more than half of the population makes a living in agriculture. Families in the dry mountains and deserts depend more on sheep and goat herding.

Pakistan has five provinces: Punjab, Sind, Baluchistan, the North-West Frontier Province, and the Northern Areas. India claims part of the Northern Areas, too. Over the years, this claim has led to much fighting between India and Pakistan. In 1949, the United Nations started a cease-fire between the two countries. A cease-fire is an agreement to stop fighting. Pakistan was given control of the northern portion of Kashmir, or Azad Kashmir, which means "Free Kashmir." India controls the southern portion of Kashmir. Fighting over Kashmir still continues, however.

Most Pakistanis live in Punjab, where the nation's capital, Islamabad, and the nation's most productive farms are located. Much of the land is low and flat. Four rivers flow south through Punjab and join with the Indus River. Water from these rivers make Punjab the world's single largest irrigated farm area.

Pakistan's provinces are divided along ethnic lines. Punjabis represent more than 60 percent of Pakistan's population. In general, the people of Pakistan feel more loyalty to their province than to their country. Ethnic ties are strong. Conflicts between ethnic groups are not uncommon. Each ethnic group has its own language, but many Pakistanis speak two or more languages. The official language of Pakistan is Urdu, a mixture of Hindi and Farsi.

Pakhtuns, or Pushtuns, form the main ethnic group of the North-West Frontier Province. They are known for their strong code of honor. They are also the main ethnic group of Afghanistan. The Mohajirs, or refugees, live in southern Sind. There, they form the main population group. Afghanistan has two main languages: Pushtu and Farsi. Pushtu is spoken only by the Pushtuns. Farsi is the first language of Tajiks and Hazaras, but it is a widely spoken second language for others. In the north, Turkic languages are common. There are also at least 30 other languages, each spoken by an average of 25,000 people or fewer in Afghanistan.

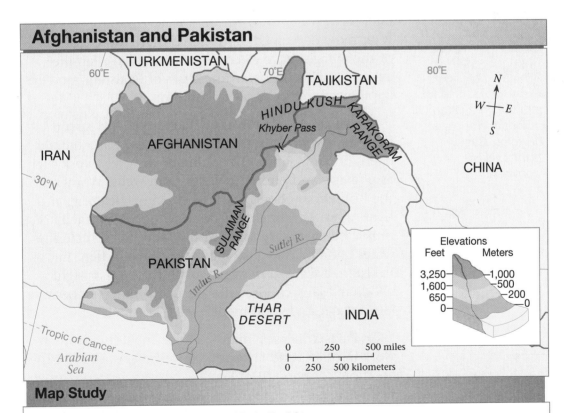

Afghanistan and Pakistan

Map Study

1. **PLACE** What is the elevation of the Hindu Kush?

2. **REGION** Would you describe the terrain of Afghanistan and Pakistan as mainly mountainous or mainly flat?

Everyday Life

One of the things that most people in Pakistan and Afghanistan have in common is their religion. They are Muslims who practice Islam faithfully. This gives everyday life a certain unity throughout the region. For example, the day is organized around the five times of prayer. Almost everybody fasts during the month of Ramadan. Almost everybody also celebrates Eid, the three-day holiday that follows Ramadan.

Both Pakistan and Afghanistan are poor countries. Most people live in small villages. Their houses are usually made of homemade mud-and-straw bricks. Few homes have running water. Most people bathe using buckets of water drawn from a well. Pakistan, however, is far more developed than Afghanistan. More than half of the villages have electricity. Some village families even own televisions. In the cities of Pakistan, modern appliances are not at all uncommon.

The streets of Pakistan are crowded with carts and bicycles. Bus and taxi travel is also common.

Men and children in the villages typically spend their days working in the fields. They use water buffalo, oxen, donkeys, and other animals for heavy work such as plowing and pumping water from wells. Women do the household chores, such as cooking, cleaning, and hauling water. Cooking is done outdoors. Women also milk whatever dairy animals the family has, including water buffalo. They also look after the children. In Pakistan, a woman may give birth to seven or eight children. Many children die as infants, however, because clean water and good medical care is scarce.

In Pakistani cities, many people, including women, work in offices and factories. However, cottage industries are more common. People make baskets, pottery, carpets, furniture, metal wares, and leather goods. Craftswomen often work at home and make lower wages than men.

Pakistan also has a thriving repair business. Because appliances and technical goods are hard to get, people tend to keep everything that can be fixed.

Like the people of India, Pakistanis eat lentils, rice, and bread nearly every day. Unlike the people of India, Pakistanis eat a lot of meat—especially lamb. However, they do not eat pork because Islam forbids it. Meat is often grilled over charcoal or baked in a clay oven. Traditionally, people eat with their hands rather than with knives, forks, and spoons.

Afghan cooking shows the influence of the cultures of India and Central Asia. From India come baked rice dishes and curry-like sauces. From Central Asia come steamed ravioli and dried yogurt products. The daily diet for many Afghans consists of bread, onions, and tea.

Traditionally, both men and women in this region wear a two-piece outfit: baggy cotton pants and a long loose shirt. Pakistanis call this outfit a shalwar qameez. It covers the body as required by Islam. Because the same outfit is worn by rich and poor alike, it stands for class equality, which is an important value of Islam. Women usually wear long scarves or shawls over their heads and shoulders. Some wear veils when they go out in public. Most Afghan men wear turbans.

✓ Check Your Understanding

Write your answers in complete sentences.

1. Why is there fighting in the Northern Areas of Pakistan?

2. In which province do most Pakistanis live?

3. What is the main religion of Pakistan?

This Pakistani man is wearing an outfit known as a shalwar qameez.

Islam and the Family

Arabs brought Islam to the subcontinent of India in the 600s. The religion quickly spread from Central Asia to the Indus River. Today, most people in Pakistan and Afghanistan are Sunnite Muslims. Both countries have strong Shiite minorities, too.

Pakistan began in 1947 as a Muslim country, but it had a British system of law. Since the 1970s, Pakistani leaders have been working to strengthen the role of Islamic law. For example, charging interest on a private loan is forbidden. In Afghanistan, Islamic laws are enforced more strictly.

Islamic laws and traditions give a definite shape to family life. Women and men live very separate lives. In most households, women have an area set aside where men from other families cannot go.

All children get a religious education. In the early years, women take care of this education. Mothers, aunts, and grandmothers teach children what it means to be a Muslim and how to say their five daily prayers. Later, boys may study further at the mosque.

Children may also go to regular schools set up by the government. In Pakistan, a low percentage of girls go to school. Girls who do get an education go to separate schools from boys. In Afghanistan, when the group known as the **Taliban** took control in 1996, it became illegal for girls and women to get an education. This was because the Taliban instituted its version of strict Islamic rule. As a result, literacy among women is low. In many parts of Afghanistan, the percentage of women who can read and write is close to zero.

Girls often are married by the time they are 15 or 16 years old. Nearly all marriages are arranged by the families. Women put much time and energy into arranging these marriages. Only they can visit other households and identify possible brides.

Dating is rare, but two people who are about to marry often know each other. Many people marry within their own clan. In fact, marriages between first cousins are common.

Weddings are important events. In some parts of this region, a man pays a bride price to the woman's family. Almost always, the bride's family gives her a **dowry** to bring to the marriage. Usually, this includes household items such as bedding, dishes, and a radio.

Nearly every family keeps a copy of the Koran at home. This book is carefully wrapped in cloth and placed on a high shelf so that nothing can be set on top of it. The Koran is not just read but is treated as a sacred object. For example, before a trip, a relative may hold the Koran above the front doorway while the family passes under it three times. Sometimes, the Koran is used as a blessing.

Remember
The Koran is the sacred book of Islam. It is written in Arabic.

The Art of Storytelling

Storytelling is important in Afghanistan and Pakistan. Because few people can read and write, storytelling helps to keep family history alive. Grandparents describe where the family came from and tell about their ancestors.

Storytelling is also part of public life. In northern Afghanistan, singing storytellers are sometimes hired to perform at weddings and parties. If a village has a good storyteller, it may invite neighboring villagers over for a storytelling session. The audience does not just sit and listen at such a session. The audience may shout approval or may argue with a storyteller's version of a tale.

In Pakistan, storytellers used to spend a lot of time in the city markets. The Pakistani city of Peshawar even has a street named for storytellers. This street is lined with teahouses where people still gather to trade tales.

Afghanistan

Afghanistan is like the Balkans in some ways. It is a mountainous area with many ethnic groups. It lies wedged between cultures that do not get along. For many centuries, warring forces have met and clashed in Afghanistan.

In the 1800s, the British were colonizing India while the Russians were moving south. Afghanistan found itself squeezed between these powers. Britain tried to conquer Afghanistan to keep it out of Russian hands, but it failed. Even so, Afghanistan ended up as a **buffer state** between Russia and British India.

After World War II, and throughout the cold war, Afghanistan remained a buffer state. To the south and west were allies of the United States—Pakistan and Iran. To the north was the Soviet Union. Afghanistan accepted money from both the United States and the Soviet Union in exchange for staying neutral. Afghanistan sent its technical students to the West and its military students to the Soviet Union.

Over time, a large Communist Party formed within the Afghan military. In 1978, this party seized power in the country, killing the Afghan president. It declared Afghanistan a Communist state. The new government tried to break up big landholdings, send girls to school, and introduce other social changes.

These changes threatened the conservative Muslim way of life. People in the rural areas rebelled. The rebels said they were fighting for Islam. They became known as **mujahideen.** Student leaders from Kabul and soldiers from the Afghan Army joined them. By 1979, the Communist government in Kabul seemed in danger of failing. The Soviet Union poured troops into Afghanistan to prop up the Communist government. Eventually, the Soviets moved 115,000 soldiers into Afghanistan.

HISTORY FACT

Some people feel that the war in Afghanistan was the most important battle in the cold war. They think it led to the fall of the Soviet Union, because it showed that the Soviet Union was weaker than many people had thought.

For ten years, the Soviet forces battled the mujahideen. More than two million Afghans were killed. At least six million Afghans fled the country and became refugees. Nearly every village suffered damage. Finally, the Soviets gave up and pulled their troops out of Afghanistan. In 1992, the Afghan Communist government collapsed. The mujahideen marched into Kabul and declared Afghanistan an Islamic state.

The mujahideen, however, were divided into seven main parties, most of which represented particular ethnic groups. In 1994, the Taliban became the strongest of the ethnic groups. Over the next few years, it managed to gain control of most of the country. It fought against one guerrilla group in a northern section of Afghanistan.

Fighting continued between the Taliban and a guerrilla group in northern Afghanistan. The fighting made movement to the north difficult for nomadic families, such as this Afghan family.

Sports and the Arts in Afghanistan

The Turkic people of northern Afghanistan play a game on horseback called buzkashi. The carcass of a calf or goat is placed on a field. The players race on horseback toward the carcass, lean down from their saddles, and try to pick up the carcass. In order to win, a rider must first carry the carcass across the playing field and back again. Then, the rider must drop the carcass where it was when the game started. All the while, other players are trying to snatch the carcass away.

Buzkashi is dangerous. Riders can be pulled off their horses and trampled. The game is a test of warrior virtues—skills, strength, and courage. During the war against the Soviets, buzkashi became popular in southern Afghanistan.

The many ethnic groups of Afghanistan have a rich tradition of artistic expression. Even everyday objects such as blankets and purses are beautifully made. Often, there is a similarity to Islamic design in their work. Afghans use the same detail in creating the fine woven carpets that both they and Iranians make. These are also called Persian rugs. They are prized around the world.

✓ Check Your Understanding

Write your answers in complete sentences.

1. What is the Taliban?

2. Why is storytelling important in Afghanistan and Pakistan?

3. Why did the people in rural areas rebel against the Communists in Afghanistan?

GLOBAL ISSUES
The Arms Race

When the United States used atomic bombs against Japan in World War II, the world changed. Ever since, the world has faced the risk of nuclear destruction.

During the cold war, both the Soviets and the Americans built a supply of nuclear weapons. Even now, both Russia and the United States have many of these bombs. Other nations have built atomic bombs, too.

India exploded its first test nuclear bomb in 1998. Much of the rest of the world was alarmed. India, however, said that it had become a major power—a nuclear power. India could protect itself from enemies such as Pakistan. Months later, Pakistan exploded its own test atomic bomb. One result of this recent arms race is a new effort to ban these bombs. No one who remembers the horrors of Hiroshima and Nagasaki wants to see them repeated.

Answer the questions below.

1. Why did India feel it needed to have atomic bombs?

2. Why might the United States believe there is a need to keep a stock of nuclear weapons today?

MAKE A DIFFERENCE
Find out what your representative in Congress feels about banning nuclear weapons in the world. Then write a letter to the representative, agreeing or disagreeing with his or her position.

Summary

Most of Pakistan and Afghanistan is dry and mountainous. Yet, most people live in villages and farm for a living.
Punjabis are the main ethnic group in Pakistan. Urdu is the official language of Pakistan.
Pushtuns, or Pakhtuns, are the main ethnic group of Afghanistan. Pushtu and Farsi are the main languages.
Nearly all people in Pakistan and Afghanistan are Muslims.
Storytelling is an important tradition in Pakistan and Afghanistan.
The Soviet Union invaded Afghanistan in 1979. Soviet troops fought a war with Muslim rebels known as the mujahideen. After the Soviet troops withdrew from Afghanistan, seven parties fought for control of Kabul.
In the mid-1990s, the Taliban emerged as the strongest of those parties. It controlled Afghanistan.

buffer state
dowry
mujahideen
Taliban

Vocabulary Review

Complete each sentence with a term from the list.

1. Rebels who fought for Islam in Afghanistan were called ____.

2. A small country that separates two large countries is a ____.

3. The ____ is the group that took control of Afghanistan in 1996.

4. Money or goods that a bride brings to a marriage is a ____.

Chapter Quiz

Write your answers in complete sentences.

1. What are the main ethnic groups in Pakistan?

2. What are the two main languages of Afghanistan?

3. Which two countries both claim parts of the Northern Areas?

4. **Critical Thinking** Why is the literacy rate among women in Afghanistan so low?

5. **Critical Thinking** Why has Afghanistan so often been a land of war?

Write About Geography

Complete the following activities.

1. The Taliban has just taken over in Afghanistan, where you live. Write about how much your life has changed.

2. You are a sports reporter at a game of buzkashi. Write an article about what you see at the game.

Group Activity

Create a timeline of Afghanistan history with your group. Divide up the time from 1800 to today. Each person finds events that happened during a time period. Then combine the information into a timeline.

Many people sell products in the floating markets of Thailand. What types of products are being sold here?

Chapter 31 / Southeast Asia: The Mainland

Words to Know

stilt	a heavy pole that, when combined with others, keeps a house above the ground and out of the water
paddy	a flooded field where rice is grown
tuberculosis	a deadly lung disease caused by bacteria
scripture	the sacred writing of a religion

Places to Know

Thailand

Laos

Cambodia

Vietnam

Myanmar

Learning Objectives

- Describe the physical geography of the Southeast Asian mainland.

- Describe the patterns of family and village life in Southeast Asia.

- Explain how colonialism affected Southeast Asia.

- Describe the Vietnam War and its consequences on the region.

- Compare the two main branches of Buddhism.

- Describe music and dance in the Southeast Asian mainland.

The Mainland of Southeast Asia

Thailand is one of five countries located entirely on the mainland of Southeast Asia. Thailand is situated on a peninsula that was formerly known as Indochina but is now generally called Southeast Asia. Laos, Cambodia, and Vietnam are on the same peninsula. Myanmar, which was known as Burma before 1989, lies west of Thailand. It separates Southeast Asia from the Indian subcontinent. Both Myanmar and Thailand extend south into the Malay Peninsula.

Both Southeast Asia and the Malay Peninsula have mountain ranges that meet together in the north. These mountains are only about 10,000 feet high, but they are rugged in places. Their slopes are covered with dense rain forests. These high hills and mountains are not very populated.

You Decide

When is a flood useful to farmers? When is it destructive and undesirable?

Between the mountain ranges are broad valleys. Great rivers run through these valleys. The Irrawaddy and Salween rivers run south through Myanmar. The Chao Phraya runs through Thailand. The Mekong River winds its way through Thailand, Laos, Cambodia, and Vietnam. These rivers flood every year, bringing silt down to the coastal plains and deltas. The silt makes the soil rich and farming easy. The valleys, plains, and deltas of Southeast Asia are, therefore, densely populated.

In the past, traffic between India and China had to move through Southeast Asia. The big peninsula of Southeast Asia is sometimes called Indochina. This is because India and China influenced the cultures in this region. The countries of Southeast Asia have a variety of political systems. Myanmar is a socialist country under military rule. Like North Korea, it is closed to the outside world.

Thailand is a constitutional monarchy. It has democratic elections. The military plays a strong role in Thailand.

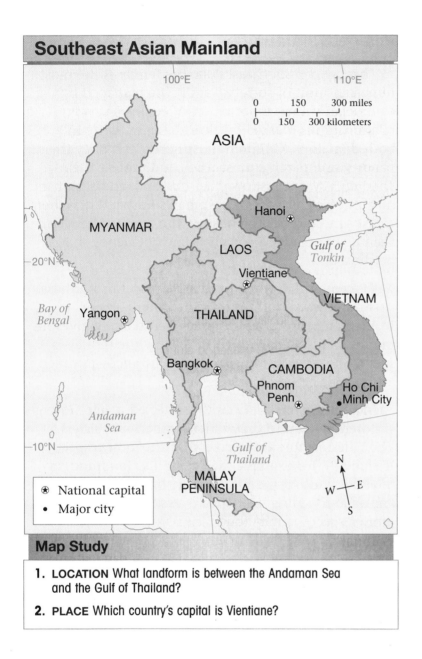

Southeast Asian Mainland

100°E   110°E

0   150   300 miles
0   150   300 kilometers

ASIA

MYANMAR

Hanoi ⊛

LAOS

Gulf of
Tonkin

20°N

Vientiane ⊛

VIETNAM

Bay of
Bengal   Yangon ⊛

THAILAND

Bangkok ⊛

CAMBODIA

Phnom
Penh ⊛

Ho Chi
• Minh City

Andaman
Sea

0
10°N

Gulf of
Thailand

MALAY
PENINSULA

N
W — E
S

⊛ National capital
• Major city

Map Study

1. **LOCATION** What landform is between the Andaman Sea and the Gulf of Thailand?

2. **PLACE** Which country's capital is Vientiane?

Laos and Vietnam have Communist governments. Cambodia once had a Communist government. In 1993, free elections were held. Cambodia now has a government based on democracy.

Village Communities

HISTORY FACT

Vietnam was ruled by China from about 100 B.C. to about A.D. 900.

Throughout Southeast Asia, the family is the most important unit of society. Family life is shaped by Confucian values, especially in Vietnam. Every relationship is marked by clear duties running in both directions. Children must honor and obey their parents, and parents must teach and protect their children. A wife must obey her husband, and a husband must protect his wife. If a woman's husband dies, her eldest son becomes the head of the family. The woman then owes her eldest son the same obedience she gave her husband.

Women do, however, have more power in Southeast Asia than they do in most of the other parts of Asia. In Vietnam, for example, a man traditionally gives his money to his wife, who controls how the money is spent. She gives her husband an allowance—as much as she feels he needs or deserves.

In Southeast Asia, status is connected to age. Younger children look up to their older brothers and sisters. The oldest people are treated with the most respect. A Thai boy, for example, will greet his grandmother by holding up his hands, pressing his palms together, and then touching his hands to his body. To show even more respect, he may touch his hands to his forehead. The grandmother will return the greeting, but the younger person must greet her first.

The extended family usually lives close together. A village may include several extended families. Therefore, villages in Southeast Asia are tightly knit communities. The villages govern themselves. Decisions are made in a village council, or gathering of married men. Everyone has a voice in these councils. The community usually elects a leader, however, to guide the process.

Life in the Tropics

The tropical climate of Southeast Asia affects daily life in many ways. For example, shelter from cold is not needed, so houses are usually small, simple, and open to the breeze. Bamboo grows quickly in this climate, so it is commonly used as a building material. Some houses are made entirely from woven grasses. Most rural homes have thatched roofs and dirt floors.

The rivers tend to flood during the summer monsoons. In the lowlands, therefore, many houses are built on **stilts**. These heavy poles keep the houses high above the ground. During flood season, people commonly get to and from their houses in boats.

Fruit grows well in Southeast Asia and is an important part of the diet there. The fruit of this region includes bananas, coconuts, papayas, pineapples, durians, lychees, and mangosteens.

Rice **paddies** generally surround each village. The rice fields are flooded to start the seeds growing. Men, women, and children work in the fields, standing in a few inches of water. Farm machinery is still rare—it costs too much for most villagers. People work by hand or with simple tools. They may use water buffalo to help with the heavier work.

Disease tends to be a problem in the tropics. Southeast Asia is no exception. Malaria is widespread. **Tuberculosis** is a growing problem. This lung disease spreads very easily through the air. It is not confined to the tropics, however. In fact, 200 years ago, it was a major cause of death in Europe. For years, scientists thought that they had conquered it. Now, it is on the rise again. Southeast Asia is one of the places where it is spreading most rapidly.

Southeast Asian houses near rivers are often built on stilts. The stilts protect the houses from floods during the monsoon season.

Remember
Malaria is a disease spread by mosquitoes.

Getting Around

Railroads and highways are scarce in Southeast Asia. In the mountains, they are hard to build. In the lowlands, they are hard to maintain. Someone has to keep cutting back the plants that grow so rapidly in the tropics. There also are many floods to cope with.

Because of these difficulties, waterways generally take the place of highways and railroads. Southeast Asia's rivers are filled with small boats. Some are powered by diesel engines or outboard motors. Some use sails. Some depend on people to row them. Canals connect the rivers and extend the network of waterways.

In the cities, many people get around on bicycles. In fact, bicycles are even used to carry around other people. Such bicycles are called pedicabs. Many poor urban people make their living as pedicab drivers. In a city such as Bangkok, these drivers have to watch out for cars, trucks, buses, and motorcycles. In Laos and Vietnam, cars are rarer. The streets of the Vietnamese city of Hanoi, for example, are filled with thousands of bicycles.

Because highways are scarce in Vietnam, junks, a type of boat, are an important form of transportation.

✓ Check Your Understanding

Write your answers in complete sentences.

1. Why is Southeast Asia sometimes called Indochina?

2. What are most houses like in Southeast Asia?

3. How do villages govern themselves in Southeast Asia?

4. What is the most common way for people to travel from one area of a country to another in Southeast Asia?

GEOGRAPHY IN YOUR LIFE
Getting Directions

Most people need to ask for directions at one time or another. To successfully get where you want to go, follow these steps. First, make sure the person helping you knows the place you are trying to find. Second, write down the directions as you hear them. If possible, have the person show you the directions on a map. Finally, repeat the directions to the person who told them to you.

From the Royal Hotel to Wat Phnom

1. Leave from front entrance of the hotel.

2. Turn right.

3. Walk three blocks east.

4. Turn right at Wat Phnom entrance.

Answer the questions below.

1. How do you get from the Royal Hotel to Wat Phnom?

2. Why should you repeat directions to the person who gave them to you?

CHALLENGE Why is it important to know where compass directions are if you are listening to directions?

Apply the Skill
Find directions from one place to another using the Internet. Use a search engine to find a map site. Using search words such as "find directions" will help you locate web sites that give directions. Use the site to find the way from your house to a friend's house in another part of town. Write or print out the directions.

From Ancient Empires to Colonialism

HISTORY FACT

The practices of both Hinduism and Buddhism in Southeast Asia reflect India's influence on the region's culture and history.

In ancient times, Southeast Asia was home to many great kingdoms. The greatest was the Khmer empire, which lasted from the 500s to the 1400s. It was centered in Cambodia, but it ruled much of what is now Thailand, Vietnam, and Laos. Its capital was called Angkor Thom. Near this city, the Khmer kings built Angkor Wat, the largest religious structure in the world. It started out as a Hindu temple to the god Vishnu. When the Khmer kings converted to Buddhism, it became a Buddhist monastery.

Two monks sit at the base of Angkor Wat, the largest religious structure in the world.

In the 1300s, two new kingdoms began competing with the Khmer empire. By 1600, the Annam kingdom ruled in Vietnam, and the kingdom of Siam ruled what we now call Thailand.

By this time, Europeans were pushing into the region. They came as traders and missionaries, but they stayed on as conquerors. Myanmar became part of the British colony of India. France colonized all of what is now Cambodia, Laos, and Vietnam.

Only Siam remained free. King Mongkut of Siam let the British and French colonizers keep each other out of his country. His son Chulalongkorn continued this policy. Siam was never colonized by a European power. That is why it is now called Thailand, which means "land of the free." Thailand still has a king. He is directly descended from Mongkut and Chulalongkorn.

In Southeast Asia, the French built rice, rubber tree, and tea plantations, and mined tin and lead. They used the native people as low-wage laborers. The French also trained local people to help run the colony. Southeast Asian people who were educated in the West worked as clerks, technicians, and bureaucrats.

In the 1900s, many Western-educated Vietnamese people began demanding independence from France. The movement spread throughout Southeast Asia. After World War II, the French found themselves at war with the people of Southeast Asia. In 1954, the French suffered a terrible defeat at Dien Bien Phu. This forced France to give up their colonies in Southeast Asia.

Cambodia and Laos became independent nations. Vietnam, however, was divided between two rival groups. The Communists, led by Ho Chi Minh, were strong in the northern part of Vietnam.

Another group, led by Ngo Dinh Diem, was strong in the southern part. The two sides agreed to let the people choose which form their government would take in an election. The election was scheduled for 1956, but it never took place. Diem backed out, sensing that he was going to lose. He declared South Vietnam an independent country. This led to the Vietnam War.

The Vietnam War

To block the spread of communism during the cold war, the United States decided to support Diem and the government of South Vietnam. This government was not fighting North Vietnam directly. It was fighting South Vietnamese Communists known as the Viet Cong. The Viet Cong fought mainly in small groups that staged sudden surprise attacks and then scattered into the jungle. Their weapons came from North Vietnam, which had received them from China and the Soviet Union.

At first, the United States sent only weapons and advisers to Vietnam. After 1964, it began sending troops. In 1965, the United States started bombing North Vietnam. By 1968, the United States had 550,000 troops stationed in Vietnam.

The Viet Cong kept fighting, and the government of South Vietnam fell slowly apart. Diem had been overthrown by his own generals in 1963. The leaders who took his place were corrupt and had no popular support. In 1972, Richard Nixon, then President of the United States, began to pull American troops out of the war. He had decided to let the South Vietnamese army defend itself against the Viet Cong.

Geography Fact

Saigon was renamed Ho Chi Minh City to honor the Communist leader of what was North Vietnam.

However, the South Vietnamese army had no strength left to fight. In 1975, the Communists captured Saigon, the capital of South Vietnam. They changed its name to Ho Chi Minh City. Vietnam was finally united under Communist rule.

Today, the government of Vietnam is still struggling with problems left over from the war. More than a million Vietnamese people were killed in the fighting. The country was bombed more heavily than all of Europe was during World War II. Vietnam is still filled with unexploded mines and bombs, which are slowly being collected.

War in Southeast Asia

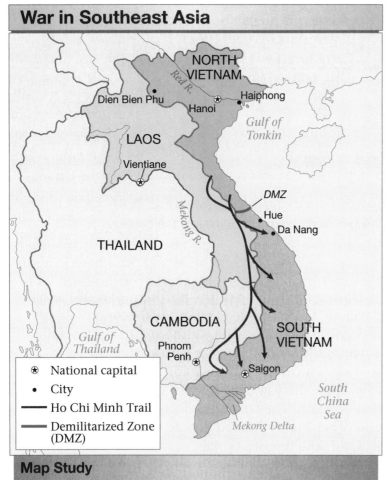

Map Study

1. **LOCATION** Describe where the Demilitarized Zone is.

2. **REGION** The Mekong River forms a border between Laos and what country?

Vietnam's lovely coast is becoming a destination for tourists as the country has begun to end its isolation.

During the war years, the northern part of Vietnam developed a disciplined Communist economy based on central planning. The southern part developed a free-market economy geared toward serving U.S. soldiers. Putting the two economies together was not easy. After the war, hundreds of thousands of people fled Vietnam. They included doctors, engineers, teachers, and other highly trained people. Vietnam is now lacking skilled professionals.

The war left Vietnam isolated for many years. The country had little contact with Western nations. It was also on bad terms with China. The Vietnamese felt that their giant, northern neighbor wanted to control them. Vietnam's only close ally was the Soviet Union.

Since the collapse of the Soviet Union, Vietnam has sought ties with other nations. It has begun to trade with Australia, Japan, some European nations, and even the United States. As Vietnam has opened up, its ancient culture and beaches have brought new visitors. In 1997, 1.7 million tourists visited Vietnam.

$ Economics Fact

Vietnam's first stock exchange opened in 2000. Four companies were allowed to list their shares on the exchange.

The Khmer Rouge

In the 1960s, the war in Vietnam spread to Laos and Cambodia. Ho Chi Minh had been sending soldiers and supplies into these two countries down a path called the Ho Chi Minh Trail. To stop the flow of arms and soldiers, the United States bombed the Ho Chi Minh Trail. U.S. bombing killed more than 100,000 people in Cambodia.

The Communists used such attacks to build support for their own cause. By 1970, both Laos and Cambodia had powerful Communist guerrilla movements. The main Cambodian Communists were called the Khmer Rouge—the "Red Khmers." Their leader was Pol Pot. Many of the fighters were teenagers. The Khmer Rouge captured the capital, Phnom Penh, in 1975. They renamed Cambodia Kampuchea.

Pol Pot and his supporters wanted to change the way the country was run and influenced. They wanted to turn Kampuchea into a self-sufficient, isolated, rural nation. They drove people out of the cities and into the countryside. Thousands of people died on these forced marches. The survivors were made to work in the fields. Many of them died of overwork, starvation, or disease.

The Khmer Rouge killed everyone who was either well-to-do or influenced by Western culture. People who wore glasses, for example, were considered "westernized" and were killed. More than a million people died under Pol Pot's rule. Hundreds of thousands escaped to live as refugees in Thailand or elsewhere.

In 1979, some Cambodians asked the Vietnamese to help them fight the Khmer Rouge. The Vietnamese invaded Cambodia. They drove out the Khmer Rouge. Then Vietnam set up a new Communist government under their control. The Khmer Rouge, however, took over the northern hills. There, they began to fight the new government. They bought guns from China with money from gems they had mined and timber they had cut in the north.

Two non-Communist guerrilla groups also fought the government. One of the groups was headed by Norodom Sihanouk, Cambodia's last prince. In June 1993, Cambodia had an election run by the United Nations. Sihanouk's group won. Sihanouk was once again the head of the Cambodian government. The Khmer Rouge took no part in the elections. In fact, they declared that they no longer wished to fight. Pol Pot died in 1998.

Cambodia is governed by a constitutional monarchy today. Norodom Sihanouk is Cambodia's king. However, the country still struggles with civil war. The prime minister and president of Cambodia battle Sihanouk for more power.

Two Branches of Buddhism

In Thailand and Myanmar, at least 95 percent of the people are Buddhists. They practice Theravada Buddhism—a main school of Buddhist thought. Another school of thought is Mahayana Buddhism. It is also practiced in China, Japan, and Korea.

Both Theravada Buddhists and Mahayana Buddhists seek release from endless rebirth and believe in the goal of enlightenment. Both agree that a way of living called Buddha's "Eightfold Path" is the way to reach enlightenment. Both believe in the law of karma.

The disagreement between these two schools is a matter of emphasis and centers on the Buddha himself. Mahayana Buddhists see Buddha as a saint. They point out that Buddha not only became enlightened but also came back as a saint to help others. Such a saint is called a Boddhisatva. Buddha was the first and greatest Boddhisatva, but there are many others. Mahayana Buddhists believe that people can get help from Buddha and from other Boddhisatvas through prayers and rituals.

In the Theravada school of thought, Buddha is seen as a model who showed the way. Others can follow the same way, but they get no special help from Buddha or other saints. To become enlightened, people have to live and do exactly as Buddha did. For Theravada Buddhists, the ancient Buddhist **scriptures** are of special importance. They show exactly what Buddha said and thought.

Mahayana Buddhism is very much a part of everyday life for its practitioners. For Theravada Buddhists, however, religion is a full-time occupation. Those who wish to make serious progress in this faith must become monks. Most men become monks at some point in their lives. Some enter a monastery for just a few weeks or months. Some become monks after they retire. Some spend their lives as monks. For this reason, monasteries, or wats, play a big role in Theravada Buddhism. In Thailand and Myanmar, almost every town has a wat.

Thai males can become monks at any age.

Buddhist monks in Southeast Asia wear yellow-orange robes. They own nothing but a bowl, a needle, a razor, and a mat. They mend their own clothes and keep their heads shaved. Each morning, they go out with their bowls to get food. In the afternoon, the monks study and read scriptures and meditate. People in this region believe that by giving to monks they improve their own karma.

Music and Dance

Southeast Asia has many groups of isolated people who live in the hills. These groups are known for their fine folk arts. The Hmong of Laos, for example, create beautiful weavings and embroidery.

Music is important to the hill dwellers. Lullabies, for example, teach children good behavior and other values. These hill dwellers make flutes, mouth harps, and other instruments out of bamboo.

The Cambodians have a style of dancing that began over a thousand years ago. It started as entertainment for the kings and nobles of the Khmer empire, and was based on Indian dancing. The dancers act out stories from the *Ramayana* and other Hindu tales.

Celebrations

TET FESTIVAL

Tet is the biggest holiday of the year in Vietnam. It celebrates the lunar new year. This is a time when the living honor their ancestors, whose spirits are thought to visit the Earth during Tet.

Tet Festival celebrates the lunar new year.

Preparations for the festival begin weeks in advance. City dwellers return to their home villages if they can. People clean and decorate their ancestors' graves. On the last night of the old year, the family gathers for soybean soup. Candles are lit at a family altar and prayers are said. Then, about three hours before midnight, family members start setting off firecrackers to chase off evil spirits that might otherwise hinder the ancestors. At midnight, the spirits of the ancestors enter the house.

Critical Thinking What is the biggest holiday of the year where you live? How is it similar to and different from Tet?

In this style of dancing, each position of the hands, fingers, legs, feet, and body has a meaning. The slightest change of angle can change the entire meaning. Because of this, every gesture and motion must be precise. Learning such precision takes years of training.

The Khmer Rouge nearly put an end to classical dance in Cambodia. Fewer than 20 members of the country's national ballet survived the Communist government.

The classical dance of Thailand is much like that of Cambodia. When the Thais conquered the Khmers in the 1300s, the Thais moved the whole Khmer royal dance company to their own court. Thai dancers act out stories from traditional Thai literature. The dancers wear masks, heavy makeup, rich costumes, and big headdresses.

Cambodian dancer

✓ Check Your Understanding

Write your answers in complete sentences.

1. What is the only Southeast Asian country that was never colonized?

2. Why did the United States enter the Vietnam War?

3. Who were the Khmer Rouge?

4. What beliefs do Theravada Buddhists and Mahayana Buddhists have in common?

5. Why are monasteries important in Theravada Buddhism?

6. What country influenced Cambodia's style of dance?

Summary

This region has two peninsulas: Southeast Asia and the Malay Peninsula. The mainland of Southeast Asia has sparsely populated hills and densely populated plains, valleys, and deltas. It is home to five countries: Myanmar, Thailand, Laos, Cambodia, and Vietnam.
Major rivers in Southeast Asia include the Irrawaddy, the Salween, the Chao Phraya, and the Mekong.
Most people of the Southeast Asian mainland are farmers.
Both China and India have influenced the cultures of Southeast Asia.
The most important ancient kingdom of Southeast Asia was the Khmer empire.
The Vietnam War grew out of a dispute between Communists and others in Vietnam.
The Khmer Rouge, led by Pol Pot, ruled and nearly destroyed Cambodia between 1975 and 1979.
Theravada Buddhism and Mahayana Buddism are the two branches of Buddhism that are practiced most in Thailand and Myanmar.

Vocabulary Review

Write *true* or *false*. If the statement is false, change the underlined term to make it true.

1. A <u>stilt</u> is a flooded field where rice is grown.

2. <u>Scriptures</u> are the sacred writings of a culture.

3. Heavy poles that keep a house above the ground and out of water are called <u>paddies</u>.

4. A deadly lung disease caused by bacteria is <u>tuberculosis</u>.

Chapter Quiz

Write the correct letter for each place.

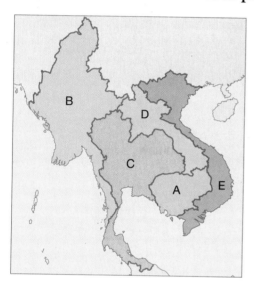

1. Thailand
2. Myanmar
3. Vietnam
4. Cambodia
5. Laos

Write About Geography

Complete the following activities.

1. Draw a poster that shows how climate affects the way of life in Southeast Asia.

2. Make a chart that explains the causes and some of the consequences of the Vietnam War.

Group Activity

Play a trivia game about this chapter. Have each person in your group create five questions about the chapter. Then divide into two teams. The teams can take turns answering the questions that the other team wrote.

The islands of Southeast Asia contain many mountainous areas. How does that affect farming?

Chapter 32 / Southeast Asia: The Islands

Words to Know

strait	a narrow strip of water between two bodies of land
kampong	a traditional Indonesian village
conservation	saving natural resources such as rain forests and wildlife
batik	a process for hand-printing colored designs on cloth by using wax and dyes
gamelan	traditional Indonesian orchestra

Places to Know

Indonesia

Malay Archipelago

Malay Peninsula

Borneo

New Guinea

Sumatra

Java

Sulawesi

Learning Objectives

- Locate and describe the Malay Archipelago.
- Describe the blend of religious traditions in Indonesia.
- Tell how the spice trade affected Indonesian history.
- Describe the Indonesian economy today.
- Identify the traditional crafts and performing arts of Indonesia.

Southeast Asia: The Islands

Indonesia is part of the Malay Archipelago, the world's biggest group of islands. These islands stretch from the Malay Peninsula almost to Australia. They separate the Indian Ocean from the Pacific Ocean. The archipelago includes over 13,000 islands, about 6,000 of which are inhabited. The Philippines, a group of islands in the north, are part of the Malay Archipelago. Culturally, however, they form a separate region. In the southern part of the archipelago, the major islands are Borneo, New Guinea, Sumatra, Java, and Sulawesi.

Five countries are located in this region: Malaysia, Singapore, Brunei, Indonesia, and Papua New Guinea. Malaysia is split between the Malay Peninsula and the island of Borneo. The tiny nation of Brunei is also located on Borneo. The rest of Borneo is part of Indonesia.

Singapore is even smaller than Brunei. It occupies the tip of the Malay Peninsula. A narrow **strait** separates it from part of Indonesia. Singapore is not only a city but also an independent country—and a wealthy one. Like Hong Kong, it is a major port and a center for world banking and trade. Almost all of the people in Singapore are of Chinese descent.

Indonesia is the largest country in this region. If all 6,000 of its islands were put together, they would cover about one-fifth of the United States. In terms of population, Indonesia is the fifth-largest country in the world. It has 193 million people, two-thirds of whom live on Java, an island no bigger than New York State.

Indonesia's islands arc from Sumatra in the west to New Guinea in the east—about the distance between New York and San Francisco. Only the western half of New Guinea—called Irian Jaya—belongs to Indonesia. The eastern half of the island is the independent country of Papua New Guinea.

Islands of Southeast Asia

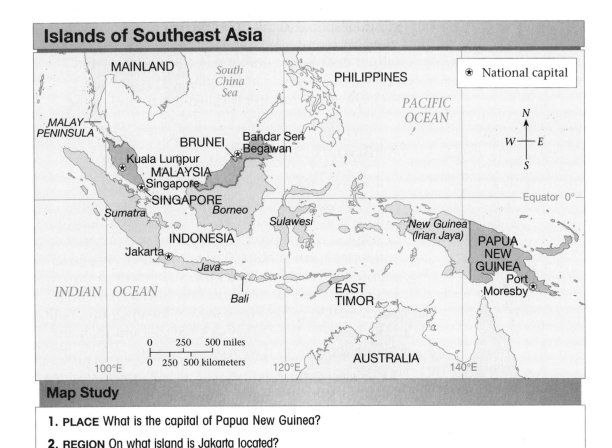

Map Study

1. **PLACE** What is the capital of Papua New Guinea?

2. **REGION** On what island is Jakarta located?

Hundreds of volcanoes dot the Malay Archipelago, which is part of the Ring of Fire. At least once a year, a volcano erupts somewhere in Indonesia. In 1883, the eruption of Krakatoa blew up an entire island. The sound of the eruption was heard in Africa. The ash caused a hard winter in Europe. A new volcanic island is still forming where old Krakatoa used to be.

Rich kingdoms flourished in this region between A.D. 200 and A.D. 1500. These kingdoms controlled the narrow strait between Sumatra and the Malay Peninsula. Later, Europeans colonized the entire region. The modern countries of this region took shape after World War II.

Remember
Japan and Korea are also part of the Ring of Fire. This great ring circles the entire Pacific Rim.

Indonesia has about 300 different ethnic groups. Living on many separate islands has increased the cultural differences among Indonesians. Over 125 languages are spoken in Indonesia. The official language of the country is called Bahasa Indonesia.

Religion in Indonesia

Most Indonesians are Muslims. This makes Indonesia the largest Muslim nation in the world. Islam in Indonesia, however, is very different from the religion that is practiced in places such as Arabia. In Indonesia, Islam has mixed with earlier religions. Animist and Hindu traditions are still practiced. For example, Indonesian Muslims burn incense in honor of local nature spirits. They leave gifts on shrines built to Hindu gods. They often seek advice from shamans, who are thought to have magical powers.

A widespread Indonesian custom called the selamatan is really a religious ritual. It is a feast that is meant to bring about a desired event or result. For example, a person who wants a new job may hold a selamatan. Certain foods, such as flavored rice cones, are eaten at the feast. Guests burn incense and perform other rituals. Then they join their host in Islamic prayers.

Almost all of the people of Bali are Hindus. A number of Buddhists and Christians also live in Indonesia. Like the Muslims, however, the Buddhists and Christians of Indonesia feature rituals and customs from other traditions in their religious practices.

✓ **Check Your Understanding**

Write your answers in complete sentences.

1. Name the largest country in the Malay Archipelago.

2. Where is Singapore?

3. What is a selamatan?

GEOGRAPHER'S TOOL KIT
Reading Population Density Maps

A population density map shows the average number of people living per square mile in an area. To read this kind of map, first look at the key. Often, colors tell different densities. Then, compare the map to the key to see where the least and most densely populated places are located.

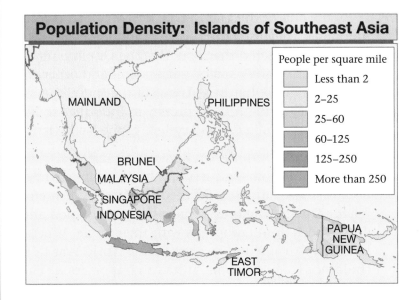

Population Density: Islands of Southeast Asia

People per square mile

Less than 2

2–25

25–60

60–125

125–250

More than 250

MAINLAND

PHILIPPINES

BRUNEI

MALAYSIA

SINGAPORE

INDONESIA

PAPUA NEW GUINEA

EAST TIMOR

Answer the questions below.

1. What color on the map shows a population density of fewer than two people per mile?

2. What are the two most densely populated islands in Indonesia?

CHALLENGE Why might someone in business find a map like this useful?

Apply the Skill

Use this population density map to write three questions. Exchange questions with a classmate, and use the map to answer each other's questions.

Spice, Rice, and Timber

In the 1500s, Indonesia was the world's main source of nutmeg, cloves, pepper, and many other spices. Because these spices attracted European traders, they affected Indonesian history. At that time, spices were considered precious in Europe. Spices were used to preserve food. When Columbus stumbled upon America, he was looking mainly for a route to the East Indies, as the islands of Indonesia were called.

By the end of the 1600s, Dutch people had colonized Indonesia. They used the people of Indonesia as low-paid workers and treated them poorly. The Dutch built plantations to grow spices, coffee, rice, and other cash crops. They took hardwoods out of the Indonesian forests. They made enough money in Indonesia to build canals, dikes, and a railroad system in the Netherlands.

Meanwhile, Indonesian agriculture suffered. Indonesian people grew less and less food for themselves because more land was devoted to growing cash crops for the Dutch. The Indonesians had to buy food and other goods from Europeans with their wages. When Indonesia became independent after World War II, it could not feed its people. It had to import food. This food shortage was the first problem that the leaders of the new nation had to tackle.

Another problem was ethnic unrest. The most violent uprisings were in the region of East Timor. Indonesia, as a republic, elected Abdurrahman Wahid as president in 1999. He hoped to bring stability back to the region.

Indonesia's Economy Today

Agriculture remains important in Indonesia. About 60 percent of the people work as farmers. The hot, wet climate is perfect for growing rice. It allows farmers to grow two or even three crops per year.

Indonesia still grows spices, but rice is the major crop. In fact, it is now the world's largest rice producer. Even so, Indonesia can barely feed its people because its population has been growing so quickly.

Indonesia's main export is oil. It is a member of OPEC—the Organization of Petroleum Exporting Countries. Indonesia sells oil mainly to Japan, South Korea, and Taiwan. In the 1980s, a sudden drop in oil prices hurt Indonesia. Its leaders decided that the country depended too much on oil exporting. Therefore, Indonesia has been trying to develop other exports, such as liquid natural gas.

Indonesia hopes to decrease its dependence on oil exports. Tourism is one way to bring money into the country. In Bali, which is well known for its ceremonies, dance, and beaches, tourism is a major industry.

Another of Indonesia's strongest resources is its people. There are more than 94 million workers in the country. Those workers, and Indonesia's low wages, draw industry to the country. In the 1960s, Indonesia made little more than textiles for export. In the past 15 years, the country has doubled its manufacturing.

Companies have built most of their factories on Java. Besides willing workers, this island has good roads, an airport, and a port. Sending finished goods overseas from Java is easy. Many of the factories make goods that are labor-intensive. That is, they need many hours to produce. Some examples of these kinds of goods are footwear, glassware, and clothing.

HISTORY FACT

Coffee is sometimes nicknamed "java." This reflects the fact that, at one time, Java was a major source of the world's coffee.

Millions of people have moved to the few cities that have become industrial centers. About nine million people live in Jakarta now. That is two-thirds of all Indonesians. Right outside Jakarta, and other cities, are **kampongs**, or villages, where many more people live.

Another way that Indonesia brings in money is through exporting wood. About half of the land is covered with rain forest where valuable hardwoods such as teak and ebony grow. Foreign companies pay the Indonesian government for the right to log. These companies have cut too much wood too quickly, though. They have not planted enough new trees. As the rain forest disappears, wildlife is threatened. The rain forest also reduces flooding and holds soil in place. Losing rain forest would be a disaster for Indonesia.

In the 1980s, **conservation** laws were passed to try to save the rain forest. Companies are supposed to plant new trees whenever they cut down old ones. Also, raw lumber can no longer be exported. Instead, now it must be processed in Indonesia.

Eating and Cooking Indonesian Food

Indonesian cooking has been influenced by many cultures: Indian, Chinese, Middle Eastern, and European. Rice is eaten at nearly every meal. Usually, it is cooked in a bamboo steamer. One popular dish is fried rice with vegetables and spices. Another is sate. To make sate, a cook soaks strips of meat in spices and juices, and then grills them over charcoal. Sate is served with a spiced peanut sauce.

Other ingredients in Indonesian dishes include tofu, or soybean cake, coconut, and red chilis. Lemon grass appears in many dishes as well. It is a wild grass that has a lemony smell. Lemon grass is also used in Thai, Vietnamese, and Chinese cooking, as well.

Dutch immigrants contributed the rijstafel to Indonesian cooking. Rijstafel means "rice table" in Dutch. Rice is central to this meal. It is served in a large dish or bowl. Around it, as many as 20 other foods are served in small dishes.

Indonesian Textile Arts

Indonesia is famous for its textile arts. People skilled in crafts spin, dye, and weave cotton and silk. Designs and colors both have special meanings. In the past, weaving itself was seen as a symbol. It stood for creating life. For this reason, in many cultures, only women were allowed to weave cloth.

The most outstanding textile art of Indonesia is **batik**, a way of creating colorful designs on cloth. First, the artist draws a design on the cloth with melted wax. Then, when the wax cools, the cloth is dipped in dye. Only the parts without wax take the color. After the cloth dries, the wax is ironed out. Many batik designs reflect Hindu myths and legends. Blue, yellow, and brown are traditional colors.

The designs and colors of Indonesian batik fabric have special meanings.

Traditional Indonesian Entertainment

Picture 20 musicians sitting cross-legged on woven grass mats. In the background is a temple with a golden roof. The musicians are tapping out tones on bronze gongs and on long, double-ended drums. The music is gentle but lively—like the sound of frogs in rice fields at night. This is a **gamelan** orchestra.

Gamelan is traditional Indonesian music. It sounds as if it is being made up on the spot. Actually, however, this music is carefully planned and follows complicated rules. For example, high-pitched instruments play more notes than low-pitched instruments.

A gamelan orchestra plays traditional Indonesian music.

Each instrument plays a different melody, and the parts are woven together. As one melody is ending, another may just be starting. Thus, the music has a simmering, flowing quality.

The combination of instruments differs from one gamelan orchestra to another. Generally, the instruments include gongs, drums, flutes, stringed instruments, and xylophones. Some orchestras also have singers.

There are many styles of gamelan. In Java, gamelan can be slow and formal. This music was created for the royal courts. In Bali, gamelan is often fast-paced and exciting. People dance to it. Gamelan orchestras play at festivals and celebrations. They also play in temples and at government events. Indonesian radio stations and television shows feature gamelan music.

Gamelan orchestras also provide music for puppet shows. One type of Indonesian puppet show is called wayang kulit. In this type of show, puppets perform behind a screen, their shadows falling on the screen. The people in the audience see only the shadows, never the puppets. Wayang kulit companies perform stories from the *Ramayana* and other Hindu legends. A wayang kulit performance may last from five o'clock in the evening until dawn. People are free to come and go during the performance, and many people do so.

✓ Check Your Understanding

Write your answers in complete sentences.

1. Why did Indonesian agriculture suffer under the Dutch?

2. Why do companies like to open factories on Java?

3. Why were women often weavers?

4. What is the difference between gamelan in Bali and gamelan in Java?

Summary

The five largest islands in Southeast Asia are Borneo, New Guinea, Sumatra, Java, and Sulawesi.

Malaysia, Singapore, Brunei, Indonesia, and Papua New Guinea are nations located in the Malay Peninsula and the Malay Archipelago.

Indonesia is the largest Muslim country in the world. Indonesian Islam, however, has borrowed much from other religious traditions.

Java and Bali are the most crowded islands of Indonesia. About two-thirds of Indonesians live on Java.

batik
conservation
gamelan
strait
kampong

Vocabulary Review

Write a term from the list that matches each definition below.

1. A narrow strip of water between two bodies of land

2. Saving natural resources such as rain forests and wildlife

3. A process for hand-printing colored designs on cloth

4. A traditional Indonesian village

5. Traditional Indonesian orchestra

Chapter Quiz

Write your answers in complete sentences.

1. The countries of Malaysia, Indonesia, and Brunei share what island?

2. Traders from which country colonized the Malay Archipelago?

3. What are shadow puppets, a traditional form of entertainment in Indonesia, called?

4. **Critical Thinking** Two-thirds of all Indonesians live in the city of Jakarta. What might life be like there?

5. **Critical Thinking** Why are some people concerned about logging in Indonesia?

Write About Geography

Complete the following activities.

1. Trace the Pacific Ocean on a map and mark where the Ring of Fire is located. Write a caption that explains the Ring of Fire.

2. It is the late 1970s. Write a letter to a newspaper editor that explains why laws to conserve the forests are needed.

Group Activity

Your job is to create a book about the Indonesian islands for cruise-ship passengers. Each person can choose an island and find out basic facts and information about the island's food, people, and arts.

Coconuts are one of the main exports of the Philippines. Some of the products made from coconuts are coconut oil, furniture, clothing, and rugs. What happens to the local economy if the coconut harvest is poor?

Words to Know

typhoon	a tropical storm in the Pacific Ocean that brings high winds and heavy rainfall
abaca	a plant used to make rope
surname	a person's family name
barangay	local government in the Philippines

Places to Know

Philippines

Luzon

Visayas

Mindanao

Manila

Learning Objectives

- Identify the original settlers of the Philippines.
- Tell how Spanish and U.S. occupation influenced Filipino culture.
- Describe the barangays and their role in Filipino life.
- Describe Catholicism in the Philippines.

The Land and the People

Geography Fact

Only about 7 percent of the islands of the Philippines are larger than one square mile. Only about one-third of the islands have names.

The Philippines is a group of about 7,100 islands northeast of Borneo. The Philippines is part of the Malay Archipelago. The people who live in the Philippines area are called Filipinos. Most Filipinos live on Luzon, the largest island in the Philippines. A group of Philippine islands called the Visayas is heavily populated, too. The second-largest island, Mindanao, is not very populated.

The landmass of the Philippines is about as big as the state of Nevada. The country's coastline, however, is twice as long as that of the U.S. mainland. The Philippines, like the rest of the Malay Archipelago, is part of the Ring of Fire. Earthquakes and volcanic eruptions are common. So are **typhoons**, which are large storms that blow in from the Pacific Ocean.

The climate in the Philippines is tropical. The winter monsoon creates a dry season from December to May. The rest of the year is wet. The islands have many mountains that slope down to fertile coastal plains. About 40 percent of the land is covered with forests.

Most Filipinos live in the countryside, where they farm or fish for a living. Pineapples, coconuts, bananas, sugar, rice, corn, and **abaca** are exported from the Philippines. Abaca plants are used to make rope. Because the land is so mountainous, rice is often grown on terraces cut into the lower mountain slopes. In Luzon, a people called the Ifugaos cut many long terraces almost to the tops of the mountain. These terraces were built over 2,000 years ago.

Remember
A land bridge also existed between Siberia and North America.

Filipinos are descended mainly from Asians who migrated to the Philippine Islands more than 22,000 years ago. At that time, the oceans were lower. Land bridges connected many islands of the Malay Archipelago. People were able to walk from mainland Southeast Asia to the Philippines.

The Philippines

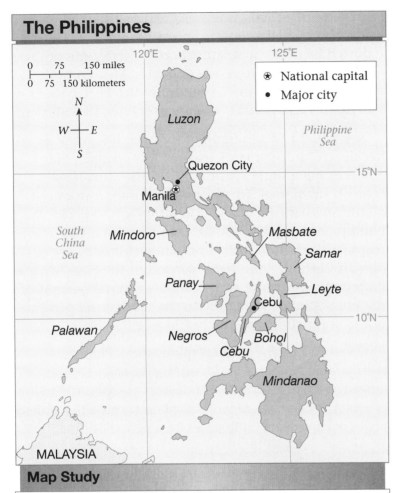

0 75 150 miles
0 75 150 kilometers

N
W—E
S

- ⊛ National capital
- • Major city

120°E

125°E

Luzon

Philippine Sea

Quezon City

15°N

Manila

South China Sea

Mindoro

Masbate

Samar

Panay

Leyte

Cebu

10°N

Palawan

Negros

Bohol

Cebu

Mindanao

MALAYSIA

Map Study

1. **LOCATION** What is the national capital of the Philippines?

2. **PLACE** The island of Cebu lies between three other islands. Name these islands.

Later, the waters rose, and the land bridges disappeared. People from Australia and Asia then came to the Philippines by boat. In the 1100s, some immigrants from China settled on the islands. In the 1300s, Arabic traders introduced Islam to the southern islands.

In the early 1500s, a Spanish explorer named Ferdinand Magellan landed in the Philippines. He was followed by other Spaniards shortly after. Some of the same Spanish soldiers who conquered Mexico came to fight for control of these islands. By the 1570s, the Philippines had become a Spanish colony, like Mexico.

Spain ruled the Philippines for over 300 years. As in Mexico, the Spaniards married local people. Many Filipinos have some Spanish ancestors. Most have Spanish **surnames**. The Catholic Church, introduced by the Spaniards, had a strong influence, too. The Philippines is the only Asian country with a Catholic majority. In fact, 85 percent of Filipinos today are Roman Catholic. Another 9 percent of the Filipinos are Protestants. Muslims, who make up about 5 percent of the population, live mainly in the south. One percent of the population consists of Chinese Buddhists.

About 90 percent of the Filipinos speak Pilipino, the national language. It is based on Tagalog, a Malay language. About 100 different dialects are spoken. English is widely spoken as a second language because the United States occupied the Philippines for a period of time.

The United States in the Philippines

In 1898, a war broke out between Spain and the United States. Spain lost the war and was forced to sell the Philippines to the United States for $20 million. The United States ruled the Philippines until World War II, when, for a short time, Japan took control. In 1946, the United States declared the Philippines an independent nation. The new country had a government modeled on that of the United States.

The United States had large military bases on the Philippines. By treaty, it kept these bases after Philippine independence. The bases made the United States a military power in east Asia.

Many businesses developed around the bases. Most of them were restaurants and clubs. They were places for U.S. military service members to spend their money and free time. Filipinos left farms and shops to work in these businesses. Many Filipinos did not like the way the bases affected the culture of the Philippines. It was as if the United States still controlled their country.

In the 1950s, a group of Filipino Communists rebelled against the newly independent government. The rebels were called the Huks. They fought, in part, to get rid of the U.S. military bases. The United States joined forces with the Philippine government to crush the Huk rebellion. A new guerrilla group called the New People's Army rose in place of the Huks.

Then in the 1970s, another rebellion occurred. This time, the rebels were the Muslims of Mindanao. They complained of unfair treatment by the Catholic majority and demanded the right to govern themselves.

Ferdinand Marcos was president of the Philippines at the time of these rebellions. He had been democratically elected in 1965, but he used the rebellions as an excuse to make himself a dictator. He canceled the elections of 1972 and declared martial law. He said that he had to do this in order to fight the rebels. The United States supported Marcos and thought that he could stop the Communists from taking over the Philippines.

Marcos's tactics did not succeed in wiping out the New People's Army. This group still stages violent attacks in rural areas from time to time. He also failed to resolve the issues of the Muslim population. Mindanao remains a troubled area in the Philippines.

Under Marcos, the Philippine economy lost ground. The poor of the country became poorer. Marcos became one of the richest men in the world. He and his family moved billions of dollars out of the country into foreign banks.

You Decide

In what ways might the U.S bases have affected the culture of the Philippines?

In 1983, Filipinos poured into the streets to demonstrate against Ferdinand Marcos. Ronald Reagan, then President of the United States, asked Marcos to step down as president of the Philippines. Marcos could not rule without U.S. support. He and his wife Imelda were forced to leave the country. A democratically elected government took over the Philippines again. The country has remained a democracy. In 1992, the U.S. military bases in the Philippines were closed.

Problems remain, however. The economy has improved dramatically, but promises of land reform have not been kept. The gap between rich and poor is still very wide. In fact, about 2 percent of the people control most of the country's wealth.

Metro Manila

Manila, the capital of the Philippines, is located on the island of Luzon. It began in 1571 as a walled fortress built by the Spanish. Old Manila grew up around this fort. In 1976, Marcos joined several surrounding cities with Old Manila to create Metro Manila. About ten million people live in Metro Manila—almost one-sixth of the Philippine population. Metro Manila stretches about 100 miles from edge to edge. It is one of the biggest cities in Asia—and it is growing.

Economics Fact

The United States is the Philippine's largest trading partner.

Metro Manila is the industrial center of the Philippines. Goods are produced for export to the United States, Japan, and Taiwan. The government encourages small industries, which are growing quickly in Manila. These small industries include clothing, furniture, and craft businesses. For trained professionals, however, there are not enough jobs in the Philippines. Many educated Filipinos emigrate to more developed countries such as the United States.

When the United States closed its bases in the Philippines, the military left behind vehicles that have been converted into jeepneys such as this.

Life in Manila is fast-paced. Traffic is heavy. Jeepneys fill the crowded streets. A jeepney is a small bus converted from a U.S. Jeep. Because tourism is a large part of Metro Manila's economy, there are many fine hotels, restaurants, clubs, and movie houses. Filipino music has a strong Latin dance beat. It also shows the influence of American folk, pop, and rock music.

Life in the Barangay

In the Philippines, the local government in both rural and urban areas is the **barangay**. Each has a leader who speaks for the community in dealings with the larger government. A barangay board advises the leader. Most barangays have their own church.

The word barangay comes from the name of the sailboats that first brought settlers to the Philippines from Borneo. Each boat carried a family, with the head of the family in charge. Even now, in rural areas, a barangay is based on a network of relationships like that of an extended family.

Today barangay boards start credit unions. They raise money for community projects. They begin day care centers. In 1978, the Philippine government saw that courts were clogged. To solve the problem, the government formed the Barangay Justice Programme. In each of the 42,000 barangays, a board of people solves disputes. The people in the barangay trust the decisions. The government saves money and the courts are less clogged.

Spotlight On

TRADITIONAL DANCES OF THE PHILIPPINES

The singkil is a traditional Filipino dance of Islamic origin. A female dancer moves between two pairs of bamboo poles, which form a tic-tac-toe pattern near the ground. Four helpers hold the bamboo poles and clap them together, quickening the pace. The dancer steps gracefully and quickly between the poles. She represents a proud, elegant princess. As she dances, she sweeps lace fans across her body. Her dress and fans are styled with gold designs.

Another Filipino folk dance is called tinikling. This dance mirrors the flying movements of a blue-gray water bird called the heron. The jota and curacha are two dances that grew out of Spanish folk dances.

Bamboo poles are used during this performance of a folk dance in Mindanao, Philippines.

Critical Thinking Why do you think traditional dances are important?

The Catholic Church in the Philippines

The Catholic Church is a major presence in the Philippines. Almost all Filipino children are baptized. This ceremony names children and brings them into the church. Godparents are usually chosen at the baptism.

Catholicism in the Philippines is unique. In Filipino Catholicism, local saints are very important. Filipinos look to their saints for help with everyday problems. For example, Filipinos pray to saints to help bring in a good crop or to find a spouse. Many communities have healers who claim to be inspired by saints. These healers are thought to have special powers.

Most families have religious icons in their homes. These icons may include pictures or sculptures of the Virgin Mary and the infant Jesus. Every day, the family kneels in prayer before the icons. Religious icons are found in public places, too. Stories and legends about miracles are connected to many icons.

Easter week is the most important holiday season in the Philippines. The holiday begins with mourning. On Good Friday—the day when Christ was nailed to the cross—Filipino men parade down the streets. The men beat their bare backs with whips to remind everyone of the pain that Christ suffered. Then, on Easter Sunday, the country explodes with joy as Filipinos celebrate the day Christ was said to have risen from the dead.

✓ **Check Your Understanding**

Write your answers in complete sentences.

1. What country first colonized the Philippines?

2. Why did Ferdinand Marcos leave power?

3. How is Catholicism unique in the Philippines?

Summary

The Philippines is a group of islands in the northern part of the Malay Archipelago. The main islands are Luzon, Mindanao, and a group of islands called the Visayas.

Filipinos are descended mainly from Asians who settled on the Philippine Islands long ago.

The Spanish colonized the Philippines for over 300 years and left a strong mark on Filipino culture, including the introduction of the Catholic Church.

The United States controlled the Philippines from about 1898 to 1946. The U.S. government owned and operated large military bases in the Philippines until 1992.

The national government of the Philippines is a democracy modeled after that of the United States.

barangay
typhoon
surname
abaca

Vocabulary Review

Complete each sentence with a term from the list.

1. A _____ is a tropical storm in the Pacific Ocean.

2. A plant used to make rope is an _____ plant.

3. The local Philippine government is called a _____ .

4. A _____ is a person's family name.

Chapter Quiz

Write your answers in complete sentences.

1. What is the tropical storm that is very much like a hurricane called?

2. What is the Malay language on which Pilipino is based?

3. What impact did Ferdinand Marcos have on the Philippines?

4. **Critical Thinking** Why is a barangay so closely knit?

5. **Critical Thinking** Why is Manila important to the Philippines today?

Write About Geography

Complete the following activities.

1. Create a chart of the groups that came to the Philippines. Write what each contributed to the country.

2. You are the U.S. President in 1983. Write a letter to Ferdinand Marcos telling him why he needs to step down as president of the Philippines.

Group Activity

Your group is a barangay board. Elect a leader. Then make a decision about an issue that people are concerned with at your school. Decide how your leader should speak to the larger "government," the school.

Unit 9 Review

Comprehension Check
Answer each question in a complete sentence.

1. How does Islam shape family life in Pakistan and Afghanistan?

2. Why are monasteries important in Thailand and Myanmar?

3. Why do many Vietnamese people speak French?

4. How is Indonesia working to improve its economy?

Building Your Skills
Answer each question in a complete sentence.

1. What geographical feature runs along India's northern border?

2. What is the first thing to do when you are getting directions from someone?

3. How can you tell what the population density is of an area on a population density map?

Where Is It?
Write the name of the place based on the information below.

1. Was once called Bombay

2. The province where most Pakistanis live

3. The Indonesian island where Jakarta is located

Writing an Essay
Answer one of the following essay topics.

1. Describe how Hinduism affects the lives of people in India.

2. Explain what has happened to Communism in Vietnam and Cambodia in recent years.

3. Explain how the United States' relationship with the Philippines has changed.

Geography and You

Weather such as monsoons has a huge affect on areas of South and Southeast Asia, such as India. What weather patterns affect your life?

Chapter 34 Australia and New Zealand

Chapter 35 Oceania

Australia and New Zealand are similar culturally but different physically. In what ways does that affect life in the region?

TRAVEL LOG

The South Pacific has some animals and landforms that are not found anywhere else in the world. Write about three of the animals or natural landforms that you have seen while visiting this region.

Australian boomerang

Australia's Opera House in Sydney is known throughout the world. What conclusions can you draw about Sydney from this style of architecture?

Chapter 34 / Australia and New Zealand

Words to Know

Eurasia	a geographical term for the landmass that is made up of the continents of Europe and Asia
biogeography	the study of the geographic distribution of animals and plants
marsupial	a type of mammal that is born before it is fully developed, and then completes its development in its mother's pouch
Outback	the name given to Australia's vast, mainly desert, interior
clinic	a hospital that serves a specific population

Places to Know

Great Dividing Range

Ayers Rock

Great Barrier Reef

North Island

South Island

Learning Objectives

- Explain the wildlife found in Australia and New Zealand.
- Explain why Australia and New Zealand are culturally different from their Asian neighbors.
- Trace the history of the Maoris.
- Tell what life is like on an Australian sheep station.
- Describe the arts of Australia and New Zealand.

The Continent of Australia

Australia is the only continent that is also a country. In the east, it faces the Pacific Ocean. In the south and west, it borders the Indian Ocean. It is the world's sixth-largest country and is about the size of the United States.

Australia was isolated for most of the last 55 million years. Animals could not roam in and out of this continent as they could between Africa, **Eurasia**, and the Americas. As a result, the **biogeography** of Australia is different from that of any other part of the world. Many animals and plants that are found in Australia cannot be found on other continents. For example, the platypus and the spiny anteater—the world's only two egg-laying mammals—are found in Australia. Australia also has the emu—a large, flightless bird much like the African ostrich.

The most striking feature of Australia's wildlife is the large number of **marsupials**, a kind of mammal that is born before it is fully developed. When a marsupial is born, it crawls into a pouch on its mother's belly, where it completes its development. Marsupials are rare in most parts of the world. In Australia, however, they are common. Some Australian marsupials are kangaroos, koalas, wallabies, and wombats.

Australia is the flattest of all the continents. Most of Australia is low, too—not more than 900 feet above sea level. One mountain chain—the Great Dividing Range—runs along Australia's eastern edge. This range is just high enough to prevent moist ocean air from moving inland. The east coast of Australia receives plenty of rain, but the bulk of the continent stays dry. In fact, most of Australia's interior is desert. This vast, dry wilderness is called the **Outback**.

Kangaroos are marsupials found only in Australia and on nearby islands.

The Outback has many strange and beautiful landscapes. Here and there, huge lumps of bare, round rock stick up from the dry plateau. Near the very center of the Outback is Ayers Rock. This red rock is six miles around and about 1,260 feet high. To the aboriginal people of Australia, Ayers Rock is a sacred place.

Mining is important to Australia. The country has reserves of gold, bauxite, iron ore, copper, uranium, coal, oil, natural gas, and other minerals. Many of these minerals are exported. Australia also exports a lot of beef and wool, which come from the cattle and sheep on huge ranches called stations. These ranches are located in the Outback. Only 6 percent of the people work on ranches, but they raise enough food for the entire nation. About 85 percent of Australians live in cities, where most of them work in sales and service jobs.

The Great Barrier Reef lies off the northeastern coast of Australia. The reef is made of coral. The animals that make up this coral reef, called coral polyps, live in groups. When they die, their stony skeletons remain. More polyps grow on top of the old skeletons. In this way, coral keeps building up. Huge underwater ridges of coral form over time. Finally, the coral ridges may poke up above the water, thus forming coral islands.

Coral reefs are found in warm, shallow, tropical waters throughout the South Pacific. The Great Barrier Reef is the world's longest coral reef—about 1,200 miles long. It has the richest variety of underwater plants and animals in the world. The calm water between the reef and the land is good for swimming and other sports. Because of this, Australia's Great Barrier Reef draws many tourists. Unfortunately, along with the tourists come powerboats, hotels, and other services that create harmful pollution. Too much tourism may be damaging the reef.

Economics Fact

Australia's agriculture is not limited to ranches. There are also many farms that produce goods such as wheat, barley, sugar cane, and fruit.

Remember
Coral is made up of the hard outside skeletons of billions of tiny sea animals.

Australia and New Zealand

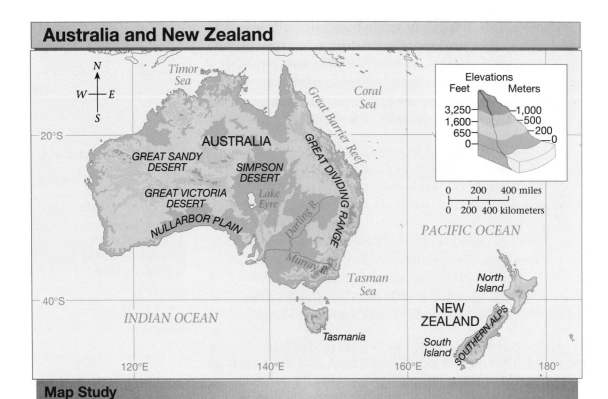

Map Study

1. REGION Which body of water lies between Australia and New Zealand?

2. LOCATION Where are the Southern Alps?

The Two Islands of New Zealand

About 1,200 miles southeast of Australia lies New Zealand. This nation is made up mainly of two islands—North Island and South Island. New Zealand is about the size of the state of Colorado.

New Zealand is much like Australia culturally. Physically, however, New Zealand is quite different. Unlike Australia, New Zealand gets plenty of rainfall. New Zealand has many tall mountains. Between these tall mountains are green valleys.

New Zealand is even more isolated geographically than Australia. There are hardly any native mammals in New Zealand. There are, however, many rare birds. For example, the kiwi is a small, brown, flightless bird that lives only in New Zealand.

Like Australia, New Zealand has many sheep ranches, or stations. Wool and lamb are the country's main exports. New Zealand also exports dairy products such as butter and cheese. In New Zealand, 84 percent of the people live in cities.

Immigration and Land Rights in Australia

The first people arrived in Australia about 40,000 years ago and probably came from Southeast Asia. These people were the Kooris, or the aboriginal people. They were the only people to live in Australia until the 1500s, when Europeans arrived. At that time, the number of Koori people was about 300,000. They were nomadic hunters who traveled in small clans and lived in rough camps.

One tool that the Kooris used in hunting was called a boomerang. This was a flat piece of wood shaped like a wide "V." When it was thrown, it took a curving path through the air. If it missed its target, it circled back to the hunter. Other kinds of boomerangs were used as digging tools, clubs, and even musical instruments.

In 1769, a British sea captain named James Cook landed in Australia and claimed it for Britain. At that time, British jails were overflowing—mainly because British law was harsh. For example, people could be sentenced to years of prison for stealing bread, or for their political ideas. For years, Britain had been sending prisoners, or convicts, to its colonies in America. In 1783 after the Revolutionary War ended, the American colonies won their freedom. Britain, therefore, started sending its prisoners to Australia.

You Decide

What made the British think that Australia would be a good place to send prisoners?

During the next 80 years, about 160,000 British convicts arrived in Australia. Eventually, the flow of convicts slowed, when gold was discovered in Australia. This discovery brought a new wave of settlers, who came from many parts of Europe, not just Britain. The Kooris were chased off land that the European settlers wanted for mining, farming, and ranching. The European settlers killed the Kooris who resisted. Many Kooris also died of European diseases. By 1860, their population had dropped to about 25,000. Australia became independent of Britain in 1901. A policy of only allowing immigrants from Europe into Australia began under British rule and continued until 1966. Once the policy was changed, immigrants also came from many parts of Asia. The largest group of immigrants were refugees from Southeast Asia.

Today, 95 percent of Australians are descended from Europeans. Another 4 percent have Asian roots. The Kooris make up less than 1 percent of the population. Because of prejudice, the Kooris remain at the bottom of the Australian society. Few Kooris have good jobs. Most are poor and cannot read or write. About half of Australia's Kooris live in urban areas. City life often forces them to abandon their own culture.

Today, many Kooris are trying to restore their cultural traditions. They are also fighting to regain lands and mineral rights that they lost to European settlers. So far, progress has been slow.

 Check Your Understanding

Write your answers in complete sentences.

1. Why are there so many marsupials in Australia?

2. Where do most people in New Zealand live?

3. Why did the population of the Kooris drop so much?

GLOBAL ISSUES
Protecting the Coral Reefs

The Great Barrier Reef may be 5.3 million years old. In the past few decades, though, people have put it in greater danger than in all the previous centuries combined.

Fishing, tourism, and mining put the reef at risk. One type of fishing, bottom trawling, scrapes the life off the bottom of the ocean. Tourism, with its roaring boats and pollution, is another problem. The 1960s brought an interest in drilling for oil in the reef. This was one reason Australians first decided to guard this unique place.

In 1981, the reef was added to the United Nations' World Heritage List. Australia is working to protect the reef. Mining and spear fishing with scuba gear are banned. In some areas of the reef, almost no people are allowed. Australia has good reasons to protect the reef. It is protecting a $1 billion-a-year tourist industry. It is also preserving a world treasure.

Answer the questions below.

1. Why is the Great Barrier Reef more at danger now than in previous centuries?

2. Which of the activities threatening the reef do you think is the biggest threat? Explain why.

MAKE A DIFFERENCE
There are places worth protecting near where you live. Find out from local conservation groups or on the Internet what natural areas are in danger. Choose one of these areas to help protect. Then ask what you can do to make a difference.

Immigration and Land Rights in New Zealand

The original people of New Zealand, called the Maoris, have fared much better than the Kooris in Australia. They probably came to New Zealand by canoe from such islands as Tahiti and Hawaii. Most of the Maoris arrived between the 1200s and the 1400s. By the time Europeans set foot on the islands, the Maoris were settled farmers living in villages. Before 1840, Europeans had set up only a few small trading posts on New Zealand. Traders, whale hunters, and missionaries lived there. Even so, these Europeans harmed the Maoris by bringing diseases with them, as they had done elsewhere in the world. They also brought guns, which made traditional Maori intergroup warfare much more deadly. The Maori population began to shrink.

In 1840, the British signed a treaty with the Maoris that made New Zealand a British colony. The treaty promised the Maoris certain rights. Soon, however, European settlers began taking over Maori lands. The Maoris fought back, but they lost their lands eventually. Then, in the twentieth century, under new leaders, the Maoris began to rebuild their culture. They strengthened their position in New Zealand. Their population began to grow again.

Today, about 87 percent of the people in New Zealand trace their roots to Europe. Most of them are descended from British settlers. They belong to Protestant churches such as the Church of England. The Maori people, however, make up almost 10 percent of New Zealand's population. Maori is one of the country's official languages. New Zealand's courts are taking a new look at the treaty of 1840. Some parts of the treaty may be judged unfair and may be changed. The government of New Zealand has programs to support Maori arts and culture.

Life in the Outback

In the Outback of Australia, cattle and sheep ranching is a way of life. A typical Australian station is huge. The land is so dry and bare of vegetation that each sheep needs about 50 acres of grazing range. One station may, therefore, cover a thousand square miles. Workers ride the range on horseback.

Ranchers are busy at sheep shearing time, when the wool is shaved off the sheep. Most Australian sheep are grown for wool rather than for meat. Ranch owners hire extra workers who labor hard for several weeks. After shearing, the sheep are turned loose to graze—at which point, most of the station workers are let go.

Ranching families often live hundreds of miles from the nearest towns. Children cannot go to school, so the school comes to them—by radio. This is called School of the Air, which began in 1951. Teachers who live in the main towns talk with their students each day by two-way radio. Most teachers never actually meet their students. Teenagers usually receive their textbooks and lessons— and send their homework to the teacher—by mail.

A worker can shear 300 sheep a day. Each sheep produces about 9 pounds of wool. A big ram, however, can produce as much as 50 pounds.

Another program designed to help people in the Outback is the Royal Flying Doctor Service. It began in 1927 and is still going strong. In this program, doctors and nurses, working from an air base, use an air ambulance to reach patients who need immediate medical care. People in need use a two-way radio to call the air base. Even tiny Outback towns have **clinics**, which the doctors and nurses of the Flying Doctor Service visit regularly.

Two railroad lines cross the Outback. Along one of the lines, a slow train brings groceries and other supplies to isolated communities. This train is called the Tea and Sugar. The Tea and Sugar is thus like a traveling store.

A Nation Against Nuclear Weapons

Remember
Nuclear weapons are bombs like the ones dropped on Japan during World War II.

In the 1980s, New Zealand declared itself a "nuclear-free zone." It banned nuclear weapons from entering New Zealand. Only the United States has used such weapons, but many nations make and store them. No nations with nuclear weapons may dock their warships in New Zealand.

U.S. military leaders were angered by New Zealand's decision to ban nuclear weapons. In fact, the United States canceled an agreement it had to protect New Zealand in case of war.

There were people, however, who saw New Zealand as a model for their movement. In 1985, a ship called the *Rainbow Warrior* docked in Auckland, New Zealand. The ship belonged to the environmental group Greenpeace. The *Rainbow Warrior* was on its way to protest nuclear weapon tests by France in the South Pacific. However, while the ship was in harbor, French spies bombed it. One person was killed. The bombing created great tension between France and New Zealand.

The United States helped to smooth the differences between France and New Zealand. New Zealand still remains a nuclear-free zone, and most New Zealanders strongly support their government's antinuclear policy.

The Arts

Australia and New Zealand have many museums, galleries, cultural festivals, and other art events. In Australia, some museums and galleries specialize in Koori art. The country has several communities of Koori artists whose art has become prized. Some of these artists paint in realistic styles. Most of these artists, however, take their inspiration from traditional Koori art. They use images from ancient art that was painted on rocks and cave walls.

The Sydney Opera House is a fine example of Australia's interest in the arts. The building is an architectural wonder and a work of art in itself. Ballet groups, opera companies, orchestras, and theater groups perform inside the Opera House. Australia also has its own movie industry. Although the Australian movie industry is small, it is older than the film industry in the United States.

Traditional Maori artists are best known for their wood carving. For centuries, Maori artists have carved rich decorations into the doorways, roof beams, and side posts of their community buildings. They decorated canoes, storage boxes, tools, and musical instruments. They even carved finely detailed designs into clubs, ax handles, and digging sticks.

Modern Maori artists work in wood, stone, ivory, and bone. In their carvings, Maori artists use the forms of gods, animals, humans, and ocean waves to tell their history. The Maoris do not value art just for its beauty. They also believe that, in the hands of an artist, beautifully carved stone, bone, or wood becomes partly sacred and has spiritual power.

At one time, European settlers collected Maori artwork and sold it to art dealers in Britain. The Maoris do not want this to happen again. They feel that they lose some of their spiritual power—and a part of themselves—when their art goes to people of other cultures. Therefore, the Maoris do not let their art out of the country unless it is protected by a Maori leader.

Maori artists are known for their wood carving. They decorate canoes, tools, and musical instruments.

✓ Check Your Understanding

Write your answers in complete sentences.

1. Describe New Zealand's population.

2. Why are ranches in the Outback so huge?

3. What is New Zealand's nuclear-free zone?

Summary

Australia is the only country that is also a continent. Most of Australia is low, flat, and very dry.
The Great Barrier Reef, which lies off the northeastern coast of Australia, is the world's longest coral reef.
Australia was first settled about 40,000 years ago by the Kooris. The Maoris settled in New Zealand between the 1200s and 1400s.
New Zealand is a nation made up of two main islands. It is mountainous and gets plenty of rainfall.
Sheep ranching is an important industry in both Australia and New Zealand. Australian sheep are raised mainly for their wool.
Descendants of European settlers make up most of the population of Australia and New Zealand today.

Vocabulary Review

Write *true* or *false*. If the statement is false, change the underlined term to make it true.

1. A <u>clinic</u> is a hospital that serves a specific population.

2. <u>Eurasia</u> is the study of the geographic distribution of animals and plants.

3. The geographic term for the landmass that is made up of the continents of Europe and Asia is the <u>Outback</u>.

4. A type of mammal that is born before it is fully developed is a <u>marsupial</u>.

5. <u>Biogeography</u> is the name given to Australia's, mainly desert, interior.

Chapter Quiz

Write your answers in complete sentences.

1. When Europeans arrived in New Zealand, by whom were the islands inhabited?

2. Kangaroos and wallabies are what kind of mammals?

3. What did nomadic hunters in Australia use to hunt small game long ago?

4. **Critical Thinking** In what ways is Australia like the United States?

5. **Critical Thinking** How do people cope with the isolated life of the Outback?

Write About Geography

Complete the following activities.

1. You are growing up on a ranch in the Outback. Write the best and worst things about living there.

2. It is the 1980s. Write the arguments for and against New Zealand becoming a nuclear-free zone.

Group Activity

Design a way to teach this chapter for the School of the Air. Assign a person to teach each section. Ask questions about this chapter or find another way to teach students who learn by listening.

Scientists and tourists visit Oceania to see its beautiful coral reefs. How could this attention threaten or help the reefs?

Chapter 35 / Oceania

Words to Know

atoll	a ring-shaped coral island surrounding a lagoon
outrigger	a canoe with a frame that holds a float on each side
copra	the dried meat of a coconut

Places to Know

Polynesia

Melanesia

Micronesia

Learning Objectives

- Describe the three main areas of Oceania.
- Compare volcanic islands and coral islands.
- Explain how Oceania became populated.
- Explain how most people of the Pacific islands make a living.

Three Areas of Oceania

Oceania is a huge area of the South Pacific. It includes New Zealand and parts of Indonesia. From east to west it stretches about 7,000 miles. At least 20,000 small islands are located in this area. Many are so small that no one lives on them.

Oceania can be divided into three regions. The islands of the east make up Polynesia. These islands include Hawaii, Samoa, Tonga, the Cook Islands, Tahiti, Easter Island, and hundreds more. In the west are the islands of Melanesia. The biggest of these islands is New Guinea. The eastern half of the island is Papua New Guinea, which became an independent nation in 1975. Melanesia also includes Fiji, New Caledonia, the Solomons, and hundreds of other islands.

Remember
The western half of New Guinea is Irian Jaya, which belongs to Indonesia.

The third group of islands is called Micronesia, which is north of Melanesia. The word *micro* means "small." Guam, the largest island in Micronesia, is only 210 square miles. Other islands in this region include the Carolines, the Marianas, and the Marshalls.

Most of Melanesia is south of the equator, and most of Micronesia is north of the equator. Both island groups lie generally west of the international date line. Polynesia lies generally east of it. This imaginary line is 12 time zones away from the prime meridian. People who cross the date line from west to east go back 24 hours in time. For example, if it is Monday just west of the date line, it is Sunday just east of it.

Some islands in Oceania are actually the peaks of volcanic mountains that rise from the ocean floor. The Hawaiian Islands are examples of such volcanic islands. Two active volcanoes in this island group are Kilauea and Mauna Loa. Volcanic islands receive much more rainfall than coral islands do. Volcanic islands also have richer soil, which is better for farming.

Other islands in Oceania are the tops of coral reefs. The Cook Islands of Polynesia are coral islands. Since coral needs water to grow, a coral island never rises much more than sea level. In fact, the highest point on a coral island may be just 10 or 20 feet above sea level. When many small coral islands are grouped together, they form an **atoll**. On coral islands, water for drinking may be scarce. These islands have no streams or rivers because they have no mountains. Ground water is limited, too, because a coral island has just a thin layer of soil. Below this layer lies coral and salty ocean water.

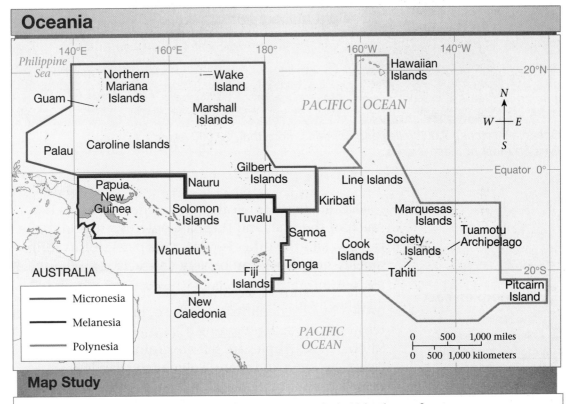

Oceania

Map Study

1. **LOCATION** The Northern Mariana Islands are a part of what island group?

2. **REGION** What continent is closest to Oceania?

Oceania stretches 7,000 miles and contains more than 20,000 islands. No one lives on most of these islands.

Oceania has a tropical climate. The weather is hot much of the year, and there are only two seasons. One is rainy, and the other is rainier. Tropical storms form quickly here. They can be very destructive.

Many islands of Oceania are territories that are owned by other countries. Even so, most of these territories are self-governing. Guam and American Samoa, for example, are self-governing U.S. territories. New Caledonia and many Polynesian islands are French territories. Some islands, such as the Cook Islands, are territories of New Zealand. There are also nine independent island nations, including Palau, Fiji, Samoa, Tonga, Vanuatu, and Kiribati.

$ Economics Fact

The Northern Marianas is a U.S. territory in the Pacific. Melons, nuts, and vegetables are its primary agricultural products.

Early Sea Voyages

At least 30,000 years ago, people from Southeast Asia moved to the island of New Guinea. Over time, they continued to move east across Melanesia. Much later, people traveled to the other South Pacific islands by boat. Micronesia and Polynesia probably were not populated until about 3,500 years ago.

Ancient peoples probably drifted on the warm ocean currents on rafts. Later, people built large, double-framed boats that could carry dozens of people as well as animals, food, and other supplies. Later still, islanders invented **outriggers**. These canoes have floats on each side that prevent the boats from tipping over. Using outriggers, people were able to row from island to island. Trade became possible, especially among the islands of Polynesia.

Spotlight On

THE EASTER ISLAND STATUES

When European explorers came to Easter Island, they found a stunning sight. All around the edge of the volcanic island stood huge, gray stone statues. Each statue consisted of the top half of a human form, 15 to 40 feet high.

The statues were carved out of the stone from a volcanic mountain in the middle of the island. No one is certain how the statues were moved down from the mountain. Each statue is a single stone weighing as much as 50 tons. The statues on the island's edge marked burial places and probably had a religious purpose.

Critical Thinking Why are the Easter Island statues so mysterious?

Easter Island was given its name by a Dutch explorer who spotted the island on Easter Sunday in 1722.

When people first migrated from Asia to the South Pacific islands, they brought pigs, chickens, dogs, and other animals. They also brought plants and seeds to grow on the islands. Some seeds also drifted to the islands in ocean currents. Birds and the wind also carried seeds. Yams and potatoes, which are staple foods in Polynesia, must have come from South America. How they got there is a mystery.

European explorers first visited the Pacific Islands in the 1500s. Much later, Captain James Cook, a British explorer, mapped many of the islands and left a detailed record of his observations. Captain Cook described the people and their way of life. He charted racial and ethnic differences among the islanders.

French, Spanish, and Dutch explorers also sailed to the Pacific Islands. Each claimed different territories for their home countries. As usual, the Europeans brought new diseases. Smallpox, measles, tuberculosis, and other illnesses killed entire populations.

Christian missionaries arrived in the late 1600s. They nearly destroyed the islanders' culture. For example, many island people were accustomed to wearing little or no clothing in the hot climate. The missionaries, however, found it shocking and forced the islanders to cover up. The missionaries also tried to keep the islanders from performing traditional dances.

Later missionaries were more understanding of Oceania's cultures. In the 1900s, Christianity took root in the region. Today, churches are often the center of village life. Protestant churches are especially common.

✓ Check Your Understanding

Write your answers in complete sentences.

1. What two types of islands form Oceania?

2. Where did the first peoples of Oceania come from?

3. How did missionaries try to change life in Oceania?

Earning a Living on the Islands

Tourism is the main industry in many parts of Oceania. The tropical climate, sandy beaches, and relaxed way of life on these islands are resources because they attract tourists. Tourism brings trade and provides jobs. Islanders work in hotels and restaurants, and artists and craftspeople sell their works to tourists.

Many people come to the islands to swim and to explore the coral reefs from underwater. The coral is dying out in some places. It is being killed by soil erosion and ocean pollution. The main threat to the coral reefs, however, is from a starfish called the crown-of-thorns starfish. Since the 1960s, the population of this starfish has been growing very quickly. Scientists are trying to control this starfish in order to protect the reefs.

Hawaii's white beaches and tropical weather draw tourists.

Coconuts are the main agricultural crop of the Pacific islands. The meat inside the coconuts is dried to produce **copra**, which contains coconut oil. Many islands have factories that press coconut oil out of copra and process it for export. Coconut oil is used in cooking oil, soap, suntan lotion, brake fluid, and many other products.

Farmers also grow bananas, pineapples, cocoa, sugar cane, ginger, vanilla, and other cash crops. The coral islands support little agriculture. The way of life of coral island residents depends on fishing.

Only a few islands have any mineral resources. Nickel, iron ore, chrome, and copper are mined in New Caledonia. Phosphate, a mineral used in fertilizer, is found on Nauru in Micronesia. The Solomons export seashells, which are mostly used as a building material. All of these natural resources are limited, however, and could soon run out.

Oceanic Arts

Until the Europeans arrived, the people of Oceania had no written language. They had a rich tradition of stories handed down from generation to generation. These stories contain images from nature, such as trees, animals, and fish. The stories tell of love, pleasure, death, and the island way of life. They also carry information about the past. Storytelling is a way of remembering ancestors and ancient sea voyages.

Throughout Oceania, dance is an important social activity. Each region has its own dances. For example, the Hawaiian hula uses mainly hand and arm movements. In the Tongan dance called me'etu'upaki, the dancers' movements imitate the paddling of a boat.

In Melanesia, dances are often ritual acts with a religious purpose. The dancers wear costumes and masks in order to look like certain spirits. Through their movements, the dancers hope to make contact with these spirits. In some ceremonies, dancers act out events that took place in the past. For example, dancers may act out an entire battle with an enemy group.

Artists in Oceania make beautifully decorated masks. They also weave baskets and make woodcarvings. Another traditional art in Oceania is the painting of tapa cloth, which is made from the bark of mulberry trees. The bark is soaked in water and pounded to make a thin sheet. Then, one or more artists draw designs on the cloth. These designs may tell stories about the culture. Sometimes, people hang tapa cloth in their houses to divide an open space into two rooms.

The Hawaiian lei is a well-known native art form. This necklace of flowers is given with a kiss as a welcome or goodbye gift. Travelers have a tradition of tossing the leis back onto the water as their ship leaves. That shows the traveler's wish to return to Hawaii.

Dancing is an important activity in Oceania. Each region has its own dances that may have a religious purpose.

✓ Check Your Understanding

Write your answers in complete sentences.

1. What is the main threat to the coral in the Pacific?

2. How is tapa cloth made?

3. What does throwing a lei on the water mean?

GEOGRAPHER'S TOOL KIT
Comparing Maps and Graphs

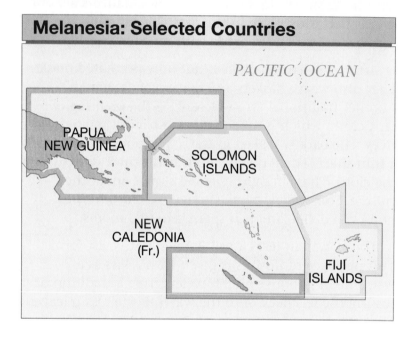

Melanesia: Selected Countries

PACIFIC OCEAN

PAPUA
NEW GUINEA

SOLOMON
ISLANDS

NEW
CALEDONIA
(Fr.)

FIJI
ISLANDS

Both maps and graphs provide information. Maps show information about places. Graphs present numbers. When you compare these different kinds of information, you can often learn more about a region.

Here is how to compare the data on a map and graph. First, look at the titles. Then, look for information about the same places on both the map and the graph. Compare the information on each. That should help you to draw conclusions about those places.

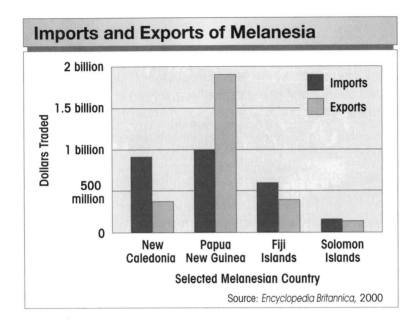

Imports and Exports of Melanesia

Dollars Traded

- 2 billion
- 1.5 billion
- 1 billion
- 500 million
- 0

Imports
Exports

New Caledonia Papua New Guinea Fiji Islands Solomon Islands

Selected Melanesian Country

Source: *Encyclopedia Britannica,* 2000

Answer the questions below.

1. Explain how this map and graph are related.

2. Look at both the map and the graph. Why might imports and exports of the Solomon Islands be smaller than those of Papua New Guinea?

CHALLENGE Look at the map and the graph. Why do you think most of the countries of Melanesia import more than they export?

Apply the Skill

Look at a landform map of Australia. Then make a graph that shows the population of the major cities. Write questions about the map and graph. Exchange questions with a classmate. Try to answer each other's questions based on information shown on the map and the graph.

35 Review

Summary

The three areas of Oceania are Polynesia, Micronesia, and Melanesia.
Oceania is a vast region in the South Pacific Ocean. It contains about 20,000 islands, both coral and volcanic. Coral islands are always low and fairly flat. Volcanic islands are higher and more mountainous.
Most Pacific islanders are descendants of Southeast Asians who migrated to these islands thousands of years ago.
Many Oceanic islands were colonized by Europeans and became territories of those countries.
Tourism helps support the economy. Copra is the main cash crop in Oceania. The Oceanic islands have little industry and few natural resources.

copra

atoll

outrigger

Vocabulary Review

Write a term from the list that matches each definition below.

1. The dried meat of a coconut

2. A canoe with a frame that holds a float on each side

3. A ring of coral islands that surround a lagoon

Chapter Quiz

Write your answers in complete sentences.

1. What line marks the division between Polynesia and Micronesia?

2. What are islands that rise very little above the ocean's surface called?

3. The economy of many islands in Oceania depends on which resource?

4. **Critical Thinking** Which kind of island is more likely to be inhabited, volcanic or coral? Explain your answer.

5. **Critical Thinking** How do the arts and crafts of Oceania depend on the environment there?

Write About Geography

Complete the following activities.

1. You live on an Oceania island. Write what your daily life is like.

2. Find a picture of Oceania in this chapter. You are visiting the place or the person in the photograph. Write a postcard about it.

Group Activity

Design a brochure that will attract tourists to the islands of Oceania. Some people in the group can research tourist attractions. Others can find or make drawings, write the copy, and design the brochure.

Unit 10 Review

Comprehension Check

Answer each question in a complete sentence.

1. Why is nearly all Australian farmland located along the east coast?

2. How did Australia come to be a colony of Britain?

3. How is the physical geography of New Zealand different from that of Australia?

4. Why is copra important to the people of Oceania?

Building Your Skills

Answer each question in a complete sentence.

1. Where are the North Island and South Island located?

2. How can comparing a map and a graph be useful?

Where Is It?

Write the name of the place based on the information below.

1. The area of Australia with huge ranches

2. The island group that includes Hawaii

Writing an Essay

Answer one of the following essay topics.

1. Compare the treatment of the Kooris and the Maoris, both in previous centuries and today.

2. Describe the impact that Europeans had on Oceania.

Geography and You

In what ways are Oceania, New Zealand, and Australia different from where you live? In what ways are they similar?

Appendix

Glossary

abaca a plant used to make rope (p. 496)

acid rain rain water that carries large amounts of chemicals (p. 360)

adobe a sun-dried brick made of mud and straw (p. 104)

ally a close partner (p. 139)

animism a belief that many spirits live within the natural world (p. 150)

anthropologist a scientist who studies the origins and development of human life and culture (p. 180)

apartheid a system of laws developed in South Africa to keep racial groups separate (p. 198)

aqueduct a structure that carries water from one place to another (p. 119)

arable suitable for use as farmland (p. 216)

archaeologist a scientist who studies items that people made long ago in order to learn about how they lived (p. 195)

archipelago a chain of islands (p. 134)

atoll a ring-shaped coral island surrounding a lagoon (p. 525)

Balkanization breaking up into small groups that fight each other (p. 352)

barangay local government in the Philippines (p. 501)

batik a process for hand-printing colored designs on cloth by using wax and dyes (p. 489)

biogeopgraphy the study of the geographic distribution of animals and plants (p. 510)

bog a wet, spongy area (p. 258)

boycott an attempt to change the actions of a company or country by refusing to buy its products (p. 199)

buffer state a small country that separates two large countries and prevents a conflict between them (p. 454)

bureaucracy any organization made up of appointed officials organized into many ranks (p. 336)

cacao the plant from which chocolate is made (p. 120)

capital good a manufactured product—such as steel, tractors, or factory machinery—used to produce other products (p. 336)

capitalism an economic system in which land, factories, and businesses are privately owned and run for profit (p. 291)

cash crop a crop grown to be sold; a cash crop usually provides a farmer's or landowner's main source of income (p. 107)

caste a fixed social class into which one is born and from which one cannot move (p. 437)

cease-fire an agreement to stop fighting (p. 344)

chernozem a rich, black soil, which is common in cool or dry climates (p. 341)

civilian a person who is not a soldier (p. 234)

civilization a high level of culture that includes writing (p. 89)

class struggle the struggle between the upper class and the lower class (p. 389)

classless society a society in which no group of people has more wealth, power, or status than any other (p. 389)

climate the pattern of weather in a place over many years (p. 7)

clinic a hospital that serves a specific population (p. 517)

cold war a sharp conflict between countries without actual war (p. 292)

collective farm a large farm run by a group of people working together under government supervision (p. 324)

colony a territory owned and governed by another country (p. 91)

commercial done for the purpose of making money (p. 31)

commonwealth a self-governing political unit that is part of a nation or states; a group of self-governing states (p. 137)

communism an economic system in which the government owns all property and businesses (p. 139)

conservation saving natural resources such as rain forests and wildlife (p. 488)

constitution the basic laws that set up the rules of government for a nation (p. 59)

consumer good a product that satisfies people's wants or needs (p. 336)

contra a rebel fighting the Sandinista government in Nicaragua (p. 109)

copra the dried meat of a coconut (p. 530)

coral the stony outside skeletons of tiny sea animals; billions of such skeletons pile up to form underwater ridges called coral reefs (p. 135)

cottage industry a small-scale manufacturing operation in which people make goods by hand in their own homes (p. 261)

coup the sudden violent overthrow of top government leaders by another group of leaders (p. 325)

culture everything people make, think, and do (p. 30)

currency the type of money used in any particular country (p. 296)

custom a pattern of behavior followed by a whole group of people (p. 36)

delta a flat, sandy area where a river enters an ocean (p. 17)

demilitarized zone   an area where no military forces are allowed (p. 418)

democracy   a form of government in which people choose their own leader (p. 48)

descendant   a person born later in a family line (p. 58)

desertification   a process by which dry grassland turns into desert (p. 162)

dictator   a leader who rules with complete power (p. 109)

dike   a barrier built to hold back sea water (p. 287)

discrimination   treating some people worse than others because of prejudice (p. 74)

dowry   money or goods that a bride brings to a marriage (p. 453)

dynasty   a series of rulers who belong to the same family (p. 244)

ejido   a communal farm in Mexico, on which farmers either work the land together or individually (p. 93)

embargo   an order that forbids trade with a certain country (p. 139)

empire   a group of countries or cultures under a single ruler (p. 90)

endangered species   an animal in danger of dying out because its numbers are few (p. 187)

epic   a long poem or story (p. 249)

equator   an imaginary line around the middle of the Earth (p. 5)

erg   a huge sand dune that shifts over time (p. 211)

erosion   the wearing away of the Earth's surface by wind or water (p. 17)

estate   a large area of land or property usually owned by one person or family (p. 323)

ethnic cleansing   a policy in which members of one ethnic group drive away or kill members of other ethnic groups (p. 358)

Eurasia   a geographical term for the landmass that is made up of the continents of Europe and Asia (p. 510)

export   to sell goods or resources to other countries; the goods sold are called exports (p. 49)

extended family   a social unit consisting of parents, their children, and other relatives (p. 30)

famine   a serious food shortage that causes many people to die of starvation (p. 177)

fascism   a form of government headed by a dictator who supports private property but strictly controls industry and workers (p. 310)

fertile   capable of producing a great deal (p. 227)

fjord   a long, narrow bay surrounded by cliffs (p. 274)

fossil fuel   coal, oil, or natural gas that formed over millions of years from the remains of plants and tiny animals (p. 23)

fundamentalist a person who believes that the basic beliefs of a religion should be followed exactly (p. 248)

gamelan traditional Indonesian orchestra (p. 490)

game reserve a large area set aside for wild animals (p. 186)

geography a study of the Earth's surface, focusing on descriptions of places and the people who live in them (p. 4)

ghetto a neighborhood where a particular ethnic group is forced to live because of prejudice (p. 74)

glacier a huge, moving mass of ice (p. 16)

glasnost a policy that allows open discussion about Soviet life and politics (p. 325)

guerrilla a soldier who fights outside a regular army, often against a government (p. 105)

hacienda in Latin America, a large estate or ranch (p. 93)

hieroglyphic related to a system of writing in which pictures called hieroglyphs stand for ideas (p. 213)

Holocaust the mass murder of Jewish and other people by Nazi forces (p. 234)

homeland a special reserve in South Africa where many black South Africans were forced to move (p. 198)

hurricane a violent tropical storm (p. 47)

hydroelectric power electricity made by machines that are operated by rushing river water (p. 166)

igloo a dwelling made of sod, wood, rock, or domed ice (p. 61)

immigrant a person who moves to another country to settle (p. 48)

import to buy goods or resources from other countries; the goods bought are called imports (p. 52)

incarnation the particular physical form that a spirit takes in this world (p. 435)

Industrial Revolution a period of rapid industrialization in many Western countries that began in the 1700s (p. 261)

industry businesses that make finished products (p. 32)

inhabited having people living on the land (p. 135)

intifada an organized rebellion by the people of Palestine against Israel (p. 235)

invader an outsider who comes into an area to conquer or destroy it (p. 151)

invest to spend money for something, such as a business, that may return a profit (p. 390)

irrigation the watering of dry farm land by means of ditches or pipes (p. 88)

ivory a valuable white bone that comes mainly from elephant tusks (p. 170)

jade a hard stone that is usually green (p. 392)

junta a small group of military leaders who take power and rule a country by force (p. 128)

kabuki a form of popular Japanese theater that uses elaborate stage settings (p. 410)

kampong a traditional Indonesian village (p. 487)

karma a fate or destiny shaped by one's past actions in this lifetime or in a previous lifetime (p. 435)

landlocked surrounded by land (p. 116)

latitude distance, measured in degrees, north and south of the equator (p. 4)

long house a large wooden dwelling (p. 59)

longitude distance, measured in degrees, east and west of the prime meridian (p. 4)

location where a place is (p. 4)

loot to seize and carry away goods (p. 371)

manufacturing the making of products (p. 51)

map projection a way to draw the curved areas of the Earth on a flat surface (p. 18)

marine having to do with the sea (p. 302)

marsupial a type of mammal that is born before it is fully developed, and then completes its development in its mother's pouch (p. 510)

martial law a state of emergency in which a government suspends citizens' rights and uses its army to control its people (p. 199)

meditation quiet, focused thought (p. 404)

mestizo a person who has both Spanish and American Indian ancestry (p. 91)

migration the movement of a group of people from one place to another (p. 8)

minaret a tower of a mosque (p. 250)

mineral a natural resource found inside the Earth (p. 50)

monarchy a government run by a single ruler, usually a king or queen, who inherits the position (p. 209)

monotheism the belief that there is only one god (p. 231)

monsoon a seasonal wind that creates a strong pattern of wet and dry seasons in parts of Asia (p. 432)

moor a rolling plain covered with grasses and low shrubs (p. 258)

mosque an Islamic place of worship (p. 151)

mujahideen   warriors who fight for Islam (p. 454)

multicultural   involving many cultures mixed together (p. 80)

mythology   the study of traditional stories known as myths (p. 280)

nationalism   a strong feeling of loyalty to one's country (p. 181)

neutral   not supporting either side in a disagreement or struggle (p. 354)

nirvana   in Buddhism, the condition of having reached enlightenment (p. 404)

noh   a form of traditional Japanese theater that uses minimal stage settings (p. 410)

nomad   a person who travels all the time in search of food (p. 38)

nonrenewable resource   a resource that cannot be replaced by natural resources or is replaced extremely slowly (p. 23)

nuclear family   a social unit consisting of parents and their children (p. 30)

oasis   an area in a desert where water springs are found (p. 211)

occupied   controlled by a foreign military force (p. 417)

ore   a natural mixture of rocks or soils that contains metal (p. 50)

Outback   the name given to Australia's vast, mainly desert, interior (p. 510)

outrigger   a canoe with a frame that holds a float on each side (p. 527)

overpopulated   having more people in a given area than the resources can support (p. 162)

paddy   a flooded field where rice is grown (p. 465)

pension   money paid regularly to a person who has retired or grown too old to work (p. 278)

perestroika   a policy that allows the rebuilding of the Soviet economy (p. 325)

permafrost   permanently frozen layer of soil just beneath the Earth's surface (p. 318)

pesticide   a chemical used to kill insects or other pests (p. 302)

pharaoh   the ruler of ancient Egypt (p. 213)

philosopher   a thinker who seeks knowledge and wisdom (p. 305)

pilgrimage   a trip to a place that has special religious importance (p. 224)

plain   a flat landform (p. 17)

plantation   a large farm that grows a single crop (p. 73)

plateau   a high, flat landform (p. 17)

population   the whole group of people in an area (p. 33)

prejudice   judging people without knowing them (p. 73)

prime meridian   the line of 0 degree longitude from which east and west locations are measured (p. 5)

privatization the act of private companies taking over farms, factories, and other businesses (p. 337)

proverb a short saying that expresses the values or morals of a culture (p. 156)

pueblo a dwelling with many rooms made of stone or clay (p. 59)

pyramid a structure with a square base and four triangle-shaped sides that rise to a point (p. 90)

quipu a knotted string used by the Inca to keep records (p. 119)

quota a limited amount (p. 79)

radioactive giving off the kind of energy used in nuclear bombs and power plants (p. 276)

rain forest any dense forest that grows in a moist area; a tropical rain forest is near the equator (p. 107)

Reformation the sixteenth-century religious movement that began the Protestant branch of Christianity (p. 290)

refugee a person who flees his or her home because of war, political danger, famine, or economic hardship (p. 80)

reincarnation rebirth into a new body or physical form in this world (p. 435)

Renaissance a creative period in European history, lasting roughly from 1400 to 1600 marked by widespread interest in exploration, invention, and the arts (p. 306)

renewable resource a resource that can be replaced as it is used (p. 23)

republic a government in which laws are made by a small group of citizens elected by the people (p. 209)

reservation a piece of public land set aside by the government for use by a certain group of people; called a reserve in Canada (p. 64)

reunification to come together again after being divided (p. 292)

rift a crack or separation in the Earth's crust, usually caused by forces deep beneath the surface (p. 177)

ritual an activity that has a sacred meaning and is part of the practice of a religion (p. 150)

rural in the country (p. 32)

sacred deeply respected and usually having religious meaning (p. 105)

saga a long, detailed story or account of an event (p. 280)

Sahel a strip of grassland along the southern edge of the Sahara (p. 148)

sanction a step taken by several nations acting together to punish another nation for breaking international laws (p. 199)

satellite a country that is independent in name but is actually controlled by a bigger, more powerful country (p. 373)

savanna a grassland region near the tropics (p. 148)

scripture the sacred writing of a religion (p. 475)

secular not having to do with religion (p. 242)

seismograph   a device for measuring earthquakes (p. 386)

serf   a peasant who cannot legally leave the land on which he or she works (p. 323)

service   a useful task that people perform to earn a living without making a product (p. 52)

shrine   a sacred place or structure where people go to pray (p. 403)

smuggle   to move goods in or out of a country illegally, often to avoid paying taxes (p. 121)

socialism   a political system in which the government controls farms and businesses (p. 228)

solidarity   a complete coming together (p. 355)

staple   a main food eaten by a people (p. 90)

steppe   land that is dry, flat, and covered with grass (p. 319)

stilt   a heavy pole that, when combined with others, keeps a house above the ground and out of the water (p. 465)

strait   a narrow strip of water between two bodies of land (p. 482)

strategic   important to carrying out a war or for defending against attack (p. 373)

strike   to stop work, as a group, until certain demands are met (p. 263)

subcontinent   a large portion of a continent that is geographically isolated from the rest of the continent (p. 432)

sub-Saharan   the region of Africa south of the Sahara (p. 148)

subsistence   providing only the basic needs of life (p. 31)

surname   a person's family name (p. 498)

swamp   an area that has shallow standing water (p. 167)

sweatshop   a factory that pays very low wages to laborers who work long hours in crowded conditions (p. 422)

Taliban   the group of Sunnite Muslims who instituted Islamic fundamentalist rule in Afghanistan (p. 452)

technology   the use of science for practical purposes (p. 32)

terrace   a long step cut into a slope to create level land for farming (p. 118)

terrorism   violence directed against civilians in order to put pressure on governments (p. 234)

theocracy   a country whose government is run by religious leaders (p. 248)

tipi   a cone-shaped, portable dwelling made of poles and animal skins (p. 59)

trade union   an organization of workers who are in the same industry; a labor union (p. 263)

trade wind   a tropical wind that blows from the northeast and southeast toward the equator (p. 135)

treaty   an agreement between nations or peoples (p. 64)

tropical   related to regions near the equator; a tropical climate is very warm and moist (p. 23)

truce   a temporary agreement to stop fighting (p. 418)

tsetse fly   a bloodsucking African fly that often carries deadly parasites to humans, animals, and plants (p. 167)

tsunami   a huge sea wave caused by an undersea earthquake or volcanic eruption (p. 400)

tuberculosis   a deadly lung disease caused by bacteria (p. 465)

tungsten   a metal used in light bulbs (p. 374)

typhoon   a tropical storm in the Pacific Ocean that brings high winds and heavy rainfall (p. 496)

United Nations   an international organization whose purpose is to keep peace between nations (p. 110)

urban   in or around a town or city (p. 32)

vegetation   the main plant life of an area (p. 194)

velvet revolution   a revolution without bloodshed (p. 356)

wage   money paid to workers (p. 262)

welfare state   a country in which government money is used to provide people with social services (p. 278)

yurt   a movable round tent covered in felt or animal skins (p. 374)

Index

Acknowledgments

Grateful acknowledgment is made to the following for illustrations, photographs, and reproductions on the pages indicated: **Cover:** Money: Ron Wise/ www. banknoteworld.com; lei: Ann Cecil Photography; Map: Stone; pottery: Jerry Jacka Photography; Junk: Nik Wheeler/CORBIS; sun: The Image Bank **Unit 1:** p. 1: PhotoDisc; p. 2: Stone; p. 7: Jeremy Horner/CORBIS; p. 8: Sygma/CORBIS; p. 14: Dave G. Houser/CORBIS; p. 16: Andre V. Malok; p. 17: Andre V. Malok; p. 24: Wil McIntyre/Photo Researchers, Inc.; p. 25: Pat Lacroix/ The Image Bank; p. 28: Doug Menuez/Photo Disc; p. 31: Shama Balfour, Gallo Images/CORBIS; p. 36: United States Postal Office; p. 37: M. Bryan Ginsberg **Unit 2:** p. 43: Pearson Education Corporate Digital Archive; p. 44: Nik Wheeler/CORBIS; p. 48: Telegraph Colour Library/FPG; p. 50: Wells Fargo Bank and Union Trust Company Historical Museum; p. 51: Matthew McVay/Stock Boston; p. 56: Stone; p. 59: Dave Bartruff/Stock Boston; p. 61: Marie-Louise Brimberg/National Geographic; p. 64: Kevin Flemming/CORBIS; p. 65: Tom Bean/CORBIS; p. 70: The Granger Collection; p. 72: The Stock Market; p. 73: Library of Congress; p. 74: SuperStock, Inc.; p. 77: ©Seattle Post-Intelligencer Collection; Museum of History and Industry/CORBIS; p. 78: The Granger Collection **Unit 3:** p. 85: Transparency no. 5003 (3) Photo by John Bigelow Taylor/Courtesy Department of Library Services/American Museum of Natural History; p. 86: Macduff Everton/CORBIS; p. 90: CORBIS; p. 93: Jack Kurtz/Impact Visuals; p. 95: Danny Lehman/ CORBIS; p. 96: Art Resource; p. 100: Arvind Garg/ CORBIS; p. 105: The Bowers Museum of Cultural Art/CORBIS; p. 107: Gail Shumway/FPG; p. 108: Bill Gentile/CORBIS; p. 111: Anna Clopet/CORBIS; p. 114: Hubert Stadler/CORBIS; p. 119: Robert Frerck/The Stock Market; p. 120: Stone; p. 122: Kirk Condyles/Impact Visuals; p. 124: Tom Brakefield/The Stock Market; p. 132: ©David Cumming/Eye Ubiquitous/CORBIS; p. 138: Roberto Bora/AP World Wide Photos; p. 140: Wexley Bicxe-Upon/Photo Researchers, Inc.; p. 141: Fran-Marc Frei/CORBIS **Unit 4:** p. 145: Anthony Johnson/Image Bank; p. 146: Paul Almasy/CORBIS; p. 150: Queen Mother Head Benin: Reproduced by courtesy the Trustees of the British Museum # 38365 (MOPM); p. 153: James L. Stanfield/National Geographic; p. 155: Margaret Courtney-Clarke/CORBIS; p. 160: George Gerster/Photo Researchers, Inc.; p. 162: Magnum Photos, Inc.; p. 165: G. Holton/Photo Researchers, Inc.; p. 174: Charles and Josette Lenars/CORBIS; p. 181: Bertrand/Explorer/Photo Researchers, Inc.; p. 186: Sharna Balfour/Gallo Image/CORBIS; p. 190: Torleif Svensson/The Stock Market; p. 193: Kerstin Geier/Gallo Images/CORBIS; p. 195: MIT Collection/CORBIS; p. 200: AP/Wide World Photos **Unit 5:** p. 205: ©Greg Stott/Masterfile; p. 206: Stephanie Dinkins/Photo Researchers, Inc.; p. 210: Charles and Josette Lenars/CORBIS; p. 214: Photo Researchers, Inc.; p. 215: Will and Deni McIntyre/ Photo Researchers, Inc.; p. 217: ©Kenneth Garrett; p. 220: Fred J. Maroon/Photo Researchers, Inc.; p. 224: CORBIS; p. 225: ©David H. Wells/CORBIS; p. 231: Index Stock; p. 232: ASAP, LTD./Index Stock; p. 238: Harvey Lloyd/The Stock Market; p. 242: Chris Hellier, CORBIS (kids); p. 244: AP/Wide World Photos; p. 247: Beatriz Schiller/International Stock Photo; p. 248: David Turnley/CORBIS **Unit 6:** p. 255: Corbis Digital Stock; p. 256: Robert Houser/Index Stock; p. 259: SuperStock, Inc.; p. 262: Photo Researchers, Inc.; p. 265: Farrell Grehan/CORBIS; p. 266: The Granger Collection; p. 272: Harvey Lloyd/The Stock Market; p. 274: Donnezan/Explorer/Photo Researchers, Inc.; p. 276: Joe Viesti/Viesti Associates; p. 280: PhotoDisc, Inc; p. 284: Jose Fuste Raga, The Stock Market; p. 291: Greg Edwards, Captured Moments; p. 293: AP/Wide World Photos; p. 295: Musee d'Orsay, Paris/Lauros-Giraudon, Paris/SuperStock, Inc.; p. 297: Musees Louvre Plan, "The Paris Pages"/www.paris.org; p. 300: Ed Viesti/Viesti Photography; p. 304: Jamie Squire/Allsport; p. 307: Stuart Dee/The Image Bank **Unit 7:** p. 315: Bob Daemmrich/Stock Boston; p. 316: Wolfgang Kaehler/CORBIS; p. 324: Library of Congress; p. 326: Novosti/Sovfoto; p. 327: Paolo Koch, Photo Researchers, Inc.; p. 328: Bill Demichelle/Sovfoto/Eastfoto; p. 332: Jeff Greenberg/International Stock Photo; p. 338: Mahaux Photo/Image Bank; p. 340: Robert S. Semeniuk/The Stock Market; p. 343: Sovfoto/Eastfoto; p. 345: Sovfoto/Eastfoto; p. 348: SuperStock, Inc.; p. 356: Peter Turnley/CORBIS; p. 357: SuperStock, Inc.; p. 358: AP/Wide World Photos **Unit 8:** p. 365: Corbis Digital Stock; p. 366: SuperStock, Inc.; p. 374: ©Landau, Photo Researchers, Inc.; p. 375: Baysgulang/Eastfoto; p. 376: Sovfoto; p. 382: Will and Deni McIntyre/Photo Researchers, Inc.; p. 388: Owen Franken/CORBIS; p. 391: Cary Wolinsky/Stock Boston; p. 392: Dean Conger/CORBIS; p. 393: Peter Beck/The Stock Market; p. 394: Impact Visuals; p. 398: David Ball/The Stock Market; p. 404: The Stock Market; p. 408: Paul Chesley/Tony Stone Images; p. 409: Charles Gupton/ Stock Boston; p. 410: Paolo Koch/Photo Researchers, Inc.; p. 414: AP/Wide World Photos; p. 422: Allen Green/Photo Researchers, Inc.; p. 423: ©Timespace/ The Viesti Collection, Inc. **Unit 9:** p. 429: Spencer Grant/Stock Boston; p. 430: ©Charlie Westerman/International Stock; p. 434: Telegraph Colour Library/FPG; p. 435: Charles and Josette Lenars/CORBIS; p. 436: Museum of Chandigarh, Chandigarh,India/Explorere/SuperStock, Inc.; p. 438: Jermey Horner/CORBIS; p. 446: Elain Evrard/Photo Researchers, Inc.; p. 450: Photo Researchers, Inc.; p. 451: Ric Ergenbright/CORBIS; p. 455: AP/Wide World Photos; p. 460: Jean-Marc Truchet/Tony Stone Images; p. 465: Michele Burgess/Stock Boston; p. 466: J. Du Boisberran/ The Image Bank; p. 468: Simeone Huber/Stone; p. 472: Paul Stepan-Vierow, Photo Researchers, Inc.; p. 475: Robert Semeniuk, The Stock Market; p. 476: ©Joe Viesti, Viesti Associates, Inc.; p. 477: Thomas Ives/The Stock Market; p. 480: Denis Waugh/Tony Stone Images; p. 489: SuperStock, Inc.; p. 490: Susan McCartney/Photo Researchers, Inc.; p. 494: Sean Sprague/Stock Boston; p. 501: Alain Evrard/Photo Researchers, Inc.; p. 502: Blair Seitz/Photo Researchers, Inc. **Unit 10:** p. 507: David Cimino/International Stock; p. 508: Dale Boyer/Photo Researchers, Inc.; p. 510: David Barnes/ The Stock Market; p. 517: Paul Steel/The Stock Market; p. 519: Jon Allan/Photo Researchers, Inc.; p. 522: Stuart Westmoreland/Photo Researchers, Inc.; p. 526: Amos Nachoum/The Stock Market; p. 527: George Holton/Photo Researchers, Inc.; p. 529: Bill Bachmann, Photo Researchers, Inc.; p. 531: Porterfield/Chickering/ Photo Researchers, Inc.